"九五"国家重点图书

国 际 工 程 管 理 教 学 丛 书
INTERNATIONAL PROJECT MANAGEMENT TEXTBOOK SERIES

国际工程管理英汉/汉英词汇
An English-Chinese/Chinese-English Dictionary
of International Project Management

主 编 何伯森
副主编 周可荣 张水波
    洪柔嘉 孔德泉

中国建筑工业出版社

图书在版编目（CIP）数据

国际工程管理英汉/汉英词汇/何伯森主编-北京：
中国建筑工业出版社，1999
（国际工程管理教学丛书）
ISBN 978-7-112-03945-6

Ⅰ．国… Ⅱ．何… Ⅲ．对外承包-项目管理-词汇-英、汉 Ⅳ．F740.4-61

中国版本图书馆CIP数据核字（1999）第20246号

国际工程管理教学丛书
INTERNATIONAL PROJECT MANAGEMENT TEXTBOOK SERIES
国际工程管理英汉/汉英词汇
An English-Chinese/Chinese-English Dictionary of
International Project Management
主编　何伯森
*
中国建筑工业出版社出版、发行（北京西郊百万庄）
各地新华书店、建筑书店经销
北京同文印刷有限责任公司印刷
*

开本：850×1168毫米　1/32　印张：17½　字数：465千字
1999年9月第一版　2008年7月第五次印刷
印数：6501—7500册　定价：33.00元
ISBN 978-7-112-03945-6
（9300）

版权所有　翻印必究
如有印装质量问题，可寄本社退换
（邮政编码100037）

本词汇为国际工程管理专业词汇，包含了国际工程管理所涉及的工程咨询、工程采购、货物采购、项目管理、合同管理、法律、谈判、对外贸易、国际金融、财务、会计、保险、仲裁以及土建类工程实施等多个学科的英汉词汇10000余条及汉英词汇近11000条。注意选收了一些伴随管理科学和语言发展而产生的新词。后附有"有关中外机构团体名称表"和"各国和地区货币一览表"两个附录。

　　本词汇可供从事国际工程项目咨询、监理、设计、施工、安装、招标、投标等工作的管理人员、翻译人员、技术人员、财会人员、物资采购和管理人员、保险人员、仲裁人员、科研人员以及高等学校有关专业师生使用。

* * *

责任编辑　程素荣　朱首明

国际工程管理教学丛书编写委员会成员名单

主任委员
  王西陶 中国国际经济合作学会会长

副主任委员（按姓氏笔画排列）
  朱传礼 国家教育委员会高等教育司副司长
  陈永才 对外贸易经济合作部国外经济合作司原司长
       中国对外承包工程商会会长
       中国国际工程咨询协会会长
  何伯森 天津大学管理工程系原系主任，教授（常务副主任委员）
  姚　兵 建设部建筑业司、建设监理司司长
  施何求 对外贸易经济合作部国外经济合作司司长

委员（按姓氏笔画排列）
  于俊年 对外经济贸易大学国际经济合作系主任，教授
  王世文 中国水利电力对外公司原副总经理，教授级高工
  王伍仁 中国建筑工程总公司海外业务部副总经理，高工
  王西陶 中国国际经济合作学会会长
  王硕豪 中国水利电力对外公司总经理，高级会计师，国家级专家
  王燕民 中国建筑工程总公司培训中心副主任，高工
  刘允延 北京建筑工程学院土木系副教授
  汤礼智 中国冶金建设总公司原副总经理、总工程师，教授级高工
  朱传礼 国家教育委员会高等教育司副司长
  朱宏亮 清华大学土木工程系教授，律师
  朱象清 中国建筑工业出版社总编辑，编审

陆大同	中国土木工程公司原总工程师，教授级高工	
杜　训	全国高等学校建筑与房地产管理学科专业指导委员会副主任，东南大学教授	
陈永才	对外贸易经济合作部国外经济合作司原司长 中国对外承包工程商会会长 中国国际工程咨询协会会长	
何伯森	天津大学管理工程系原系主任，教授	
吴　燕	国家教育委员会高等教育司综合改革处副处长	
张守健	哈尔滨建筑大学管理工程系教授	
张远林	重庆建筑大学副校长，副教授	
张鸿文	中国港湾建设总公司海外本部综合部副主任，高工	
范运林	天津大学管理学院国际工程管理系系主任，教授	
姚　兵	建设部建筑业司、建设监理司司长	
赵　琦	建设部人事教育劳动司高教处副处长，工程师	
黄如宝	上海城市建设学院国际工程营造与估价系副教授，博士	
梁　鏐	中国水利电力对外公司原副总经理，教授级高工	
程　坚	对外贸易经济合作部人事教育劳动司学校教育处副处长	
雷胜强	中国交远国际经济技术合作公司工程、劳务部经理，高工	
潘　文	中国公路桥梁建设总公司原总工程师，教授级高工	
戴庆高	中国国际工程咨询公司培训中心主任，高级经济师	

秘书（按姓氏笔画排列）

吕文学	天津大学管理学院国际工程管理系讲师
朱首明	中国建筑工业出版社副编审
李长燕	天津大学管理学院国际工程管理系副系主任，副教授
董继峰	中国对外承包工程商会对外联络处国际商务师

序

对外贸易经济合作部部长 吴仪

欣闻由有关部委的单位、学会、商会、高校和对外公司组成的编委会编写的"国际工程管理教学丛书"即将出版,我很高兴向广大读者推荐这套教学丛书。这套教学丛书体例完整、内容丰富,相信它的出版能对国际工程咨询和承包的教学、研究、学习与实务工作有所裨益。

对外承包工程与劳务合作是我国对外经济贸易事业的重要组成部分。改革开放以来,这项事业从无到有、从小到大,有了很大发展。特别是近些年贯彻"一业为主,多种经营"和"实业化、集团化、国际化"的方针以来,我国相当一部分从事国际工程承包与劳务合作的公司在国际市场上站稳了脚跟,对外承包工程与劳务合作步入了良性循环的发展轨道。截止到1995年底,我国从事国际工程承包、劳务合作和国际工程咨询的公司已有578家,先后在157个国家和地区开展业务,累计签订合同金额达500.6亿美元,完成营业额321.4亿美元,派出劳务人员共计110.4万人次。在亚洲与非洲市场,我国承包公司已成为一支有较强竞争能力的队伍,部分公司陆续获得一些大型、超大型项目的总包权,承揽项目的技术含量不断提高。1995年,我国有23家公司被列入美国《工程新闻记录》杂志评出的国际最大225家承包商,并有2家设计院首次被列入国际最大200家咨询公司。但是,从我国现代化建设和对外经济贸易发展的需要来看,对外承包工程的发展尚显不足。一是总体实力还不太强,在融资能力、管理水平、技术水平、企业规模、市场占有率等方面,与国际大承包商相比有明显的差距。如,1995年入选国际最大225家承包商行列的23家中国公司的总营业额为30.07亿美元,仅占这225家最大承包商总营业额的 3.25%；二是我国的承包市场过分集中于亚非地区，不利于我国国际工程咨询和承包事业的长远发展；三是国际工程承包和劳务市场竞争日趋激烈，对咨询公司、承包公司的技术水平、管理水平提出了更高的要求，而我国一些大公司的内部运行机制尚不适应国际市场激烈竞争的要求。

商业竞争说到底是人才竞争，国际工程咨询和承包行业也不例外。只有下大力气，培养出更多的优秀人才，特别是外向型、复合型、开拓型管理人才，才能从根本上提高我国公司的素质和竞争力。为此，我们既要对现有从事国际工程承包工作的人员继续进行教育和提高，也要抓紧培养这方面的后备力量。经国家教委批准，1993年，天津大学首先设立了国际工程管理专业，目前已有近10所高校采用不同形式培养国际工程管理人才，但该领域始终没有一套比较系统的教材。令人高兴的是，最近由该编委会组织编写的这套"国际工程管理教学丛书"填补了这一空白，这套教学丛书总结了我国十几年国际工程承包的经验，反映了该领域的国际最新管理水平，内容丰富，系统性强，适应面广。

我相信，这套教学丛书的出版将对我国国际工程管理人才的培养起到重要的促进作用。有了雄厚的人才基础，我国国际工程承包事业必将日新月异，更快地发展。

1996年6月

前　言

　　自从十几年前我们开始涉足国际工程这一领域，从事国际工程承包、咨询、教学、培训、编写教材以及翻译 FIDIC、ITC 等国际组织编写的多种合同文件以来，深感需要一本国际工程管理的工具书——国际工程管理英汉/汉英词汇。基于这样的指导思想，多年来，我们一直在有意识地收集有关单词和词组，也曾在我们出版的教材中编辑词汇作为附录。但是由于日常工作繁忙，编写一本正式的词汇需要付出大量的时间和精力，因而一直未能了却这一宿愿。

　　国际工程管理教学丛书编委会将编写"国际工程管理英汉/汉英词汇"的任务交给我们后，我们感到能够有机会为我国千千万万奋战在五大洲的国际工程事业的开拓者们奉献一本大家需要的工具书是一件十分有意义的工作。国际工程管理在我国属于新兴的学科，同时又是跨多种专业的交叉学科，在国际上也是一个不断发展的学科，其中有许多新词和词组还没有标准的中文译词，完成这一任务需要有广阔的专业知识和深厚的英语功底，因而也是一项艰巨的任务。

　　为了编好这本词汇，我们从两种途径入手汇集有关专业单词和词组：一方面从我们过去翻译的大量书刊以及教学、培训采用的教材中，特别是世界银行贷款项目有关文件和 FIDIC 编写的各种文件的最新文本中挑选单词和词组；同时也从先期出版的十四本国际工程管理教学丛书中挑选了一批单词和词组；另一方面，由于在国际工程实际工作中必然涉及到法律、合同、项目管理、外贸、谈判、金融、保险、财会以及有关经济和技术等领域的内容，为此，我们邀请校内外各有关专业的专家和教师从各自的专业领域内挑选与国际工程管理有关的单词和词组，考虑到工程技术涉及多种技术方面的专业，在本词汇中只汇集了那些土建工程实施最常用的单词和词组，合计共约15000余条。最后，经过专业教师与英语教师本着尽量选用英文文献、书刊、词汇中的通用词汇和新词的原则，共同推敲，精选出我们认为适宜的、可能最为常用的英/汉单词和词组10000余条，同时编出国际工程管理汉/英单词和词组近11000余条。

由于这是一本国际工程管理专业性质较强的词汇，所以，在单词和词组释义中我们考虑的主要是单词和词组的专业概念与含义，同时也考虑到所选单词和词组的习惯用法，并结合我们翻译国际工程有关书籍和文件的实际体会，在可能的条件下查阅有关专业词典，对某些疑难词组，专门请教了富有国际工程实践经验的专家，在此基础上，最后确定了单词和词组的释义。

参加提供专业词汇的专家和教师有何伯森、洪柔嘉（项目管理、合同管理方面）；周可荣（经济方面）；张水波（法律、仲裁方面）；刘尔烈（工程技术方面）；鹿丽宁（外贸方面）；潘文（谈判方面）；梁秀伶（保险方面）；梅世强（财会方面）；王秀琴（金融方面）。汇编附录的有张水波、洪柔嘉、王秀琴、邓斐等。

孔德泉负责词汇的计算机处理及编排。

本词汇主编何伯森，副主编周可荣、张水波、洪柔嘉、孔德泉。全部词汇由何伯森、周可荣、张水波审定。全书由周可荣、洪柔嘉、孔德泉通校。

在疑难词义推敲过程中，得到潘文、梁鉴、王世文、汤礼智等专家的指导；在词汇的编写过程中，得到房宇、王辉、张俊萍、谢亚琴、刘常华、林立等同志的协助，在此向他们表示衷心的感谢。同时也向先期出版的国际工程管理教学丛书各书作者表示衷心的感谢。

三年来，我们为这本词汇的编写付出了大量的心血，多次易稿，反复推敲和筛选，力求尽我们的最大努力向读者送上一本收词覆盖面较广、词条释义较为准确恰当，并且较为实用的工具书。但由于受专业知识和水平的限制，作为第一次尝试必然会有许多不足以至错误之处，为此，热忱希望各位读者多加指教，以便再版时订正。多谢！

来函请寄"天津市 天津大学 管理学院 何伯森收"（邮编300072）

体 例 说 明

英 汉 部 分

一、英语词条包括单词、词组两类，均按英语字母顺序排列
二、单词条目均标注词性。若同一单词含有不同词性时，视情况，或分别标出，
  如：address *n.* 地址   *v.* 处理，解决；
  或同时标出，如：appeal *n. v.* 上诉；呼吁。
三、圆括号的用法
  1、英语词条中（ ）表示该处可替换前面紧连接的词，
   如：become (fall) due，表示 become due 和 fall due 为两个同义词；
  2、汉语释义中（ ）用于表示补充说明，
   如：attachment of risk   风险责任的起期（即保险责任开始生效）；
  3、释义中（ ）中带"或"的释义，表示可替换前面的释义部分，
   如：entitle *v.* 给予权利（或条件、资格），表示 entitle 可译为：给予权利，给予条件，给予资格。
四、方括号的用法
  方括号［ ］或为国别、语种，或为单复数说明，如：［英］表示"英国"，［拉］表示"拉丁语"，［复］表示"复数"。
五、凡同一词条有不同拼写方法时，均同时列出并用逗号分隔。
六、释义中词意相近的词用逗号分隔，词意较远的词用分号分隔。
七、本词汇所用缩略语

n. 名词   *v.* 动词   *a.* 形容词   *ad.* 副词   *prep.* 介词。

汉 英 部 分

一、选词原则

　　一般选择国际工程管理中最常用的词汇，同时兼收少量有关的普通词汇。

二、汉语词条按汉语拼音排序。

三、释义原则

　　从国际工程管理专业角度，最常用英语单词或词组在前，余此类推。

四、英语单词不标注词性。

五、圆括号的用法

1、少量汉语词条带有（ ），用于解释和说明，以防误解。

2、英语释义中（ ）表示该处可替换前面紧连接的词。

　　　如：备用现金　till money (cash)，表示备用现金可译为：till money 或 till cash。

目 录

1 英汉部分 ·· 1
2 汉英部分 ·· 241
3 附录一 ·· 509
4 附录二 ·· 516
5 主要参考书目 ··· 538
6 跋 ·· 539

A

abandon *v.*
抛弃,放弃,废弃
abandoned assets
废弃资产
abandoned property
废弃财产
abandonee *n.*
受委付人,财产受领人
abandonment *n.*
撤销;放弃;让与;委托
abandonment of appeal
放弃上诉
abandonment of claim
放弃索赔权利
abandonment of contract
放弃合同
abandonment of right
放弃权利
abate *v.*
减价;废止
abate a price
还价
abatement *n.*
折扣;减税;冲销,扣减
abatement of action
撤销诉讼
abatement of debt
免除债务,减轻债务
abatement of tax
减税
ABC analysis
ABC 分析,ABC 分类控制法
abeyance *n.*
产权待定,暂缓
abide *v.*
遵守(合同、法律、决定、诺言等);坚持
abide by the agreement
遵守协议
abide by the contract
遵守合同
ability *n.*
能力
ability to monitor contract
监督合同能力
ability to pay
支付能力;纳税能力;购买力
ability to work
工作能力
abnormal *a.*
不正常的,异常的
abnormal cost
非正常成本,特别成本
abnormal depreciation
非常折旧,特别折旧
abnormal gains
非正常收益
abnormal loss
非正常损失
abnormal profit
非正常利润,特别利润
abnormal risk
特殊风险
abolish *v.*
废除
abortive *a.*
(计划等)失败的
above par
超过票面,超过面值,溢价
abroad *n.*
国外,海外
abrogate *v.*
取消(条约、法令等)
abrogate the original contract
废除原合同
absence *n.*

缺席;缺乏;不存在;旷工
absence of proof
缺乏证据
absent *a.*
缺勤的
absolute *a.*
绝对的,完全的,纯粹的
absolute acceptance
绝对承担,无条件接受
absolute advantage
绝对优势
absolute condition
绝对条件
absolute endorsement
单纯背书,无条件背书
absolute fact
确凿事实
absolute interest
绝对权益
absolute quota
绝对配额
absolute title
绝对产权,绝对所有权
absorb *v.*
吸收;吞并
absorb the price difference
分担差价
absorption *n.*
分摊(费用等);合并,吸收
absorption cost
完全成本
absorptive capacity
(对援助的)吸收能力,承受能力
abstract *n.*
文摘;摘要 *a.* 抽象的
abstract of account
账目摘要
abstract of particulars
细则;摘要
abstract of title
产权简史;产权归属说明书
abstract quotation
抽象报价

abundance *n.*
充足,丰富
abundance of capital
资金充足
abundance of labour
劳动力充裕,劳动力过剩
abuse *v. n.*
滥用,妄用
abuse of authority
滥用职权
abuse of law
滥用法律
abuse of power
滥用权力
abuse of trust
滥用信用
abutment *n.*
支座;拱座;桥台;边墩
accede *v.*
继承;同意
accelerate *v.*
加快,加速
accelerated completion
加速竣工,提前完工
accelerated cost recovery system
加速成本回收制度
accelerated curing of concrete
混凝土快速养护
accelerated depreciation
加速折旧
accelerated method of depreciation
加速折旧法
accelerating admixture
促凝外加剂
acceleration *n.*
加速施工
acceleration clause
加速偿还条款,提前偿付条款,加速清还条款
acceleration cost
加速施工费
acceleration order
加速施工指令

accelerator n.	促凝剂
accept v.	承兑；接收；承诺
accept a claim	接受索赔
accept a quotation	接受报价
accept an invitation	接受邀请
accept an offer	接受报价，接受发盘
accept an order	接受订单
accept the bid (tender)	接受投标
acceptable a.	可接受的，合格的
acceptable accounting principle	公认会计原则
acceptable date	可接受日期
acceptable deviation	可接受的偏离
acceptable local procedures	可接受的当地程序
acceptable material	合格材料
acceptable price	可接受价格
acceptable to the bank	可为银行所接受的
acceptable variation	可接受的变更
acceptance n.	接受；承保；承兑；承诺；验收
acceptance amount	承兑金额
acceptance bank	承兑银行
acceptance bill	承兑票据，承兑汇票
acceptance by owner	业主认可
acceptance certificate	验收证书
acceptance certificate of the contract goods	合同货物验收证书
acceptance commission	承兑汇票手续费
acceptance contract	承兑合同
acceptance credit	承兑信用证；承兑汇票
acceptance criteria	验收准则
acceptance for honor	接受承兑
acceptance L/C	承兑信用证
acceptance of a project	工程验收
acceptance of bribes	受贿
acceptance of offer	接受报价
acceptance of risks	承担风险
acceptance of the bid (tender)	接受投标书
acceptance of works	工程验收
acceptance payable	应付承兑票据
acceptance rate	票据贴现率
acceptance receivable	应收承兑汇票
acceptance register	承兑票据登记簿
acceptance specification	验收规范
acceptance test	验收试验
acceptance with reservation	

有保留接受
accepted bill
已承兑汇票
accepted contract amount
接受的合同款额,中标合同额
accepted letter of credit
已承兑信用证
accepted risk
被接受的风险
accepting bank
承兑银行
accepting house
承兑商行
acceptor *n.*
承兑人,承付人
access *n.*
通道;接近;通过;进入权
access right
进入权;查阅权
access to data
资料查阅
access to site
进入现场
access to works
进入工程现场
accession tax
财产增益税
accessory *a.*
附加的 *n.* 附件;附属物
accessory contract
附加合同,附约
accessory debtor
从属债务人
accessory risk
附加风险
accident *n.*
意外事故,事故,偶然事件
accident compensation
意外事故赔偿
accident damage
意外损害
accident insurance
事故保险

accident prevention
安全措施;事故预防
accident report
事故报告
accident to workmen
人身事故,伤害工人的事故
accident work injury
工伤事故
accommodation *n.*
膳食供应;生活设施;提供方便;融通;贷款
accommodation bill
融通票据
accommodation check
融通支票
accommodation endorsement
融通背书
accommodation endorser
融通背书人(或担保人)
accommodation note
融通票据
accommodation paper
融通票据
accomplished bill of lading
已提货提单
accomplishment *n.*
完成
accord and satisfaction
和解和清偿
account *n.*
账,账户;账目,会计科目;账单
account as recorded in a ledger
分类账科目
account balance
账户余额
account balanced
账户结平,收支两讫
account book
账簿,会计账册
account chart
会计科目一览表
account classification
账户(或科目)分类

account conversion	会计年度
账户转换	accountability *n.*
account current	负有责任,有义务
往来账户	accountability verification
account day	责任证明
结算日	accountable document
account form of balance sheet	应加说明的文件
账户式资产负债表	accountancy *n.*
account holder	会计工作
账户人,客户	accountant *n.*
account in transit	会计师,会计人员
在途账,未达账	accountant bill
account in trust	账单
信托账户	accountant book
account law	会计账簿
会计法	accountant general
account number	总会计师
账户编号,账号	accounting *n.*
account of receipts and payments	会计;会计学;会计工作,核算
收支表	accounting changes
account officer	会计变更
会计主管	accounting control
account payable	会计控制,会计监督
应付账款	accounting convention
account payable ledger	会计惯例
应付账款明细账	accounting document
account payable register	会计凭证
应付账款登记簿	accounting entity
account purchase	会计主体,会计单位
赊购,赊买	accounting entry
account receivable	会计分录
应收账款	accounting equation
account receivable financing	会计恒等式,会计等式
应收账款融资	accounting evidence
account receivable ledger	会计凭证
应收账款明细账	accounting firm
account title	会计事务所
账户名称;会计科目	accounting income
account transfer	账面收益
账户转换	accounting method
account turnover	会计方法
周转账户	accounting period
account year	会计期间,会计分期

accounting principles
会计原则；会计原理
accounting procedure
会计程序
accounting records
会计记录
accounting released
公布账目
accounting statement
会计报表
accounting unit
会计单位，记账单位
accounting valuation
会计计价
accounts n.
会计账簿；会计报表
accounts payable ledger
应付账款分类账
accounts receivable collection period
应收账款周转天数，应收账款回收期
accounts receivable turnover
应收账款周转率
accredited a.
被委任的；被鉴定为合格的
accredited degree
合格程度
accredited party
被授权方
accretion n.
自然增值
accrual a.
应计的 n. 积累，增长，应计
accrual basis accounting
权责发生制会计
accrual of interest
累计利息；应付利息
accrual system
权责发生制
accrue v.
应收、应计（利息等）；自然增长
accrued account
应计账户
accrued and deferred accounts
应计和递延账户
accrued payroll
应付工资
accruing amount
累计金额
accumulate v.
积累；累计
accumulated depletion
累计折耗
accumulated depreciation
累计折旧
accumulated earnings
累计盈余，当存盈利
accumulated funds
积累资金
accumulated loss
累计损失
accumulated surplus
累计盈余
accumulation cost
累计成本
accumulation settlement
累计结算
accuracy n.
准确性
accusation n.
诉讼，控告
accuse sb. of a crime
指控某人有罪
accused person
被控告人，被告
accusing party
控告方
accusing person
控告人
acetylene welding
乙炔焊接，气焊
achieve v.
达到；完成
achievement n.
成就
acid-proof material
耐酸材料

acid-resisting concrete
耐酸混凝土
acknowledgment *n.*
承认,确认;收讫通知书,收据,收货回单
acknowledgment of receipt
回执,收据
acoustical board
吸声板,隔声板
acquire a new market
获得新市场
acquiring enterprise
引进方企业,购方企业
acquiring of control
取得控制权
acquiring party
引进方,获得方,购买方
acquisition *n.*
获得,取得;收购
acquisition cost
购置成本
acquisition of property
购置财产
acquisition of technology
技术引进,获得技术
acquit *v.*
释放;赔偿,偿还
acquit sb. of a crime
宣判某人无罪
acquittance *n.*
债务清偿收据,契约废除证明
acquittance of a debt
免除债务
act *n.*
行为,行动;法案,法令,条例 *v.* 代理;采取行动
act against duty
违反义务行为
act in excess of authority
越权行为
act of bankruptcy
破产法
Act of God
天灾
act of insolvency
破产法
act of omission
懈怠行为
acting manager
代理经理
action *n.*
诉讼;行动
action commitments
采取行动的承诺
action for possession
占有诉讼
action item
采取行动项目,诉讼项目
action programme
行动纲领
active account
活跃账户(指存款、取款频繁的账户)
active balance
顺差
active debt
有息债务
active trust
有经营权的信托
activities of project
项目业务
activity *n.*
单项活动,作业
activity bill of quantities
单项工程量清单
actual *a.*
实际的 *n.* 任何有形商品
actual additional cost
实际附加成本
actual breach
实际违约
actual cash value
实际现金价值
actual cost
实际成本
actual cost method
实际成本法

actual delivery
实际交货
actual loss
实际损失
actual loss ratio
实际损失率
actual price
实际价格
actual purchase order price
实际购货定单价格
actual tare
实际皮重
actual total loss
实际全损;绝对全损
actual value
实际价值
actuary n.
精算师,固定资产统计师
ad damnum clause
损坏赔偿条款
ad hoc
[拉]特定的,为某目的而安排的;尤其,特别
ad hoc arbitration
临时仲裁,特设仲裁
ad valorem bill of lading
货值提单,从价提单
ad valorem duties
从价税
ad valorem freight
从价运费
ad valorem import duty
从价进口税
ad valorem rate of duty
从价税率
ad valorem tariff
从价关税率
ad valorem tax
从价税
adaptive planning
适应性规划
add v.
添加,附加

added value
增值
added-value tax
增值税
addendum n.
附录;附加物;补遗;修改书,补充通知
addition n.
增加,增添
additional a.
附加的;追加的
additional charge
附加费用
additional clause
附加条款
additional contract clauses
附则,合同补充条款
additional cost
附加费用;新增成本
additional freight
附加运费
additional input of labour
增加人工投入
additional order
追加定单,追加订货
additional payment
额外付款
additional premium
附加保险费,加保费
additional provision
附加条款
additional rate
附加费率
additional risk
附加险
additional service
附加服务
additional survey
补充勘测
additional tax
附加税
additional transit period
补加期限

additional work
附加工作;新增工作
additive n.
添加剂,外加剂
add-on
比例运价,比例附加
add-on interest
追加利息
address n.
地址 v. 处理,解决
address book
通讯录
address correction
地址更正
address modification
地址变更
addressee n.
收电人,收件人
addresser n.
发电人,发件人
adequacy n.
充分,足够;适当
adequacy of insurance
保险的完备性
adequate supply
充足的供应
adhere v.
坚持
adhesion n.
粘结
adhesive tape
胶带
adjacent land
邻地,邻近地域
adjoining owner
毗邻产业主,相邻(土地、房屋的)所有者
adjudication n.
裁决
adjudication division
审判庭
adjudication fee
法庭费用

adjudication of bankruptcy
宣告破产
adjudication order
裁决令
adjudication rule
裁决规则
adjudicator n.
裁决人,调解人
adjust v.
调整;校正;理算
adjustable unit price
可调单价
adjustable-rate mortgage
可调利率抵押贷款
adjusted bank balance
调整后银行余额
adjusted book balance
调整后账面余额
adjusted price
调整后价格
adjusted trial balance
调整后试算表
adjuster n.
调解人;海损理算师
adjustment n.
调整;校正;理算
adjustment letter
海损理算书,海损精算书
adjustment of average
海损理算
adjustment of claim
赔偿理算,索赔理算
adjustment of claim for general average
共同海损赔偿理算
adjustment of general average
共同海损理算
admeasurement n.
测量,计量;分配
admeasurement type of contract
计量型合同
administer v.
管理;实施,执行

administer claim
解决索赔案件
administering authority
行政当局
administration n.
行政管理
administration cost
管理成本
administration expense account
管理费账户
administration expenses
管理费
administration fee
管理费
administration law
行政法
administration measure
行政措施
administration of assignment
委派管理
administration practice
管理规定,行政惯例
administration suit
遗产管理诉讼
administrative overhead
行政管理费用
administrative personnel
行政管理人员
administrative risk
可管理风险
administrative staff
行政管理人员
administrative tribunal
行政法庭
administrator n.
行政管理员;遗产管理人
administrator in a bankrupt estate
破产产业管理人
admissible document
可作证据文件
admissible evidence
可接受证据
admissible load
容许荷载
admission n.
准许进入;录用,任命;承认
admonition n.
警告;劝告
adopt v.
采用
adoption n.
采纳,通过
adulterate v.
掺假,掺杂
advance a.
预先的 n. 垫款,预付款;增长 v. 贷款;增长
advance by overdraft
透支
advance call
预垫款
advance collections
预收款项
advance freight
预付运费
advance payment
预付款
advance payment for contract
合同预付款
advance payment guarantee
预付款保函
advance remittance
预付汇款
advanced planning
预先计划
advanced price
已上涨的价格
advancement n.
进展;预付
advances n.
预付款
advances to subcontractor
预付分包商款
advancing n.
价格上涨
advantage n.

优势；利益
adventure *n*.
冒险
adverse *a*.
不利的，有害的，逆的
adverse balance
逆差
adverse balance of international trade
国际贸易逆差
adverse physical conditions
不利自然条件
adverse physical conditions or obstructions
不利自然条件或障碍
adverse possession
逆向占有，非物主占有，相反占有权
adverse weather conditions
不利气候条件
advertise *v*.
为…做广告
advertisement *n*.
通告；广告，宣传
advice *n*.
建议；通知
advice for collection of documentary bill
跟单汇票托收委托书
advice note
通知单
advice of arrival
到货通知
advice of authority to pay
授权付款通知书
advice of payment
付款通知
advise *v*.
通知
adviser, advisor *n*.
顾问
adviser service
咨询服务
advising bank

通知银行，通知行
advising charges
通知手续费
advisory *a*.
顾问的，咨询的
advisory committee
咨询委员会，顾问委员会
aerial insurance
空运保险
aeroconcrete *n*.
加气混凝土
affect *v*.
影响
affidavit *n*.
[拉]宣誓书，保证书
affidavit of claim
权利要求书，索赔书
affidavit of document
文件证明书
affiliate *n*.
会员；分支机构，分公司，附属公司
 v. 联营，隶属于
affiliate company
联营公司
affiliation *n*.
联营；附属
affirmation of contract
批准合同
affirmative warranty
确认保证
affix *v*.
附加；签署；盖(印章) *n*. 附件
afloat cargo
已装船货物，路货
afloat goods
已装船货物，路货
after date（A.D）
出票后
after sight（A.S）
见票后
after sight bill
见票后(若干天)付款期票
aftercare engineer

后照管工程师
after-sales service
售后服务
after-tax profit
税后利润
age of vessel
船龄
agency *n.*
代理；代理机构；代理权
agency agreement
代理协议
agency commission
代理手续费(或佣金)
agency contract
代理合同
agency fee
代理费
agenda *n.*
记录,备忘录
agent *n.*
代理人,代理商；外加剂,添加剂
agent bank
代理银行
agent firm
代理公司
agent for owner
业主的代理人
agent's tort
代理人侵权行为
aggregate *n.*
合计,总计；骨料
aggregate amount of letter of credit
信用证总限额
aggregate bin
骨料仓
aggregate-cement ratio
骨料水泥比
aggregate gradation
骨料级配
aggregation *n.*
集团；聚集
aggregative planning
总体规划

agio *n.*
折扣,贴水；银行手续费
agitating truck
搅拌运料车
agree *v.*
达成协议；同意,赞成
agreed compensation
商定的补偿
agreed port of destination
约定目的港
agreed rate
协定运费率
agreed sum
商定金额
agreed terms
商定条件
agreement *n.*
协议,协定,契约
agreement form
协议书格式
agreement of understanding
非正式协议
ahead of schedule
提前完成计划
aide-memoire *n.*
[法]备忘录
air brick
空心砖
air carrier
空运承运人
air compressor
空气压缩机
air conditioner
空气调节器
air consignment note (ACN)
空运发货单,航空托运单
air entrained agent
(混凝土)加气剂
air flue
风道,烟道
air freight
航空运费；航空货运,空运货物
air hammer

气锤
air inlet
进风口
air receipt
空运收据
air risk
空运险
Air Transportation Cargo Insurance
航空运输货物保险
airport tax
机场税
airway bill (AWB)
空运提单
airway bill of lading
空运提单
alcohol n.
酒精,乙醇
alien a.
外国的
alien bank
外国银行
alien corporation
外国公司
alien merchant
外商
alienate v.
转让,产权转移
alienation n.
转让
alignment n.
定线,准线;组合,联盟
all expected benefits
全部预期效益
all expected costs
全部预期费用
all parties
各方
all parties to a contract
合同各方
all risks (a/r, A.R.)
一切险,综合险,全险
all risks insurance
一切险保险
all risks marine insurance
海上综合保险
allied company
联营公司
all-in contract
整套承包制合同
all-in price
总价格
all-in rate
综合单价,总括性利率
all-in-one program
一揽子项目
allocate v.
分配(资金);分派;拨(款);分摊
allocate cost
分摊成本
allocate price
调拨价格
allocated cost
已分摊成本
allocation n.
分配;分摊;拨款
allocation of business profits
营业利润分摊
allocation of funds
资金分配
allocation of responsibility
责任分担
allocation of risks
风险分担
allotment n.
拨款,分配
allotment advice
拨款通知
allowable cost
允许成本
allowable load
容许荷载
allowable soil pressure
容许土压力
allowance n.

津贴,补助费;允许;折扣,备抵
allowance clause
短溢装条款,宽容条款
allowance for bad debts
备抵坏账
allowance for profit
允许利润
allowance for sales discount
备抵销货折扣
all-purpose financial statement
通用财务报表
all-risk policy
一切险保险单
alongside bill of lading
船边交货提单
alter *v.*
改动,变更
alteration *n.*
改动,更改,变更,修订
alteration of works
工程变更
alteration work
变更工作
altered check
涂改的支票
alternate *a.*
交替的,轮流的
alternative *a.*
两者挑一的,备选的 *n.* 备选方案,替代方案
alternative duty
选择税
alternative goods
供选择的货物
alternative material and equipment
替代材料与设备
alternative of financial nature
商务备选方案,商务选择性报价
alternative provisions
替代条款
alternative solution
替代方案
alternator *n.*
交流发电机
amalgamated balance sheet
合并资产负债表
amalgamation *n.*
合并;混合
ambiguity *n.*
含义不明确,模棱两可
amend *v.*
改正,修改
amend the amount of L/C
修改信用证金额
amend the terms of L/C
修改信用证条款
amendment *n.*
修改,更正,修订
amendment advice
修改通知单
amendment of bidding (tender) documents
招标文件的修改
amendment of contract
修正合同
amendment of letter of credit
信用证修改(书)
amenity *n.*
(环境,建筑物等)舒适,方便
amicable *a.*
友好的
amicable settlement
友好解决
amicable settlement of dispute
争端的友好解决
amortization *n.*
分期偿还;转让(不动产);摊销
amortization cost
折旧费
amortization rate
分期偿还率
amortized mortgage loan
分期偿还抵押贷款
amount *n.*
数额;总数;金额
amount allocated

分配额, 拨款额
amount insured
保险金额
amount not recovered
未能收回的金额
amount of a draft
汇票金额
amount of an annuity
年金金额
amount of claim
索赔额
amount of insurance
保险金额
amount of the credit
信用证金额
amusement *n.*
娱乐
analysis *n.*
分析
analysis and evaluation methodology
分析和评估方法
analyze a market
分析行情
anchor *n.*
锚杆, 锚筋 *v.* 锚固
anchor bar
锚杆, 锚筋
anchor bolt
锚栓, 地脚螺栓
anchorage *n.*
锚固; 锚座; 锚具
anchorage dues *n.*
停泊税; 停泊地; 锚固, 锚座
ancillary *n.*
附属物; 助手
ancillary restrictions
附加限制
angle steel
角钢
Anglo-American Law System
英美法系
annex *n.*
附录, 附件 *v.* 附加

announce *v.*
宣布
announced bid price
唱标价
announcement *n.*
通告
annual *a.*
年度的, 每年的
annual account
年度决算
annual budget
年度预算
annual cash ceiling
年度支付最高限额
annual closing
年度结算
annual costs
年度费用
annual disbursements
年度支付额
annual income
年收入
annual inflation rate
年通货膨胀率
annual interest rate
年利率
annual leave
年度休假
annual percentage rate (APR)
年利息率
annual precipitation
年降水量
annual production capacity (APC)
年生产能力
annual rental
年租
annual report
年度报告
annual sales
年销售量
annual sales volume
年销售额
annual statement

年度决算书
annuity *n.*
年金
annul *v.*
取消,废除,使无效
annulling of the contract
撤销合同
antedate *v.*
填早日期,倒填日期
antedated check
倒填日期支票
anti-avoidance measures
反避税措施
anticipate *v.*
预期,预料;提前偿付(或支取)
anticipated acceptance
预先承兑,提前支付的承兑汇票
anticipated cost
预期成本
anticipated gain
预期收益
anticipated interest
预期利息
anticipated price
预期价格
anticipated profit
预期利润
anticipation *n.*
预期;提前偿付(或支取)
anticipatory breach
先期违约
anticorrosive paint
防锈漆
anti-dumping duty
反倾销税
anti-evasion measures
反逃税措施
antiquities *n.*
古董
antirust *a.*
防锈的
antiseepage *n.*
防渗
antiseismic *a.*
抗地震的
anti-trust law
反托拉斯法
apparatus *n.*
仪器,装置
appeal *n. v.*
上诉;呼吁
appeal board
上诉委员会
appeal bond
上诉保证书
appeal to arbitration
诉诸仲裁
appear *v.*
刊登;出庭
appearance in court
出庭
appendix *n.*
附录,附件
appendix to bid
投标书附录
appendix to contract
合同附件
applicable *a.*
适用的
applicable law
适用的法律
applicant *n.*
申请人;投保人
applicant for insurance
投保人
application *n.*
申请(书);应用
application fee
申请费
application for arbitration
仲裁申请
application for business
营业申请
application for employment
求职申请
application for export licence

出口许可证申请书
application for insurance
投保单
application for letter of credit
信用证开证申请书,信用证申请书
application for payment
付款申请,支付申请
application for shipment
装运申请
application for special commitment
申请特别承诺
application for withdrawal
申请撤回;提款申请
application form
申请表
apply *v.*
申请;适用于
apply for reimbursement
报销
apply to the customs
报关
appoint *v.*
委派,约定
appointed bank
指定的银行
appointing authority
任命机构
apportion *v.*
分配,分摊
apportionment n.
分摊;拨款;(共同海损的)分摊数额
apportionment of damages
损害赔偿的分担
apportionment of liability
责任分担
appraisal *n.*
评估,评价;评价书;鉴定
appraise *v.*
评估,评价;鉴定
appraised value
评定价值,评估确认价值
appraiser *n.*
估价人,评价人,鉴定人

appreciation *n.*
升值,涨价,增值
approaches *n.*
方法,步骤
approbate *v.*
(依法)认可,批准
appropriate *v.*
拨给(款项等);挪用 *a.* 适当的
appropriate a fund
拨款
appropriate money
拨款
appropriation *n.*
拨款;挪用,占用
approval *n.*
批准,赞同
approval notice of the contract
合同批准通知
approval process
审批过程
approve *v.*
批准,授权,许可
approved *a.*
批准的,通过的
approved bidders list
批准的投标人名单
approved change order
批准的变更命令
approved vendors list
批准的供货商名单
approximate *a.*
近似的,大约的
approximate bill of quantities
近似工程量清单
arbiter *n.*
仲裁员,公断人,裁决人
arbitrage *n.*
套利;套汇
arbitral *a.*
仲裁的
arbitral award
裁决书
arbitral decision

仲裁裁决
arbitral procedure
仲裁程序
arbitral tribunal
仲裁庭
arbitrate *v.*
仲裁,裁决
arbitrate a dispute
仲裁争端
arbitration *n.*
仲裁
arbitration act
仲裁法案
arbitration agreement
仲裁协议
arbitration award
仲裁裁决,公断书
arbitration board
仲裁委员会
arbitration clause
仲裁条款
arbitration fee
仲裁费
arbitration law
仲裁法
arbitration of disputes
争端仲裁
arbitration panel
仲裁人员,仲裁小组
arbitration procedure
仲裁程序
arbitration rules
仲裁规则
arbitration tribunal
仲裁法庭
arbitrator *n.*
仲裁员,公断人,裁决人
arch bridge
拱桥
arch dam
拱坝
architect *n.*
建筑师

architectural design
建筑设计
architectural engineer
建筑工程师
architectural perspective
建筑透视图
architectural working drawing
建筑施工图
architecture *n.*
建筑学;建筑设计
area *n.*
地区;面积
area allotted for the construction
施工划拨用地
argument *n.*
争论
arm's length quotation
正常报价;公平交易
arrange *v.*
安排;调解
arrangement *n.*
安排;协议;调解
arrangement of reinforcement
钢筋布置
arrears *n.*
拖欠,欠款
arrest *vt. n.*
扣留(船只,货物),扣押(财产)
arrested property
被扣押的财产
arrestment *n.*
财产扣押
arrival *n.*
到达
arrival contract
到货合同
arrival notice
到货通知;抵埠通知
arrival quality
到货品质,到货质量
arrival terms
到货条件
arrive *v.*

到达
art of negotiation
谈判艺术
article *n.*
(法律的)条,条款;项目;物品
articles *n.*
章程,法规,规章,条例;物品
articles of agreement
协议条文
artificial *a.*
人造的;虚假的
artificial obstruction
人为障碍,人为拖延手段
artificial person
法人
artificial risk
人为风险
as a last resort
作为最后一着(手段)
as constructed
实际建成的
asbestos *n.*
石棉
asbestos tile
石棉瓦
as-built documents
竣工文件
as-built drawing
竣工图纸
as-built schedule
实际工期
ask for loan
借债,告贷
ask for payment
催付,催缴
ask for samples
要样
asked (asking) price
要价,索价
aspect *n.*
方面;(建筑物的)方位,方向
asphalt *n.*
沥青

asphalt concrete
沥青混凝土
asphalt concrete pavement
沥青混凝土路面
asphalt felt
油毛毡
asphalt mixing unit
沥青搅拌设备
as-planned schedule
计划工期
assemble *v.*
装配,组装
assembling reinforcement
绑扎钢筋
assembly *n.*
装配,组装
assembly drawing
安装图,装配图
assembly line
生产线,装配线
assembly shop
装配车间
assertion *n.*
主张,断言
assess *v.*
评价,估价;确定,评估
assess the damages
确定损害赔偿额
assessed value
估定价值
assessment *n.*
评价,评估,估算,估价
assessor *n.*
估价财产人,确定税款的人
assets *n.*
资产;财产
assets account
资产账户
assets and liabilities
资产与负债
assets cover
资产担保,资产抵偿
assets depreciation

资产折旧 | 协会,社团
assets turnover | **assumed loss ratio**
资产周转率 | 预定损失率
assets valuation | **assurance** *n.*
资产估价,资产计价 | 保险;保证
assign *v.* | **assure** *v.*
分配;指定;转让财产 | 对…进行保险;保证,使…放心
assignable *a.* | **assured** *n.*
可转让的 | 投保人,被保险人,保险受益人
assignee *n.* | **assurer** *n.*
受让人,代理人 | 保险人,承保人
assignee in bankruptcy | **at a discount**
破产资产管理人 | 折扣,低于票面价值,贴水
assigner, assignor *n.* | **at a premium**
转让人,委托人 | 溢价
assignment *n.* | **at buyer's option**
转让;转让证书;权益转让 | 由买方选择
assignment of contract | **at discretion**
合同转让 | 随意,任意
assignment of debt | **at liberty**
债务转让 | 有权
assignment of lease | **at market**
转租 | 按市价
assignment of policy | **at maturity**
保险单转让 | (远期汇票等的)到期
assigns *n.* | **at odds**
受让人,代理人 | 有矛盾,有分歧
assistance *n.* | **at par**
协助,援助 | 按面值,平价
assistant *n.* | **at risk**
助理 | 有风险
assistant engineer | **at seller's option**
助理工程师 | 由卖方选择
assistant project manager | **at sight**
项目经理助理 | 见票即付
assistant superintendent | **at the lower of cost or market**
助理监理员 | 按成本或市价孰低计价
associate *v.* | **attach** *v.*
联合 *a.* 非正式的,副的 *n.* 同事,合伙人 | 随附,附上;扣押,查封
 | **attached account**
associate member | 被查封账户
准会员 | **attached clause**
association *n.* | 附加条款

attached list
附表
attachment *n.*
附件；附加装置；传票，查封(财产)
attachment of risk
风险责任的起期(即保险责任开始生效)
attendance *n.*
出席；出工
attention *n.*
注意；由…经办(商务信函用语)
attestation *n.*
证明，证词，证据；宣誓
attorney *n.*
代理人，律师；受权人，受托人，代办人
attractive price
具有吸引力的价格
attributable to
可归因于…
auction *n. v.*
拍卖
audit *n. v.*
审计，查账；清算，决算
audit findings
审核结果
audit trail
审计线索，查账追踪
audited annual report
年度审计报告
audited financial statement
财务审计报表
auditing clauses
审计条款，查账条款
auditor *n.*
审计员，审核人，查账人
authenticate *v.*
认证；证明；出具证据；转开(保函)
authenticated *a.*
权威性的；可信的，可靠的
authenticity *n.*
真实性，可靠性
authoritative interpretation
权威性解释
authoritative precedent
权威性判例
authorities concerned
有关当局
authority *n.*
权力(机构)，官方当局；职权，权限
authority limits
权力范围
authority to delegate
权力委托，授权的权力
authority to pay
授权付款
authorization *n.*
授权，认可；委任；核准
authorization to proceed
授权进行
authorize *v.*
授权，核准，审定
authorized *a.*
被授权的；核准的，审定的
authorized bank
指定银行，授权银行
authorized capital
核准资本
authorized capital stock
法定股本；核定股本
authorized representative
授权代表
authorized signature
授权人签名
authorizing engineer
授权(给他人)的工程师
autocratic acts
专制行为
autograph *n.*
签署，亲笔签名
automatic transfer service
自动转账服务
autonomous tariff
自主税率
autonomous tariff system
自主税则

auxiliary book
辅助账簿
auxiliary enterprise
附属企业
auxiliary structures
附属建筑物
availability n.
可得性；可用性；有效性
available a.
可得的；可用的；有效的
available balance
可动用结余
average n.
海损；平均数 a. 平均的，一般的
average agent
海损代理人，理赔代理人
average agreement
海损协议
average bond
共同海损保证书
average contribution
（共同）海损分摊
average cost per unit
平均单位成本
average life
平均使用年限
average method of depreciation（or amortization）
直线折旧（或摊销）法
average policy
海损保险单
average price
平均价格
average service conditions
一般使用条件，正常使用条件

average statement
（共同）海损理算书
average taker
海损理算人
average tare
平均皮重
avoid a contract
废止合同
avoidable accident
可避免的事故
avoidable cost
可避免成本
avoidance n.
废止，避免
avoidance of double taxation
避免双重征税
avouch v.
保证，担保
award v.
判给，授予 n. 判决，裁决书；奖励
award criteria
授标准则
award decision
授标决定
award notification
授标通知
award of contract
中标，授予合同，授标
awarded by court
经法庭判定
awarded contract price
中标合同价
axis n.
轴线，轴

B

back n.
背面 v. 背书（支票等）a. 拖欠的，过期的；背面的
back a bill
在票据上背书
back a check

背书支票
back bond
退还担保
back charges
决算后诸项费用
back door
非法途径,后门
back freight
退货运费,回程运费
back money
拖欠款,过期未付款
back order
延交定货,未交付订单
back pay
欠薪
back tax
退税
backdate *v.*
倒填日期,填早日期,追溯
backed bond
已背书债券,有担保债券
backfill *v.*
回填 *n.* 回填料
background *n.*
背景
background material
背景材料
backhoe excavator
反铲挖土机
backlog *n.*
储备;积压的工作,定单积压
back-stopping cost
资助费用
back-to-back account
对开账户
back-to-back (letter of) credit
背对背信用证,转开信用证
backup *n.*
贮存备用;待用品;后备人员
backup data
备查资料
bad account
呆账,坏账

bad cheque
空头支票
bad debt
坏账,呆账
bad packing
包装不良(提单批语)
baffling *a.*
不能理解的,困惑的
bail *v.*
将(财物)委托于…;保释 *n.* 保释金
bail bond
保释金保函
bailee *n.*
(财产)受托人,被保释人
bailer, bailor *n.*
(财产)委托人,保释人
bailment *n.*
寄托;保释
balance *n.*
平衡,收支平衡;结余,余额
balance due
所欠余额,结欠余额
balance of account
账面余额
balance of amount
款项余额
balance of current account
经常项目差额,往来账结余
balance of international indebtedness
国际借贷差额
balance of payment (BOP)
(国际)收支差额
balance of payments deficit
(国际)收支逆差
balance of payments surplus
(国际)收支顺差
balance of revenue and expenditure
财政收支平衡
balance sheet
资产负债表,平衡表
balance sheet data
资产负债数据
balancing account

结账,平衡账户
bale *n.*
包,捆
bale capacity
包装容量
ban *v.*
禁止;禁令
ban on export
禁止出口
ban on import
禁止进口
bank *n.*
银行
bank acceptance
银行承兑汇票
bank accommodation
银行资金融通
bank account
银行账户;银行账
bank balance
银行存款余额
bank bill
银行票据
bank book
银行存折
bank cable transfer
银行电汇
bank charge
银行手续费
bank check
银行支票,支票
bank credit
银行信贷
bank deposit
银行存款
bank discount
银行贴现
bank financed consulting services
银行资助的咨询服务
bank financing
银行贷款,银行资助
bank guarantee
银行保证书,银行保函

bank holding company
银行控股公司
bank loan
银行贷款
bank of deposit
存款银行
bank overdraft
银行透支
bank prime rate
银行优惠利率
bank protection work
护岸工程
bank rate
银行贴现率,银行利率
bank remittance fee
银行汇款手续费
bank statement
对账单
bank transfer
银行间的转账;银行汇款
bankable bill
可在银行贴现的票据
bankable project
银行愿担保的项目
banker's acceptance
银行承兑票据
banker's acceptance credit
银行承兑信用证
banker's invoice
银行发票
banker's L/G
银行保函
banker's lien
银行留置权
bank-financed project
银行贷款项目
bankrupt *n.*
破产者;破产 *a.* 破产的
bankruptcy *n.*
破产,破产倒闭
bankruptcy act
破产法案
bankruptcy administrator

破产管理人
bank's draft
银行汇票
bank's order
银行本票
bar *n.*
障碍,限制;线条;律师业 *v.* 限制,阻止
bar association
律师协会
bar chart
线条图
bar council
司法委员会,律师委员会
bar cutter
钢筋截断机
bar spacing
钢筋间距
bareboat charter
光船租赁
bargain *n. v.*
买卖合同;议价,成交;商定
bargaining position
价格谈判的地位,议价能力
barge *n.*
驳船,平底船
bar-mat reinforcement
钢筋网配筋
barometer *n.*
气压表
barrage *n.*
堰;坝;挡水建筑物
barratry *n.*
欺诈行为,不法行为
barred claim
失去时效的债权
barred debt
受时效限制的债务
barred obligation
受时效限制的债务
barrister *n.*
专门律师,大律师
barter *n.*
易货,物物交换
barter trade
易货贸易
base cost estimate
基本成本估计,基本费用估计
base date
基准日期
base freight rate
基本运费
base lending rate
基本贷款汇率
base level
基准面,基面
base line
基线,底线
base line budget
基线预算
base line cost
原始费用,基线费用
base price
标底,基价
base price index
基本价格指数
base stock
基本库存
base value
基期价值
base year
基准年
basic contractual responsibilities
基本合同责任
basic design
基本设计
basic interest rate
基本利率
basic item
基本分项工作
basic price
基本价格
basic rates
基本费率
basic salary
基本工资

basic wages 基本工资
basis *n*. 基础,根据
basis for budget and schedule 预算与进度的依据
basket purchase 整套购买
batch *n*. 配料;一批
batch bin 配料仓
batch budgeting 分批预算
batch costing 分批成本预算法
batch production 批量生产
batching plant 混凝土搅拌厂
beam *n*. 梁;横杆
beam and slab structure 梁板结构
bear *n*. 空头,卖空 *v*. 承担
bear a loss 负担损失
bear expenses 承担费用
bear legal liability 承担法律责任
bearer *n*. 持票人;持有人 *a*. (证券等)不计名的
bearer B/L 不记名提单
bearer bond 不记名债券
bearing capacity 承载力
bearing pile 承重桩,支承桩

bearing wall 承重墙
beat down 跌价,杀价
beat down price 压价
become (fall) due 到期的,应付的
bedrock price 最低价格,底价
before tax income (or profit) 税前收益(或利润)
beginning balance 期初余额
behavior criterion 行为标准
behavioural characteristics criteria 行为标准
behind schedule 拖期,跟不上进度
belated *a*. 误期的
belated claim 过期的索赔,迟索的赔款
belt conveyor 传送带,皮带运输机
belt loader 带式装料机
belt-bucket elevator 斗式提升机
benchmark *n*. 水准点
benchmark rate 基准利率
benchworker *n*. 钳工
bender *n*. 弯筋机
beneficial *a*. 有权益的,受益的
beneficial interest 受益权
beneficial owner

受益业主
beneficiary *n.*
受益人
benefit *n.*
利益,效益;补助金
benefit of agreement
协议利益
benefit of insurance
保险利益
benefit-cost ratio（BCR）
效益成本比率
benefited interest
利益,权益;补助金
benefited party
受益方
berth *n.*
泊位,船位
berth charter
舱位包租,班轮条件租赁
berth clause
泊位包租条款
betterment *n.*
改良;不动产增值;[复]修缮经费
betterment and extension
修缮和扩建
bid *v. n.*
投标;报价;标价;买方递盘
bid addenda
投标书补遗
bid bond
投标担保,投标保函
bid clarification meeting
投标澄清会议
bid clarifications
投标书中问题的澄清
bid cost
投标费用
bid currencies
投标货币
bid due date
投标日期
bid evaluation
评标

bid examination
投标核查
bid form
投标格式
bid guarantee
投标保函,投标保证书
bid invitation
招标,招标通知
bid invitation contents
招标内容
bid invitation letter
投标邀请函
bid language
投标语言
bid opening
开标
bid opening minutes
开标纪要
bid opening procedure
开标程序
bid package
投标文件包
bid package contents
投标文件内容
bid period
投标期
bid phase
投标阶段
bid preparation
投标准备,编标
bid price
投标价,投标总报价
bid procedure
投标程序
bid process
投标步骤
bid receipt
投标书签收
bid requirement
投标要求
bid review and evaluation
投标书的审查与评估
bid schedule of prices

投标价目表
bid security
投标保证
bid shopping
投标压价
bid substance
投标实质内容
bid summary
投标汇总
bid tabulations
投标表册
bid unit price
投标单价
bid validity period
投标有效期
bid withdrawal
撤回投标书
bidder *n.*
投标人,投标者
bidder selection
选择投标人
bidder selection criteria
选择投标人准则
bidder's obligation
投标人的义务
bidder's prequalification
投标人资格预审
bidder's qualification
投标人资格
bidder's return of documents
投标人退还文件
bidding *n.*
投标
bidding advice
投标通知
bidding and award
投标与授标
bidding documents
招标文件
bidding price
投标报价
bidding time
投标时间

bid-rigging
操纵投标
bilateral agreement
双边协议
bilateral contract
双边合同
bilateral document
双边文件
bill *n.*
票据;账单;汇票,期票;清单;起诉书
bill at sight
见票即付汇票
bill discounted
已贴现票据
bill endorsed in blank
空白背书汇票
bill for collection
托收汇票
bill of approximate quantity contract
估计工程量单价合同
bill of credit
取款凭单,付款通知书
bill of entry (B/E.)
报关单
bill of exchange (B/E.)
汇票
bill of lading (B/L.)
提单,提货单
bill of materials
用料清单
bill of parcels
发货单,包裹单
bill of payment
付款清单
bill of quantities
工程量表,工程量清单
bill of quantities contract
工程量表合同
bill of sale
卖据,发货单
bill of sufferance
待检查物品单,免税单
bill of variations

工程变更单
bill of works
工程报表
bill payable
应付票据
bill payable at fixed date after sight
见票后定期付款汇票
bill payable at sight
见票即付汇票,即期汇票
bill payable by installments
分期付款汇票
bill payable on demand
即期汇票
bill purchased
买入的汇票
bill rate
票据贴现率
bill receivable
应收票据
bill undue
未到期汇票
bill-of-lading freight
提单运费
bills for collection (BC)
托收票据
bind *v.*
约束;使(协定)确定不变;负法律义务(或责任)
binder *n.*
临时协议;承保协议;暂保单
binding *a.*
有约束力的,必须遵守的
binding contract
有约束力的合同
binding power
约束力
binding receipt
暂保收据
binding signature
有约束力的签字
bitumen *n.*
沥青
bituminous concrete
沥青混凝土
bituminous grouting
沥青灌浆
bituminous layer
沥青层
bituminous water-proof coating
沥青防水层
blade machine
平地机
blank *a.*
空白的,未填写的
blank bill
空白票据
blank bill of lading
空白提单
blank check
空白支票
blank endorsement
空白背书,不记名背书
blank (letter of) credit
空额信用证,空白信用汇票
blank note
空白支票
blanket acceptance
全部接收
blanket approval
全部认可,全部同意
blanket bond
总括保证
blanket contract
一揽子合同
blanket purchase contract
一揽子采购合同
blocked account
冻结账户
blocked currency
冻结货币
blocked deposit
冻结存款
blocked fund
冻结资金
blotter *n.*
临时分录账;原始账,流水账

blower *n.*
鼓风机,吹风机
blue print of the project
工程蓝图
blueprint *n.*
蓝图,规划
blueprinter *n.*
晒图机
board *n.*
委员会,董事会,部门理事会
board chairman
董事会主席,董事长
board foot
板英尺(木材的英制计量单位)
board meeting
董事会会议
board of control
管理局
board of directors
董事会
board of executive directors
执行董事会
board of governors
理事会
board of reference
咨询委员会
board of review
评审委员会;上诉委员会
board presentation
提交董事会
bodily injury
人身伤害,身体伤害
bolt *n.*
螺栓
bona fide *a.*
[拉]真诚的,善意的
bona vacantia
无人继承权;无主物
bona-fide bidder
善意投标人
bona-fide endorsee
善意被背书人
bona-fide holder
善意持有人,合法持票人
bond *n.*
担保;债券,公债
bond market
债券市场
bond payable
应付债券
bonded area
保税区
bonded goods
保税货物
bonded port
保税港
bonded stores
保税仓库
bonded warehouse
保税仓库
bonding agent
担保代理人
bonding capacity
担保能力;担保额度
bonding company
担保公司
bonding rate
担保费率;债券利率
bonus *n.*
奖金;额外津贴;红利
bonus clause
奖励条款
bonus for completion
竣工奖金
bonus for early completion
提前竣工奖金
bonus issue
派发红股
bonus share (stock)
红利股
boojee pump
气压灌浆泵
book *n.*
账簿;账面 *v.* 记账;订货;预订
book balance
账面余额

book cost
账面成本
book inventory
账面盘存
book loss
账面损失
book of account
会计账簿
book profit
账面利润
book surplus
账面盈余
book value
账面价值
bookkeeper *n.*
簿记员；记账员
bookkeeping *n.*
簿记
boom *n.*
繁荣(期)，(经济的)景气
boom hoist
臂式吊车
bordereau *n.*
[法]分保明细表；业务报表
borderline cases
难以确定的情况
bore hole
钻孔
bored pile
钻孔桩
boring rig
钻架；钻机；钻探设备
borrow *v.*
借款；借入
borrower *n.*
借款人，借用人
borrowing *n.*
借贷，贷款
borrowing bank
借款银行
borrowing cost
借贷成本
borrowing country
借款国
both parties
双方
both sides clear
银货两讫
bottom price
最低价格
bounced cheque
(因存款不足)被银行退回的支票
bouncer *n.*
空头支票
bound *a.*
受约束的，有义务的
bound labour
合同工
boundary *n.*
分界线；边界
box girder
箱型大梁
boycott *v.*
联合抵制
branch *n.*
分公司，分支机构
branch pipe
叉管，支管
brand *n.*
商标；品牌
brand name
标牌
brand-new
全新的，最新出品的
breach *n.*
违反，破坏，不履行
breach of contract
违约，违反合同
breach of contractor
承包商违约
breach of duty
失职
breach of law
违法
break *v.*
(股票等)暴跌；使…破产，耗尽…的

资产;取消;违反
break a contract
违反合同
break down clause
机损条款
breakage n.
破坏;[复]损耗量;索赔费
breakdown n.
分类;分析;明细表
breakdown of lump sum bid price
投标包干价格分解
breakdown of price
单价分析
breakdown price
分项价格
break-down test
破坏试验
break-even analysis
保本分析;损益平衡分析;盈亏平衡分析
break-even chart
保本图,损益平衡图
break-even point
保本点,盈亏平衡点
breakwater n.
防波堤
bribe n.
贿赂,贿赂物 v. 行贿,收买
bribery n.
行贿
brick n.
砖
brick masonry structure
砖石结构
bricklayer n.
瓦工
bridge crane
桥式吊车,桥式起重机
bridge deck
桥面板
bridge financing
过渡性融资
bridge loan

过渡贷款
bridge pier
桥墩
bridge rail
桥栏杆
bridge the price gap
解决差价
brief n.
大纲,提要,摘要
bring down prices
降价
broke a.
破产的
broken period
非标准期限
broken space
空余舱位;舱位损失
broken stowage
亏舱;损失舱位,积载空隙
broker n.
经纪人,代理人,中介人
brokerage n.
经纪人佣金;经纪业;回扣
broking n.
经纪业
bucket n.
水桶;(浇混凝土的)吊罐;(挖土机的)铲斗
bucket loader
斗式装载机
budget n.
预算,预算费
budget allocation
预算拨款
budget and cost control
预算与成本控制
budget control
预算控制
budget document
预算书
budget estimate
概算
budget of expenditure

支出预算
budget proposal
概算
budget summary
预算汇总
budgeted cost
预算成本
budgeted man-hour
预算工时
buffer fund
缓冲基金
buffer inventory
缓冲库存;保险储备存量
buffer stock
安全存货
builder *n.*
建造商;[英]建造师,营造师
building loan
建筑贷款
building owner
房产主
building permit
建筑执照,建设许可证
building regulations
房屋建造规章
building tax
建筑物税,房产税
Build-Operate-Sell (BOS)
建设—运营—出售
Build-Operate-Transfer (BOT)
建设—运营—移交(或转让)
Build-Own-Operate (BOO)
建设—拥有—运营
Build-Own-Operate-Maintain (BOOM)
建设—拥有—运营—维护
Build-Own-Operate-Subsidize-Transfer (BOOST)
建设—拥有—运营—补贴—移交
Build-Own-Operate-Transfer (BOOT)
建设—拥有—运营—移交
Build-Own-Sell (BOS)

建设—拥有—出售
Build-Rent-Transfer (BRT)
建设—出租—移交
Build-Transfer-Operate (BTO)
建设—移交—运营
bulk *n.*
散装货物;大量 *a.* 散装的
bulk cargo carrier
散装货船
bulk cement
散装水泥
bulldozer *n.*
推土机
bullet loan
一次还款式贷款
bunker adjustment factor
燃油附加调整率
burden *n.*
负担;义务;负荷,载重;间接费用
bureau of shipping
船级社
buried pipe
暗管
business *n.*
生意;商业,商行;工商企业;事情
business cycle
商业周期
business development
业务开发
business environmental risk index (BERI)
企业环境风险指数
business interruption insurance
经营中断保险
business license
营业执照
business place
营业地点
business report
营业报表
business transaction
商业交易
business-like

讲究实际的
buy off
买通
buy-back
返销,回购
buy-back agreement
返销协议
buy-back of product
产品返销,回购产品
buyer *n.*
买方,买主
buyer credit
买方信贷
buyer's market
买方市场
buying expenses
进货费用
buying offer
买方递盘,买方发价,购买要约,购货发盘
buying order
购货单
buying price
买价
buyout *n.*
收购
by contract
按照合同,承包
by measurement
按体积(计运费)
by share
按份额
by volume
按体积(计运费)
by-law
细则;地方法规

C

cable *n.*
电报
cable crane
缆索起重机
cable hoist
卷扬机,绞车
cable rate
电汇费率
cable suspension bridge
悬索桥
cable-stayed bridge
斜拉桥
cadastre *n.*
土地清册,不动产清册
caisson foundation
沉箱基础
caisson pile
管柱桩;沉箱桩
calamity *n.*
灾害,灾荒
calcium lime
生石灰
calculate *v.*
计算,核算
calculated risk
计划风险,预计风险
calculations
计算书
calendar *n.*
历法;日历;月历;日程表
calendar day
日历日
calendar month
日历月,历月
calendar year
日历年,年度
call *v.*
催缴;通知偿还

call deposit
通知存款
call for bids (tenders)
招标
call for funds
集资
call in a loan
收回贷款
call letter
催款信；推销商品的信件
call loan
通知贷款；短期同行拆借；活期贷款
call money
活期贷款
call price
赎回价格
callable *a.*
可赎回的；可随时支取的；应要求即付的
callable bond
可赎回公司债券
calling *n.*
职业；行业
calling for proposals
要求（承包商）提出建议书
cambist *n.*
汇兑商；各国货币比值手册
camp *n.*
营地
camp equipment
营房设备
camps and housing
现场营地与住房
cancel *v.*
取消，注销；删去，省略；作废
cancel a contract
撤销合同
canceled check
注销的支票，付讫支票
cancellation *n.*
取消，注销；删去，省略；作废
cancellation of a contract
撤销合同

cancellation of licence
吊销执照
candidate for tendering
投标候选人
cap *n.*
（利率）上限
capability *n.*
能力
capacity *n.*
职位；资格；权力；容量；能力
capacity for duties
承担义务的能力
capacity for right
行使职权能力
capacity operating rate
设备利用率
capacity to contract
缔约能力
capital *n.*
资本；资金；资方
capital account
资本性账户；固定资产账户
capital and labour
劳资双方
capital assets
固定资产，资本性资产
capital bonus
股票股利，资本红利
capital budget
资本预算
capital charges
资本支出
capital composition structure
资本结构
capital construction
基本建设
capital cost
基本建设费用
capital expenditure
资本支出
capital flight
资金外逃
capital formation

资本形成
capital fund
资本基金,基建资金
capital intensive project
资金密集项目
capital investment
资本投资
capital market
资本市场
capital outlay
资本支出;基建投资
capital return
资本收益率
capital stock
股本
capital stock authorized
法定股本
capital surplus
资本盈利,资本盈余
capital transfer tax
资本转移税
capital turnover rate
资本周转率
capitalizable cost
可资本化成本
capitation *n.*
按人计算,按人收费
caption *n.*
标题
caption of account
会计科目
card *n.*
卡片;会员证;信用卡;名片
card holder
持卡人
card issuer
发卡人
cardinal changes
根本性变更
cargo *n.*
船货;货物
cargo accounting advice
货物账款通知单

cargo damage adjustment
货损理算
cargo delivery notice
提货通知
cargo document
货运提单
cargo inspection
货物检查
cargo insurance
货运保险
cargo marine insurance
海洋货运保险
cargo mark
货物标志,货运唛头
cargo paper
货运单证
cargo policy
货物保险单
cargo transportation insurance
货物运输保险
carpenter *n.*
木工
carriage *n.*
货运,运输;运费
carriage and insurance paid to (CIP)
运费、保险费付至
carriage by air
空运
carriage by land
陆运
carriage by rail
铁路运输
carriage by road
公路运输
carriage expenses
运费
carriage forward
运费由收货人付,运费待付
carriage paid
运费已付
carriage paid to (CPT)
运费付至…(价)
carrier *n.*

承运人;运输公司;运输工具
carrier's liability insurance
承运人责任保险
carrier's lien
承运人留置权
carry *v.*
运载;结转;执行
carry out a contract
履行合同
carrying cost
置存成本
carrying value
账面价值;置存价值
cartage *n.*
搬运费,运货费
case *n.*
箱;案例
case estimate
案件(赔付)估价
case stated
判案要点陈述
cash *n.*
现金 *v.* 把……兑现
cash a cheque
支票兑现
cash account
现金账户,现金账
cash against delivery
交货付款
cash against document (CAD)
交单付款
cash allowance
现金额度
cash and delivery
付款交货
cash assets
现金资产
cash at bank
银行活期存款
cash bonus
现金奖金,现金红利
cash book
现金簿,现金账

cash credit
现金支出;现金贷方
cash deposit
保证金;现金存款
cash deposit as collateral
保证金,押金
cash disbursement journal
现金支出日记账
cash discount
现金折扣
cash dispenser
自动取款机
cash dividend
现金股息
cash flow
资金流动;现金流量
cash flow analysis
资金流分析
cash flow diagram
现金流图
cash flow estimate
现金流估计
cash flow statement
现金流量表
cash fund
现金基金
cash guarantee
现金担保
cash in order
订货付现
cash in treasury
库存现金
cash inflows
现金流入(量)
cash losses
现金赔款
cash management account (CMA)
现金管理账户
cash market
现金交易市场
cash on delivery (COD)
货到付款
cash on hand

手头现金,库存现金
cash on shipment（COS）
装船付现;装运付款
cash outflows
现金流出(量)
cash over and short
现金溢缺
cash payment
现金支付
cash purchase
现购,现金购买
cash realizable value
可变现价值
cash receipts journal
现金收入日记账
cash register
现金出纳机
cash sales
现金销售
cash settlement
现金结算
cash with order（CWO）
订货付现
cashed check
已兑现支票
cashier *n.*
出纳员
cashier's check（cheque）
银行本票
cashier's order
银行本票
cast *v.*
浇注
casting vote
决定性的一票
cast-in-place diaphragm wall
就地浇灌地下连续墙
cast-in-situ concrete
现浇混凝土
casual worker
临时工
casualty *n.*
灾难,意外事故;[复]伤亡人员
casualty insurance
意外事故险
casualty loss
意外损失
catalogue *n.*
种类,分类;商品目录
catalogue and summary
目录与摘要
catastrophe loss
巨灾损失
catch pit
集水坑,截水坑
catchment *n.*
流域;集水
category *n.*
种类,类型,类目
caterpillar crane
履带式起重机
caterpillar excavator
履带式挖掘机
caterpillar loader
履带式装载机
cause *n.*
原因,起因,诉因
caution money（security）
保证金
caveat *n.*
停止支付通知;停止诉讼申请
caveat emptor
[拉]买方负责,出门不换
caveat venitor
[拉]卖方负责,包退包换
cave-in *n.*
塌方
cease *v.*
停止,休止,终止
cease work
收工,停工
ceded company
分保公司,再保险公司
ceding company

再保险分出公司
ceiling *n.*
顶棚,天花板;最高限额
ceiling amount
最高限额
ceiling price
最高限价
cement block
预制水泥砌块
cement brand
水泥牌号
cement bunker
水泥仓
cement grout
水泥(压力)灌浆
cement injection
水泥喷浆
cement mortar
水泥砂浆
central bank
中央银行
centrifugal pump
离心泵
ceramsite concrete
陶粒混凝土
certificate *n.*
证明,证书;执照;单证
certificate fee
签证费
certificate for completion
竣工证书
certificate for export
出口检验证
certificate for payment
付款证书
certificate of clearance
清关证书
certificate of completion
竣工证明,竣工证书
certificate of credit standing
资信证明
certificate of deposit
存款单
certificate of dishonour
拒付证书
certificate of expenditure
支出证明书
certificate of inspection
(商品)检验证书
certificate of insurance (C/I)
保险单,保险凭证,保险证书
certificate of manufacture
(出口商)制造证明书
certificate of occupancy
占有证明书
certificate of origin (C/O)
产地证书,原产地证明书
certificate of quality
货物品质证书
certificate of re-export
再出口证书
certificate of registry
注册证书
certificate of release
债务解除证书
certificate of seaworthiness
适航证明书
certificate of testing
检验证书
certified accountant
注册会计师
certified check (cheque)
保付支票
certified cost engineer
注册成本工程师
certified public accountant (CPA)
[美]执业会计师
certify *v.*
证明
cessation *n.*
停止,休止,终止
cessation of liability
终止责任
cessation of work

停工
cesser clause
中止条款
cession *n.*
(财产,权利等)转让
cestui que trust
信托受益人
CFR (cost and freight)
成本加运费(价)
chain of command
指挥系统
chain risks
连锁风险
chairman *n.*
董事长;主席
chamber *n.*
议院;会议厅;会所
chamber of commerce
商会
chamber of trade
贸易协会
chance *n.*
机会;可能性;风险,意外
chance of loss
损失机会
change *v.*
变更,改动;兑换 *n.* 零钱
change notice
变更通知
change order
变更命令,变更指令
change order log
改变订单日志
change order procedure
改变订单程序
changed conditions
已变更的条件
changes in financial position
财务状况变动
changes in legislation
立法的变动
changes in personnel
人员的更换,职员的变更

channeller *n.*
凿沟机,挖槽机
character *n.*
品行证明书,(给雇员的)推荐信;标志,符号
characteristics *n.*
特点,性能
charge *n.*
收费,费用;指控 *v.* 要价;收费;使承担;控告
charge for storage & freight of goods
物资储运费
charge for trouble
手续费;酬劳费
charge off
冲销,销账
charge sales
赊销,赊售
charges for customs clearance
清关费
charging line
供电线路,供水管线,供料线
chart *n.*
图表;海图
chart of accounts
账户一览表,会计科目表
charter *n.*
公司执照;章程;契约;租船 *v.* 租;发执照;特许
charter by voyage
航次租船;程租
charter money
租金
charter of company
公司章程
charter party
租船合同;租船方
chartered accountant (CA)
[英]特许会计师,注册会计师
chartered engineer
注册工程师
chartered freight
租船运费

chartered period
租期
chartered quantity surveyor
注册工料测量师
chattel *n.*
动产
chattel mortgage
动产抵押
cheap credit
低息贷款
cheap labour force
廉价劳动力
cheap money
低息借款
check *n.*
[美]支票;检查 *v.* 检查,制止
check and accept
验收
check book
支票簿
check book stubs
支票簿存根
check mark
核对符号
check outstanding
未兑现支票
check register
支票登记簿
checkable *a.*
可用支票付款的
checking account
支票账户,活期账户
checking of estimate
概算书的检查
checklist *n.*
核对清单
checkout *n.*
结账
cheque *n.*
[英]支票
chief *a.*
主要的,首席的 *n.* 主任;重要部分
chief arbitrator
首席仲裁员
chief architect
总建筑师
chief delegate
首席代表
chief designer
总设计师
chief engineer
总工程师
chief resident engineer
驻地首席工程师
chipping machine
混凝土打毛机
choice of law
法律的选择
chose *n.*
动产;财产
chronological books
序时账簿
circuit breaker
断流器,断路开关
circular credit
旅行信用证,流通信用证
circulate *v.*
使…流通
circulating assets
流动资产
circulating fund
流动资金
circulating liabilities
流动负债
circulation tax
流通税
circumstances *n.*
事项,情况
civil *a.*
公民的;民用的;民事的;国内的
civil action
民事诉讼
civil architect
民用建筑师
civil architecture
民用建筑

civil code
民法典

civil commotion
民间骚乱

civil damages
民事损害赔偿

civil engineer
土木工程师

civil engineering
土木工程

civil engineering firm
土建公司

civil engineering procedure
土木工程程序

civil engineering standard method of measurement
土木工程工程量计算规则

civil law
民法,大陆法

civil legal relation with foreign element
涉外民事法律关系

civil liability
民事责任

civil liability insurance
民事责任险

civil responsibility
民事责任

civil status
公民地位

civil work
土建,土木工程

claim $v.$
索赔,索取,要求 $n.$ (权利)主张,索赔,要求权

claim against carrier
向承运人索赔

claim by owner
业主索赔

claim consciousness
索赔意识

claim cost components
索赔款的组成部分

claim event
索赔事件

claim for adjustment of price
要求调整合同价

claim for compensation
索赔补偿费

claim for damages
索赔损害赔偿费

claim for extension of time
延长工期索赔

claim for extra cost
额外费用索赔

claim for loss and expenses
损失与开支索赔

claim money
索赔款

claim ratio
赔付率,索赔率

claim settlement
理赔

claim settling agent
理赔代理人

claimant (claimer) $n.$
索赔人;原告;债权人;请求人

clamshell crane
抓斗式起重机

clarification $n.$
澄清

clarification of bidding (tender) documents
招标文件的澄清

clarify $v.$
阐明,澄清

class rate
分级费率

classification $n.$
类别,等级

classified depreciation
分类折旧

clause *n.*
条款,项目
claused bill of lading
附批注提货单,不洁提单
clay *n.*
粘土
clean bill
光票
clean (bill for) collection
光票托收
clean bill of lading
清洁提单,无暇疵提单
clean draft
光票,普通汇票
clean (letter of) credit
光票信用证,无跟单信用证
clean up the site
清理现场
cleanliness of site
现场整洁状况
clean-on-board bill of lading
已装船清洁提单
clear *v.*
清除;结关 *a.* 纯的;清楚的
clear a port
出港;结关
clear a ship
卸货
clear certificate
结关证明书
clear income
净收入
clear off
清偿
clear profit
净利润
clearance *n.*
清理;许可(证);结关,清关
clearance permit
出港许可证
clearance procedure
结关手续
clearance through customs
结关
clearing *n.*
结关;清除;结算
clearing account
暂记账户,待清账户
clearing agreement
结算协定
clearing bank
清算银行
clearing (clearance) agent
报关代理人;清算代理人
clerical *a.*
职员的;文书工作的
clerical cost
办公费用
clerical error
笔误,记录错误
clerk *n.*
管理员,职员,秘书
clerk of works
工程管理员,监督员
client *n.*
委托人,业主;当事人;顾客,客户
client adviser
业主顾问
client concerned
当事人
client's approval
业主的批准
client's personnel
业主的职员
client's property
业主的财产
client's representative
业主的代表
climate *n.*
气候
climate extremes
气候异常情况
close books
结账
closed account
已结清账户

closed bidding
非公开招标
closed market
封闭式市场
closed-end investment fund
定额投资基金
closing n.
收盘,停业,收市,结账
closing balance
期末余额
closing date
结账日期,截止日期
closing entry
结账分录
closing price
收盘价
closing rate
收盘汇率
closing stock
期末存货
closing techniques
成交技巧
closing trial balance
结账后试算表
co-acceptor
共同承兑人
coassignee n.
合伙受让人;合伙受托人
co-assurer
共同承保人
co-beneficiary
共同受益人
co-borrower
共同借款人
co-contractor
联营承包商
code n.
法规,法典;代码;准则,规范
code of accounts
账目编号
code of international conduct
国际行为准则
code of practice
施工规范
code requirement
法规要求
code-allowable
法规允许的
co-debtor
共同债务人
codes and standards
法规与标准
coding n.
编码
cofferdam n.
围堰
cofinancing n.
联合融资;共同资助
cognovit
[拉]n. 被告承认书,债务确认书
co-guarantor
共同担保人
coincide v.
符合,一致;巧合
co-insurance n.
共同保险,联合保险
co-insured a.
被共同保险的
cold-drawn bar
冷拉钢筋
collaboration n.
协作,合作
collapse v. n.
塌方,塌陷;毁坏
collateral n.
从属抵押品,附属担保品 a. 间接的,附属的
collateral acceptance
担保承兑
collateral bond
担保债券
collateral contract
附属合同
collateral evidence
旁证
collateral loan

抵押贷款
collateral mortgage
担保品抵押
collateral warranty
副担保书,附带担保
collateralized loan
有抵押品的贷款
collect *v.*
收取;托收;提取(货物)
collect a bill
托收汇票
collect data
收集资料
collect duties
征税
collecting agent
代收人;收账代理人
collecting bank
代收银行;托收银行
collection bill
托收汇票
collection on clean bill
光票托收
collection on documents
跟单托收
collection order
托收委托书
collection period
账款回收期
collections *n.*
收账;应收账款
collective bargaining agreement
劳资集体谈判协议
collision *n.*
碰撞
collision insurance
碰撞险
collusion *n.*
串通,舞弊
collusive agreement
勾结性协议
collusive bid (tender)
串通投标,勾结投标

co-manager
联合经理;共同管理人
combination *n.*
合并,联合
combination of bids
组合投标
combined carriage of goods
联合运货
combined certificate
联合凭证
combined financial statement
合并财务报表
combined offer
合并发盘
combined policy
联合保险单
combined quotation
合并报价(单)
combined transport bill of lading (C.T.B/L)
联运提单
come into collision with
跟…相撞
come into force
生效
command *n. v.*
命令,指挥
commence *v.*
开工,开始
commencement *n.*
开工,开始
commencement date
开工日期
commencement of cover
保险责任开始
commencement of work
开工
comment *n. v.*
注释;解说;评论
commerce *n.*
商业,贸易,商务
commercial *a.*
贸易的,商业的 *n.* 商业广告

commercial acceptance
商业承兑汇票
commercial affairs
商务
commercial agency
商业代理行
commercial articles
商务条款
commercial attaché
商务专员
commercial bank
商业银行
commercial bill
商业汇票
commercial claim
商务索赔
commercial code
商业法规
commercial company
商业公司,贸易公司
commercial correspondence
商业信函
commercial counselor
商务参赞
commercial court
商事法庭
commercial discount
商业折扣
commercial draft
商业汇票
commercial insurance
商业保险
commercial invoice
商业发票
commercial letter of credit
商业信用证
commercial loan
商业贷款
commercial paper
商业票据,商业单据
commercial registration
商品注册
commercial representative
商务代表
commercial set
成套商业单据
commercial treaty
贸易条约
commission $n.$
委托(书),代办;委员会;佣金;手续费
commission broker
佣金经纪人
commission charges
手续费;佣金
commission contract
贸易代理合同
commission of conciliation
调解委员会
commission trade
委托贸易
commissioner $n.$
专员;政府特派员;地方长官
commissioning $n.$
试运行;调试;试车
commissioning period
试运行期
commissioning team
试车组
commissioning test run
投料试生产
commit $v.$
承诺;委托;提交
commitment $n.$
承诺,约定,承担义务;承诺付款额
commitment and award
承诺与授予
commitment authority
承诺权
commitment authorization
承诺授权书
commitment charge (fee)
承诺费
commitment document
承诺文件
commitment letter

commitment time
承诺时限,约定时间
commitment value
承诺价值
committed amount
已承诺数量
committee n.
委员会
commodity n.
商品,货物
commodity inspection
商品检验
commodity price
商品价格,物价
commodity price index
物价指数
common facilities
公共设施
common law
普通法,判例法
common law system
普通法系,英美法系
common market
共同市场
common mistake
共同错误
common requirement clause
通用要求条款
communal facilities
公共设施
communication n.
信函,通讯;交通;[复]通讯系统
community n.
社团
compact n.
契约,合同 a. 结实的 v. 使结实;压实
compaction n.
压实,夯实
compactor n.
夯具;压实工具
compactor n.
压土机,夯具
company n.
公司,商号
company act
公司法;公司条例
company law
公司法
company limited by shares
[英]股份有限公司
company property
公司财产
comparability n.
可比性
comparable a.
可比的
comparable cost
可比成本
comparative balance sheet
比较资产负债表
comparative financial statement
比较财务报表
compensation n.
赔偿(费);补偿;报酬
compensation for cancellation of contract
解除合同补偿费
compensation for damage
损害赔偿
compensation for removal
遣散费,迁移费
compensation insurance
补偿保险
compensation of additional cost
附加费用的补偿
compensation terms
补偿条款
compensation trade
补偿贸易
compensatory damages
应予赔偿的损失
compete v.
竞争
competence n.

能力;权限,权力
competent *a*.
有法定资格的;有能力的;主管的
competent authorities
主管当局
competent court
主管法庭
competition *n*.
竞争
competitive *a*.
具有竞争力的
competitive bidding
竞争性招标
competitive daywork
有竞争性的计日工(报价)
competitive price
竞争性价格
competitive shopping
竞争性购置
competitiveness *n*.
竞争能力
competitor *n*.
竞争者,竞争对手
compilation of budget
编制预算
complain *v*.
申诉,投诉
complainant *n*.
申诉人,起诉人,原告
complaint *n*.
控诉,申诉,起诉
complement *v*.
补充
complementary *a*.
补充的,补足的
complete *v*.
完成,履行 *a*. 完全的,全部的
complete cost
总成本,全部成本
complete payment
(按合同)最后的支付
complete set of bills of lading
全套提单

complete set of drawings
成套图纸
complete trust
完全信托
completed product
成品
completed project
完成的工程
completion *n*.
竣工,完成
completion certificate
竣工证书
completion date
完工日期
completion drawings
竣工图
completion of contract
完成合同
completion of works
工程竣工
completion report
竣工报告
complex *n*.
综合企业;综合结构,综合体 *a*. 复杂的,综合的
complex of equipment
成套设备
complex tariff
复式税则
compliance *n*.
依从,遵守,按照
compliance with a schedule
符合进度表,符合计划
compliance with the contract
遵守合同
comply with
符合,遵守,照做
component *n*.
组成部分,部件,构件
components of price
价格组成的各部分
composite *a*.
综合的,复合的

composite depreciation method
平均折旧法
composite index
综合指数
composite price
综合价格
composite rate of tax
综合税率
composition *n.*
债务和解,偿债协议;构成
compound *a.*
复合的 *v.* 组成;和解;以复利计算
compound amount
(复利)本利和
compound claim
综合索赔,一揽子索赔
compound duties
复合关税
compound interest
复利
compound rate
复利率
compound settlement
综合解决办法
compound tariff
复合关税,混合关税
compounded monthly
以月复利计算的
compounding *n.*
复利计算
compounding a debt
一次性付清债务
comprehensive *a.*
综合的
comprehensive tender documents
综合招标文件
compressive modulus
抗压模量
compressive strength
抗压强度
compressor *n.*
压缩机
comprise *v.*
包括
compromise *n.*
和解,妥协
compulsory clause
强制条款
compulsory insurance
强制保险
compulsory liquidation
强制清理
compute *v.*
计算
computed tare
约定皮重
computed value
计算价值
computer aided design (CAD)
计算机辅助设计
conceal *v.*
隐瞒(事实等)
conceptual design
概念设计
conceptual estimate
概念估算
concerned *a.*
有关的
concession *n.*
特许权,优惠,让步
concession agreement
特许协议,租让协议
concession of tariff
关税减让
concessional *a.*
让步的,特许的,优惠的
concessional line of credit
优惠贷款限额
concessional loan
优惠贷款
concessional rate
优惠利率
concessional tariff
优惠关税
concessionary *n.*
特许公司 *a.* 特许的,优惠的

concessionary period
特许期

conciliate *v.*
调解；安抚；和解

conciliation *n.*
调解,和解

conciliation committee
调解委员会

conciliation procedure
调解程序

conciliator *n.*
调解人

concise *a.*
简明的

conclude *v.*
结束,完成；达成,缔结

conclude a contract
缔结和约,订立合同

conclude an agreement
签订协议

conclude business after viewing samples
看样成交

conclusion *n.*
结论；缔结

conclusion of contract
合同缔结

conclusive *a.*
确定性的,最后的

concrete *n.*
混凝土

concrete admixture (additive)
混凝土外加剂

concrete aggregate
混凝土骨料

concrete brick
混凝土砖,混凝土块

concrete core wall
混凝土心墙

concrete cover
混凝土保护层

concrete curing
混凝土养护

concrete formwork
混凝土模板

concrete mixer
混凝土搅拌机

concrete mixing plant
混凝土拌和楼

concrete pavement
混凝土路面

concrete paver
混凝土摊铺机

concrete placement
混凝土浇筑

concrete pump
混凝土泵

concrete reinforcement
混凝土配筋

concrete retarder
混凝土缓凝剂

concrete sample
混凝土试件

concrete strength
混凝土强度

concrete test cube
混凝土试块

concrete vibrator
混凝土震捣器

concurrent delay
共同延误,同时发生的延误

condemnation *n.*
谴责；宣告不适用

condemned work
不合格的工作

condition *n.*
条件,状况

condition precedent
先决条件

condition subsequent
后继条件

conditional loan
有条件的贷款

conditions concurrent
并发条件

conditions for employment

雇佣条件
conditions of carriage
货运条件
conditions of contract
合同条件
conditions of contract of air waybill
空运单条款
conditions of engagement
雇佣条件
conditions of grant
让与条件
conditions of hire
租用条件
conditions of labour
劳动条件
conditions of particular application
特殊应用条件,专用条件
conditions of sale
销售条件
conditions precedent to commencement
开工的先决条件
conduct *v.*
指导;实施;经营,管理;行动
conduct negotiations
进行谈判
conduit *n.*
管道,输水道
confederation *n.*
同盟,联盟
conference *n.*
会谈,会议
conference rate
班轮公会运价;同盟费率;海运公会运价
confidence *n.*
信任;信心
confidential *a.*
保密的,机密的
confidential clause
保密条款
confidential details
机密的细节

confidential document
机密文件
confidentiality *n.*
保密,机密,保密性
confine *v.*
限制 *n.* [复]界限,范围,区域
confirm *v.*
确定,确认;批准;保兑
confirmation *n.*
确认书,证据
confirmation in writing
书面确认
confirmation of award
确定授标
confirmation of oral instruction
口头指令确认书
confirmation sample
确认样品
confirmed letter of credit
保兑信用证
confirming bank
保兑银行;确认银行
confiscate *v.*
没收,征用
confiscation *n.*
没收
conflagration *n.*
大火灾,(战斗等的)爆发
conflict *n. v.*
冲突,抵制
conflict of interests
利益的冲突
conflict of laws
法律冲突;冲突法
conflict rules
冲突法规
conform *v.*
符合;遵从
conformed copies
与原本一致的文本
conformity *n.*
符合,一致
confute *v.*

驳斥
conjuncture n.
行情;局面
consecutive a.
连续的
consecutive days
连续日
consensus rate
协商一致的利率
consent n. v.
同意,赞成
consequence n.
后果
consequential damage (loss)
(保险)间接损失,从属损失
consideration n.
考虑;报酬,补偿;对价;体谅
considering
鉴于;考虑到
consign v.
托运,委托
consigned goods
寄销品
consignee n.
收货人,受托人;代销人
consignment n.
托付;发货;寄售;托运
consignor, consigner n.
发货人;委托人;托运人
consistency n.
一惯性(原则)
consistent a.
一致的
consistent policy
一贯方针
consolidate v.
合并;调整,巩固
consolidated balance sheet
合并资产负债表
consolidated financial statement
合并财务报表
consolidated income statement
综合收益表

consolidation grouting
固结灌浆
consolidation test
固结试验
consortium n.
联合集团;联合体,国际财团;国际性协议
consortium guarantee
联合财团保函
consortium of contractors
承包商联合体
constant cost
固定成本,不变成本
constitute v.
任命;设立(机构);构成
constituted authority
合法当局
constitution n.
章程;法规;宪法;任命;组成
constrain v.
限制,强制
constraint n.
约束条件,强制
construct v.
建造,施工
constructed value
估定价值,推定价值
construction n.
施工,建设,建筑;解释;法律释义
construction access road
施工进场道路
construction account
建筑账户
construction accounting
建筑会计
construction activities
施工作业
construction agreement
施工协议书
construction and addition
建筑和扩建
construction and installation
施工与安装

construction balance sheet
建筑资产负债表
construction bridge
施工桥
construction budget
基建预算
construction business
建筑业
construction calendar
施工日历
construction change directive
施工变更指示
construction claim management
施工索赔管理
construction claims
施工索赔
construction concession
建筑许可
construction contract
施工合同,建筑合同
construction contract management
施工合同管理
construction coordinator
施工协调员
construction cost
施工成本
construction cost control
施工成本控制
construction cost estimating
施工成本预算
construction cycle
建造周期
construction delay
工期拖延
construction diversion
施工导流
construction document
施工文件
construction drawings
施工图
construction engineering corporation
建筑工程公司
construction equipment
施工设备
construction equipment status report
施工设备情况报告
construction facilities
施工装备
construction in progress
在建工程,未完工程
construction industry
建筑业
construction intermediate schedule
施工中间进度表
construction joint
施工缝;建筑缝
construction layout
施工布置图
construction management (CM)
建筑管理
construction management contract
施工管理合同
construction management contracting
施工管理承包
construction manager
施工经理
construction map
施工场地图
construction material
建筑材料
construction means
施工方法,施工手段
construction method
施工方法
construction of buildings
房屋建筑
construction of policy
保险单的解释
construction of references
权限的解释
construction organization
施工单位
construction period
施工期限,工期
construction phase
施工阶段

construction plan
施工(平面)布置图
construction planning
施工规划
construction plant
施工设备,施工装置
construction procedure
施工程序
construction program
施工计划
construction progress
施工进度
construction progress control
施工进度控制
construction schedule check list
施工进度核查单
construction sequence
施工顺序
construction service
施工服务
construction site
工地,建筑工地
construction specifications
施工技术规程(或规范)
construction stage
建造阶段
construction subcontract
施工分包合同
construction summary schedule
施工进度汇总表
construction superintendent
施工管理员
construction supervision
施工监督,施工检查
construction surpluses
施工剩余物资
construction technique
施工技术
construction way
施工手段
construction work policy
建筑工程保险单
construction works
建筑工程
constructional equipment
施工设备
constructional mechanism
建筑机械
constructional plant
建筑设备
construction's all risks insurance
工程施工一切险
constructive a.
建设性的;推定的
constructive acceleration
可推定的加速施工
constructive change
可推定的工程变更
constructive change order
可推定的工程变更指令
constructive clause
推定条款
constructive possession
推定占有,法律确认的占有
constructive suspension
可推定的暂停施工
constructive total loss
推定全损
constructive variation
可推定的工程变更
constructor n.
[美]建造者,建造师
construe v.
解释,把…逐字译出 n. 分析,直译
consular invoice
领事发票
consulate n.
领事馆
consult v.
协商;咨询;查阅
consultant n.
顾问,咨询专家,咨询人员
consultant company (corporation)
咨询公司
consultant engineer
咨询工程师

consultant's fee
咨询费
consultation n.
磋商,协商;(专家等的)会议;咨询
consultative committee
咨询委员会
consulting agreement
咨询协议
consulting engineer
咨询工程师
consulting firm
咨询公司
consulting service
咨询服务
consumables n.
消耗品
consume v.
消费
consumer credit
消费信贷
consumer durable
耐用消费品
consumer goods
消费品
consumer loan
消费贷款
consumer price index
消费品价格指数
consumption n.
消费;消耗(量)
consumption of material
材料消耗
consumption tax
消费税
contact v.
交往,接触 n. 门路;熟人
contactor n.
接触器
contain v.
包含,容纳
container n.
集装箱;容器
container freight station (CFS)
集装箱货物集散站
container ship
集装箱船
container yard
集装箱堆场
contamination n.
污染,污物
contemporary records
同期记录
content n.
内容
contention n.
争论,论点
contestant n.
争执方,争辩者
continental law system
大陆法系
contingency n.
意外事故,偶然事件;意外开支
contingency allowance
应急用款
contingency clause
偶发事故条款
contingency cost
不可预见费,应急费
contingency evaluation
不可预见性评估
contingency fund
应急基金;意外损失基金
contingency insurance
意外事故保险
contingency plan
应急计划
contingency reserve
应急储备金
contingent a.
偶有的,意外的,或有的
contingent expenses
或有费用,意外开支
contingent interest
或有权益
contingent liabilities
或有负债

contingent profit
或有利润
continuation n.
(合同等的)展期;继续
continuation clause
展期条款
continuing contract
连续合同
contour line
等高线,轮廓线
contra n.
抵消,对消
contra account
抵消账户
contraband n.
违禁品,走私货
contract n.
合同,契约 v. 承包;缔约;把…承包给
contract administration
合同管理
contract agreement
合同协议书
contract amount
合同价格
contract authorization
合同授权
contract award
授标
contract awarded
中标合同
contract based on unit price
单价合同
contract bond
合同担保
contract cancellation
取消合同
contract clause
合同条款
contract construction
承包工程
contract currency
合同货币

contract debt
合同债务
contract deposit paid
已付合同保证金
contract deposit received
已收合同保证金
contract dispute
合同争端
contract document analysis
合同文件分析
contract documents
合同文件
contract draft
合同草稿
contract duty
合同义务
contract engineer
合同工程师
contract expiry
合同期满
contract files
合同卷宗
contract for consulting services
咨询服务合同
contract for goods
订货合同
contract for labour and materials
包工包料合同
contract for project
项目合同
contract for service
服务合同
contract for the supply of labour
提供劳务合同
contract for work
包工合同
contract form
合同格式
contract formation
合同构成
contract general
合同综述
contract interface

合同接口
contract labour（worker）
合同工
contract language
合同语言
contract law
合同法
contract ledger
合同分类账
contract negotiation
合同谈判
contract obligation
合同义务
contract of association
协作合同,联合合同
contract of carriage
运输合同,货运合同
contract of carriage by sea
海运合同
contract of design
设计合同
contract of employment
雇用合同
contract of hire of labour
雇工合同
contract of insurance
保险合同
contract of lease
租赁合同
contract of marine insurance
海上保险契约
contract of privately performed work
私营工程合同
contract of sales
销售合同
contract of services
劳务合同
contract package
合同包
contract package scope
合同范围
contract performance
执行合同

contract period
合同期,合同有效期
contract policy
合同保险单
contract price
合同价格,合同价
contract price receivable
应收合同款
contract price received in advance
预收合同款
contract project
合同项目
contract provisions
合同规定
contract records
合同记录
contract renewal
合同续订
contract risks
合同风险
contract scope changes
合同范围变更
contract serial number
合同序号
contract signature date
合同签署日期
contract sum
合同价
contract suspension
合同暂停
contract termination
合同终止
contract terms
合同条款
contract under seal
盖章合同,正式合同
contract value
合同价值
contract variation
合同变更
contract version
合同文本
contract void

无效合同
contract work
承揽工作
contracting approach
签订合同方法
contracting parties
签订合同各方
contracting strategy
签订合同策略
contraction joint
收缩缝
contractor *n.*
承包商；订约人
contractor-financed contract
承包商带资承包合同
contractor unit
承包单位
contractor's affidavit
承包商宣誓书
contractor's all risks insurance（C. A. R）
承包商全险保险,承包工程一切险
contractor's capacity and capability
承包商的资格与能力
contractor's default
承包商违约
contractor's drawings
承包商的图纸
contractor's entitlement to suspend work
承包商的停工权利
contractor's equipment
承包商的设备
contractor's equipment floater
承包商设备保险单
contractor's facilities
承包商的设施
contractor's fee
承包商的酬金
contractor's financing
承包商融资
contractor's joint venture
承包商联营体
contractor's liability
承包商的责任
contractor's liability insurance
承包商责任保险
contractor's license
承包商的许可证
contractor's obligation
承包商的义务
contractor's profit
承包商的利润
contractor's representative
承包商的代表
contractor's staff
承包商的职员
contractor's total maximum liability
承包商的最高赔偿额
contractor's undertaking
承包商的许诺
contractual *a.*
合同的；承办的
contractual arrangement
合同安排
contractual claims
合同涉及的索赔
contractual commitments with the client
对业主的合同承诺
contractual fines
违约罚金
contractual input
合同项下的投入
contractual joint venture
契约式合营
contractual liabilities
合同责任
contractual obligation
合同义务
contractual practice
合同惯例
contractual procedure
缔约程序
contractual relationship
合同关系

contractual release
合同的解除
contractual restrictions
合同的约束
contractual right
合同权利
contradict *v.*
反驳,否认;同…相矛盾
contrary *a.*
相反的;矛盾的
contrast *n.*
对比
contravene *v.*
触犯(法律);违反;反驳;侵犯
contribute *v.*
贡献;促成;捐助
contributed capital
捐赠资本;实缴股本
contributing insurance
分摊保险
contribution *n.*
捐献;分担;分配
contribution clause
责任分担条款
contribution margin
贡献毛利,创利额
contribution value
分摊价值
control *v.*
控制 *n.* 控制权;管理
control（controlling）account
统驭账户,控制账户
controllable cost
可控成本
controlled company
受控公司
controlled float
受控浮动汇率
controlled price
管制价格
controller *n.*
总会计师;主管人;审计师
controversial issue
有争议的事项
controversy *n.*
争论
convene *v.*
召集(会议)
convener *n.*
会议召集人
convention *n.*
惯例,常规;公约,协定;会议
Convention on the Recognition and Enforcement of Foreign Arbitration Awards
承认及执行外国仲裁裁决公约
conventional price
协定价格
conversion *n.*
兑换,转换
conversion of currency
货币兑换
conversion price
兑换价格
conversion rate
兑换率
convertibility *n.*
货币兑换性
convertible *a.*
可兑换的,可转换的
convertible bond
可转换债券
convertible currency
可自由兑换的货币
convertible money（paper）
可自由兑换的纸币
conveyance *n.*
传递;运输工具
conveyance insurance
运输工具保险
conveyance of estate
财产转让
conveyer belt
输送带
conveying system
传送系统

conveyor, conveyer *n.*
传送设备
convict *v.*
证明有罪 *n.* 犯罪
cooperation *n.*
合作,协作
cooperative *a.*
相互协作的
cooperative joint venture
协作型合资经营
coordinate *v.*
使…协调 *a.* 同等的
coordination *n.*
协调
coordination center
协调中心
coordination of work
工作协调
coordinator *a.*
协调人
co-production *n.*
合作生产
copy *n.*
副本,复印件
copyright *n.*
版权
corporate *a.*
法人组织的,公司的,社团的
corporate acquisition
公司收购
corporate bond
公司债券
corporate charter
公司执照
corporate income tax
公司所得税
corporate merger
公司合并
corporate owner
法人业主,企业业主
corporate tax
公司税
corporation *n.*
团体,法人;公司;[美]股份有限公司
corporation act (law)
公司法
corporation by-laws
公司章程
corporation regulation
公司条例
corporation seal
公司印章
corporation tax act (CTA)
公司税法
corporation tax (CT)
公司税
corpus *n.*
本金
correct *v.*
校准;纠正,修改;制止
correct delays
纠正延误
corrected bid price
校正后的投标价
corrective action
纠正措施
correspondent *n.*
代理行;客户 *a.* 符合的,一致的
correspondent bank
代理银行,往来银行
corrupt *v.*
使腐化,贿赂 *a.* 腐化的
corrupt practice
贪污行为
corruption *n.*
受贿;腐化
cost *n.*
成本,费用;[复]诉讼费,审理辩护费用 *v.* 花费,估算成本
cost account
成本账
cost accounting
成本会计
cost allocation
成本分摊
cost analysis

成本分析
cost and commitment
成本与承诺费
cost and commitment program
成本与承诺费用计划
cost and freight（CFR）
离岸成本加运费（价）
cost and insurance（C&I）
离岸成本加保险费（价）
cost breakdown detail
成本分类细则
cost budgeting
成本预算
cost ceiling
最高成本
cost clerk
成本管理员
cost code
成本编码
cost consultant
成本咨询顾问
cost contribution
成本分摊
cost control
成本管理，成本控制
cost cutting
成本削减
cost distribution
成本分配
cost engineer
成本工程师
cost escalation
费用上涨
cost estimate
费用估算
cost factor
成本因素
cost forecasting
成本预测
cost impact analysis
成本影响分析
cost index
费用指数

cost, insurance and freight（CIF）
成本、保险费加运费（价），到岸价格
cost, insurance, freight and commission（CIF and C.）
成本、保险费、运费加佣金（价），到岸价格加佣金
cost, insurance, freight, ex-ship's hold（CIF ex-ship's hold）
成本、保险费、运费加船舱底交货（价），到岸轮船舱底交货（价）
cost, insurance, freight, landed（CIF landed）
成本、保险费、运费加卸货费（价）、到岸价格加卸货费
cost, insurance, freight, liner terms（CIF liner terms）
成本、保险费、运费加班轮条件（价），到岸价格加班轮条件（价）
cost items
成本项目
cost of bond
担保成本
cost of capital
资本成本
cost of civil engineering works
建筑工程造价，土木工程造价
cost of delay
误期费用
cost of erection
安装费
cost of fire protection
防火费用
cost of goods purchased
购货成本
cost of goods sold
销货成本
cost of insurance
保险费
cost of living
生活费
cost of overhaul
大修费用
cost of production

生产成本
cost of repatriation
遣散费
cost of safety program
安全计划费用
cost of set-up
开办费
cost of site security
现场安全费用
cost of suspension
暂时停工费用
cost of tendering
投标费用
cost of upkeep
维护费用
cost of works
工程造价
cost overrun
费用超支,成本超支
cost recovery
成本回收
cost reduction
降低成本
cost reimbursement contract
成本补偿合同
cost schedule
成本明细表
cost sheet
成本单
cost target contract
成本目标合同
cost variance
成本差异
cost-and-fee contract
成本加酬金合同
cost-benefit analysis（CBA）
成本效益分析
cost-effective analysis
成本效益分析
costing n.
成本计算
costing details and allocations
成本计算的细则与分配

costing of labour
劳务成本计算
costing of plant
设备成本计算
cost-plus contract
成本加成合同
cost-plus pricing
成本加成计价法
cost-plus-award-fee contract
成本加奖金合同
cost-plus-fee contract
成本加酬金合同
cost-plus-fixed-fee contract
成本加固定酬金合同
cost-plus-fluctuating-fee contract
成本加浮动酬金合同
cost-plus-incentive-fee contract
成本加奖金合同
cost-plus-percentage-fee contract
成本加定比酬金合同
costs and damages
诉讼费加损害赔偿费
cost-sharing formula
成本分摊公式（或准则）
cost-volume-profit analysis
成本、数量、利润分析,本量利分析
council n.
会议；委员会
counselor n.
顾问,律师,法律顾问
count v.
计算
count of lawsuit
诉讼理由
counter a.
相反的；对立的
counter guarantee
反担保函
counter offer
还价,还盘
countercharge n. v.
反控诉
counterclaim n. v.

反索赔,反诉
counterclaim for contractor's defaults
对承包商违约的反索赔
counterclaim for remedying defaults
对施工缺陷的反索赔
counterfeit v.
假冒,伪造
countermeasure n.
对策
counterpart n.
副本;相对应的物(或人)
counterpurchase n.
反购,互购
countertrade n.
反向贸易,对等贸易
countervailing credit
背对背信用证
countervailing duty
反补贴税,反倾销税,抵消税
country damage
产地损害
country of destination
目的地国家
country of dispatch
发货国
country of embarkation
装货国
country of origin
原产地(国)
country of payment
付款国
country quota
国别配额
coupon n.
息票,票证;赠券
courior charges
服务小费
court n.
法庭,法院
court cost
诉讼费
court fee
法庭费用
court of arbitration
仲裁法庭
covenant n.
缔约;契约;合同条款;违反合同的诉讼
cover v. n.
包括;覆盖;保险;抵偿
cover bid（tender）
掩护性投标
cover note（C/N）
暂保单,承保单
cover of payment
抵补支付款
coverage n.
承保险别;保险总额
CPM（critical path method）
关键路径方法
crack n.
裂缝
craft n.
工艺;行业;船
craft union
同业工会
craft wage
行业工资
craftsman n.
工匠
crane n.
吊车,起重机
crane barge
起重机船
crash n. v.
市场崩溃;暴跌
crawler crane
履带式起重机
credit n.
信用;信贷,贷款;贷方 v. 贷记
credit agreement
信贷协议
credit analysis
信用分析
credit balance

贷方余额
credit bank
信贷银行
credit card
信用卡
credit column
贷方栏
credit guarantee
信贷保函
credit insurance
信用保险
credit line
贷款额度
credit market
信贷市场
credit memorandum (memo)
贷项通知单
credit note
贷项通知单,欠条
credit policy
信贷政策,信用保险单
credit purchase
赊购
credit sale
赊销
credit side
贷方
credit standing (status)
资信状况
credit terms
信贷条件,付款条件
creditor n.
债权人,贷方,贷项
creditor beneficiary
债权受益人
creditor of bankruptcy
破产人的债权人
creditworthiness n.
借贷信用
crest n.
坝顶;峰值
crime n.
犯罪,罪行
criminal law
刑法
criminal liability
刑事责任
criminal responsibility
刑事责任
criterion n.
准则,标准,尺度
critical a.
关键的,紧急的;临界的
critical items list
关键项目清单
critical point
关键点
cross (crossed) check (cheque)
划线支票,横线支票
cross discounts
交叉折扣
cross exchange
交叉汇兑,套汇
cross license
互换许可证
cross rate
套算汇率
cross road
交叉路
cross section
横断面,断面
cross walk
人行横道
cross-default
交叉过失
cross-default clause
交叉过失条款
cross-sectoral effect
跨部门影响
crushed gravel
碎砾石
crushed stone
碎石
crusher n.

碎石机
cube *n.*
立方形,立方体
cubic *a.*
立方的
cubic centimeter(cu. cm)
立方厘米
cubic foot(cu. ft)
立方英尺
cubic inch(cu. in)
立方英寸
cubic measure
按立方度量,体积
cubic meter(cu. m)
立方米
cubic yard(cu. yd)
立方码
culture relics
文物
culvert *n.*
涵洞;排水渠
cumulative *a.*
累计的,追加的,附加的
curing mat
(混凝土)养护覆盖物
currency *n.*
货币,通货
currency adjustment factor
币值调整因数
currency appreciation
货币升值
currency availability
货币的可获得性
currency conversion
货币兑换
currency convertibility
货币可兑换性,货币自由兑换性
currency depreciation
货币贬值
currency devaluation
货币贬值
currency futures contract
货币期货合同

currency hedge
货币套期保值
currency inflation
通货膨胀
currency of account
记账货币
currency of agreement
协议书规定的货币
currency of contract
合同规定的货币
currency of payment
支付货币
currency option
货币期权
currency proportion
货币比例
currency quotation
间接标价法(以外币表示的标价方法)
currency rate
(对本国货币的)外汇汇率
currency reserve
货币储备
currency restriction
货币限制
currency revaluation
货币升值
currency risk
货币风险
currency swap
货币互换
current *a.*
现时的,当前的;流通的,流动的
current account
活期账户,往来账户
current assets
流动资产
current capital
流动资本
current cost
现行成本
current debt
短期债务,流动债务

current decrees
现行法令
current deposit
活期存款
current investment
短期投资
current labour rates
现时工资
current liabilities
流动负债
current loan
短期银行贷款
current market value
现行市价
current price
现行价格,时价
current price index
现行价格指数
current programme
现行的进度计划
current ratio
流动比率(流动资产与流动债务的比例)
current repair
小修,经常性修理
current replacement cost
现行重置成本
current revenue
当期营业收入
current wage bulletin
当前工资简报
curriculum vitae(CV)
履历表
custody n.
保管,管押
custom n.
风俗习惯;惯例;常规;习惯法
custom of the port (C.P.)
港口习惯,港口惯例
custom of trade
贸易惯例
custom union
关税同盟

customary law
惯例法,习惯法
customary tare
习惯皮重
customer n.
顾客,买主
customer's account
客户账,应收账款账户
customer's deposit
客户定金
customs n.
海关,关税,进口税
customs agency
报关代理行
customs appraised value
海关估价
customs barrier
关税壁垒
customs bond
海关保税保证书
customs broker
报关行;报关经纪人
customs brokerage
海关佣金
customs clearance
清关,海关放行证,结关
customs clearing agent
清关代理人
customs clearing charges (fee)
报关费
customs consignee
海关委托人
customs declaration
报关单
customs duty
关税
customs entry
海关进口手续,海关登记,报关单
customs examination
海关检验,验关
customs examination list
海关验货单
customs formalities

海关手续
customs house
海关
customs house officer
海关官员
customs import tariff
海关进口税则
customs inspection
验关
customs invoice
海关发票
customs law
海关法
customs pass
海关通行证
customs permit
海关许可证
customs procedures
海关手续

customs receipt
海关收据
customs regulations
海关条例
customs tariff
海关税则
customs territory
海关境域,关境
customs valuation
海关估价
cutback *n*.
削减
cut-off *n*.
截水墙,防渗墙
cut-off date
截止日期
cut-off period
不得超过的期限
cutting *n*. 挖掘;截断

D

D/A（documents against acceptance）
承兑交单
D/A draft
承兑汇票
daily *a*.
每日的,每天一次的 *ad*. 每日
daily cash report
现金日报表
daily construction report
施工日报表
daily interest
日息
daily pay（wage）
日工资
daily premium
每日保险费,每日贴(或升)水
daily rainfall
日降雨量
daily record of construction
施工日志

daily statement
日报表
daily technical service fee
日技术服务费
dam *n*.
坝
damage *n. v*.
损害,损失,破坏
damage claim
损害索赔
damage to persons and property
人身与财产损害
damage to works
对工程的损害
damages *n*.
赔款,损害赔偿金
damages for default
违约赔偿金
damp-proof coating
防潮层

danger area
危险区
danger money
危险工作津贴
danger signal
危险信号
dangerous *a.*
危险的
dangerous building
危险建筑物
dangerous goods（articles）
危险品
data *n.*
数据,资料
data on individual consultant（DI-CON）
个人咨询专家注册资料
data processing
数据处理
database *n.*
数据库
date draft
定期汇票
date due
到期日
date for inspection
检查日期
date for testing
试验日期,检验日期
date of arrival
到达日,到港日期
date of availability
有效期限
date of balance sheet
资产负债表日期,决算日
date of commencement
开工日期
date of contract
签约日期
date of delivery
交货日期
date of departure
开航日期

date of discharge
卸货日期
date of expiration（expiry）
期满日,截止日期
date of landing
卸岸日期
date of letter
发函日期
date of loading
装货日期
date of postmark
邮戳日期
date of shipment
装船日期
date of survey
检查日期,测量日期
date of termination
终止日期
date of validity
有效日期
date of value
起息日
date off-project
项目停止使用日期
date on-project
项目投入使用日期
datum *n.*
基准
datum level
基准面
datum line
基准线
datum point
基准点
daughter company
子公司
day allowances
每日津贴
day bill
定期票据
day loan
按日计息贷款
day rate

计日工资率,日工资
day shift
白班
day to day communication
日常通讯
day to day construction activities
每日施工作业
day wage
计日工资
days of grace
宽限日期,优惠期
day-time
白天
daywork n.
零工,计日工,散工
daywork rate
计日工资,每日单价
DCF method (discounted cash flow method)
资金流动折现评估法
D/D (demand draft)
即期汇票
dead account
呆账
dead capital
呆滞资本
dead freight
空舱费
dead loss
纯损失
dead money
闲置资金
dead season
淡季
dead security
不起作用的保证,无价值担保
dead stock
呆滞存货,滞销货
deadline n.
截止日期,截止时间
deadline for receipt of tenders
接收投标的截止时间
deadlock n.
僵局
deadweight n.
(船舶总)载重量;(车辆的)自重,皮重
deal n.
交易,买卖
dealer n.
经销商
dear a.
昂贵的,高价的
dear money
高息贷款
debasement n.
(货币)贬值
debenture n.
信用债券,公司债券,无担保债券;海关退税单
debit n.
借方,借记,借项 v. 记入(账户的)借方
debit and credit
借贷
debit balance
借方余额
debit card
借方卡,记账卡
debit column
借方栏
debit entry
借项
debit instrument
欠据
debit item
借项
debit memorandum (note)
借项通知单
debit side
借方
debris n.
废弃物
debt n.
债务,欠债,欠款
debt at call

即期债务
debt certificate
债务证明书
debt crisis
债务危机
debt outstanding
未偿债务
debt relief
免除债务
debt rescheduling
重订还债期限
debt service
债息,还本付息
debt side
借方
debt-equity ratio
负债与资产比,债务与股本比(率)
debtor n.
债务人,负债人;(会计)借方
deceit n.
诈骗
decide v.
决定,判决
decipherable a.
可译出的;可辨认的
decision n.
决定,决议
decision to proceed with the project
工程项目实施的决定
decision tree
决策树
decision-making
制定决策
declarant n.
报关人;申请人;申诉人
declaration n.
声明;报关单;纳税申报表
declaration for exportation
出口报关单
declaration for importation
进口报关单
declaration form
申报表

declaration inwards
进口报关单,入境报关单
declaration of acceptance
接受声明
declaration of shipment
装船通知
declaration of trust
信托书
declaration outwards
出口报关单
declaration policy
申报保险单
declare v.
申报,声明
declare at the customs
报关
declare goods
申报货物
declared value
申报价值,设定价值
decline an offer
不接受报价
declining balance method of depreciation
余额递减折旧法
decrease v. n.
减少,递减
decrease in cost
费用的减少
decree n.
法令,政令;判决 v. 颁布;判决
decrement n.
贬值,减量
deduct v.
扣除,减去,折扣
deductible n.
[复]免赔额,自负额 a. 减除的,扣除的
deductible average
绝对免赔额
deductible clause
自负责任条款,免赔条款
deduction n.

扣除,扣除额
deed *n.*
契约;行为,行动
deed of appointment
任命证书
deed of assignment
财产转让契约
deed of conveyance
转让证书
deed of indemnity
赔偿契约
deed of mortgage
抵押契约
deed of partnership
合伙契约
deed of transfer
转让契据
deed of trust
信托契约
deem *v.*
表明,认为
defalcation *n.*
侵吞(或挪用)公款
default *n.*
违约,过错,拖欠 *v.* 不出庭,不履行义务
default of contractor
承包商违约
default of employer
业主违约
default of owner
业主违约
default of payment
不履行付款义务
default party
违约方
default risk
违约风险,拖欠风险
defeat *n.*
败诉;无效 *v.* 战胜;使无效
defeated party
败诉方
defect *n.*

缺陷
defect repair
缺陷修补
defective material
有缺陷的材料
defective work
有缺陷的工作
defects correction certificate
缺陷改正证书
defects correction period
缺陷改正期
defects liability certificate
缺陷责任证书,养护合格证书
defects liability period
缺陷责任期
defects notification period
缺陷通知期
defence against claim
防范索赔
defence counsel
(被告方)辩护律师
defence, defense *n.*
辩护,防御;被告方
defend *v.*
保卫,为…辩护
defendant *n.*
被告人,被要求索赔一方
defer *v.*
推迟,延期
defer payment
延期付款
deferment charge
延期费用
deferment of a project
工程延期
deferred annuity
延期年金
deferred assets
递延资产
deferred charges(expenses)
递延费用
deferred cost
递延成本

deferred credits 递延贷项
deferred debits 递延借项
deferred delivery 延期交货
deferred equity 递延股权
deferred income 递延收益
deferred interest 延期利息
deferred liabilities 递延负债
deferred payment 延期付款
deferred payment credit 延期付款信用证
deferred payment guarantee 延期付款保函
deferred payment sale 延期付款销售
deferred premium 递延保险金
deferred revenue 递延收入
deficiency n. 不足额；缺陷；不足数
deficiency guarantee 资金缺额担保
deficiency judgement 清偿不足额判决
deficit n. 赤字，亏空
deficit account 亏损账户
deficit balance 收支赤字
deficit budget 赤字预算
deficit financing 赤字财政
deficit spending 赤字开支
definite a. 明确的，一定的，肯定的
definite appropriation 定额拨款
definite price 固定价格
definition n. 定义；解释；限定
definitive schedule 最终进度
deflation n. 通货紧缩；缩小
defray v. 支付（经营费用等），准备支付
degree of risk 风险度
degressive depreciation 递减折旧
delay v. n. 延期，延误
delay in completion 竣工拖延
delayed completion 拖期竣工
delayed payment 拖期付款
delayed shop drawings 拖期交付的施工图
delaying tactics 拖延策略
delays by subcontractor 分包商的误期
delays caused by authorities 当局造成的延误
delays in engineering 设计延误
delegate n. 代表 v. 委派…为代表，授权
delegation n. 代表团；(代表的)委派
delegation of authority 授权

delegation of duties
职责委托
delegation of power
权限的委托
delete v.
取消,删除
deleted work
取消的工作
delict n.
不法行为
delinquent tax
滞纳税款
deliver v.
递交,交付
delivered at frontier (DAF)
边境交货(价)
delivered duty paid(DDP)
完税后交货(价)
delivered duty unpaid (DDU)
未完税后交货(价)
delivered ex quay (duty paid) (DEQ)
(目的港)码头交货(关税已付)(价)
delivered ex ship (DES)
(目的港)船上交货(价)
delivered on board the ship
交到船上
delivered price
交货价格(指包括包装和运输费用在内的货价)
delivered terms
(运至买方指定地点的)交货条件
delivering carrier
交货承运人
delivery n.
交货,交付;转让
delivery advice
交货通知
delivery against acceptance
承兑交货
delivery against payment
付款交货
delivery date
交货日期
delivery of materials
交付材料,运送材料
delivery on call
通知交货
delivery order
提货单,交货清单
delivery period
交货期
delivery point
交货地点
delivery schedule
交货时间表
delivery terms
交货条件
demand v. n.
请求,正式要求;征收;需求;即期
demand bill
即期汇票,见票即付票据
demand deposit
活期存款,即期存款
demand draft(D/D)
汇票,即期汇票
demand forecast
需求预测
demand guarantee
即付保函
demand loan
活期贷款
demand note
即期票据
demarcation n.
分界,界线;划分
demise n. v.
遗赠;让位
demobilization n.
遣散
demobilize v.
遣散
demolish v.
拆除
demolition n.
拆迁;爆破

demolition cost
拆除费
demolition works
拆除工程
demoulding *n.*
脱模
demurrage *n.*
滞留;滞期费;装运误期费
denote *v.*
指示
denounce *v.*
通告废除(条款、协定等)
denunciation clause
废除条款;退约条款
depart *v.*
出发;违背
department *n.*
部门
department manager
部门经理
departure *n.*
离开,出发
dependent *a.*
从属的,依赖的
depict *v.*
叙述,描述
depicting progress
叙述情况
depletion *n.*
损耗,折损
depletion allowance
折耗备抵
depletion reserve
耗减准备
deportation *n.*
驱逐出境
deposit *n.*
存款,保证金,押金;保存处;沉淀 *v.* 存款;存放;浇注
deposit premium
预付保险费
deposit rate
存款利率

deposit slip
存款单
depositor *n.*
存储者,储户
depreciable assets
应计折旧资产
depreciate *v.*
(资产等)折旧;(货币等)贬值
depreciated cost
折余成本
depreciated value
折余价值
depreciation *n.*
折旧;贬值
depreciation base
折旧基数
depreciation charge
折旧费
depreciation cost
折旧成本
depreciation fund
折旧基金
depreciation method
折旧方法
depreciation of capital
资本折旧
depreciation of currency
货币贬值
depreciation of equipment
设备折旧
depreciation of machinery
机械设备折旧
depreciation rate
折旧率
depreciation reserve
折旧准备
depreciation-straight line method
平均折旧法
depression *n.*
萧条,不景气
deprive *v.*
剥夺;免职
deputy *n.*

副手;代表
deputy general manager
副总经理
deputy manager
副经理
dereliction *n.*
玩忽职守;放弃
derogation *n.*
部分废除,减损
describe *v.*
描述,说明
description *n.*
描述,摘要,说明
description of goods
货物说明书
description of items
条目的说明,分项的说明
description of materials
材料说明
description of project
工程说明书
description of works
工程描述
desiccation fissure
干缩裂缝
design *v. n.*
设计,计划
design and build
设计和建造
design and engineering
设计和规划
design approach
设计方案
design audit
设计审查
Design-Build-Operate-Transfer (DBOT)
设计—建设—运营—移交
design capacity
设计能力
design code
设计规范
design-construct
设计—建造
design criteria
设计准则
design data
设计数据
design details
详细设计,设计细则
design documentation
设计文件
design draft
设计图样
design drawing
设计图纸
design engineer
设计工程师
design load
设计负荷
design objective
设计目标
design professional
专业设计师
design proposal
设计方案
design quantities
设计工作量
design requirement
设计要求
design review
设计审查
design subcontractor
设计分包者
design team
设计组
design unit
设计单位
designate *v.*
指定,选派,任命
designated representative
指定的代表
design-build contract
设计—建造合同
designer *n.*
设计师,设计者

designer's consultant
设计师的顾问
designer's estimate
设计师的估价
despatch, dispatch v.
急送(电报,信件);调度;迅速处理
destination n.
目的地
destination port
目的港
destruction n.
破坏;毁灭
detail n.
细节
detailed account
明细账目,详细报表
detailed audit
详细审计
detailed budget
详细预算
detailed construction schedule
详细的施工进度表
detailed cost
详细费用
detailed design
详细设计
detailed design approach
详细设计法
detailed drawing
详图,大样
detailed engineering
详细设计,施工设计
detailed estimation
详细概算
detailed ledger
明细分类账
detailed packing list
详细装箱单
detailed particulars
细节,详细申述
detailed program
详细计划
detailed project report
工程详细报告
detailed schedule
详细计划表
detailed take-off
详细估计
details n.
详图;细则
detained goods
被扣货物
detainment n.
扣留
deterioration n.
损坏,变质,恶化,损蚀
determinable liability
确定性负债
determination n.
决定,终结,裁定
detonator n.
雷管
devaluation n.
贬值
devaluation adjustment
货币贬值调整
Develop-Operate-Transfer (DOT)
开发－运营－移交
developer n.
开发商
development n.
开发,发展
development bank
开发银行,发展银行
development capital
开发资本
development corporation
开发公司
development cost
开发成本
development credit agreement
开发信贷协议
development fund
发展基金
developmental program
开发规划

deviate *v.*
偏离,使偏离
deviation *n.*
偏差,偏离,越轨
device *n.*
方法,手段;装置
diagram *n.*
图表,图解,简图
difference *n.*
差额,差异
differing site conditions (D.S.C)
不同的现场条件,现场条件变化
dilemma *n.*
窘境,进退两难
diligence *n.*
勤奋,努力
dimension *n.*
尺寸;范围;方面
diminish *v.*
减少,降低
diminishing assets
递耗资产
diminution *n.*
减少
direct B/L
直达提单
direct cost
直接成本,直接费用
direct costing
直接成本计算法
direct current
直流电
direct damage
直接损害
direct debit
直接借记,直接付款
direct financing
直接融资
direct labour cost
直接人工费
direct loss
直接损失
direct material
直接材料
direct method of allocation of cost
成本直接分摊法
direct overhead
直接管理费
direct overhead account
直接管理费账户
direct payment
直接支付
direct port
直达港
direct purchase
直接采购
direct quotation
直接报价;直接比价
direct sale
直接销售
direct shipment
直达运输,直接装运
direct tax
直接税
direct trade
直接贸易
direct verdict
直接裁决
direction *n.*
指导;指令
director *n.*
董事;主任
dirty bill of lading
不洁提单
disadvantage *n.*
不利条件
disagreement *n.*
异议
disassembly *n.*
拆迁
disburse *v.*
拨款,支付
disbursement *n.*
支出费用,偿付款
disbursement clause
船舶费用条款

disbursement insurance
船舶费用保险
disbursement percentage
支付百分比
disbursement procedure
付款程序
disbursement voucher
支付凭单
disbursements to date (DTD)
已付金额
discharge n. v.
解雇;履行,完成;结清;卸货;结清单
discharge canal
排水渠
discharge cost
装卸费用
discharge duct
排气管道;排水管道
discharge hopper
卸料斗
discharge of contract
合同的履行
discharge of debt
清偿债务
discharge of duty
履行职责
discharge pump
排水泵
discharged workers payroll
被解雇工人工资
discharging port
卸货港
discipline n.
纪律;学科
disclaim v.
不索取,放弃;否认
disclaimer n.
放弃(权利等);放弃者;不承认
disclaimer clause
弃权条款;限制索赔条款
disclaimer of responsibility
放弃责任
disclose v.
泄露
disclosure n.
泄露
discontinue n.
停止,中断
discount v. n.
贴现;折扣,减价
discount bank
贴现银行
discount broker
贴现经纪人
discount factor
折扣系数;贴现系数
discount for price
价格贴现
discount of draft
汇票贴现
discount on purchases
进货折扣
discount on sales
销售折扣
discount period
折扣期限;贴现期
discount rate
折扣率;贴现率
discounted bid price
打折后的投标价
discounted cash flow (DCF)
贴现的现金流量
discounted notes
已贴现票据
discounted value
贴现值
discrepancy n.
不符合;差异,不一致
discretion n.
处理权,酌处权;判断
discretionary account
无条件账户
discretionary client
全权委托客户
discretionary cost
任意成本,自定成本

discretionary funds
可自由支配的基金
discretionary power
自行决定权
discretionary trust
全权信托
discrimination n.
区别,辨别,歧视
disentangle v.
解决(纠纷等);清理
dishonor n. v.
拒付,拒绝承兑,退票
dishonor a bill
不承兑期票,不支付期票
dishonor by non-acceptance
退票,票据迟到拒绝承兑
dishonor by non-payment
退票,票据迟到拒绝付款
dishonored notes (bill)
拒付的票据,退票
disinfection inspection certificate
消毒检验证书
dismantle v.
拆除
dismantlement n.
拆除
dismantling of plant
设备的拆除
dismiss v.
解雇;驳回
dispatch v.
派遣,发送 n. 快信,急件
dispatch money
速遣费
displacement n.
位移;排水量
disposal n.
处理,处置;出售;自由处置权
disposal cost
清理费用
disposal of fixed assets
固定资产的处置
disposal of surplus
剩余物的处理,废弃物的处理
dispose v.
处理,安排
disposing capacity
行为能力,处置能力
disproof v.
驳斥,反驳
dispute n. v.
争执,争议,争论,争端
dispute adjudication board (DAB)
争端裁决委员会
dispute settlement
争端解决
disputes review board (DRB)
争端审议委员会
disputes review expert
争端审议专家
disqualification n.
不合格,取消资格,无资格
disqualified goods
不合格货物
disqualify v.
取消…的资格;使不合格;使不能
disruption of progress
扰乱进度
dissolution n.
(公司等)解散,解体;(契约等)解除
dissolution of contract
合同的解除
distrain v.
扣押
distraint n.
扣押财物
distributable cost
可分摊的成本
distribution n.
分配,分销,分摊
distribution network
分销网;配电网
distribution of risks
风险分散
distribution outlet
销售渠道

distributor n.
批发商,经销商

disturbance n.
扰乱;(对财产、权利的)侵犯

disturbed soil
扰动土

ditch n.
排水沟

ditcher n.
挖沟机

diurnal n.
日志,日记簿

dive culvert
倒涵管,倒虹吸管

diversion n.
导流;引水

diversion channel
导流渠

diversion road
分支道路

divert v.
使转向

divestiture n.
剥夺,放弃(权利等)

dividend n.
红利,股息;债权人从破产人处得到的赔偿金

dividend earned
股利收入

dividend payable
应付股利

dividend payout ratio
股利支付(或分发)率

divisible contract
可分割合同

divisible L/C
可分割的信用证

division n.
部门,分公司

division controller
部门主会计师

division services manager
部门服务经理

divulge v.
泄漏

document n.
文件;票据,单据;凭证

document for claim
索赔文件

document of title
所有权凭证

document on customs clearance
结关文件

documentary bill (draft)
跟单汇票

documentary collection
跟单托收

documentary evidence
书面证据

documentary letter of credit
跟单信用证

documentary of carriage
运输单据

documents comprising the bid
组成投标的文件

dodge v.
掩饰,逃避

dollar credit
美元信贷

domain n.
产业所有权,土地征用权;领土

domestic a.
本国的,国内的,国产的

domestic cargo transportation insurance
国内货运保险

domestic contract
国内合同

domestic cost
国内费用

domestic exchange
国内汇兑

domestic finance
国内财政,国内财务

domestic inflation rate
国内通货膨胀率

domestic market price
国内市场价格
domestic preference
国内优先,国内优惠
domestic product
国货,国产品
domestic project
国内工程项目
domestic remittance
国内汇兑
domestic resources cost
国内资源成本
domestic sales
内销(额)
domestic tax
国内税
domestic trade
国内贸易
domestic turnover
国内销售额
domestic waste
生活污水,生活垃圾
domiciled bill (draft)
外埠付款汇票
donated assets
捐赠资产
donated capital
捐赠资本
donor
捐赠人
double insurance
双重保险
double shift
两班制
double taxation
双重税收
double taxation relief
免除双重税收
double-account system
复式账户制
doubtful account (debt)
呆账
Dow-Jones Index
道·琼斯指数
down payment
定金,(分期付款的)初次付款
down payment guarantee
定金保函
downstream *a*.
下游的 *ad*. 在下游
downtime *n*.
停工时间,窝工时间,停机时间
D/P (documents against payment)
  after sight
远期付款交单
D/P (documents against payment) at
  sight
即期付款交单
draft *n*.
草稿,草案;草图;汇票 *v*. 起草,草拟
draft a contract
起草合同
draft final statement
最终付款申请初稿,最终报表草稿
draft tube
通风管,尾水管
drain *n*.
排水;排水沟 *v*. 排水
drain pipe
排水管
drainage *n*.
排水,排水系统
drainage by well point
井点排水
drainage channel
排水渠
drainage conduit
排水管
drainage culvert
排水涵洞
draw *v*.
起草;提款;开(支票);吸引
draw up a contract
起草合同
draw-back *n*.
退税,退款

drawdown n.
提款;消耗
drawee n.
(汇票的)受票人,付款人
drawer n.
(汇票的)开票人,出票人
drawing n.
图纸;提款;草拟
drawing account
提存账户,提款账户
drawing list
图纸目录
dredger n.
挖泥船
drifter n.
凿岩机;风钻工
drilled well
钻井
drill-hole
钻孔
drilling n.
钻进;钻孔
drilling machine
钻机
drowned lime
熟石灰
drum mixer
筒式搅拌机
dry density
干容重
dry-stone masonry
干砌石圬工
dual a.
双重的,二元的
dual currency bond
双重货币债券
dual currency record
双重货币记录
dual tariff
双重关税
due a.
应付的,到期的;适当的;预定的 n.
[复]应得权益

due arrival
及时到达
due care and attention
应有的小心和注意
due consultation
充分协商
due date
到期日,支付日期
due date checklist
到期清单
due from
应收…款
due to
到期应付…;由于
dues n.
应付款;税款
duly ad.
及时地,适当地
duly authorized
经正式授权的
dump truck
自卸卡车
dumper n.
翻斗车,自卸车
dun v.
催债
duplicate n.
抄件,副本;复制品 v. 复制
duplicate invoice
发票副本
durability n.
耐久性
duration n.
期间,(工程期)持续时间
duration of contract
合同期限
duration of liability
责任期限
duration of licence
执照有效期
dust-proof a.
防尘的
dutiable value

完税价值
duty *n.*
关税；责任，义务
duty paid
关税已付
duty unpaid
关税未付
duty-free *a.*
免税的
duty-free goods
免税货物
duty-free importation
免税进口
duty-free shop
免税商店
duty-free zone
免税区
duty-paying value
完税价值
dwelling district
居住区
dyke *n.*
堤；沟 *v.* 筑堤；挖沟

E

earlier completion
提前竣工
early start date
最早开工日期
early withdrawal penalty
提前取款罚金
earmark *v.*
拨（款项），拨归…专用
earmarking of taxes
税款专用
earn *v.*
获得，获利，赚得
earned income
已获收益
earned man-hours
已完成的工时
earned premium
已赚保险费，赚取的保险费
earned revenue
已获营业收入
earned surplus
营业盈余
earnest *n.*
定金，保证金 *a.* 认真的，重要的
earnest money
定金，保证金
earning rate
收益率
earning statement
收益表
earning surplus
营业盈余，留存收益
earnings *n.*
盈利，收益，利润
earnings after tax (EAT)
税后收益
earnings before interest and tax (EBIT)
息前税前收益
earnings per share (EPS)
每股收益
earnings power
盈利能力
earnings report
利润表
earth dam
土坝
earth fill
填土
earth pressure
土压力
earth work
土方工程
earthquake *n.*

地震
earth-rock dam
土石坝
earthwork *n.*
土方工程
easement *n.*
地役权;附属建筑物;土地通行权
easy money
低息贷款
easy payment
分期付款
easy purchase
分期付款购置
easy terms
优惠条件
economic *a.*
经济的,经济上的
economic aid
经济援助
economic appraisal
经济评估
economic benefit
经济效益
economic blockade
经济封锁
economic contract
经济合同
economic cost
经济成本
economic crisis
经济危机
economic cycle
经济周期
economic entity
经济实体
economic interest
经济权益
economic internal return rate (EIRR)
经济内部收益率
economic law
经济法,经济规律
economic life
经济寿命
economic life and salvage value
经济寿命与残值
economic lot size
经济批量,最优批量
economic net present value (ENPV)
经济净现值
economic reckoning
经济核算
economic result
经济效益
economic risk
经济风险
economic unit
经济单位
economist *n.*
经济师,经济学家
economy *n.*
节约;经济
effect *n.*
效果;效力;影响;[复]财产 *v.* 实施,实行;使生效
effect insurance
投保
effective contract price
有效合同价
effective date
生效日期
effective date of contract
合同生效日期
effective duration of delay
实际延误的工期
effective guarantee
有效保证
effective interest rate
实际利率
effective terms
有效条款
effectiveness *n.*
有效性,有效程度
efficiency *n.*
效率,功效
efficient *a.*

有效的
elaborate *v.*
推敲,详尽阐述
elastic modulus
弹性模量
elbow *n.*
弯头
electric arc welder
电弧焊机
electric generator
发电机
electric motor
电动机
electric welding
电焊
electrical engineer
电气工程师
electrical installation
电气安装
element *n.*
因素;单元
elemental bill of quantities
单元工程量清单
elements of cost
费用要素
elevation *n.*
高程;立面图
elevation drawing
立面图
elevator liability insurance
电梯责任保险
eligibility *n.*
合格性,资格
eligible *a.*
合格的,适宜的
eligible acceptance
合格承兑票据
eligible bidders
合格投标者
eligible bill
合格票据
eligible dependents
合格家属

eligible for financing
符合资助条件
eligible source country
合格来源国
eligible termination payment（ETP）
合法的中止付款
eliminate *v.*
消除,排除
elimination *n.*
冲销,删除,抵消
embankment *n.*
土堤;填方,填土
embargo *n. v.*
禁运,禁止
emergency *n.*
紧急情况,遇险
emergency act
紧急法令
emergency action
紧急行为
emergency circumstances
紧急情况
emergency door
太平门,安全门
employ *v.*
雇佣;聘请
employee *n.*
雇员,职员,受雇者
employee experience profile
雇员履历表
employee's pension fund
职工养老金
employer *n.*
雇主,业主
employer's default
雇主违约
employer's equipment
业主的设备
employer's liability
雇主的义务,雇主的责任
employer's liability insurance
雇主的责任保险
employer's prevention

雇主的干预
employer's risks
雇主的风险
employment act
就业法
employment security
就业保障
empower *v.*
授权；准许
enable *v.*
授权；使能够
enameled tile
琉璃瓦
encamp *v.*
建立营地
enclose *v.*
附上
enclosure *n.*
附件；封入；围墙
encroach *v.*
侵占，侵入
encumbrance, incumbrance *n.*
阻碍；不动产债权，资产留置权
ending balance
期末余额
ending inventory
期末存货
end-of-project evaluation
项目期末评估
endorse a passport
签护照
endorse, indorse *v.*
背书；签注；认可；批注；转递（保函）
endorsee, indorsee *n.*
被背书人，受让人
endorsement *n.*
背书；签注；认可；批单
endorsement in blank
空白背书，不记名背书
endorser, indorser *n.*
背书人；转让人
endowment *n.*
捐赠，赠款

end-product *n.*
最终产品
enforce *v.*
实施，使生效，强制执行
enforceable contract
可强制履行的合同
enforcement *n.*
执行，贯彻，履行，强制执行
engage *v.*
任用，聘用；保证；约定；使从事
engagement clause
保证条款
engineer *n.*
工程师 *v.* 设计；管理；策划
engineer in charge
主管工程师
engineer in chief
总工程师
engineering *n.*
工程，工程学；方案设计；策划
engineering all risks (E. A. R)
设计工程一切险
engineering consultancy firm
工程咨询公司
engineering consulting contract
工程咨询合同
engineering contract
工程合同
engineering design
工程设计
engineering design plan
工程设计方案
engineering insurance
工程保险
engineering manager
设计经理
Engineering, Procurement and Construction Contract (EPC Contract)
设计、采购与施工合同
engineering scope database
工程范围数据库
engineering service loan
工程服务贷款

engineer's decision
工程师的(复审)决定
engineer's interim certificate
工程师的期中支付证书
engineer's representative
工程师代表
enquiry documents
询价文件,招标文件
enquiry, inquiry *n.*
询价,询盘
ensure *v.*
保证,确保
entail *v.*
使人承担,使成为必要
enter *v.*
进入;提出;登记;报关
enter into
参与;缔结(条约等)
enter into a contract with
与…订立合同
enter into effect
生效
enter into negotiation
参加谈判
enter up an account
入账
enterprise *n.*
企业,事业,公司;计划
enterprise property insurance
企业财产保险
enterpriser *n.*
企业家,创业者
entertain claim
接受索赔
entertain offer
接受报盘
entertain order
接受订货
entire contract
完整的合同
entitle *v.*
给予权利(或条件、资格);称呼
entitlement *n.*
应得的权利
entity *n.*
主体;个体;实体
entrance *n.*
入口,入境
entrance visa
入境签证
entrepreneur *n.*
[法]企业家;中间商;承包商
entrust *v.*
委托,信托
entrusted agent
委托代理人
entruster *n.*
委托人
entry *n.*
报关手续;进入;条目;报关单
entry certificate
入境证书
entry declaration
入港申报
entry for consumption
消费品进口报关单
entry for free goods
免税货进口报关单
entry for home use
国内消费品进口报关单
entry of contract into force
合同生效
entry of goods inward
申报进口
entry of goods outward
申报出口
entry outward
出口报单
entry price
入账价格
entry value
买入价值
entry visa
入境签证
environment *n.*
环境

environment contamination
环境污染
environment engineering
环境工程
environment protection
环境保护
environmental conditions
外界条件,周围情况
environmental impact assessment
环境影响评价
environmental monitoring system
环境监测系统
environmental pollution
环境污染
epoxide-resin paint
环氧树脂涂料
equal opportunity
同等机会
equal opportunity clause
同等机会条款
equal treatment of bidders
平等对待投标者
equality and mutual benefit
平等互利
equipment $n.$
设备,装备;(企业除房地产外的)固定资产;器材
equipment charge out rates
施工机械台时费
equipment cost estimating
施工机械费预算
equipment depreciation
设备折旧
equipment installer
设备安装商
equipment leasing
设备租赁
equipment list
设备清单
equipment maintenance
设备维修,设备保养
equipment procurement
设备采购

equipment rental
设备租用费
equipment supply loan
设备供货贷款
equitable $a.$
公正的
equitable mortgage
衡平法按揭
equity $n.$
产权;权益;股权;股票
equity capital
产权资本,权益资本
equity financing
增股筹资
equity fund
股票基金
equity holder
股本持有者
equity joint venture
产权式合营,投资入股型联营体
equity market
股票市场
equity ownership
产权所有权
equity ratio
权益比率
equity receiver
(企业财产)清算管理人
equity share
普通股
equivalency $n.$
等同性
equivalent $a.$
同等的,等效的 $n.$ 相等物
erection $n.$
安装,组装,竖起
erection all risks (EAR)
安装工程一切险
erection cost
安装费
erection diagram
装配图
erection information

安装资料
erection of equipment
设备安装
erection of plant
设备安装
erection on site
现场安装
erection works
安装工程
erratum *n.*
书写错误,勘误
error *n.*
错误,误差
error in good faith
善意过失
error of omission
过失罪,遗漏错误
error range
误差范围
escalate *v.*
使上升,上涨
escalating price
上涨的价格
escalation *n.*
上升,涨价
escalation charges
上涨费用
escalation clause
调价条款
escalation cost
涨价后的费用
escalation formula
涨价公式
escalation index
物价上涨指数
escalation lump sum contract
调值总价合同
escalation price
调价价格
escapable cost
可避免成本
escape clause
免责条款
escrow *n.*
有待完成契据
escrow account
第三方托管账户
escrow deposit
代理存款
essence *n.*
本质
essence of insurance
保险要素
establish *v.*
建立;安置
established *a.*
成立的;确定的
established international practice
公认的国际惯例
establishment *n.*
企业机构;建立,成立;经营场所
establishment charges
开办费
estate *n.*
不动产,房地产,地产
estimate *v. n.*
估算,估价,评估,预算
estimate documentation
估价文件,预算书
estimate guideline
预算导则
estimate of cost
成本估算
estimated contract payment
预计的合同支付
estimated cost
预计费用,预算成本,估算成本
estimated liabilities
估计负债
estimated physical life
预计使用年限
estimated residual value
估计残值
estimated salvage value

估计残值
estimated time of arrival (ETA)
预计到达时间
estimated time of departure (ETD)
预计离港时间
estimated time of finishing discharging (ETFD)
预计卸货完成时间
estimating *n.*
评估,估算
estimating and costing
预算和成本核算
estimation *n.*
评估,估算
estimator *n.*
估价者,估算师
estoppel *n.*
禁止翻供
ethical standard
道德标准
ethics *n.*
道德准则,规矩
Eurobank *n.*
欧洲银行
Eurocommercial paper
欧洲商业票据
Eurocurrency *n.*
欧洲货币
Eurodollar *n.*
欧洲美元
Euromarket *n.*
欧洲市场
European Currency Unit (ECU)
欧洲货币单位
Eurosyndicated loans
欧洲银团贷款
evade taxes
逃税,偷税
evaluated bid price
评标价
evaluation *n.*
评价,评算,核算,评估
evaluation criteria
评价标准
evaluation of bids
评标
evaluation process
评估过程
evasion of tax
偷税
evenness *n.*
平整度
evergreen credit
常用贷款
evidence *n.*
证据;证人;证词;证件
evidence in chief
主要证据
evidence of title
所有权证据
ex dock (EXD)
目的地码头交货
ex gratia claim
道义索赔,通融索赔
ex gratia payment
优惠支付,道义上的支付
ex parte *a. ad.*
单方面,片面
ex store
仓库交货
ex works (EXW)
工厂交货(价)
exacerbate *v.*
使加剧,恶化,激化
exact *a.*
正确的,精确的;严格的
exaggerated claim
夸大的索赔
examination *n.*
测验,检查
example *n.*
例证,范例
excavation *n.*
挖掘
excavator *n.*
挖掘机

exceed v.
超过
exceed the budget
超出预算
except v.
除外,删除 prep. 除…之外,不包括
excepted risk
除外风险
exception n.
例外,除外;异议,抗辩
exception clause
除外条款,免责条款
exceptional a.
例外的,特殊的
exceptional remedy
特殊补救办法
exceptional service
额外服务
exceptional urgency
特殊紧急事件
exceptionally adverse climatic conditions
异常恶劣的气候条件
exceptionally inclement weather
特别恶劣的天气
excess n.
超出;超出额;免赔额 a. 过量的;额外的
excess clause
超额条款,自负额条款
excess of loss reinsurance
超额损失再保险
exchange v.
换汇;交换 n. 兑换;汇票;交易所
exchange control
外汇管制
exchange control regulations
外汇管理规定
exchange dealings
外汇交易
exchange quota
外汇额度
exchange rate
汇率,兑换率;汇价
exchange restriction
外汇限制
exchange risk
汇兑风险,外汇风险
exchange tax
外汇税
excise
货物税,消费税,执照税
exclude v.
除外,把…排除在外,不包括
excluded liability
除外责任
exclusion n.
免除,除外;除外责任条款;不保事项
exclusion clause
除外条款
exclusive a.
专一的,独有的;除外的
exclusive agency
唯一代理,独家代理
exclusive contract
专营合同
exclusive dealer
独家经销商
exclusive distribution
独家经销,总经销
exclusive licence
(技术)独占许可证
exclusive market
独销市场
exclusive patent right
独家专利权
exclusive selling agent
独家销售代理商
exclusive use for the works
工程专用
ex-contractual claims
超越合同规定的索赔,非合同规定的索赔
exculpatory a.
开脱罪责的,无责任的
exculpatory clause

开脱性条款
excusable and compensable delays
可原谅并应给予补偿的拖期
excusable but not compensable delays
可原谅但不给予补偿的拖期
excusable delays
可原谅的拖期
execute v.
实施,履行;使(证书,契约等)生效;使合法
execute a contract
签署合同
executing agency
执行委员会,执行机构
execution n.
实施,执行,履行;施工;签署
execution of contract
合同的签署
executive n.
高级管理人员 a. 执行的;行政的
executive committee
执行委员会
executive director
执行董事
executor n.
执行人;遗嘱执行人
executory consideration
待结付的补偿
executory contract
待履行的合同
exempt a.
被免除的,被豁免的 v. 免除,豁免 n. 被免除义务者;免税人
exemption n.
免除,豁免;免税
exemption clause
免责条款;免税条款
exemption from duty
免税
exemption from liability
免除责任
exercise v. n.
行使;运用;实行

exercise of authority
行使职权
exercise power
行使权力
exercise right
行使权利
ex-factory price
出厂价
exhibit n.
展示件,附件,物证 v. 出示证据
ex-interest n.
无利息
existing mortgage
处于抵押状态的抵押物
exit value
脱手价值
exit-visa n.
出境签证
expansion joint
伸缩缝;伸缩接头
expansive cement
膨胀水泥
expatriate n.
移居国外者 a. 在国外居住的
expatriate craftsmen
外国技工
expatriate labour
外籍劳工
expectancy n.
期望
expected life
预计使用年限
expedite v.
加快速度;赶工
expedite deliveries
催促交货
expeditiously ad.
迅速地
expel v.
驱逐;开除
expellable a.
可驱逐的;应开除的
expendable fund

备用资金
expenditure *n.*
费用；支出；消费
expenditure of fund
资金支出
expenditure on administration
行政管理费
expense *n.*
费用；[复]开支；花费
expense account
报销费用账；开支账
expense allocation
费用分摊
expense ratio
费用率
expenses for administration
办公费
expenses for labour protection
劳动保护费
expenses for social intercourse
交际费
expenses for survey & design
勘测设计费
expenses in local currency
用本国货币支付的费用
experience *n. v.*
经验；经历
experiment *n.*
实验，试验
expert *n.*
专家，内行 *a.* 专门的，熟练的
expert committee（council）
专家委员会
expert consultant
咨询专家
expert opinion
专家意见，鉴定意见
expert witness
鉴定人
expertise *n.*
鉴定，专家评价；专业技能
expiration *n.*
（协定等的）期满；终止

expiration date
到期日
expiration of contract
合同到期，合同期满
expire *v.*
期满；(期限等)终止
expired cost
已耗成本
expiring laws
失效法律
expiry *n.*
（协定的）期满；(期限)终止
explanation *n.*
解释
exploitation *n.*
开发，开采
exploration *n.*
勘察，勘探；考察；测定
exploratory shaft
探井
explore *v.*
勘探；考察，仔细调查
explosive *n.*
炸药；[复]爆破材料
export *n.*
出口
export bank guarantee
出口银行保函
export bond
出口担保
export credit
出口信贷；出口信用证
export documents
出口单证
export duty
出口税
export entry
出口报单
export invoice
出口发票
export license（permit）
出口许可证
export of cash surpluses

剩余现金的汇出
export price
出口价
export restriction
出口限制
export shipping instructions
出口装船须知
export subsidy
出口补贴
export tax
出口税
exportation *n.*
出口
ex-post evaluation
项目影响评估,后评价
exposure *n.*
暴露;风险
express *v.*
明确表达 *n.* 快件;快运物品 *a.* 明确的;快捷的
express agreement
明示协议
express assignment
明示转让
express collect
运费到付
express consent
明示同意
express delivery
快递
express provision
明示规定
express terms
明示条款
express undertaking
明示承诺
express waiver
明示放弃;明示弃权书
expression *n.*
措辞,表达;表达方式
expressway *n.*
高速公路
expropriation *n.*

征用;剥夺所有权
expropriation of land
土地征用
ex-quay（EXQ）
目的港码头交货(价)
ex-ship（EXS）
目的港船上交货(价)
extend *v.*
扩大;发展;给予;延长
extend a contract
延长合同
extendible bond
可延期债券
extension *n.*
延长,延期;扩展,扩建
extension fee
延期费
extension of defects liability period
缺陷责任期的延长
extension of time
延期,工期延长
extension of time for completion
竣工期限的延长
extension of works
工程扩建
extent of agreement
协议范围
extent of damage
损害程度
extent of liability
责任范围
extent of power
权限
external *a.*
与外国有关的;对外的;外界的
external affairs
对外事务
external debt
外债
external interest rate
境外利率
extinguish *v.*
偿清(债务);取消

extra *a.*
特别的；额外的，外加的
extra allowance
额外津贴
extra charges（expenses）
额外开支
extra cost
额外费用，额外成本
extra premium
附加保险费
extra work
额外工作
extralegal *a.*
超出法律权限的
extraneous risks
附加风险，外来风险

extraordinary *a.*
非常的；非惯例的；特别的
extraordinary gains and losses
非常损益
extraordinary item
非经常性项目
extras *n.*
外加费用
extreme *a.*
极端的
extrovert *a.*
外向型性格的 *n.* 外向型的人
ex-warehouse
仓库交货价
ex-works price
工厂交货价

F

fabricate *v.*
装配,制作,结构加工；伪造
fabricated claim
虚构的索赔
fabricating yard
装配场
fabrication check points
加工制造的检验点
face amount（value）
票面金额,面值
face brick
面砖
face clause
（提单）正面条款
face to face negotiation
面洽,当面谈判
facilitation of trade procedures
贸易手续的简化
facilities for other contractors
为其他承包商提供方便
facility *n.*
[复]便利,方便；设施,设备,工具
facing stone
饰面石
facsimile（fax）*n.*
传真
facsimile telegraph
传真电报
facsimile transmission
传真发送
fact sheet
情况说明书
factor *n.*
因素；系数；代理人
factorage *n.*
代理业；代理商佣金；手续费
factoring charges
代理融通费,委托收债费
factoring company
代理融通公司,收债公司
factory cost
制造成本
factory expenses
制造间接费用
factory gate price
出厂价

factory order 生产通知单
factory price 出厂价格
factory tax 出厂税
factual record 真实记录
facultative *a.* 临时的；任意的；授权的
facultative reinsurance 临时再保险
fail *v.* 失败；破产；违约
fail in negotiation 谈判失败
fail the test 未通过检验
failure *n.* 失败；不履行；破产；无支付能力
failure to deliver 未能交货
fair *a.* 公平的；光明正大的；尚好的
fair average quality (FAQ) 良好平均品质,中等品质
fair competition 公平竞争
fair dealing 公平交易
fair dismissal 合理驳回；正当解雇
fair market price 公平市价
fair presentation 公允表达
fair price 公平价格
fair trading act 公平交易法
fair wages 公平工资
fall due （付款）到期
false document 伪造的文书
false entry 伪造记录；假账
false profit 虚盈实亏,虚假利润
false report 假报告
fan blower 鼓风机
fast track method 高速轨道方式
fast-setting cement 速凝水泥
fast-setting concrete 速凝混凝土
fatal accident 死亡事故
fatigue *n.* 疲劳,劳累
fatigue crack 疲劳裂缝
fatigue test 疲劳试验
fault *n.* 断层；故障
fault detector 探伤仪
faulty work 工作缺陷
favour *n. v.* 有利于；赞同；优惠；支持
favourable *a.* 优惠的；赞同的；有利的
favourable balance of trade 贸易顺差
favourable condition 优惠条件
favourable interest rate 优惠利率
favourable price 优惠价

favourable terms 优惠条件
favourable treatment 优惠待遇
feasibility *n.* 可行性
feasibility study 可行性研究
federal budget 联邦预算
federation *n.* 联盟;联合会;联邦政府
fee *n.* 费(用);酬金;手续费
fee for inspection 检验费
fee for permit 牌照费,执照费
feed hopper 进料斗,供料斗
feed pipe 供水管
feedback *n.* 反馈
feedstock *n.* 原料
festival *n.* 节日 *a.* 节日的
fiber board 纤维板
fiction *n.* 捏造,编造
fidelity bond（insurance) 职工忠诚保险
fiduciary loan 信用贷款
fiduciary service 信托服务
field *n.* 工地,场地;现场;领域
field book 工地记录本
field construction manager 现场施工经理
field erection 现场安装
field inspection 工地视察;实地调查
field inspection staff 现场检查人员
field investigation 现场勘察
field laboratory 工地试验室
field measurement 现场量测
field procurement supervisor 现场采购主管
field project staff 现场项目人员
field reporting 工地报告
field representative 现场代表
field sales 现场销售
field service 现场服务
field survey 现场调查
field test 现场试验
field work 野外作业;现场工作
figure *n.* 图形;数字;金额;价格
file *n.* 档案,文件 *v.* 提出;备案
file a claim 提出索赔
file copy 入档备案文件
file data 档案资料
filler *n.* 填料

filling pile
灌注桩
final acceptance
最终验收
final acceptance certificate
最终验收证书,竣工验收证书
final account
决算表,最终账目
final certificate
最终证书
final certificate of payment
最终支付证书
final cost
最后成本
final decision maker
最后决策人
final design
最终设计
final inspection
最后检查
final invoice
最终发票
final payment
最终付款
final review and assessment
最终审查与评定
final settlement of account
决算
final statement
最终报表,决算表
final value
终值
final verdict
最终裁决
finance *n.*
财政,金融;[复]资金 *v.* 筹资,融资
finance company
金融公司,信贷公司
finance lease
融资租赁
financial *a.*
财务的,金融的,财政的
financial accounting
财务会计
financial accounts
财务账目
financial aid
财务援助,财政资助
financial analysis
财务分析
financial assets
金融性资产,财务资产
financial audit
财务审计
financial budget
财务预算
financial capacity
财务能力
financial center
金融中心
financial claim
经济索赔;债权
financial commissioner
财务专员
financial community
金融界
financial compensation
经济补偿
financial condition
财务状况
financial cost
财务成本
financial counselling
金融咨询,财务咨询
financial consultant (counsellor)
财务顾问
financial data
财务数据
financial expenses
财务费用
financial futures
金融期货
financial guarantee
财务担保
financial institution
金融机构

financial instrument 金融票据;金融工具
financial intermediation 金融中介
financial lease 财务租赁
financial leverage 财务杠杆;举债经营
financial management 财务管理
financial market 金融市场
financial penalty 罚款
financial position 财务状况
financial projection 财务预测
financial proposal 财务建议书
financial ratio 财务比率
financial report 财务报告,财务报表
financial resources 财政资源;资金
financial risk 金融风险
financial security 经济担保
financial settlement 财务结算
financial statement 财务报告
financial viability 金融偿付能力
financial year 会计年度;财政年度
financier $n.$ 金融家;金融机构
financing $n.$ 融资;筹资;理财
financing charges 融资费
financing cost 筹资成本
financing interest rates 融资利率
financing plan 融资计划;资助计划
financing structure 融资结构
financing terms 融资条件
finder $n.$ 中介人,经纪行
finder's fee 中介人佣金
fine $n.$ 罚金 $v.$ 处…以罚款 $a.$ 细微的;优良的
finish $v.$ 完成
finished cost 完工成本,加工成本
finished goods 成品
finishing $n.$ 装修,抹面;精加工
finishing work 装修工程
finishing-machine 抹面机
fire $n.$ 火,火灾 $v.$ 解雇,开除
fire brick 耐火砖
fire extinguisher 灭火器
fire hydrant 消防栓
fire insurance 火灾保险
fire on the sea 海上火灾
fire perils

火灾风险事故
fire prevention
防火
fire prevention safety inspection
防火安全检查
fireproof *a.*
防火的,耐火的
fire-resisting concrete
耐火混凝土
firm *n.*
商行;公司 *a.* 确定的,约定的
firm commitment
不变承诺
firm lump sum contract
固定总价合同
firm offer
实盘
first aid
急救
first cost
最初成本;主要成本
first loss insurance
第一损失保险
first mortgage
第一抵押权
first priority
绝对优先权,第一优先权
first-hand data
原始数据
first-hand information
第一手资料
first-rate *a.*
第一流的
fiscal *a.*
财务的;财政的;会计的
fiscal agent
财务代理人
fiscal crisis
财政危机
fiscal law
会计法
fiscal measures
财政措施

fiscal policy
财政政策
fiscal revenue
财政收入
fiscal year
会计年度;财政年度
fitting *n.*
装配;修整;[复]装置,零配件
fitting out
安装
fitting out elements
安装配件
fitting out handbook
装配手册
fitting shop
装配车间
fix *v.*
安装;修理;固定
fixed assets
固定资产
fixed assets net value
固定资产净值
fixed assets salvage value
固定资产残值
fixed assets tax
固定资产税
fixed capital
固定资本
fixed charges
固定费用
fixed cost
固定成本,固定费用
fixed credit line
固定信贷额
fixed equipment
固定设备
fixed exchange rate
固定利率;固定汇率
fixed expenses
固定开支
fixed intangible assets
无形固定资产
fixed labour norm

劳动定额
fixed labour rates
固定劳工工资等级
fixed overhead
固定管理费
fixed price basis of payment
按固定价格付款
fixed price contract
固定价格合同
fixed price contract with adjustments
可调价的固定价格合同
fixed price contract with incentives
带奖励的固定价格合同
fixed property
不动产；固定资产
fixed rate
固定汇率；固定利率
fixed rate loan
固定利率贷款
fixed royalty
固定提成
fixed tangible assets
有形固定资产
fixed unit price contract
固定单价合同
fixed wages
固定工资
fixed-percentage-of-cost method (of depreciation)
成本定率(折旧)法
fixed-percentage-on-declining-balance method
定率递减(折旧)法
fixed-term contract
定期合同
fixture *n.*
附属装置，夹具，支架
fixtures *n.*
装置
flat rate
统一费率；统一税率；比例税率
flat truck(lorry)
平板车

flaw detector
探伤仪
fleet policy
车(船)队保险单
flexible budget
弹性预算，变动预算
flexible exchange rate
弹性汇率
flexible pavement
柔性路面
float *v.*
浮动；发行，使流通；浮时
float bridge
浮桥
floating *a.*
浮动的，流动的，不固定的
floating assets
流动资产
floating capital
流动资本
floating debt
短期债务，流动债务
floating exchange rate
浮动汇率
floating interest rate
浮动利率
floating property
流动财产
floating rate note (FRN)
浮动利率票据
flood *n.*
洪水；水灾
flood discharge
洪水流量
flood insurance
水灾险
flood level
洪水位
flood peak
洪峰
floor *n.*
地板，地面；最低额，底价
floor broker

(交易所)场内经纪商
floor of the court
诉讼人席位
floor price
最低价格
floor space
居住面积
floorage *n.*
使用面积
flow *n.*
流动;流量
flow chart
流程图,程序图
flow diagram
流程图
flow meter
流量计
flow of funds
资金流转
fluctuating price contract
浮动价格合同
fluctuation *n.*
波动;涨落;起伏
fluctuation of price
价格波动
fluid *a.*
流动的;易变的;流体的
fluid assets
流动资产
fluid capital
流动资本,流动资金
fly ash
粉煤灰
follow the international practice
遵守国际惯例
follow-up investment
后续投资
foot bridge
人行桥
foot-note *n.*
附注,脚注
for reference only
仅供参考

forbearance *n.*
债务偿还期的延展;宽容
force *n.*
力量;影响;效力;约束力 *v.* 迫使
force account
自营工程
force down prices
压价
force majeure
[法]不可抗力,人力不可抵御的自然力
force majeure clause
不可抗力条款
force of bind
约束力
force of law
法律效力
forced insurance
强制保险
forced liquidation
强制清算
forecast *n. v.*
预测,预报
foreclosure *n.*
取消赎回权
foredate *v.*
填早日期,倒填日期
foreign agency
外国代理机构
foreign branch
国外分支机构
foreign currency
外币
foreign currency requirements
外币需求
foreign debt
外债
foreign draft
国外汇票
foreign exchange
外汇,外币
foreign exchange control
外汇管制

foreign exchange earning
外汇赢利
foreign exchange exposure
外汇风险
foreign exchange gains and losses
汇兑损益
foreign exchange risk
外汇风险
foreign exchange transaction
外汇交易
foreign investment
外国投资;国外投资
foreign market
国外市场
foreign trade
对外贸易
foreman n.
工长,领班
foresee v.
预见
foreseeability n.
预见性
foreseeable losses
可预见的损失
foreseen damages
预见到的损害赔偿费
forfeit n.
(因违约,失职等)被没收的财产;罚金 v. 丧失,失去
forfeiture n.
罚金;没收物;丧失,权利的丧失
forfeiture clause
没收条款
forfeiture of payment
取消付款
forge v.
伪造;锻造
forged document
伪造文件
forged signature
伪造签字
form n.
表;格;格式;方式;方法;模板 v. 构成,组成
form of agreement
协议书格式
form of payment
支付方式
form of proxy
委托书格式
form of report
报告书格式
form of tender
投标书格式
form removal
模板拆除
form support
模板支撑
formal a.
正式的;形式的
formal acceptance
正式验收;正式承兑
formal agreement
正式协定
formal clause
正式条款
formal confirmation
正式确认
formal contract
正式合同
formal invoice
正式发票
formal law
成文法
formal notice
正式通知
formalities n.
手续
formula n.
公式,方程式,计算式
formula price adjustment
公式调价法
formulate v.
编制;系统的阐述;用公式表示
formwork n.
模板;模板工程

fortuitous *a.*
偶然的

fortuitous accident
意外事故

fortuitous event
意外事件

forward *a.*
预约的；期货的；远期的 *v.* 转交；发送 *n.* 期货

forward contract
远期合同

forward cover
期货抵补

forward dealings
期货交易

forward delivery
远期交货，将来交货

forward exchange
远期外汇，期汇

forward exchange rate
远期汇率，期货汇率

forward margin
远期差价，期货差价

forward payment
预付款

forward price
期货价格

forward rate
远期汇率

forwarder *n.*
转运公司，代运人，货运代理行

forwarding charges
运输费用

foul B/L
不洁提单

foundation *n.*
基础；基金

foundation settlement
地基沉降

foundation work
基础工程

foundation works
基础工程

fragile *a.*
易损坏的

frame *n.*
构架，结构

frame crane
龙门吊

framed structure
框架结构

franchise *n.*
特许权，专营权；免赔额 *v.* 给予特许

franchise agreement
特许协议

franchise clause
免赔额条款

franchise taxes
特许经营税

franchisee *n.*
特许权受让人

franchiser *n.*
特许权出让人

franco *a.*
[法]全部费用在内价格的，目的地交货价的

franco invoice
全部费用在内价的发票

fraud *n.*
欺骗；舞弊

fraudulent act
欺诈行为

fraudulent misrepresentation
欺骗性的不正确陈述

free *a.*
自由的，不受限制的；免费的，无偿的

free alongside ship (F.A.S)
（装运港）船边交货价

free carrier… (named point) (FCA)
货交承运人（指定地点）（价）

free competition
自由竞争

free convertible currency
自由兑换货币

free currency
自由货币

free export
出口免税
free from particular average (FPA)
单独海损不赔偿,平安险
free import
进口免税
free in and out
船方不负担装卸费用
free loan
无息贷款
free medical treatment
免费医疗
free of charge
免费
free of duty
免关税
free of tax
免税
free on board (FOB)
(起运港)船上交货价,离岸价格
free on rail (FOR)
铁路交货价
free port
自由港
free-stone *n.*
毛石,乱石
free-trade area
自由贸易区,免税区
free-trade zone
保税区
freeze *v. n.*
冻结
freight *n.*
运费;货运;运送的货物
freight audit
运费审查
freight bill
运费单
freight charges
运费
freight clause
运费条款
freight collect

[美]运费由提货人支付
freight cost
运费
freight forward
[英]运费由提货人支付
freight forward cost
货物发运费用
freight forwarder
运输代理行
freight insurance
运费保险
freight list (F/L)
运价表
freight note
运费单
freight paid
运费已付
freight policy
运费保险单
freight prepaid
运费已预付
freight rate
运费率
freight to be paid
运费到付
freight to collect
运费到付
freight-in
进货运费
frequency *n.*
频率
friendly cooperation
友好合作
fringe benefits
附加福利
frog rammer
蛙式打夯机
front loaded
前重后轻的(报价),不平衡(报价)
frost-resisting concrete
抗冻混凝土
frozen account
冻结账户

frozen assets
冻结资产
frustrated contract
落空的合同,不能履行的合同
frustration *n.*
受挫,落空,不能履行,被迫终止
frustration of contract
合同落空(指不可抗力引起)
fuel *n.*
燃料
fuel cost
燃料费
fulfill *v.*
完成,履行(职责)
fulfill a contract
履行合同
fulfillment *n.*
完成,履行(职责)
fulfillment of schedule
完成进度计划
full cost
全部成本,完全成本
full coverage
完全承保
full insurance
全额保险
full liability
完全责任
full replacement cost
全部重置成本
full set of bills of lading
全套提单
full set of clean on board bills of lading
全套清洁已装船提单
full set of documents
全套文件
function *n.*
职能;功能;职责;用途
fund *n.*
基金;资金 *v.* 提供资金,资助
fund flow
资金流转
fundamental breach
根本性违约
funded debt
长期债务
furnish *v.*
提供,供应
furnishing and erecting
供货与安装
furnishings *n.*
供应;装备
furniture and office appliances
家具及办公用具
future value
未来价值,终值
futures *n.*
期货交易
futures market
期货市场
futures price
期货价
futures trading
期货贸易

G

gage *n.*
抵押品
gain *n.*
获利,收益,盈余,利润 *v.* 获得,赚
gain and loss
损益,盈亏
gale *n.*
定期交付的租金(或利息);大风
galloping inflation
恶性通货膨胀

galvanized iron
镀锌铁皮,白铁皮
galvanized iron wire
镀锌铁丝
gang *n.*
小组,施工队
ganger *n.*
领班,监工
gantry crane
门式起重机,龙门吊
Gantt chart *n.*
甘特图,线条图,横道图
garnishee order
(向第三债务人下达的)扣押令
gasoline *n.*
汽油
gauge *n.*
标准;规格;测量计
general *a.*
总的;普遍的,一般的;通用的
general acceptance
普通承兑
general account
总账
general agency
一般代理;总代理
general agent
总代理人
general arrangement drawings
总体布置图
general arrangements
总布置图
general average act
共同海损行为
general average adjustment
共同海损理算
general average clause
共同海损条款
general average contribution
共同海损分摊
general average deposit
共同海损保证金
general average disbursement insurance
共同海损费用保险
general average fund
共同海损基金
general average (G. A.)
共同海损
general average guarantee
共同海损担保书
general average loss
共同海损损失
general average security
共同海损担保
general average statement
共同海损理算书
general conditions
通用条件,一般条件
general conditions of contract
通用合同条件
general container
普通集装箱
general contract
总承包合同
general contractor
总承包商,总包商
general contractual liabilities
合同的一般责任
general equilibrium analysis
综合分析,宏观分析,全面均衡分析
general expenses
日常费用
general foreman
总监工
general journal
普通日记簿,普通日记账
general labour
普工
general layout
总平面布置图
general ledger account
总分类账户
general lien
一般留置权
general manager

总经理
general mortgage
一般抵押,总抵押
general obligation
一般义务
general overhead
总部管理费
general partnership
普通合伙
general plan
总体布置图;总体规划
general price level
一般物价水准
general procurement notice
总采购通告
general requirements
总体要求
general responsibilities
一般义务,一般责任
general right
一般权利
general specification
总体规定
general terms and conditions
一般(交易)条件
general theory of law
法的一般原理
general tort
一般侵权行为
general trade system
总贸易体系
generalized system of preferences documents
普惠制单据
generalized system of preferences (GSP)
普遍优惠制,普惠制
generation *n.*
发电;发生;产生
gentleman's agreement
君子协定
geographic(al) position
地理位置;经纬度

geological condition
地质条件
geological investigation
地质勘探
geological profile
地质剖面图
geotextile fabrics
土工织物
gift *n.*
礼品,赠品;赠与
girder *n.*
主梁,大梁
give-and-take *n. a.*
平等交换(的);互让(的)
glazier *n.*
玻璃工
global corporations
全球公司
global quota
全球配额
glued board
胶合板
go into force
生效
go into operation
投入运营
goal *n.*
目标,目的
godown *n.*
货仓,仓库
godown entry
入库单
godown keeper
仓库管理员
godown receipt
仓库收据
good faith
诚信,善意;良好信誉
goods *n.*
货物,商品;私人财产(尤指动产)
goods in stock
存货,现货
goods in transit

在途货物
goods-ordering contract
订货合同
goods-out on consignment
寄销品
goodwill *n.*
商誉;友好
governing law
适用的法律,管辖的法律
government *n.*
政府;管理机构
government bond
政府债券,公债
government budget
政府预算
government commitment
政府的承诺
government credit
政府信贷
government decree
政令
government department
政府部门
government enterprise
国营企业
government intervention
政府干预
government investment
政府投资
government owner
政府业主
government procurement policy
政府采购政策
government revenue
政府税收
grace *n.*
恩惠;(票据等到期后的)宽限期
grace of payment
支付宽限
grace period
宽限期
grade *n.*
级别,等级

grade separation bridge
立交桥
graded aggregate
级配骨料
grader *n.*
平土机;(骨料)分选机
grading elevation
路基标高
graduated payment
累进偿付
graphic(al) *a.*
图示的,图解的
granite *n.*
花岗岩
grant *n.*
同意,转让;补贴;赠款 *v.* 授予,转让
grant a certificate
签发证书
grant of representation
代表权的授予
graph *n.*
图表,图解
gratuitous *a.*
免费的,无偿的
gratuity *n.*
赏钱,小费
gravel *n.*
砾石,卵石
gravel road
砾石路
gravity dam
重力坝
gross *a.*
总的,毛的
gross domestic product（GDP）
国内生产总值,国内总产值
gross earnings
毛利,总收益
gross fixed investment
固定投资总额
gross floor area
总建筑面积
gross for net

以毛(重)作净(重)
gross income
总收入
gross margin（profit）
毛利
gross misconduct
严重渎职
gross national income（GNI）
国民收入总值
gross national product（GNP）
国民生产总值
gross operating spread
营业毛利
gross pay
工资总额
gross premium
保险费总额
gross price
毛价,总价
gross profit
毛利润
gross profit on sales
销货毛利
gross profit ratio
毛利率
gross rate
毛费率
gross value
毛值,总值
gross weight
毛重,总重
ground *n.*
场地;理由
ground bolt
地脚螺栓
ground elevation
地面高程
ground improvement
地基加固;地基处理
ground lease
土地租约
ground works
土方工程
groundage *n.*
停泊费;港口费
groundwater *n.*
地下水
groundwater level
地下水位
group action
集体行为
group boycotts
集体抵制
group method of depreciation
分类折旧法
group of piles
群桩
group sense
群体意识
grout mixer
砂浆搅拌器
grouting *n.*
灌浆
grouting machine
灌浆机
growth *n.*
增长,发展,扩大
growth rate
增长率
guarantee *v.* 保证,担保 *n.* 保函,担保;抵押物
guarantee for re-export of equipment
设备再出口保函
guarantee loan
抵押贷款
guarantee of insurance
保险担保书
guarantee on the first demand
首次要求即付保函,无条件保函
guarantee period
保证期
guarantee slip
保单
guaranteed maximum cost contracts
最高成本限价合同
guaranteed maximum price

保证最大价格
guarantor *n.*
保证人,担保人
guaranty period
保证期
guesstimate *n. v.*
粗估;猜测
guideline *n.*
指南

guidelines for procurement
采购指南
gully *n.*
排水沟
guniting *n.*
喷浆
gypsum *n.*
石膏

H

half finished goods
半成品
hallmark *n.*
品质证明,优质标记
hand rail
扶手,栏杆
hand worker
手工工人
handbook *n.*
手册
handbook of users of consulting services
咨询服务用户手册
handing-over certificate
移交证书
handle *v.*
处理;经营
handle with care
小心轻放
handling charge
装卸费;手续费
handling cost
装卸费;管理费
handling in field
现场搬运
hand-over *a.*
移交的
handstone *n.*
小石子
harbor dues
停泊费,港务费;入港税
harbor duty
港口税
harbor project
港湾项目
harbor regulation
港口条例
harbor works
港湾工程
hard currency
硬通货;硬币
hard loan
硬通货贷款;条件苛刻的贷款
hard-copy
硬副本,打印副本
hardhat *n.*
安全帽
hardware *n.*
硬件
harsh duties
苛捐杂税
haul distance
运输距离
haulier *n.*
承运人;运输工
hauling equipment
运输设备
have charge of
主管着…
hazard *n.*

危险,风险因素,公害
H-brick
空心砖
head *n*.
水头;渠首;首长;主管,主任
head of pile
桩头,桩帽
head office
总部,总公司
head office cost
总部费用
head office overhead
总部管理费
head tax
人头税
headquarters *n*.
总部
health certificate
健康证明
health insurance
健康保险;医疗保险
hearing *n*.
审理;受理申诉;听证会
heating and ventilating
采暖与通风
heating system
供暖系统
heat-insulating material
绝热材料,隔热材料
heavy clay
重粘土
heavy construction
大型工程
heavy lift
重型起重机
heavy weather damage
恶劣天气损失
heavy-duty truck
重型卡车
hedging *n*.
套期保值
heir *n*.

继承人
helmet *n*.
安全帽
hereby *ad*.
特此,据此;兹
hidden loss
隐蔽损失
high pressure pump
高压泵
high priced bid
高标价投标
highest bidder
报价最高的投标人
high-flying highway
高架公路
high-level talks
高层谈判
high-quality cement
高标号水泥
high-rise building
高层建筑
high-strength cement
高强水泥
high-tensile steel bar
高强度钢筋
highway *n*.
公路
highway engineering
公路工程
hillside *n*.
山坡
hire *v*.
雇用,租赁,租借 *n*. 租用;租金;工钱
hire purchase
[英]分期付款购买,租购
hired labour
雇工
hirer *n*.
雇主;租借者
historical cost
历史成本,过去成本
hoist *n*.

卷扬机
hold *v.*
认为;相信;持有;举起;约束
hold harmless
免除责任;转移责任
hold in pledge
抵押
holder *n.*
持票人;持证人
holder in due course
正当持票人
holding company
控股公司
holiday *n.*
假日,节日,[复]假期
holiday with pay
带薪假日
hollow brick
空心砖
home consumption
国内消费
home country
本国
home leave
探亲假
home made
国内制造
home office cost
公司本部费用
Hongkong Interbank Offered Rate (HIBOR)
香港银行同业拆放利率
honorary certificate
荣誉证书
honored *a.*
已付款的;荣誉的
honour *v.*
承兑;执行 *n.* 荣誉;信用
honour a bill
支付期票
honour one's liability
承担赔偿责任
honour the contract
信守合同
honouring contract and acting in good faith
重合同、守信誉
hook damage
钩损险
hoop reinforcement
环筋,箍筋
horizontal agreement
横向协议
horse power
马力
host *n.*
主人,主持人
host country
东道国
host government
东道国政府
hostilities *n.*
敌对行为
hot money
游资;短期流动资金
hot-rolled bar
热轧钢筋
hot-rolling *n.*
热轧
hourly wage rate
小时工资
house *n.*
房屋,住宅;商业机构;商号
house bill
公司汇票,商号票据
housing *n.*
住房;住房建筑
housing development
住宅建设
housing fund
住宅建设基金
hull insurance
船舶保险
hull policy
船体保险单
human resources

人力资源
hush money
贿赂费
hydraulic engineering
水利工程
hydraulic excavator
液压式挖土机
hydraulic power station
水电站
hydraulic resources
水利资源
hydraulic structure
水工建筑,水工结构
hydraulic works
水利工程
hydrological *a.*
水文的
hydrological and geological data
水文地质资料
hydrological station
水文站
hypothecate *v.*
抵押,典质
hypothecated assets
被抵押资产,抵押资产
hypothecation *n.*
财产抵押行为

I

I-beam *n.*
工字梁
IDA credit
国际开发协会信贷
identification *n.*
鉴别,确定,识别;身份
identification card
身份证
identification of risks
风险辨识
identify *v.*
验明,鉴别
identity *n.*
身份;一致性
idle *a.*
空转的;无效的;闲置的;窝工的
idle capacity
闲置生产能力
idle cost
窝工费用
idle equipment
闲置设备
idle money
闲置资金

idle time
停工时间
ignorant error
出于无知的错误
ignore *v.*
驳回;不理,忽视
illegal *a.*
不合法的,非法的
illegal act
违法行为
illegal contract
非法合同
illegal payment
非法支付
illegal profit
非法利润
illegality *n.*
非法行为,违法
illicit *a.*
被禁止的,违法的
illustration *n.*
举例说明,例述,用图表说明
imitation trade mark
冒牌商标

immaterial capital
无形资本,非物质资本
immediate *a.*
立即的,即时的,直接的
immediate beneficiary
直接受益人
immediate cause
直接原因
immediate compensation
立即赔偿
immediate delivery
立即交货
immediate payment
立即付款
immediate shipment
立即装运
immovable property
不动产
immovables *n.*
不动产
immunities of the carrier
承运人责任的豁免
immunity *n.*
豁免
impact *v.*
影响 *n.* 影响力,冲击
impact evaluation report
(项目)影响评价报告
impartial *a.*
公正的,不偏袒的
impartial and unbiased manner
公正无偏的态度
impartiality *n.*
公正性;中立性
impasse *n.*
死胡同,僵局
impeach *v.*
控告;弹劾
impediment *n.*
妨碍,阻碍
imperfect *a.*
不完善的
impersonal entity
法人单位
implement *v.*
落实;执行,实施 *n.* [复]用具,工具
implementation *n.*
实施,执行;履行(契约,诺言等)
implementation of contract
合同的履行
implementation schedule
执行进度
implication *n.*
隐含,含义,言外之意
implied *a.*
默认的,默示的;隐含的
implied contract
默示合同
implied meaning
隐含的意思
implied objection
默示异议
implied power
默示权力
implied terms
默示条件
implied warranty
默示保证
implied work
隐含的工作,默示工作
imply *v.*
暗示,默示,隐含
import *v.*
进口;表明 *n.* 进口;含义
import admission
进口许可
import agent
进口代理商
import and export license
进出口许可证
import announcement
进口通知
import ban
进口禁令,禁止输入
import contract
进口合同

import declaration
进口申报单
import duty
进口税
import duty memo
货物进口完税单
import entry
进口报关单
import license (permit)
进口许可证,进口批件
import licensing
进口许可制
import limit
进口限额
import material
进口材料
import procedure
进口手续
import prohibition
禁止进口
import quota
进口配额
import restraint
进口限制
import substitution
替代进口
import surplus
贸易入超
import surtax (surcharge)
进口附加税
import tax
进口税
import trade
进口贸易
importer's currency
进口国货币
impose v.
征(税等);把…强加在
imposition n.
课税,税款;强加
impossibility of performance
不可能履行
impost n.

进口税,关税
impound v.
扣押
impracticability n.
无法实行
imprest n.
预付款;垫付款
imprest cash
定额备用现金
imprest fund
定额备用金
imprest system
定额备用制
imprint v.
盖印 n. 印记
improper a.
不合格的,不恰当的
improvement n.
改进;改建
improvement cost
改进成本;改建费用
in a manner prescribed by law
依法定程序
in charge of
负责,领导
in fault
有责任,有过错
in favour of
以…为受款人,付款给…人;有利于;赞同
in force
有效,在有效期中
in short supply
供不应求
in situ
现场的,就地的
in the interests of
对…有利的
inactive a.
不活动的;不使用的,闲置的
inactive money
呆滞资金
inactive stock

呆滞存货
inactive trust
不主动信托
inadequate *a.*
不充分的,不适当的
inalienable *a.*
不可分割的;不可剥夺的
inapplicable *a.*
不适用
incapability *n.*
不胜任,无资格
incentive *n.*
刺激,鼓励,奖励
incentive fee
奖金
incentives for early completion
提前完工的奖励
inception stage
(项目)开始阶段
inch *n.*
英寸
incidental *a.*
伴随的;临时性的 *n.* 附带事件;[复]杂项;杂费
incidental expenses
附带费用
incidental revenue
附带收入
incidental service
附带服务,相关服务
inclement weather
恶劣天气
inclusive *a.*
包括的
income *n.*
收益,收入,所得
income account
收益账(户)
income deduction
收益扣除额
income distribution
收益分配
income insurance
收入保险
income sheet(**statement**)
收益表,损益表
income summary account
收益汇总账户
income tax
所得税
income tax payable
应付所得税
income tax return
所得税申报表
incoming material
进库材料
incompetent *a.*
不胜任的,无能力的
inconsistent *a.*
不一致的,不符的
incontestable *a.*
不可争辩的,不可否认的
inconvertibility *n.*
不可兑换,(证券)不可兑换性
inconvertible currency
不能自由兑换的货币
incorporate *v.*
结合,合并;组成公司;纳入
incorporated companies
股份公司
incorporated (INC) *n.*
[美](放在公司名后)有限责任公司
incorporation *n.*
公司;社团;结合,合并
incorporator *n.*
公司创办人;社团成员
increase *v. n.*
增长,增加
increase in cost
费用的增加
increased cost
增加的费用
increased value clause
增值条款
increased value insurance
增值保险

increasing cost
递增成本
increment *n.*
增值,增额
incumbent *a.*
负有义务的,义不容辞的
incur a heavy loss
招致重大损失
incur obligation
负有义务
indebtedness *n.*
债务
indemnification *n.*
赔偿,补偿;保障
indemnify *v.*
补偿;使免于受罚;赔偿;保障
indemnifying party
保障方
indemnity by employer
雇主提供的保障
indemnity for damage
损坏赔偿
indemnity liability
赔偿责任
indemnity of insurance
保险赔偿
indent *n.*
订货单,契约 *v.* 订货;订合同
indenture *n.*
契约,凭单
independent *a.*
独立的
independent accountant
独立会计师,开业会计师
independent agent
独立代理人
independent claim settling clerk
独立理赔人
independent contractor
独立承包商;独立订约人
independent engineer
独立工程师
independent insurer
独立保险人
independent party
独立一方
indeterminate *a.*
不确定的,模糊的
index *n.*
索引;指数;指标
index of construction costs
建筑费用指数
index of prices
物价指数
index of wage
工资指数
indexed rate
与……指数挂钩的利(或关税,兑换)
率
indication *n.*
指示;标识
indicative mark
指示性标志
indicator *n.*
指标;指示物
indices for contract price adjustment formula
合同价格调整公式指数
indirect cost
间接成本
indirect damage
间接损害
indirect expenses
间接开支
indirect financing
间接融资
indirect labour cost
间接人工成本
indirect liability
间接责任
indirect loss
间接损失
indirect loss insurance
间接损失保险
indirect material cost
间接材料费用

indirect quotation
间接标价法
indirect tax
间接税
indirect trade
间接贸易
individual *n.*
个人,个体;独立单位 *a.* 个人的,单独的
individual check
私人支票
individual consultant
个人咨询专家
individual depreciation
单独折旧
individual enterprise
个体企业
individual income
个人所得
individual income tax
个人所得税
individual job procedure
单项工作程序
individual owner
个体业主
individual proprietorship
独资
indivisible *a.*
不可分割的
indivisible obligation
不可分债务
indorse, endorse *v.*
背书;签注;认可;批注
indorsee, endorsee *n.*
被背书人,受让人
indorsement, endorsement *n.*
背书;签注;认可;批单
indorser, endorser *n.*
背书人,转让人
industrial act
劳工法
industrial and commercial income tax
工商所得税
industrial architecture
工业建筑
industrial dispute
劳资争端
industrial injury
工伤
industrial property right
工业产权,工业所有权
industry *n.*
工业;产业
industry tax
产业税
ineffective *a.*
无效的
inefficient *a.*
低效的;无能的
inequality *n.*
不平等
inevitable *a.*
不可避免的
inexorable *a.*
铁面无私的
inexpensive *a.*
廉价的
inexperienced *a.*
缺乏经验的
inferior *a.*
劣等的,低档的
inflammable *a.*
易燃的 *n.* 易燃品
inflammable material
易燃材料
inflation *n.*
通货膨胀,物价暴涨
inflation adjustment
通货膨胀调整
inform *v.*
通知
informal agreement
非正式协定
informal contract
非正式合同

informal record
非正式记录
information *n*.
情况；资料，信息
information data bank
信息数据库
information management system (IMS)
信息管理系统
infrastructure *n*.
基础设施
infrastructure project
基础设施项目
infringement *n*.
侵权行为
infringement of a contract
违反合同
infringement of patent
侵犯专利权
inherited property
继承的财产
inheritor *n*.
继承人
in-house *a*.
机构内部的
in-house capabilities
机构内部能力，机构自身能力
in-house capacity
厂内生产能力
initial *v*.
草签，小签 *a*. 初步的；词首的 *n*. 首字母
initial a contract
草签合同
initial balance
期初余额
initial budget
初始预算
initial costs (expenses)
开办费
initial data
原始数据
initial payment
首期付款
initial price
初期价格
initial setting time
初凝时间
initial strength
初始强度
initial stress
初始应力
initialling *n*.
草签，缩写的签名
initiate procurement
开始采购
injunction *n*.
禁止令，强制令
injure *v*.
伤害
injury *n*.
伤害
injury insurance
伤害保险
injury on job
工伤
injustice *n*.
不公平
in-kind
以货代款
in-kind payment
实物支付
inland *n*.
内陆 *a*. 内陆的，内地的
inland bill of lading
国内提单；陆运提单
inland bill of lading clause
国内提单条款
inland exchange
国内汇兑
inland marine insurance
内河运输保险
inland transit policy
内陆运输保险单
inland transportation
内陆运输

inlet *n*.
进水口
innovation *n*.
革新,创新;新方法
input *n*.
投入,输入
inquire *v*.
问询,查询,询价
inquirer *n*.
询问者,调查人
inquiry *n*.
询价,询盘,查询
in-situ concrete pile
现浇混凝土桩
insolvency *n*.
无力偿付债务,破产
insolvency assignee
破产清算人
insolvent *n*.
破产者,无偿付能力者 *a*. 无偿付能力的
insolvent debtor
破产债务人
insolvent law
破产法
inspect *v*.
检查,视察,查阅
inspection *n*.
检查,检验,视察
inspection well
检查井
inspection certificate
检验合格证书
inspection certificate of origin
产地检验证书
inspection certificate of quality
品质检验证书
inspection certificate of quantity
数量检验证书
inspection certificate of value
价值检验证书
inspection certificate of weight
重量检验证书

inspection of accounts
查账
inspection of documents
文件审查,文件查阅
inspection of site
现场视察
inspection of works
检查工作
inspector *n*.
检查员,视察员
install *v*.
安装;设置,安置
installation *n*.
安装;安置;设施
installation diagram
安装图
installation fee
安装费
installation supplying
设施供应
installment *n*.
分期付款;分期分批
installment accounts receivable
应收分期账款
installment buying
[美]分期付款购买;租购
installment contract
分期付款合同
installment payment
分期付款
installment sale
分期付款销售,延期付款销售
installment shipment
分批装船,分批装运
institute *n*.
学会;协会;研究所;学院
Institute Cargo Clauses (A)
(伦敦保险)协会货物保险条款(A)
  (一切险)
Institute Cargo Clauses (B)
(伦敦保险)协会货物保险条款(B)
  (水渍险)
Institute Cargo Clauses (C)

(伦敦保险)协会货物保险条款(C)(平安险)
Institute Cargo Clauses (ICC)
(伦敦保险)协会货物条款
Institute Strikes, Riots and Civil Commotions Clauses
(伦敦保险)协会罢工、暴动及民变险条款
Institute War Clauses (IWC)
(伦敦保险)协会战争险条款
institution *n.*
设立;制定;条例;学会,协会
Institution of Civil Engineers' Conciliation Procedure
[英]土木工程师学会调解程序
institution of proceedings
起诉
institutional *a.*
机构的,组织的
institutional infrastructure
公共基础设施
instruct a bank
向银行下达通知
instruction *n.*
指导;指示;[复]命令;说明书
instruction for variation
变更命令
instruction to contractor
给承包商的指示
instructions to bidders
投标人须知
instrument *n.*
证件;票据;仪器;工具
insulation *n.*
绝缘,绝缘体
insurable *a.*
可保险的
insurable interest
可保权益
insurable property
可保财产
insurable risks
可保风险

insurable value
可保价值
insurance *n.*
保险;保险额;保险费;保障
insurance against accident to workmen
工伤事故保险
insurance against loss in weight
承保短量险
insurance agent
保险代理人
insurance amount
投保金额
insurance assessment
保险估价
insurance certificate
保险凭证,保险证书,保单
insurance clauses
保险条款
insurance company
保险公司
insurance contract
保险合同
insurance cover (coverage)
保险范围;保险总额
insurance documents
保险单据
insurance estimating
保险费估算
insurance expenses
保险费
insurance for liability
责任保险
insurance fund
保险基金
insurance group
保险集团
insurance in transit
运输保险
insurance incident
保险事件
insurance interest
保险利益

insurance law
保险法
insurance liability
保险责任
insurance of client's property
业主财产保险
insurance of damage
损害保险
insurance of goods
货物保险
insurance of workmen
劳工保险
insurance of works
工程保险
insurance period
保险期限
insurance policy
保险单,保单
insurance policy in force
生效的保险单
insurance premium
保险金,保险费
insurance rate
保险费率
insurance risk
保险风险
insurance surveyor
保险鉴定人
insurant n.
被保险人,受保险人,投保人
insure v.
给…保险,保险,承保
insure against
投保…险,为…办理保险
insured n.
被保险人,受保险人,保险客户 a. 保险的
insured amount
保险金额,投保金额
insured item
投保项目
insured liability
保险责任

insured loss
被保损失
insured object
保险对象
insured perils
被保风险
insured person
被保险人
insured property
被保险财产
insured value
保险价值
insurer n.
承保人,保险人,保险公司
insuring party
投保方
intangible a.
无形的,触摸不到的
intangible assets
无形资产
intangible fixed assets
无形固定资产
intangible goods
无形商品
intangible movables
无形动产
intangible property
无形资产,无形财产
intangible value
无形价值
integrated a.
整体的,综合的
integrated service
整套服务
integrity n.
正直
intellectual property right
知识产权,智力财产
intelligence n.
情报;智力
intend v.
打算;意思是
intendment n.

（法律上的）含义；意旨
intensity of rainfall
降雨强度
intent *n.*
意向，目的
intention *n.*
意向，蓄意
intention agreement
意向协定
intentional act
故意行为
intentional tort
故意侵权行为
interactive *a.*
相互影响的
inter-bank loan
银行间贷款
inter-company elimination
公司间往来抵销账项
inter-company loan
公司间贷款
inter-company transactions
公司间往来业务
interest *n.*
利息；权益；股权；兴趣；[复]利益
interest for delayed payment
延迟付款利息
interest margin
利息差额
interest on loans
贷款利息
interest payable
应付利息
interest per annum
年息
interest per diem
日息
interest per mensem
月息
interest rate
利率
interest rate adjustment
利率调整

interest rate arbitrage
套利率，利率套购
interest-bearing note
带息票据
interest-free credit
无息信贷，无息贷款
interface *n.*
接口，连接
interface of responsibilities
责任分界线
interference *n.*
干扰，干涉，妨碍
interim *n.*
间歇 *a.* 期中的，期间的；暂时的，临时的
interim acceptance certificate
期中验收证书
interim audit
期中审计
interim certificate
期中（付款）证书
interim determination of extension
临时延期决定
interim financial statement
期中财务报表
interim payment
期中付款；临时付款
interim procedures
暂行办法
interim provisions
暂行规定
interim regulations
暂行条例
interim results
期中业绩
interior decoration
内部装修
intermediary *n.*
中间人；调解人；中介物 *a.* 中间的
intermediary business
中介业务
intermediate *n.*
中间人；调解人；中介人 *a.* 中间的

intermediate term
中期
intermediation *n.*
中介；媒介；调解
intermodal carrier
联运承运人，联合运输人
intermodal container
联运集装箱
intermodal transportation
联合运输
internal *a.*
（公司）内部的；国内的；本地区内的
internal accounting
内部会计
internal auditing
内部审计
internal benefits
内部效益
internal control
内部控制
internal cost
内部成本
internal debt
内债
internal rate of return（IRR）
内部收益率；内部回收率
internal risk
内部风险
internal tax
国内税
international *a.*
国际的，国际上的
international arbitral award
国际仲裁裁决书
international arbitral tribunal
国际仲裁法庭
international cargo transportation insurance
国际货物运输保险
International Commercial Terms (Incoterms)
国际贸易术语
international competitive bidding (ICB)
国际竞争性招标
international construction engineering contract
国际建筑工程合同
international convention
国际公约；国际惯例
international corporation
国际公司
international currency
国际通行货币
international customs
国际惯例
international division
国际（事业）部
international double tax imposition
国际双重征税
international double taxation
国际双重征税
international fair
国际博览会
international finance
国际金融
international law
国际法
international practice
国际惯例
international price
国际价格
international project
国际工程
International Rules for the Interpretation of Trade Terms 1980 (Incoterms 1980)
1980年国际贸易术语解释通则
international sanction
国际制裁
international shopping
国际询价采购
international syndicated loan
国际银团贷款
international tax avoidance
国际避税

international tax evasion
国际逃税
international taxation agreement
国际税收协定
international trade
国际贸易
International Trade Centre (ITC)
国际贸易中心
International Trade Organization (ITO)
国际贸易组织
international trading currency
国际贸易货币
international validity
国际效力
interplay *n. v.*
相互影响
interpretation *n.*
解释;翻译,口译
interpretation of contract
合同的解释
interpretation of law
法律的解释
interpretation of statutory language
法律用语的解释
interpreter *n.*
翻译,译员
interruption *n.*
中断;干扰
inter-sectional matters
部门间的事务
interview *n.*
会见
introduce *v.*
介绍
introduction *n.*
简介;简述;介绍
introvert *a.*
内向型性格的 *n.* 内向型的人
invalid *a.*
(法律上)无效的
invalidate *v.*
使无效

invalidate the contract
废约
invalidity *n.*
无效性
invariability in price
价格不变性
invariable *a.*
不变的
inventory *n.*
存货;库存清单;详细目录
inventory allowance
存货允许限度
inventory control
存货管理
inventory cut-off date
盘存截止日
inventory data
存货数据
inventory method of depreciation
盘存折旧法
inventory reserve
库存储备量
inventory sheet
存货盘点表,盘存单
inventory turnover
存货周转
inventory valuation
存货估价
inverted filter
反滤层
inverted siphon
倒虹吸管
invest *v.*
投资;投入;授予
investigation *n.*
调查,勘查
investment *n.*
投资
investment allowance
投资补贴额
investment appraisal
投资评价
investment bank

投资银行
investment budget
投资预算
investment recovery period
投资回收期
investment return
投资回报
investment securities
投资证券
investment trust
投资信托
investment turnover
投资周转(率)
investor *n.*
投资者,投资人
invisible trade
无形贸易
invitation to bid (tender)
邀请投标,招标
invitation to negotiate
邀请谈判
invite *v.*
邀请
invite bids for
为…招标
invoice *n.*
发票;账单;发货清单
invoice value
发票价值
invoice with document attached
附有单证的发票
invoicing *n.*
开具发票
involuntary *a.*
非自愿的,强迫的
involuntary bankruptcy
强制破产
involve *v.*
涉及;参与
inward
进口
inward charges
入港费用

IOU (I Owe You)
借据,欠条
irreconcilable *a.*
不可调解的
irrecoverable *a.*
不能挽回的
irredeemable currency
不可自由兑换的货币
irrefutable *a.*
驳不倒的
irregular tax
杂税
irrelevant cost
不相关成本
irresistible force
不可抗力
irrespective of percentage (I.O.P)
无论损失如何全部赔偿
irrevocable *a.*
不可撤销的,不可取消的
irrevocable credit
不可撤销的信用证
irrevocable documentary (letter of) credit
不可撤销的跟单信用证
irrevocable L/C
不可撤销的信用证
irrevocable letter of guarantee
不可撤销的保函
irrigation channel
灌溉渠
isolation of risk
风险的分离
issuance *n.*
发布,颁布
issue *n. v.*
颁发;签发;发行
issue a bill of lading
开出提单
issue a certificate
签发证书
issue bidding documents
颁发招标文件

issuing bank
开证行
I-steel(bar) n.
工字钢
item n.
项目；项；条款
itemize v.
逐条记载，详细登记
itemized price
分项价格
itemized record
明细记录
items dismantled
已拆除的分项工程

J

jack n.
千斤顶
jack lamp
安全灯
jargon n.
行话，术语
jeopardy n.
危险
jerque note
结关单；海关检查证
jerquer n.
（海关）船货检查员
jerry a.
偷工减料的
jerry builder
偷工减料的建筑商
jerry construction
偷工减料的施工
job n.
工作；职业；零活
job changes
工作变动；工程变更
job completion
工作完成；工程竣工
job cost journal
工程成本日记账
job cost ledger
工程成本分类账
job cost record
工程成本记录
job cost sheet
分批成本单
job cycle
作业循环
job discipline
劳动纪律
job location
施工现场
job lot method
分批法
job opening
招工
job organization
工程组织机构
job out
外包，分包出去
job overhead cost
工程管理费
job performance
工作业绩
job progress
工程进度
job rate
生产定额
job site
工地，施工现场
job site clean up
工地清理
job site facilities
工地设施
job site survey
工地勘察
job specification
工作规范，操作规程

job supervisor
监工员
job title
职称
job vacancy
职位空额
jobber *n.*
批发商;临时工人
joinder *n.*
联合;共同诉讼
joint *a.*
共有的,联合的,共同的 *n.* 接缝,接头
joint account
联合账户
joint act
共同行为
joint adventure
联营体,合资企业
joint and several liability
共同的和各自的责任,连带责任
joint bid
联合投标
joint creditor
共同债权人
joint filler
接缝填料
joint financing
联合筹资
joint guarantee
联名保证,联合担保
joint insured cross liability clause
共保交叉责任条款
joint liability
共同义务,连带责任
joint loan
联合贷款
joint mortgage
联合抵押
joint ownership
共同所有权
joint rate
联运费率

joint state and private enterprise
公私合营企业
joint supervision
联合监督
joint sureties
连带保证人
joint tenant
共同租赁人
joint tendering
联合投标
joint venture agreement
合资企业协议
joint venture bank
合资银行
joint venture company
合资公司
joint venture for project
项目联营体
joint venture（JV）
联营体;合资企业
joint-stock company
联合股份公司
journal *n.*
分录簿,日记账,日志;期刊
journal entry
分录
journal voucher
转账凭证,分录凭单
journeyman *n.*
雇工;计日工;熟练工
judge *n.*
法官,审判员 *v.* 审理;判断
judgment *n.*
判决;判断;鉴定
judicial *a.*
司法的;公正的
judicial assistance
司法协助
judicial person
法人
junior *a.*
(地位或等级)较低的,年资较浅的
junior accountant

初级会计师
jurisdiction *n*.
管辖权;司法权
juristic person
法人
jury *n*.
陪审团

justifiable *a*.
正当的;有理由的
justification *n*.
证实,证明;理由
justify *v*.
证明…是正当的;为…辩护

K

keelage *n*.
入港税;停港费
keen *a*.
价格低廉的,有竞争力的
keen price
有竞争力的价格
keep account
记账
keep dry
防潮
keeper *n*.
保管人;经营人
kerb *n*.
路缘石,侧石
key *n*.
关键,重点,要点
key ledger
总分类账
key personnel
关键人员,主要人员
keystone document
核心文件,基本文件,中心文件
kickback *n*.
回扣;酬金,佣金
kite *n*.
空头支票
kite-flier *n*.
开空头支票者
kiting *n*.
开空头支票;挪用
knapping machine
碎石机
know-how *n*.
技术秘密,专门技术,技术诀窍
know-how license
专有技术许可证
knowledge *n*.
理解,知道;知识
known danger
已知危险
known loss
已知损失

L

label *v*. *n*.
标记,标签
labeled price
标明的价格
laboratory *n*.
实验室
labour *n*.
劳务,工人,劳力
labour agreement
劳务协议
labour capacity
劳动生产能力

labour contract	劳务合同
labour cost	人工费用
labour discipline	劳动纪律
labour dispute	劳资纠纷
labour disturbance	劳资纠纷,工潮
labour due	劳动报酬
labour efficiency	劳动效率,工作效率
labour force	劳动力
labour hour rate	工时率
labour income	劳务收入
labour law	劳工法,劳动法
labour monitoring	劳工监督
labour norms	劳动定额
labour permit	劳工许可证
labour planning	劳务计划
labour productivity	劳动生产率
labour protection	劳动保护
labour rate	劳务费率
labour relations	劳资关系
labour resources	人力资源
labour trouble	劳资纠纷
labour turnover rate	人工周转率
labour union	工会
labour unrest	劳资争议
labour wage	劳工工资
labour-intensive *a.*	劳动密集型的
laches *n.*	疏忽;迟误
lack *n. v.*	缺少,缺乏
lack of evidence	缺乏证据
lack of materials	材料短缺
ladder *n.*	梯子
laden in bulk	散装的
lading *n.*	船货;装载
lading permit	装船许可证
lading port	装货港
lag *v.*	滞后,落后 *n.* 延迟
land *n.*	土地
land acquisition	获得用地
land certificate	土地证,地契
land for temporary works	临时工程用地
land improvement	土地改良
land patent	(公共)土地转让证
land subsidence	地面沉陷

land tax	大型企业
土地税	**last** *a.*
land trust certificate	最后的,最终的,上一个的 *v.* 持续
地产信托证	**last invoice price method**
land warranty	最后进价法
土地转让证书	**latest date**
landed cost	最晚日期,截止日期
到岸成本	**last-in first-out（LIFO）**
landed price	后进先出法
抵岸价,卸货价格	**late acceptance**
landed quality	延迟接受
到岸品质	**late bid**
landed weight	迟到的投标书
卸货重量	**late delivery**
landing *n.*	延迟交货
上岸,登陆	**late payment**
landing account	迟到的付款
卸货记录,栈单	**late shipment**
landing charges	延迟装运
卸货费	**late start date**
landing order	最晚开工日期
卸货通知单	**latent defect**
landing place	潜在的缺陷
卸货地点	**lateral reinforcement**
landing stage	横向钢筋
浮码头,趸船	**latitude** *n.*
landscaping *n.*	纬度
绿化	**law** *n.*
landslide *n.*	法律;规律,定律
滑坡塌方	**law circle**
language of agreement	法律界
协议书语言	**law court**
language of arbitration	法院
仲裁语言	**law of company**
language of contract	公司法
合同语言	**law of contract**
lapse *n. v.*	合同法
权力失效;作废;期满	**law of enterprises**
lapse of attention	企业法
一时疏忽	**law of insurance**
lapse of time	保险法
时效终止	**law of international trade**
large-scale enterprise	国际贸易法

law of merchant
商(业习惯)法
law of nations
国际法,万国公法
law office
律师事务所
lawful *a*.
依法的;法定的,合法的
lawful money
法定货币
lawsuit *n*.
诉讼 *v*. 提起诉讼
lawyer *n*.
律师
lay *v*.
放置;铺筑,敷设
lay days
装卸期限
lay off
临时解雇
lay time
装卸时间
laydown machine
(沥青混凝土)铺设机
layout *n*.
布局,设计;草图,平面布置图
layout chart
布置图;线路图;施工流程图
leadership *n*.
领导能力,领导艺术
leading *a*.
重要的,最先的
leading company
主要公司,牵头公司
leading hand
领班
leading partner
牵头方
leading underwriter
首席承保人
leads and lags
提前与延迟(偿付债务)
lease *n*.

租赁;租约;租借期限 *v*. 出租
lease agreement
租约
lease financing
租赁融资
lease purchase
租赁购买
leaseback *n*.
回租,售后回租
leased equipment
租用的设备
leasehold *n*.
租赁权;租赁期;租借物
leaseholder *n*.
租借人,承租人
leasing *n*.
租赁
leasing company
租赁公司
leasing guarantee
租赁保函
leave *n*.
休假;许可;离去
leave pay
假期薪金
leave some leeway
留有余地
leave with pay
带薪休假
leave without pay
无薪休假
ledger *n*.
分类账,分户账;总账
ledger form
分类账表格
ledger journal
分类日记账
leeway *n*.
余地
legal *a*.
法律的,法定的;合法的;具有法律地位的 *n*. 法定权利
legal act

法律行为
legal action
诉讼
legal adviser
法律顾问
legal agent
法定代理人
legal arbitration
法律仲裁
legal assets
法定资产
legal authorization
合法授权
legal capacity
法定身份,权利能力
legal capital (value)
法定资本
legal charges
律师服务费
legal compensation
法定赔偿
legal construction
法律释意
legal consultation
法律咨询
legal costs
诉讼费用
legal document
法律文件
legal entity
法定单位,法人实体
legal fact
法律事实
legal holiday
法定假日
legal insurance
强制性保险,法定保险
legal liability
法律责任
legal liquidation
法定清算
legal mortgage
合法抵押
legal person
法人
legal personality
法人资格
legal proceedings
法律诉讼程序
legal provisions
法律规定
legal representative
法定代理人
legal right
法定权利
legal rules
法律规定
legal sanction
法律制裁
legal system
法系
legal tender
法定货币
legal title
法定所有权;法定资格
legal weight
法定重量
legality *n*.
合法;[复](法律上的)义务
legally-binding agreement
有法律效力的协议
legend *n*.
摘要说明;图例
legislation *n*.
立法;法规
legislature *n*.
立法机构,立法机关
legitimate claim
合法的请求;合理索赔
legitimate heir
合法继承人
legitimate income
合法收入
legitimate right
合法权利
lend *v*.

贷款给,借出
lender *n.*
出借人,贷款方
lending *n.*
贷款,放款
lending rate
贷款利率
lending term
贷款期限
lending terms
贷款条件
length *n.*
长度
lessee *n.*
租借人,承租人
lessor *n.*
出租人
let *v.*
出租;让与;交付(承包)
letter of acceptance
中标函,中标通知书
letter of acknowledgement
回函;确认函
letter of administration
遗产管理委任书
letter of advise
通知书
letter of application
申请书
letter of assignment
(财产权利的)转让书
letter of attorney
委任书,授权书
letter of authority from manufacturer
制造厂家的授权书
letter of award
授标函
letter of confirmation
确认书
letter of credit (L/C)
信用证
letter of general average guarantee
共同海损保函
letter of guarantee for bid
投标保函
letter of guarantee for loan
借款保函
letter of guarantee for maintenance
质量维修保函
letter of guarantee (L/G)
保函,保证书
letter of hypothecation
抵押证书
letter of indemnity
赔偿保证书
letter of intent
意向书
letter of invitation(LOI)
邀请函
letter of lien
留置权书
letter of notice
通知书
letter of patent
专利证书
letter of recommendation
推荐信
letter of trust
信托书,留置权书
letters *n.*
证书;许可证
letters of the law
法律的字面意思
level *n.*
水准仪;水位,水平面;标高 *v.* 使相等;使无差别
level premium
平均保险费
level tendering
水准投标;勾结投标
level-control point
高程控制点
leveled price
拉平的价格
leveling machine

平土机,平路机
leverage *n.*
举债经营;杠杆作用
leverage ratio
杠杆比率;举债经营比率
levy *v.*
征税;扣押 *n.* 征收税款;扣押财产
levy causae law
[拉]准据法
levy duties on
对…征税
levy on property
扣押财产
lex cause law
[拉]准据法
lex non scripta
[拉]不成文法
lex scripta
[拉]成文法
liabilities account
负债账户
liability *n.*
责任,义务;[复]债务,负债,债款
liability clause
责任条款
liability for acceptance
承兑责任
liability for damage
损害责任
liability for delay
误期责任
liability for fault
过失责任
liability for satisfaction
清偿责任
liability insurance
责任保险
liability of the client
委托人的责任,业主的责任
liability of the consultant
咨询专家的责任
liability reserves
负债准备金

liability risk
责任风险
liable *a.*
有(法律)责任的;应受罚的;有义务的
liaise *v.*
建立联络关系,与…联络
liaison office
联络办事处
liaison officer
联络官
liberty *n.*
自由;[复]特权,特许
LIBOR (London Inter-Bank offered Rate)
伦敦银行同业拆放利率
licence agreement
许可证协议
licence duty
执照税;牌照税
licence fee
牌照费
licence, license *n.*
许可证;执照
licence plate
(汽车等的)牌照
licence tax
牌照税
licencee, licensee *n.*
许可证接受人;领有执照者
licensed architect
注册建筑师
licensed contractor
注册承包商
licenser, licensor *n.*
许可证颁发人,出证方
licensing *n.*
许可证交易
licensing law
许可证法
lien *n.*
留置权,扣押权,抵押权
life expectancy

使用年限
life of product
产品寿命
life-cycle cost
使用周期成本
lift (elevator) *n.*
电梯;升降机
lift station
泵站,扬水站
lighting of the site
工地照明
lightning rod
避雷针
lime mortar
石灰砂浆
limestone *n.*
石灰岩
limit *n.*
限额;极限;[复]范围 *v.* 限制
limit of compensation
赔偿的限额
limitation *n.*
限度;(诉讼)时效
limitation of authority
权限
limitation of liability
责任限度,责任范围
limitation period
时效期限
limited *a.*
有限的;有限责任的
limited amount guarantee
限额保函
limited company
有限公司
limited competitive selected bidding
有限竞争性选择招标
limited duration guarantee
定期保函
limited liability company
[英]股份有限公司;有限责任公司
limited partnership
有限合伙(公司)

limited recourse
有限的追索
limits of authority
权限
limits of indemnity
赔偿限额
line *n.*
直线;生产线;行业;航线;管线
line manager
前线经理,生产经理
line of production
生产流程
line production method
流水生产法
linear load
线性荷载
linear metre
延米
liner *n.*
班机;班轮;(产品箱内的)衬垫物
liner transport
班轮运输
lines of credit
信贷额度
liquid *a.*
易变为现金的;流动的,液体的
liquid assets
流动资产
liquid fund
流动资金
liquid investment
短期投资
liquid liability
流动负债
liquid ratio
流动比率
liquidate *v.*
清理(破产企业);清偿(债务)
liquidated damages
协定的损害赔偿费;预定违约金
liquidated damages for delay
误期损害赔偿费
liquidation *n.*

清算,清理;变现;偿债
liquidation of debt
清还债务
liquidation value
清算价值
liquidator *n.*
资产清算人;破产清算人
liquidity *n.*
清偿能力
liquidity ratio
偿债能力比率
list *n.*
表格;目录,一览表 *v.* 刊明,刊出
list price
价目表价格,牌价
listed *a.*
上市的;表列的,列出的
listed company
上市公司
listed securities
上市证券
literal contract
成文合同,书面合同
literal interpretation
字面解释
litigant *n.*
诉讼当事人 *a.* 诉讼的
litigate *v.*
诉讼,诉诸法律
litigation *n.*
诉讼,起诉
litigation procedure
诉讼程序
Lloyd's（Llds）
[英]劳埃德保险公司,劳合社
Lloyd's policy
劳合社保险单
load *n.*
载荷;装载;装填
loading *n.*
装货
loading capacity
载重量
loading on board
装船
loading port
装货港
loading test
加载试验
loamy soil
壤土
loan *n. v.*
贷款,借出,贷与
loan agreement
贷款协议
loan ceiling
贷款限额
loan committee
贷款委员会
loan consortium
贷款财团
loan document
贷款文件
loan interest rate
贷款利率
loan note
借款单证
loan on actual estate
不动产抵押贷款
loan principal repayment
贷款本金偿还额
loan repayment
偿还借贷
loan repayment period
贷款偿还期
local *a.*
地方性的;当地的,本地的
local agent
当地代理人
local authority
地方当局
local competitive bidding（LCB）
国内竞争性招标
local contractor

当地承包商
local cost financing
国内费用筹措
local court
地方法院
local currency
当地货币
local expenditures
当地开支
local government
当地政府
local interest rate
当地利率
local labour
当地工人
local material
当地材料
local personnel
当地人员
local price
当地价格
local shopping
当地购买
local statute
当地法规
local supplier
当地供应商
local tax
地方税
local worker
当地工人
locality *n.*
地区,所在地;位置,方向
locate *v.*
找出,探出;位于
location *n.*
位置
lodge *v.*
寄宿;寄存;提起(诉讼,索赔等)
lodging quarters
住房
logistics *n.*
后勤

long length charges
超长附加费
long list
长名单
long price
高价
long term
长期
longitude *n.*
经度
longitudinal beam
纵梁
longitudinal joint
纵向接缝
longitudinal reinforcement
纵向钢筋
long-lived assets
长期资产
long-run agreement
长期协议
long-term agreement
长期保险协议
long-term claim
长期债权
long-term debt
长期债务
long-term forecast
长期预测
long-term investment
长期投资
long-term lease
长期租赁
long-term liabilities
长期负债
long-term loan
长期贷款
long-term planning
长期规划
long-term policy
长期保单
long-term rental
长期租用
loophole *n.*

（条文等中的）漏洞，空子
losing a suit
败诉
losing effect
失效
losing party
败诉方
loss *n.*
损失；损耗
loss abatement
损失的减少
loss and expenses
损失与花费
loss and gain
损益
loss clause
损失条款
loss control
损失控制
loss frequency
损失频率
loss of advanced profits insurance
预期利润损失保险
loss of efficiency
效率降低
loss of net income
净收入损失
loss of profit
利润损失
loss of profit insurance
利润损失保险
loss prevention
损失预防
loss ratio
损失率，赔付率

lost *a.*
损失的；失去的
lost or not lost clause
无论灭失与否条款
lowest bid (tender)
最低报价，最低标
lowest bidder (tenderer)
最低价投标人
lowest evaluated bid
最低评标价投标
lubricant *n.*
润滑油
lumber *n.*
木材
lump sum
包干价，总价
lump sum contract
总价合同
lump sum cost
一次性支出
lump sum items
包干项
lump sum on firm bill of quantities
固定工程量总价合同
lump sum payment
总价付款
lump sum price
总包价格
lump sum remuneration
包干酬金
lump sum with fluctuations
可调价的包干
lump work
包工，包干工作

M

machine *n.*
机器，机械；机构
machine capability
设备能力
machine hour
台时

machine idle time
设备闲置(或窝工)时间
machine life
机械寿命
machinery *n.*
(总称)机器,机械;政府等的机构
machinery breakdown insurance
机器损坏保险
machinery breakdown policy
机械故障保险单
machinery consequential loss（interruption）insurance
机械间接损失保险
machining *n.*
机械加工,切削加工
macro forecast
总体预测,宏观预测
macrostructure *n.*
宏观结构,基础设施
mail transfer advice
信汇通知书
mail transfer（M/T）
信汇
main *a.*
主要的,最重要的;总的
main budget
总预算,主要预算
main circuit
主干线路
main contract
主合同,总包合同
main contract clauses
主合同条款
main contractor
总承包商
main drain
排水干沟;排水总管
main office
总公司;总管理处;总行
main works
主包工程
maintain *v.*
保持;维修

maintenance *n.*
维修,维护;保持
maintenance bond
维修担保
maintenance certificate
维修证书
maintenance cost
维修费
maintenance guarantee
维修保函
maintenance manual
维修手册
maintenance of plant
设备的维护,设备的保养
maintenance of value
保持价值
maintenance of works
工程维修
maintenance period
维修期
major alternative
主要备选方案
major items of construction plant
主要施工设备
majority rule
多数裁定原则
majority stockholder
控股人,控股股东
majority-owned subsidiary
拥有过半数股权的附属公司
make a loss
亏损
make advance
垫付,预支
make an offer
报价,发盘
make good
赔偿;修复
make good on general average
共同海损补偿
make money
赚钱
make policy

决策
make profit
获利
make remittance
汇款
malfeasance *n.*
渎职(罪),违法乱纪
malicious damage
恶意破坏
malicious prosecution
诬告
man day
工日
man hour
工时
management *n.*
经营,管理,安排;管理部门
management accounting
管理会计
management agreement
管理协定
management by exception
例外管理
management by objective
目标管理
management consultant
管理顾问
management contract
管理合同
management contracting
管理承包
management contractor
管理承包商
management control system
管理控制系统
management fee
管理费
management function
管理职能
management information system (MIS)
管理信息系统
management of human resources
人力资源管理
management operating system (MOS)
生产管理制度
management overheads
上级管理费
management techniques
管理技巧
manager *n.*
经理;管理人员
managerial accounting
管理会计
managing director (MD)
执行董事,总经理
mandate *n.*
财产委托(书);指令,(书面)命令
mandator *n.*
委托者;委任者;命令者
mandatory *n.*
受托人 *a.* 命令的,强制的;委托的
manifest *n.*
仓单,船货清单
manipulate *v.*
操纵
man-month
人/月
man-month contract
人/月合同
man-month (day, hour) rate
人/月(日,时)费率
manner of execution
实施方法
manners and customs
风俗习惯
manpower curves
人力曲线
manual *n.*
手册,指南 *a.* 手工的,体力的
manual labour
体力劳动者
manual rates
标准保险费率
manufacture *v. n.*

制造,加工
manufacturer *n.*
制造商,厂家
manufacturing consignment
委托加工
manufacturing with orderer's sample
来样加工
manufacturer's agent
厂商代理人
manufacturer's certificate
厂商证明书
manufacturer's invoice
厂商发票
manufacturing cost
制造成本
manufacturing drawing
制造图
manufacturing expenses
制造费用
manufacturing statement
生产报表
manuscript *n.*
手稿,原稿
marble *n.*
大理石
margin *n.*
毛利,盈余;保证金;息差;边际
margin call（notice）
追加保证金的通知
margin money
保证金
margin of preference
优惠差额
margin rate
保证金比率
marginal *a.*
边际的;最低限度的;微小的,少量的
marginal cost
边际成本
marginal deposit
保证金存款
marginal income
边际收益

marginal note
旁注,附注
marginal profit
边际利润
marginal revenue
边际收入
marine *a.*
海上的,航海的;船用的
marine bill of lading
海运提单
marine insurance
海运保险,水险
marine insurance policy
海运保险单
marine law
海事法,海商法
marine premium
海运保险费
marine structure
海上建筑物
maritime *a.*
海运的,海事的;近海的;船用的;海员的
maritime arbitration commission
海事仲裁委员会
maritime claim
海事索赔
maritime court
海事法庭
maritime customs
海关
maritime law
海事法,海商法
maritime loss
海损
maritime perils
海上风险,海险
maritime transportation insurance
海洋运输保险
mark *n.*
标记 *v.* 作记号;记录;标志
mark-down *n.*
减价

mark-up *n.*
成本加成,标高金
market *n.*
市场;市价 v. 销售,买卖
market allocation
市场划分,市场分配
market analysis
市场分析
market demand
市场需求
market fluctuation
市场波动
market intelligence
市场信息
market price
市场价格
market rate
市场利率
market share
市场份额
market value
市场价值
marketable securities
可转让证券
marketing *n.*
(市场)营销(学)
marketing expenses
销售费用
marketing mix
销售组合
marketing outlet
销路
marshy area
沼泽地区
mason *n.*
泥瓦工
masonry *n.*
圬工,砌筑体
masonry wall
砌筑墙体
master budget
总预算
master control account
总控制账户
master lease
主租约
master list
总清单
master programme
总进度计划
master schedule
总进度计划
matching *n.*
拟合;匹配
material *n.*
材料;[复]用具,器材 *a.* 决定性的;
物质的;重大的
material alteration
重大修改
material assets
有形资产
material breach of contract
严重违约
material certification
材料合格证
material consumption norm
材料消耗定额
material cost
材料成本,材料费
material damage
物质损失
material delivered note
材料出库单
material deviation
重大偏离
material evidence
物证,实质性证据
material handling
材料转运
material omission
严重遗漏
material receipt
材料收据
material receiving report
材料签收报告
material release

材料发放
material requisition note
领料单
material resources
物力资源
material specification
材料明细表
material supply
材料供应
material terms
实质性条款
materiality *n.*
重要性
materialman *n.*
供应商
materials planning
材料计划
materials purchasing
材料购买
materials return report
退料单
mate's receipt
收货单；大副收据
matrix style organization
矩阵式机构
matters in dispute
争端事宜
maturity *n.*
成熟老练；(票据等)到期(日)，偿还日
maturity of a draft
汇票支付日期
maturity value
到期值，终值
maximum *a.*
最高的；最大的；最多的 *n.* 最大；最高；最多
maximum amount
最大量，最大金额
maximum guaranteed price
最高保证价格
maximum liability
最大限度的责任；最大赔偿额

maximum limit
最高限额
maximum possible loss
最大可能损失
mean *n.*
平均数，[复]方式，手段；财产，收入
mean down time
平均停工时间，平均停机时间
means of execution
实施方法
means of payment
支付手段
means of verification
验证方法
measure *n.*
措施；测量，量度 *v.* 测量
measure of indemnity
赔偿限度
measurement *n.*
计量，衡量，测量
measurement and cost reimbursement contract
测量与成本补偿合同
measurement contract
计量合同
measurement for payment
为支付进行的计量
measuring instrument
量测仪器；量具
measuring peg
测桩
mechanical *a.*
机械的
mechanical equipment installation works
机械设备安装工程
mediate *v.*
调停，调解
mediation *n.*
调停，调解，中间调解
mediator *n.*
调解人
medical certificate

体检证明,医疗证明
medical examination
体格检查
medical expense insurance
医疗费用保险
medical fee
医疗费
medical treatment
医疗
medium *n.*
中间人,调解人;媒介;手段,工具 *a.* 中等的,中间的
medium long-term
中长期
medium term
中期
meeting notes
会议记录
meeting of minds
意见一致
member of consortium
联合体成员,财团成员
membership *n.*
成员资格,会员资格
membership fee (due)
会员费
membrane *n.*
薄膜;防渗护面
memorandum *n.*
备忘录;摘要;非正式记录
memorandum of association
[英]公司章程
memorandum of deposit
存款单;抵押证书
memorandum of payment
缴款通知
memorandum of understanding
谅解备忘录
merchandise *n.*
商品,货物
merchandise credit slip
退货凭单

merchandise declaration
货物申报单
merchandise inventory
商品盘存
merchandise mark
商标
merchant *n.*
商人;零售商 *a.* 商业的;商人的
merchant bank
商业银行
merchant contract
商业合同
merchant wholesaler
批发商
merge *v.*
(使)合并,(使)结合
merger *n.*
合并
merit *n.*
优点;价值;[复]事实真相;法律依据
merit-rating
考级(制)
message *n.*
消息;信息
meteorological conditions
气象条件
method of application
申请方法
method of construction
施工方法
method of fixed percentage on cost
成本固定百分比(折旧)法
method of payment
支付方式
method of programming
计划编制方法
method of redress
补救办法
method of sampling
抽样方法
method of weighting

加权法
metric *a.*
公制的
metric conversion
公制换算
metric measure
公制计量
metric system
公制
metric ton（MT）
公吨
middleman *n.*
中间人,经纪人
mid-term evaluation
中期评估
milestone *n.*
里程碑,重大事件
milestone dates
里程碑日期
milestone schedule
里程碑进度表
minifair *n.*
小型交易会,小交会
minimize *v.*
使减到最少,使缩到最小
minimum *a.*
最低的;最小的;最少的 *n.* 最低;最少;最小
minimum amount
最小金额;最小量;最低限度
minimum amount of payment
最低支付限额
minimum fine
最低罚款
minimum premium
最低保险费
minimum price
最低价格
minister *n.*
部长;公使
ministry *n.*
(政府的)部
minor change in the work
较小的工程变更
minute *n.*
分;备忘录,笔记;[复]会议记录;审判记录 *a.* 微小的
minute book
会议记录本
minutes of meeting
会议记录;会谈纪要
minutes of proceedings
议事记录
miscellaneous *a.*
杂项的,各种的
miscellaneous expenses
杂项开支
miscellaneous local taxes
地方杂税
miscellaneous material
零星用料
misconduct *n.*
渎职;处理不当 *v.* 对…处理不当
misconduct in office
玩忽职守
misconduct offense
渎职罪
misrepresentation *n.*
讹传;虚报;歪曲
missing *a.*
失踪的,遗失的
mission *n.*
代表团;任务,使命
mission allowance
出差津贴
misstatement *n.*
虚报;错报
mistake *v.*
错误;失策;误解
mistake of decision-making
决策错误
misunderstanding *n.*
误解
mitigate *v.*
减轻(惩罚),使缓和
mitigation *n.*

减轻
mitigation of damages
损害赔偿的减轻
mixed cost
混合成本
mixed duties
混合税
mixed tariff
混合税率
mixer *n.*
拌合机,搅拌机
mixer plant
拌和楼
mixer truck
搅拌运料车
mixing of concrete
混凝土拌和
mixture ratio
拌合比,混合比
mobilization *n.*
动员
mobilization advance
动员预付款
mobilization charges
动员费
mobilization fee
准备费,启动费
mode *n.*
方式,模式
mode of payment
支付方式
model agreement
示范协议
model house
样板房
model test
模型试验
moderate price
中等价格,适度价格
modernization *n.*
现代化
modest price increase
适当涨价

modest price reduction
适当降价
modification *n.*
修改,变更
modification of bid
投标文件的修改
modification of planning
计划的修改
modification of tender
投标文件的修改
modify *v.*
修改,变更
moisture *n.*
湿度;潮湿
moisture capacity (content)
湿度,含水量
moisture density
单位容积土壤含水量
moling machine
(隧洞)全断面掘进机
monetary *a.*
货币的,金融的,财政的
monetary assets
货币性资产
monetary authorities
财政当局
monetary exchange rate
货币汇率
monetary gain or loss
货币损益
monetary item
货币性项目
monetary liabilities
货币债务
monetary policy
货币政策
monetary restraint
货币限制
monetary stability
币值稳定
monetary unit
货币单位
monetary value

币值
monetary-nonmonetary method
货币性与非货币性方法
money *n.*
货币,金钱;款项
money account
现金账(户)
money assets or liabilities
货币性资产或负债
money at call
短期放款,短期(同行)拆借
money changing
货币兑换
money equivalent
等值货币
money interest rate
货币利率
money market
货币市场
money market certificate (MMC)
[美]货币市场存单
money market deposit account
[美]货币市场存款账户
money market mutual funds
[美]货币市场互助基金
money measurement
货币计量,货币计价
money of account
记账货币
money order (M.O.)
汇款单,汇票
money returned
还债
money transaction
现金交易
money turnover
货币周转
moneyed corporation
金融公司
money's worth
等值货币价值
monitor *n. v.*
监督,监视,监控

monitor work
监控工作
monkey engine
锤式打桩机
monolithic concrete
整体浇灌混凝土
monopoly *n.*
垄断;专卖
monopoly price
垄断价格;专卖价格
monopoly right
专卖权,专利权
Monte Carla Simulation
蒙特卡罗模拟
monthly *a.*
每月的,按月计算的 *ad.* 每月
monthly allowance
月津贴
monthly detailed schedule
每月详细进度表
monthly interim payment certificate
每月期中付款证书
monthly pay
月薪
monthly payment
每月付款,按月支付
monthly report
月报告
monthly returns
月报表
monthly settlement report
月结算报告
monthly statement
月报表,月结算单
monthly summary
月汇总表
monthly wages
月工资,月薪
moral risk
道德风险
moral standard
道德准则
moratorium *n.*

延期偿付权;延缓偿付期
more or less clause (M/L clause)
短溢装条款
mortgage n.
抵押权;抵押单;抵押款 v. 抵押;(楼宇)按揭
mortgage bond
抵押债券
mortgage clause
抵押条款
mortgage loan
(房地产)抵押贷款
mortgagee n.
抵押贷款人,受押人,承押人,承按人
mortgagor n.
按揭人,抵押人,出押人,抵押借款人
most-favoured-nation clause (MFN cl.)
最惠国条款
most-favoured-nation tariff rates
最惠国关税率
most-favoured-nation treatment
最惠国待遇
mother company
母公司
motivation n.
激励
motive n.
动机
motor car insurance
汽车保险
motor car liability insurance
机动车责任险
motor flusher
洒水车
motor vehicle tax
机动车辆税
mounting n.
安装;装置
mounting drawing
安装图,装配图

mounting of equipment
设备安装
mounting rack
安装架,工作台
movable property
动产
movables n.
动产
moving expenses
搬迁费
multilateral a.
多边的,多国参加的
multilateral agreement
多边协定
multilateral aid
多边援助
multilateral clearing
多边清算
multilateral contract
多边合同
multilateral cooperation
多边合作
multilateral settlement
多边结算
multilateral tariff treaty
多边税收协定
multilateral trade
多边贸易
multinational a.
跨国的,多国的 n. 跨国公司
multinational company (MNC)
多国公司,跨国公司
multinational enterprises (MNE)
多国企业
multi-party arbitration
多方仲裁
multiple a.
复合的;多项的;多倍的 n. 倍数
multiple line insurance
复合保险,多险种保险
multiple options funding facility
多选择的融资安排
multiple perils insurance

多种风险保险
multiple tariff system
复式税则;多重关税制
multiple taxation
复税制
multiple-step income statement
分步收益表
municipal engineering
市政工程
municipal works
市政工程
municipality *n.*
市(政府),市政当局
mutual *a.*
相互的,彼此的,共同的

mutual benefit
互惠,互利
mutual consent
协议,双方同意
mutual funds
共同基金,互惠基金
mutual indemnification
相互补偿
mutual insurance company
互助保险公司
mutual understanding
相互理解,互相谅解
mutuality of contract
合同上的相互关系

N

naked *a.*
无证据的;原本的
naked contract
无担保合同
naked promise
无效诺言
naked truth
真相
name of commodity
商品名称,货名
named bill of lading
记名提单
named departure point
指定启运地
named place of destination
指定目的地
named policy
指定船名的保险单
named port of shipment
指定装船港
named principal
署名的委托人
narrow *a.*
狭窄的;有限的 *v.* 使...缩小

narrow margin
薄利
national *a.*
国家的;国民的;民族的
national bond
国家公债
national competitive bidding
国内竞争性招标
national customs
民族习惯
national customs territory
国家海关辖区
national debt
国债
national dividend
国民收入,国民所得
national enterprise
国营企业
national finance
国家财政
national insurance
国家保险
national market
国内市场

national product 国民产值
national revenue 国家岁入,国家税收
national shopping 国内询价采购
national standard 国家标准
national tax 国税
national treatment (缔约国双方)国民待遇
nationalization *n.* 国有化
nationalization of enterprise 企业国有化
nationals *n.* 国民
native *a.* 本地的;本国的 *n.* 本地人;本国人
natural *a.* 自然的;正常的
natural calamity 自然灾害
natural conditions 自然条件
natural person 自然人
natural reserve 自然保护区
natural resources 自然资源,天然资源
natural risk 自然风险
natural wastage 自然损耗
nature of agreement 协议的性质
nature of tort 侵权性质
nature of works 工程性质
necessitate *v.* 使成为必需,使需要
negative *a.* 负的;否定的;消极的
negative assets account 负资产账户,负债账户
negative cash flow 负现金流量
negative covenant 限制性契约
negative factor 消极因素
negative growth 负增长
neglect *v. n.* 忽略,忽视;玩忽
neglect of duty 失职,玩忽职守
negligence *n.* 疏忽,过失;玩忽
negligent act 过失行为
negligent crime 过失罪
negligent misrepresentation 疏忽性的误述
negligent of one's duties 玩忽职守
negligible *a.* 可以忽略的
negotiability *n.* 可流通性;可转让性
negotiable *a.* 可协商的,可谈判的;可转让的;可流通
negotiable certificate of deposit 可转让定期存单,流通存单
negotiable check 可转让支票,流通支票
negotiable credit

可转让信用证
negotiable instrument
可转让票据,流通票据
negotiable paper
可转让票据
negotiate *v.*
议定,协商,谈判;转让
negotiated bidding
谈判招标;议标
negotiated contract
经协商的合同
negotiated price
议价
negotiated settlement
协商解决
negotiating bank
议付银行,押汇银行
negotiating condition
议价条件
negotiating procedure
谈判程序
negotiating tactics and skills
谈判策略和技巧
negotiation *n.*
交涉,谈判,协商;议付
negotiation commission
议付手续费;转让手续费
negotiation contract
协商合同,议标合同
net *a.*
净的,纯的 *n.* 净值;净利;净数;净重 *v.* 净得,净赚
net amount
净额
net assets
净资产,资产净额
net benefit
净效益
net capital gains
资本净收益
net cash flow
净现金流量
net earnings
净收益
net freight
净运费
net income
净收益,净收入
net income after depreciation
折旧后净收益
net income after tax
纳税后净收益
net interest
净息
net investment income
净投资收入
net invoice price
净发票价格
net lease
净租赁
net liabilities
负债净额
net loss
净损失
net loss from operation
净营业损失
net markup percentage
净加价百分率
net national product(NNP)
国民生产净值
net pay
实付工资
net premium
净保险费
net present value(NPV)
净现值
net present value method(NPV method)
净现值法
net price
净价,实价
net profit
纯利,净利润
net rate
纯费率,净费率
net realizable value

可变现净值
net sales
净销售额
net salvage
净残值
net tare
净皮重
net tonnage
净吨位
net weight
净重
net worth
净值
net yield
净收益
network n.
网络；管网；网状系统
network analysis
网络分析
network chart (diagram)
网络图
network program
网络计划
network scheduling technique
网络进度计划法
neutral a.
中立的；中立国的 n. 中立国；中立者
news agency
通讯社
next-in-first-out method
次进先出法
night shift
夜班
nilometer n.
水位计
no damages for delay clause
无拖期赔偿条款
no price fluctuation provisions
无调价规定
no-claim bonus
无赔款奖金
no-claim discount
无赔款折扣

no-claim return
无赔款退费
no-interest-bearing note
不带息票据
nominal a.
名义上的；额定的；票面上的；象征性的
nominal account
虚账户，名义账户
nominal amount
名义金额
nominal capital
名义资本
nominal cost
名义成本
nominal dimension
名义尺寸，标称尺寸
nominal exchange rate
名义汇率
nominal interest rate
名义利率，额定利率
nominal partner
名义合伙人
nominal quantity
名义数量，名义工程量
nominal terms
有名无实的条款
nominal value
名义价值，票面价值
nominate v.
提名，任命，指定，推荐
nominated subcontractor
指定分包商
nominated supplier
指定供应商
nomination n.
提名，任命，指定，推荐
nominee n.
被提名人，被任命人，被指定者
non-acceptance
拒绝承兑，不接受
non-admitted assets
不受保资产

non-assignable
(合同等)不可转让的
non-bearing wall
非承重墙
non-cash charges
非现金支出
non-compensable delay
不予补偿的延误
non-competitive bid
非竞争性报价
noncompliance *n*.
不同意,不遵守,不符合
non-compliance with contractual conditions
不符合合同条件
non-compliance with specifications
不符合技术规范
non-contractual claim
非合同规定的索赔
non-contractual document
非契约性文件
non-controllable cost
不可控成本
non-delivery
未能送达,未交货
non-disclosure
保密,(投保时)隐瞒情况不报
non-discountable bill
非贴现票据
non-discriminatory treatment
无差别待遇,不歧视待遇
non-dollar countries
非美元国家
non-eligible country
不合格来源国
non-excusable delays
不可原谅的拖期
non-execution *n*.
不执行
non-fundamental breach
非根本性违约
non-governmental institution
非政府机构
non-implementation of contract
合同的不履行
non-installment credit
非分期还款信贷
non-monetary assets
非货币性资产
non-monetary liabilities
非货币性负债
non-negotiable *a*.
不可转让的
non-operating expenses
非营业费用
non-operating income
非营业收入
non-operating revenue
非营业收入
non-performance *n*.
未履约,违约
non-proportional reinsurance
非比例再保险
non-prosecution *n*.
不起诉
non-recourse
无追索权
non-recurring incomes and expenses
临时性收支
non-responsive bid
不符合要求的投标
non-separation agreement
不可分割协议书
non-tariff barrier
非关税壁垒
non-trade receipt
非贸易收入
non-transferable credit
不可转让信用证
non-waiver
不弃权
norm *n*.
标准,规范;定额
normal *a*.

正常的,标准的;正态的
normal condition
正常情况,正常条件
normal cost
正常费用
normal hour
标准工时
normal loss
正常损耗
normal section
正断面图
normal services
正常的服务
normal shrinkage
正常的收缩
not to insure clause
不受益条款
notarial *a.*
公证(人)的
notarial act
公证手续
notarial certificate
公证证书
notarial document
公证文件
notarization *n.*
公证
notarize *v.*
公证
notary *n.*
公证人
note *n.*
票据;借据;通知书;便条;记录
note of hand
借据;期票
note on demand
即期票据
note on discount
贴现票据
note payable
应付票据
note receivable
应收票据

notice *n.*
通知,布告;注意
notice by fax
传真通知
notice in writing
书面通知
notice of abandonment
委付通知,委弃通知
notice of claim
索赔通知书
notice of default
违约通知
notice of defect
缺陷通知
notice of dishonour
拒付通知
notice of loss
损失通知
notice of payment
通知偿还
notice of readiness
准备就绪通知
notice of shipment
装船通知
notice of test
检验通知
notice period
通知期限
notice to commence
开工通知
notification *n.*
布告,通知,通知书
notification of approval
批准通知
notify *v.*
通知;宣告
notifying bank
(信用证)通知银行
notional price
假设价格,理论价格
notwithstanding *prep.*
尽管
nude cargo

裸装货
nuisance *n*.
妨害,损害
null *a*.
无效的
null and void
无效,作废
number *n*.

数目,数字,号码
numerical error
编号错误,数字错误
numerous *a*.
大批量的
nut *n*.
螺母

O

obey *v*.
服从
obey the law
遵守法律
object *n*.
物体;标的(物);对象;目的 *v*. 反对;拒绝
object cost
目标成本
object of action
诉讼标的
object of insurance
保险标的
object of taxation
课税对象
objection *n*.
反对;反对的理由;妨碍;缺点
objective *n*.
目的,目标 *a*. 客观的,真实的;目标的
objective cause
客观原因
objective evidence
客观证据
objective fact
客观事实
objective management
目标管理
objective schedule
任务进度表
objective tax

目的税;对物税;专用税
objectivity *n*.
客观性
obligate *v*.
负有责任,负有…的义务
obligation *n*.
责任,义务,职责;契约;债务
obligation outstanding
未清偿债务
obligatory reinsurance
固定分保,自动分保
obligee *n*.
债权人,债主;权利人;受惠人
obliger *n*.
施惠人
obligor *n*.
债务人,负债者;义务人
obscurity *n*.
模糊,不明确
observance *n*.
观察;遵守;惯例
observation *n*.
观察;考察;评论
observation station
观测站
observe *v*.
遵守,奉行(法律,规章等);监视,观察
obstruct *v*.
阻止,妨碍
obstruction *n*.

障碍物;阻碍;妨碍(议事进程)
obtain *v.*
获得;达到
obtainable *a.*
可获得的;可买到的
obvious defect
明显的缺陷
occasion *n.*
机会;偶因 *v.* 引起
occupancy expenses
占用费,使用费
occupancy permit
占用许可证
occupancy rate
占用率,使用率
occupancy right
占用权
occupant *n.*
占有人,居住者
occupation *n.*
占有;职业,工作
occupier *n.*
占有人
occur *v.*
发生,出现
occurrence *n.*
发生,出现;(偶发)事件
ocean and rail (O. & R.)
海陆联运
ocean bill of lading
海运提单
ocean carriage
远洋运输,海运
ocean carrier
海运承运人;海运公司
ocean freight
海运运费
ocean liner
远洋班轮
ocean marine cargo (transportation) insurance
海洋运输货物保险

ocean marine insurance
海运保险
ocean vessel
远洋船舶
ocean waybill
海运提单
odd hand
临时雇工
odd job
临时工作;零活
odd money
零钱
odds *n.*
机会,可能性;差别
off limits
闲人莫入
off season
淡季
off-day *n.*
休息日
off-duty *n.*
下班,休假
offence *n.*
冒犯;犯法(行为)
offence of bribery
贿赂罪
offence of dereliction of duty
渎职罪
offend *v.*
违反;犯法
offer *n. v.*
报价,发盘,要约;提议
offer period
报价有效期
offered price
出售价格,报价
offeree *n.*
接受报价者,受盘人,受约人
offerer, offeror *n.*
报价人,发盘人,要约人
off-highway vehicle
越野车,越野运输车

office *n.*
办公室,办事处;公职
office expenses
办公费
office hours
办公时间,营业时间
office lawyer
顾问律师
office overhead costs
办公室管理费
officer *n.*
公务员,官员;办事员
officer's check
(银行)本票
official contract
正式合同
official gazette
官方公报
official holiday
法定假日
official invoice
正式发票
official language
正式语言
official letter
公函
official misconduct
渎职,失职
official price
官方价格,正式价格
official rate
官方兑换率
official representative
正式代表
officiate *v.*
行使职务;主持会议
offset *n. v.*
冲销,抵消
offset account
抵消账户
offshore bank
境外银行
offshore escrow account
境外第三方账户
offshore office
海外办事处
off-test *a.*
未经检验的
off-the-shelf *a.*
成品的;现货供应的
oil jack
油压千斤顶
oligopoly *n.*
少数制造商对市场的控制
oligopoly price
卖主垄断价格
oligopsony price
买主垄断价格
omission *n.*
忽略,遗漏,删去;失职
omit *v.*
省略,遗漏,删去;疏忽
omitted work
删除的工作
on a schedule
按预定计划
on a turnkey basis
采取交钥匙的形式
on account
记账,赊账;暂付
on behalf of
代表(某人)
on board
已装船,在船(或飞机等)上
on cash
现金交易
on credit
信用赊账
on deck B/L
舱面交货提单
on deck risk
舱面货物险
on demand(o/d)
见票即付
on duty
上班,值班,当班

on hand
库存；现存
on lending *n.*
转贷
on mortgage
(以房地产)作抵押
on rail
铁路交货
on the balance
两讫，收支平衡
on the ground
当场
on the ground of
以...为理由，以...为借口
oncost *n.*
间接成本，外加成本；现场杂费
onerous *a.*
繁杂的，麻烦的；[律]负有法律义务的
one-stop shopping
一次性采购
on-going consulting
日常咨询
on-going project
正在实施的项目
on-line *a.*
联机的
on-line maintenance
不停产检修
on-site inspection
现场检验，现场检查
on-site training
现场培训
on-the-job training
岗上培训
on-the-spot audit
现场审计
open account
赊账，未结清账户
open bid (tender)
公开招标，公开投标
open B/L
不记名提单

open channel
明渠
open cheque
普通支票，未划线支票
open contract
开口合同，非正式草拟合同
open cover
预约保险(合同)
open credit
开口信用证，无担保贷款
open door policy
开放政策
open endorsement
空白背书
open policy
开口保单，预约保单
open-end contract
开口合同，未定数量的契约
open-end orders
开口定货单
open-ended *a.*
非限定的，不固定的
opening an account
开户
opening balance
期初余额
opening bank
开证银行
opening entry
开始记录
opening price
开盘价
operating *a.*
营业上的；工作的；实施的；操作的
operating account
营业账户
operating capital
营业资本
operating condition
使用条件，运营条件
operating cost
运营成本，操作费用
operating cycle

营业循环,经营周(转)期
operating expenses
经营费用,业务开支
operating lease
营业租赁
operating loss
营业损失
operating performance
经营业绩
operating profit
营业利润
operating rate
开工率
operating revenue
营业收入
operating risk
经营风险
operating statement
经营报表
operating surplus
经营利润盈余
operation n.
操作,运转;作用;运用,运营
operation and maintenance contract
运营维修合同
operation and maintenance cost
操作和维修费用
operation and maintenance manuals
操作和维修手册
operation area
作业区
operation cost
运营成本
operation profit
营业利润
operation revenue
营业收入
operation statement
损益报表,经营报表
operational bill of quantities
作业工程量表
operational maintenance
日常维修
operational mission
业务代表团
operational project
执行中的项目
operational specification
操作规范
operator n.
操作工;经纪人
operator in charge
领班人员
opinion n.
意见(书);鉴定
opponent n.
对手
opportunity cost
机会成本
opportunity study
(投资)机会研究
optimal replacement cycle
(设备等)最优更新周期
optimization n.
最优化
optimum lot size
最优批量
option n.
选择(权),优先权;期权
option buyer
期权的买方
option money
期权交易定金
option purchase price
期权购买价
option seller
期权卖方
optional clause
选择条款
optional destination additional
选择目的港附加费
optional items
暂定项目,选择项目
optional port of discharge
任选目的港,任选卸货港
options analysis

备选方案分析
oral agreement
口头协议
oral contract
口头合同
oral evidence
口头证据
oral form
口头形式
oral instruction
口头指示,口头变更指令
oral notice
口头通知
order *n.*
命令;次序;订货单;汇票 *v.* 命令;订购
order bill of lading
指示提单,指定人提单
order check
记名支票,指定人支票
order file
订货卷宗,订货档案
order for collection
托收单
order for future delivery
期货定单
order for minor change in the work
较小的工程变更命令
order form
订货单格式
order of commencement of work
开工令
order of precedence
优先次序
order quantity
订货量
order sheet
订货单
order to suspend
暂时停工命令
orderer *n.*
订货人
ordering contract
订货合同
ordering cost
订货费用
ordinance *n.*
法令;条例
ordinary accident insurance
普通事故保险
ordinary annuity
普通年金
ordinary wear and tear
自然损耗
organization cost
开办费
organization of construction
建设单位;施工组织
origin *n.*
原产地;起源;起因
origin marking
原产地标志
original *n.*
原件,正本;原型 *a.* 原始的,最初的
original bill
汇票正本;原案
original capital
原始资本
original contract
原合同
original cost
原始成本
original data
原始资料
original deed
(契约等)原件,原本
original document
原始文件;原始单据
original insurance
原保险
original invoice
原始发票
original mark-up
原始成本加成
original of the contract
合约正本

original sample
原样品
original value
原始价值
original voucher
原始凭单
ostensible agent
名义代理人
ostensible partner
名义合伙人
outgo n.
支出;开支项目;消耗 v. 超过,优于
outlay n.
费用;开支
outline n.
大纲;略图;草案
outline and assembly drawings
外形图与装配图
outline programme
工程计划概要
outline proposal
建议书大纲
out-of-date check
过期支票,失效支票
out-of-date equipment
过时的设备
out-of-pocket cost
实际开支成本,付现成本
out-of-pocket expenses
现金支付费用,付现费用
output n.
产(出)量;产品;输出
output capacity
生产能力
output per man-hour
人(均小)时产量
output quota
生产定额
outside the law
超出法律范围
outstanding a.
未完成的;未付款的;悬而未决的;优秀的 n. [复]未偿清货款;未清算

账目
outstanding account
未清账款
outstanding amount
欠款
outstanding balance
未清余额
outstanding check
未兑现支票
outstanding claim
索赔悬案,未决赔款
outstanding debt
未清债务
outstanding dues
未付的应付款
outstanding losses
未偿损失,未付赔款
outstanding obligation
未清偿的债务,未履行的义务
outstanding order
未交定货
outstanding principal
未偿本金
outstanding work
未完成的工作,扫尾工作
outward port charges
出港手续费
over insurance
超额保险
over interest
过期利息
overall budget
总预算
overall construction plan
施工总平面图
overall floorage
总建筑面积
overall price index
综合物价指数
overbreak n. v.
(隧洞等)超挖
overcharge n. v.
收费过高;装载过多

overdraft *v. n.*
透支(额)
overdraft guarantee
透支保函
overdraw *v.*
透支(账户)
overdue *a.*
过期(未付)的;延误的
overdue delivery
逾期未交货物
overdue payment
过期未付款
overdue risk
延误船期保险
overexcavation *n.*
超挖
overfill *v.*
超填
overflow *n.*
溢流;溢洪道
overhanging beam
悬臂梁
overhaul *v. n.*
大检修,全面检修
overhead *n.*
管理费,行政费,企业一般管理费,间接费
overhead allocation
管理费分配,间接费分配
overhead charges (cost)
间接费用,管理费用,制造费用
overhead crane
桥式吊车,桥式起重机
overhead expenses
经常费用,日常开支
overhours *n.*
加班;加班时间;加班费
overland *a.*
陆上的,陆路的
overland bill of landing
水陆联运提单
overland common point
陆运可到达的地点,陆路共通地点

overlap *v.*
交错,重叠
overlapping insurance
重复保险
overlength charges
超长费
overload *n.*
超载
override *n.*
代理佣金;特许使用费,矿区租用费 *v.* 使无效;优先于
overriding credit
主信用证
overrun *n. v.*
超过(期限,范围,额度)
overseas *a.*
海外的,外国的
overseas allowance
海外津贴
overseas branch
国外分行;国外分部
overseas investment
海外投资
overseas market
海外市场
overseas project
国外项目
overseas training
国外培训
overseas works
国外工程
oversee *v.*
监视,监督
overseer *n.*
监视人,监工,工头
oversize *n.*
超大体积 *a.* 超大的
overstate *v.*
夸大,高估
overstep *v.*
逾越;违犯
overtime *n.*
加班;加班时间;加班费 *a.* 加班的

overtime allowance
加班津贴
overtime pay
加班费
overtime premium(bonus)
加班奖金
overtime wages
加班工资
overtime work
加班工作
overtime workhour
加班工时
overview *n*.
综述
overview schedule
宏观进度计划
overweight *n*.
超重 *a*. 超重的
owe *v*.
欠,欠债
owing *a*.
未付的,应付的
own damage
自负损害
own fund
自有资金
own risk
自负责任,自负风险

owner *n*.
业主,所有人
owner of title
产权所有人
owner's consultant
业主的咨询顾问
owner's duty
业主的义务
owner's equity
业主的权益
owner's obligation
业主的义务
owner's right
业主的权利
owner's risk
业主的风险,货主负担风险,船东自负风险
ownership *n*.
所有权,所有制
ownership of goods and materials
物资所有权
ownership of trade marks
商标所有权
ownership transfer
所有权转移
oxygen lance
氧气切割器

P

pack *v*.
包装,打包
package *n*.
包,包裹;包装;一揽子(交易)
package bid
组合投标,一揽子投标
package contract
一揽子合同
package cost
包装费用

package deal
一揽子交易
package mortgage
一揽子抵押
package of engineered data
设计数据包
packaging *n*.
包装
packing & marking
包装与标记

packing cost
包装成本
packing instructions
包装须知
packing list
装箱单
packing slip (sheet)
包装单,装箱单
pact n.
合同;公约;条约
paid a.
已付的;付清的
paid check
付讫支票
paid holiday
带薪休假(期)
paid off
付讫,付清
paid-in capital
缴清股本,已缴资本
paid-up capital
缴清股本,已缴资本
paid-up licence fee
已缴许可证费
paint n.
油漆
pallet n.
托盘,货盘
paper n.
票据;证券;纸币;[复]证件
paper gold
纸黄金(指特别提款权)
paper loss
账面损失
paper profit
账面利润,账面盈余
paper work
文书工作
par n.
等价,平价;票面价值
par exchange rate
平价汇率,固定费率
par value
票面价值
par value stock
有面值股票
parallel a.
平行的,并行的
parallel loans
平行贷款
parallel market
平行市场
parallel operation
平行作业
parallel process
平行工序
parameter n.
参数
parent company
母公司,总公司
parking lot
停车场
part shipment
分批装运
partial a.
部分的;偏袒的
partial compensation
部分补偿
partial coverage
部分赔付;部分保险
partial loss
部分损失
partial payment
部分支付
partial shipment
分批装运
participant n.
参与者
participate v.
参与,参加
participate in a tender
参与投标
participating loan
共同贷款
particular n.
单独事项;[复]细目;详细说明 a. 特

殊的,特定的;个别的;分项的
particular average
单独海损
particulars of construction
施工详细情况
parties to a contract
合同各方
parties to a project
项目有关各方
parties to an agreement
签订协议各方
partner *n.*
合伙人,合股人
partner in charge
联营体负责人
partnership *n.*
合伙,合伙关系,合伙企业
party *n.*
当事人,参与者
party in breach
违约方
pass book
银行存折
passage *n.*
通过;通道;通行权
passage of title
所有权转移
passive bond
无息债券
passive loan
无息贷款
passport *n.*
护照
past-due
过期
past-due bill(note)
过期票据
patch *v.*
修补
patent *n.*
专利,专利权 *a.* 专利的,特许的;明显的
patent agent
专利代理人
patent defects
明显的缺陷,外在缺陷
patent fee
专利费
patent holder
专利持有人
patent infringement
侵犯专利权
patent law
专利法
patent license
专利许可证
patent office
专利局
patent protection
专利保护
patent right
专利权
patent royalty
专利权使用费
patentable *a.*
可取得专利权的
pattern *n.*
样品,模型;图样;类型
pave *v.*
筑(路),铺设
pavement *n.*
路面;人行道
pavement breaker
路面破碎机
pavement roller
压路机
pavement structure
路面结构
paving *n.*
铺砌;铺面
paving machine
铺路机
pawn *n.*
抵押,典当;抵押品
pawn ticket
抵押凭证

pay *v.*
支付,付清;偿还 *n.* 支付;工资,报酬
pay by installments
分期付款
pay cash
付现
pay in advance
预支付
pay in kind
实物支付
pay off the principal and interest
付清本息
pay on delivery
货到付款
pay to bearer
付给持票人
pay to the order of ...
付给指定人…
payable *a.*
到期应付的
payable at sight
见票即付
payable on demand
见票即付
payable period
应付期,付款期
payable upon first demand
首次要求即付
pay-as-you-earn（PAYE）
所得税预扣法
payback *n.*
偿付,付还
payback method
回收期评估法
payback period
投资回收期
payday *n.*
发薪日;付款日;过户结账日
payee *n.*
收款人,受款人
payer *n.*
付款人
paying agent
付款代理人
paying bank
付款银行
paying list
付款清单
payment *n.*
付款,支付,支付的款项
payment after termination
终止后的付款
payment against provisional sums
暂定金额的支付
payment agreement
支付协议
payment bond
支付担保
payment by draft
汇票支付
payment by installment
分期付款
payment by measurement
采用计量支付
payment credit
付款信用证
payment deferred
延期付款
payment for claims
索赔的支付
payment guarantee
付款保函
payment in advance
预付款
payment in cash
现金支付
payment in due course
到期支付
payment in event of suspension
暂时停工情况下的支付
payment in foreign currencies
外币支付
payment in full
全部付讫,全额支付
payment in kind
实物支付

payment milestone
支付里程碑
payment of advance
预付款的支付
payment of duties
交税,纳税
payment of freight at destination
运费到付
payment on account
(作为部分付款)暂付,赊账支付
payment on arrival
货到付款
payment on delivery
交货付款
payment on invoice
凭发票付款
payment on statement
凭账单付款
payment on termination
(合同)终止时的付款
payment order
付款通知
payment provisions
支付条款
payment schedule
支付计划,支付进度表
payment term
付款期
payment terms
支付条件
payment withheld
扣发支付款
payment-by-results *n.*
按成果付酬工资制
payroll *n.*
工资单,发放工薪额
payroll check
工资支票
payroll form
工资表格
payroll recapitulation
工资汇总表
payroll records
工资记录
payroll tax
工薪税
peak discharge
洪峰流量
peak flow
洪峰流量
peak season
旺季
peak traffic flow
高峰交通量
peculation *n.*
挪用,贪污
pedestrian bridge
人行桥
penal sum
罚金
penalty *n.*
罚款;处罚
penalty clause
惩罚条款,罚金条款
penalty for delay
误期罚款
penalty of breach of contract
违约罚款
pending *a.*
悬而未决的
pending question
未决问题
pension *n.*
退休金;抚恤金
pension fund
养老基金
per annum
按年计,每年
per capita
每人平均值
per diem
按日计,按日计费
per diem allowance
每日津贴
percent *n.*
百分之…

percent weighting
加权百分数
percentage *n.*
百分率,百分比
percentage of profit
利润率
perform *v.*
履约,执行
perform a contract
履行合同
performance *n.*
履约,履行;表现,业绩
performance bond
履约担保
performance criteria
性能指标
performance evaluation
业绩评价
performance guarantee
履约保函;履约保证书
performance letter of credit
履约信用证
performance of contract
合同的履行,合同实施
performance security
履约保证
performance test
运行检验,性能检验
peril *n.*
危险;风险事故
perils of the sea
海上风险,海难
period *n.*
周期;期间;期限
period cost
期间成本
period for shipment
装船期
period of construction
工程期限,施工期限
period of depreciation
折旧年限,折旧期
period of grace
宽限期
period of insurance
保险期限
period of probation
试用期,见习期
period of quality guarantee
质量保证期
period of validity
有效期
period of warranty
保证期,保修期
periodic inspection
定期检查
periodic inventory
定期盘存
periodic measurement
定期测量
periodic meeting
定期会议
periodic payment
定期付款
periodic report
定期报告
permanent *a.*
永久的;长期的;固定的
permanent assets
永久资产,固定资产
permanent investment
永久性投资
permanent works
永久工程
permission *n.*
准许,允许
permit *n.*
许可证,执照;许可,允许 *v.* 允许,许可
perpetual bond
永久债券
person in charge
主管人,负责人
personal *a.*
个人的,私人的,人身的
personal accident insurance

人身意外保险,人身意外伤害险
personal assets
个人资产
personal assistant
私人助理
personal income tax
个人所得税
personal injury
人身伤害
personal insurance
人身保险
personal liability
个人责任
personal property
个人财产,动产
personal tort
个人侵权行为
personnel *n.*
全体人员,职员;人事部门
personnel manager
人事经理
perspective *n.*
透视图
pervious bed
透水层
perviousness *n.*
透水性
petition *n.*
申请,诉状,请求
petrol *n.*
汽油
petroleum *n.*
石油
petty cash
零用现金
phase *n.*
阶段
phased construction method
阶段发包方式
physical capital
实物资本

physical completion date
实际竣工日期
physical evidence
实物证据
physical hazard
自然风险因素
physical inventory method
实物盘存法
physical obstruction
外部障碍,自然障碍
physical progress
实际进度
physical resources
物力资源
physical risk
自然风险
physical volume
实际容积,实际量
piece rate
计件工资率
piece wages
计件工资
piece work system
计件工作
pier *n.*
墩,支柱
pile *n.*
桩
pile sheet
板桩
pile cap (head)
桩帽
pile driver
打桩机;打桩者
pile driver barge
打桩船
pile extractor
拔桩机
pile foundation
桩基
pile hammer

打桩锤
pile shaft
桩身
piling *n.*
打桩(工程)
pilot *n.*
导洞 *a.* 实验的
pipe *n.*
管道,水管
pipe bender
弯管机
pipe jacking method
顶管法
pipe layer
铺管机,埋管机
pipe pile
管桩
pipe run
管道
pipe sewer
污水管
pipe sweep
排水管
pipe vents
通风管
pipe work
管道工程
pipeline *n.*
管道,管线
pipeline project
管线工程项目
pipe-works *n.*
管道工程
piping *n.*
铺管
piping erection
管道安装
pitfall *n.*
陷阱,隐患
place *v.*
放置,安置;浇注 *n.* 地点;地区;位置
place of arbitration
仲裁地点

place of departure
始发地
place of destination
目的地
place of loading
装货地
place of payment
付款地点
placing plant
混凝土浇筑设备
plaintiff *n.*
原告;检举人
plan *n.*
平面图;计划,方案
plan of operations
项目实施计划,作业计划
plane *n.*
平面
plane-table *n.*
平板;平板仪
plank pile
木板桩
planned cost
计划费用
planned period
计划期限
planned project
计划中的项目
planning *n.*
规划,编制计划
planning commission
计划委员会
planning consent
规划同意书
plant *n.*
设备;机械;工厂,厂房
plant capacity
工厂生产能力
plant records
设备的记录
plasterer *n.*
抹灰工
plastic pipe

塑料管
plastic film
塑料薄膜
plastic soil
塑性土
plastics *n.*
塑料制品
plate bender
弯板机
platform truck
平板大卡车
pleadings *n.*
诉状,辩护
pledge *n.*
抵押(品);誓约;保证(人) *v.* 抵押;保证
pledgee *n.*
接受抵押人
pledgor, pledger *n.*
抵押人
plenipotentiary *n.*
全权代表 *a.* 有全权的
plumbing *n.*
(上下水)管道工程
plywood *n.*
胶合板
plywood concrete forms
胶合板混凝土模板
pneumatic mortar
压力喷浆
pneumatic tube
压缩空气管道
point in dispute
争执点
point of contract
合同要点
point of view
观点,看法
poison *n.*
毒品
police *n.*
警察

policy *n.*
保险单;政策,策略
policy holder
投保人,保险客户,保单持有人
policy maker
决策者
political risk
政治风险
pollution *n.*
污染
pollution prevention cost
环境保护费
pontoon crane
浮吊,水上起重机
pooling *n.*
联营
port *n.*
港口,口岸
port works
港口工程
port authority
港务局
port charge
入港税,港口费用
port clearance
出港货物结关(单);(船舶)出港结关
port congestion surcharge
港口拥挤附加费
port dues
港口税,停泊费
port of call
停靠港
port of delivery
交货港
port of departure
启运港,出发港
port of destination
目的港
port of discharge
卸货港
port of entry
进口港

port of exit
出口港
port of shipment
装运港
port surcharge
港口附加费
portable agitator
移动式搅拌机
portal crane
门式起重机
porterage *n.*
搬运费
portion *n.*
部分
portland cement
硅酸盐水泥
portland slag cement
硅酸盐矿渣水泥
positive cash flow
正现金流量
possession *n.*
占有,所有权;[复]财产
possession of site
现场的占有
possessory lien
占有留置权
possibility *n.*
可能性
post *n.*
邮件,邮寄;职位 v. 邮寄;(会计)过账;[前缀]后
post code
邮政编码
post evaluation
后评估,后评价
post office box
邮政信箱
post qualification
资格后审
post review
后审查
post-award meeting
授标后会议
postdate *v.*
填迟日期
posting *n.*
过账
postpone *v.*
推迟,延期
postponed payment
延期支付
postponement *n.*
推迟,延期
post-tensioned prestressing
后张法预加应力
potential *a.*
潜在的
potential market
潜在市场
potential risk
潜在风险
pour *v.*
浇注,流注
poured concrete
浇注混凝土
power *n.*
权力;能源,电力
power cable
动力电缆
power cut
停电;动力切断
power house (plant)
主厂房;发电厂;动力车间
power of attorney
授权书,委托书
power of interpretation
解释权
power of sale
销售权
power project
电力工程
power resources
电力资源,能源
power station

发电站,电厂
power to sign
签字权
practicability *n.*
可行性,实用性
practical *a.*
实际的；实用的
preappraisal *n.*
预评估
pre-award meeting
授标前会议
pre-bid meeting
(投)标前会议,投标预备会
pre-bid site visit
投标前现场调查
precast concrete
预制混凝土
precast concrete floor
预制混凝土楼板
precast hollow concrete block
预制混凝土空心砌块
precede *v.*
领先,优先
precedence *n.*
领先,优先权
precedence network
作业次序网络图
precedent *n.*
先例,惯例；判例 *a.* 优先的；在前的
preceding clause
前述条款
precise *a.*
精确的
precision *n.*
精确度
precommissioning *n.*
预调试,调试前的准备
precondition *n.*
前提,先决条件
pre-contract procedures
签订合同前的程序,签约前的程序
pre-defined *a.*
预先规定的

predicated cost
预计成本
prediction *n.*
预测,预料
preemptive right
优先购置权
preentry *n.*
预先报关单；预先申报
prefabricate *v.*
预制
prefabricated unit
预制构件
pre-feasibility study
预可行性研究,初步可行性研究
preference *n.*
优先,优先权；偏爱
preference for domestic contractors
对国内承包商的优惠
preference for domestic manufacturers
对国内制造商的优惠
preferential duties
特惠关税
preferential rate of interest
优惠利率
preferential tariff
优惠税则；特惠税率
preferential trade agreement
优惠贸易协定
preferred stock
优先股
preinvestment studies
预投资研究,投资前研究
prejudice *n.*
损害；偏见,歧视
preliminaries *n.*
预备(指步骤,措施等)；开办费；准备工作
preliminary *a.*
初步的,预备的
preliminary acceptance certificate
初步验收证书
preliminary act

预备诉讼行为
preliminary budget
初步预算
preliminary computation
初步计算,概算
preliminary design
初步设计
preliminary drawings
初步设计图纸
preliminary entry
预备进口报关单
preliminary evaluation
初步评价
preliminary expenses
开办费
preliminary feasibility study
初步可行性研究,预可行性研究
preliminary items
开办项目
preliminary survey
初步勘测
preliminary works
预备工程
premium *n.*
保险费;佣金;奖金;升水,贴水,溢价
premium bonus
节约时间奖
premium pay
加班工资,假日工资
premium payment
支付保险费
premium rate
保险费率;升水率
premium returns
额外利润,退还保险费
premoulded pile
预制桩
prepaid expenses
预付费用
prepaid freight
预付运费
preparation expenses
筹备费

preparation of bid
投标准备
preparation of contract documents
合同文件的准备
prepare *v.*
编制;准备
prepayment *n.*
预付款
prepayment clause
预付款条款
prepayment guarantee
预付款保函
pre-proposal conference
建议书提交前预备会
prequalification *n.*
资格预审
prequalification application
资格预审申请
prequalification documents
资格预审文件
prerequisite *n.*
先决条件,必要条件 *a.* 必要的,首要的
prescribe *v.*
规定;命令;指示
presence *n.*
出席;出庭
present *v.*
出示;出席;提出 *n.* [复]证书;文件 *a.* 现在的;出席的,在场的
present value
现值
present value of cost
成本现值
presentation *n.*
交单,提交
presenter *n.*
(票据)提示人;赠送人;提出者
presentment *n.*
提示;提出
presentment for acceptance
承兑提示
presentment for payment

付款提示
preservation *n.*
防腐
preservative substance
防腐剂
preserve *n.*
保持
preserving duty
维持关税
president *n.*
总裁;总经理;会长;行长
pressure culvert
压力涵洞
pressure grouting
压力灌浆
pressure tunnel
压力隧道
prestressed concrete
预应力混凝土
presumption *n.*
假定,推测
presumption of law
法律上的推定
pre-tensioned prestressing
先张法预加应力
preterlegal *a.*
无法律根据的;超出法律范围的
prevail *v.*
胜过;优先于;通行;流行
prevailing opinion
占优势的意见
prevailing party
胜诉的一方
prevailing price
时价,现行价格
prevailing rate
现行费率;通行汇率
prevent *v.*
防止,预防
prevention *n.*
阻止,预防
preventive claims management
预防性索赔管理
price *n.*
价格,价值 *v.* 给…定价,给…标价
price adjustment
价格调整
price adjustment clause
价格调整条款
price adjustment contract
价格调整合同
price adjustment factor
价格调整系数
price adjustment formula
调价公式
price after tax
税后价格
price asked
要价,开价
price bargaining
价格谈判,讨价还价
price ceiling
最高限价,最高价格
price concession
让价
price control
价格监督,价格控制
price cutting
减价,削价
price delivered alongside
船边交货价
price difference
差价
price duty paid
完税货价
price escalation
价格上涨,物价上涨
price estimated
估计价格
price floor
最低限价,最低价格
price fluctuation factor
价格波动因子,物价变化系数
price index

价格指数
price indication
参考价格
price list
价目表,价格单
price loco
购买地价格,当地价
price maker
价格的决定者
price mark down
减价,降价
price mark up
加价,提价
price of delivery to destination
目的地交货价
price of ex-factory
工厂交货价
price of transacting
交易价格
price quotation
报价(单)
price range
价格幅度
price revision clause
价格修正条款
price sensitivity
价格敏感性
price stability
物价稳定
price taker
价格的接受者
price tendered
投标价,报价
price terms
价格条件
priced bill of quantities
标价的工程量表
priced deviations
偏离折价
price-level-adjusted statement
按物价水平调整的报表
price-weighted index
物价加权指数

pricing n.
定价,计价
prima facie
初步的;表面的
prima facie case
有初步证据的案件
prima facie evidence
初步证据
primary data
原始资料,原始数据
primary deposit
现金存款
primary evidence
原始证据,基本证据
primary fact
主要事实,基本事实
primary market
初级市场;主要市场
primary record
原始记录
primary risk
一级风险,头等风险
prime a.
最初的,原始的;主要的,首要的;最好的
prime contract
主合同
prime contractor
总承包商
prime cost
主要成本,直接成本;进货价
prime cost plus fixed fee
主要成本加固定酬金
prime cost plus percentage fee
主要成本加定比酬金
prime interest rate
优惠贷款利率
prime quality
上等品
prime risk
基本风险,最低风险
principal n.
本人;委托人;当事人;本金;资本 a.

主要的,最重要的;资本的,本金的
principal amount
贷款本金
principal consultant
总咨询师,总顾问
principal contractor
主承包商
principal debtor
主要债务人
principal office
总部
principal payment
本金支付
principal place of business
主要营业地
principal to principal
当事人对当事人
principle *n.*
原则;原理
principle of equality
平等原则
principle of good faith
诚信原则
principle of measurement
计量原则
prior *a.*
预先的;优先的
prior claims
优先权利要求,优先索赔
prior consultation
事先协商
prior review
事先审查
priority *n.*
优先顺序,优先权;(保险)自留部分
priority construction
首期建筑
priority of contract documents
合同文件的优先次序
priority of debts
债务偿还的优先次序
private *a.*
私有的,私营的,个人的

private bidding (tendering)
不公开投标
private company
私营公司
private contact
私下接触
private enterprise
私营企业
private international law
国际私法
private law
私法
private ledger
机密分类账,内账
privilege *n.*
特许,特权;优惠
privity *n.*
默契;当事人间的相互关系
privity of contract
合同当事人间的相互关系
probability *n.*
概率,可能性
probation *n.*
试用;检验;鉴定
probationary period
试用期
problematical *a.*
未定的;疑难的
procedural law
程序法,诉讼法
procedural law for arbitration
仲裁使用的程序法
procedure *n.*
步骤,手续,程序
procedure for claims
索赔程序
procedure for concluding a contract
签订合同的程序
procedure of approval
批准程序
procedure of arbitration
仲裁程序
procedure of customs

报关程序
proceed *v.*
进行,开始;起诉
proceeding *n.*
程序;[复]诉讼;记录;汇编
proceeds *n.*
收入,收益
process *v.*
加工;处理;对…起诉 *n.* 过程;手续;诉讼;工序
process analysis
工序分析,操作分析
process capability
加工能力
process chart
工艺流程图
process control
工序控制
process costing
分步成本计算法
process data
处理数据,整理资料
process design
工艺设计
process diagram
工艺流程图
process engineer
工艺工程师
process flow chart
工艺流程图
process of export
出口手续
process of import
进口手续
processing cost
加工费,加工成本
processing time
加工时间
proclamation *n.*
公布,公告
procure *v.*
采购,获得
procurement *n.*
采购,购置
procurement methods
采购办法
procurement of consulting services
咨询服务采购
procurement of goods
货物采购
procurement of materials
材料采购
procurement of works
工程采购
procurement packages
采购包,一揽子采购
procurement program
采购计划
procurement restraints
采购限制
procurement schedule & status report (PSSR)
采购工作计划及进度报告
produce *v.*
生产;产生;制造;提交;出示
product *n.*
产品;乘积
product appraisal certificate
产品鉴定证书
product liability insurance
产品责任保险
product quality guarantee
产品质量保证
product tax
产品税
production *n.*
生产,制作;产量;出示
production bonus
生产奖金
production capacity
生产能力
production control
生产管理
production cost
生产成本,产品成本
production data

生产数据
production license
生产许可证
production line performance test
生产线性能考核
production manager
生产经理
production method of depreciation
产量折旧法
production plan
生产计划
production quantity guarantee
产量保证
production quota
生产指标,生产定额
production rate
生产率
production target
生产指标
production term
生产期
production volume
产量
production waste
生产污水
productivity *n.*
生产率,生产能力
profession *n.*
职业;专业;同业
professional *a.*
职业的;专业的 *n.* 专业人员
professional ethics
职业道德
professional etiquette
行规
professional fee
专业服务费
professional indemnity insurance
职业保障保险
professional liability insurance
职业责任保险
professional misconduct
渎职
professional responsibility
职业责任
professional service
专业服务
professional witness
专业证人
proficiency *n.*
熟练,精通
profile *n.*
剖面图,纵断面;轮廓;概况,简介
profit *n.*
利润,收益,收入
profit after tax
税后利润
profit and loss account
损益账
profit and loss statement
损益表
profit before tax
税前利润
profit distribution
利润分配
profit estimating
利润估算
profit forecast
利润预测
profit margin
利润额,利润率
profit mark-up
利润加成
profit pooling
利润汇总
profit rate
利润率
profit tax
利润税
profitability *n.*
获利能力;利润率;效益
profitability analysis
盈利能力分析
profiteer *n.*
投机商
proforma invoice

形式发票,预开发票
program backup
后备计划
program evaluation and reviews technique (PERT)
计划评审技术;统筹法
program flow chart
程序流程图
program(me) *n.*
方案,计划;程序
programming *n.*
计划拟定;程序设计
programming frameworks
计划的依据
progress *n.*
进度,进程
progress analysis
进度分析
progress chart
进度表
progress control
进度控制
progress of project
工程进度
progress of works
工程进度
progress payment
进度付款
progress report
进度报告
progress—actual vs scheduled
实际进度与计划进度对比
progressive *a.*
累进的,递增的
progressive payment
(按进度)累进付款
progressive tax
累进税
progressive total
累计总额
prohibit *n.*
禁止,阻止
prohibited articles (goods)

违禁品
prohibition *n.*
禁止;禁令;诉讼中止令
prohibitive duty
抑制性关税;高额关税
project *n.*
项目,工程;方案;规划
project activities
项目作业
project agreement
项目协议
project alternative
项目备选方案
project analysis
项目分析
project appraisal
项目评估
project approval process
项目审批过程
project brief
项目概要
project budget
项目预算
project completion report
项目竣工报告
project components
项目组成部分
project contract
工程合同
project contracting
工程承包
project control
项目控制
project coordination
项目协调
project coordinator
项目协调员
project cost
工程造价
project cycle
项目周期,项目循环
project definition
项目内容确定

project demands
项目要求
project description
项目说明,项目描述
project diary
项目日志
project engineer
项目工程师
project entity
项目实体;项目负责机构
project evaluation
项目评估
project execution and supervision
项目的执行与监督
project extension
项目的扩建
project financing
项目融资
project forecast
项目预测
project funding
项目筹资
project goal
项目目标
project identification
项目选定
project implementation schedule
项目执行计划
project inception
项目的起始
project inspection report
工程检查报告
project insurance
工程保险
project management
项目管理
project manager
项目经理
project manual
项目手册
project monitor
项目监督员
project monitoring
项目监控
project negotiation
项目谈判
project objective
项目目标
project officer
项目官员
project operation
项目运营
project opportunities
项目机会
project organization
项目机构
project participant
项目参与者
project performance
项目的执行
project performance assessment report (PPAR)
项目执行评估报告
project performance audit report (PPAR)
项目执行审计报告
project planning
项目计划
project post-evaluation
项目后评价
project pre-appraisal
项目预评估
project preparation
项目准备
project procedure manual
项目程序手册
project program
工程计划
project progress and performance report
工程进展与执行报告
project proposal
项目建议书
project quality test
项目质量考核
project report

项目报告
project representative
项目代表
project risk
工程风险
project schedule
项目进度计划
project scope
项目范围
project selection
项目选择
project sponsor
项目主办者
project staff
项目职员
project startup
项目筹备
project superintendent
项目监督人员
project suspension
项目暂停
project sustainability assessing
项目持续性评价
project team
项目组
projected cost
预计成本
projected financial statement
预计财务报表
projection *n.*
估算,预测
prolong *v.*
延长,拖延
prolong a contract period
延长合同有效期
prolong the period of validity
(票据等)延长有效期
prolonged delay
持续的误期
prolonged suspension
持续的暂时停工
promise *n.*
诺言 *v.* 许诺

promised delivery date
承诺的交货日期
promisee *n.*
受约人,承诺人
promisor *n.*
立约人,订约人
promissory note
期票,本票
promote *v.*
提升;促进
promoter *n.*
发起人,创办人,推销商
promotion *n.*
提升;促销;发起
prompt *n.*
催促;催款单;付款期限 *a.* 立即的;即付的
prompt cash
立即付款
prompt delivery
即期交货
prompt shipment
即刻装运
proof *n.*
证明;证词;证据,物证
proof by facts
事实证明
proof of delivery
交货证明
proof of loss
损失证明
proof to the contrary
反面证据,反证
proper law
准据法,管辖法
proper law of the contract
合同的准据法,合同管辖法
property *n.*
财产;财产权,物(权);(房)地产;性质
property assets
不动产,房地产
property claim

产权要求
property company
房地产公司
property dispute
产权纠纷
property in land
土地所有权
property insurance
财产保险
property law
准据法,管辖法
property right
产权
property tax
财产税
property valuation
资产评估
proportion *n.*
比例,比率;部分
proportion scale
比例尺
proportioning by volume
按容积配合
proportioning by weight
按重量配合
proposal *n.*
建议,提议;建议书;投保书
proposal form
投保单
proposal of insurance
投保书
proprietary *n.*
所有人,业主;所有权 *a.* 所有(人)的,业主的;专有的
proprietary articles
专利品,专卖品
proprietary company
控股公司
proprietary equity
业主权益,股东权益,业主产权
proprietary interest
业主权益

proprietary limited（Pty Ltd）
股份有限责任公司,控股有限公司
proprietary product
专利产品
proprietary right
所有权
proprietorship *n.*
独资企业
pro-rate *a.*
按比例的
prorate distribution
按比例分摊
prosecution *n.*
起诉
prospect *n.*
期望,展望,预期 *v.* 勘察,勘探
prospective bidder(tenderer)
有意投标者,预期投标者
prospective client
潜在客户
prospective market
预期的市场
prospective yield
预期收益
protect *v.*
保护
protected holder
受保护的持票人
protection *n.*
保护
protection and indemnity clause
保赔保险条款
protection duty
保护性关税
protection of environment
环境保护
protection works
防护工程
protectionism *n.*
保护主义
protective measure
保护措施,安全措施

protest *n*.
抗议;拒付证书 *v*. 证明拒付;抗诉
protest jacket
拒付通知单;退票通知单
protest of bill
票据拒付证明
protocol *n*.
草案;议定书;备忘录
prototype testing
原型试验
provide *v*.
规定;提供,供给
provision *n*.
规定;条款;预备;备抵;供应
provision for bad debts
备抵坏账
provision for depreciation
备抵折旧
provisional *a*.
临时的,暂时的
provisional acceptance
临时验收
provisional agreement
临时协议
provisional assessment
临时估价
provisional certificate
临时证书
provisional cost
临时成本
provisional index
暂定价格指数
provisional invoice
临时发票
provisional payment
临时付款
provisional sums
暂定金额;备用金
provisions of contract
合同条款,合同规定
proviso *n*.
限制性条件;保留条件
proviso clause
限制性条款,保留条款
proxy *n*.
代理(权);代理人;委托书
psychology of negotiating
谈判心理学
public *a*.
公共的,公众的;公开的;政府的 *n*.
公众
public accountant
执业会计师,开业会计师
public authority
公共当局
public bidding
公开招标
public company
公开发行股份有限公司;公营公司
public corporation
国有公司,国营公司
public enterprise
公营企业
public holiday
公共假日
public law
公法
public liability
公共责任
Public Limited Company (PLC)
公开有限公司
public money
公款
public notary
公证人
public relation
公共关系
public sale
拍卖
public utility
公用事业;[复]公共设施
public welfare
公共福利
public works
公用工程;市政工程

pull down
拆除
pump station
泵站
punitive damages
惩罚性赔偿费
purchase n. v.
购买,采购;购置
purchase commitment
购货约定
purchase contract
订货合同
purchase invoice
购货发票
purchase journal
购货日记账
purchase memorandum
采购备忘录
purchase money
定金,买价
purchase note
购货确认书
purchase order
购货单;定单
purchase price
买价
purchase requisition
采购申请单
purchase sample
购货样品
purchaser n.
买主,买方
purchasing agency
采购代理
purchasing agent
购货代理人
purchasing clerk
采购员
purchasing commission
代购佣金
purchasing cost
购货成本
purchasing department
采购部,物资部
pure interest
纯利息
pure premium
纯保险费
pure profit
净利润
pure risk
纯粹风险
purpose n.
目的;用途
pursuant to
根据,与…相关
put an embargo on
对…货物实行禁运;禁止…船只出入
put into production
投产

Q

qualification n.
资格(证明);合格;限制条件
qualification certificate
资格证书
qualified acceptance
附条件承兑
qualify v.
使合格,证明…合格;准予
qualifying clause
限制条款
quality n.
质量;品质;优质;特性
quality as per buyer's sample
质量以买方样品为准
quality as per seller's sample
质量以卖方样品为准

quality assurance
质量保证
quality audit
质量监察
quality certificate
质量证明
quality control
质量控制
quality cost
质量成本
quality guarantee
质量保证书
quality review
质量审查
quality surveillance
质量监督
quality tracking system
质量追踪系统
quantification n.
可计量性;定量;可量化
quantify v.
确定…的数量;用数量表示
quantitative analysis
定量分析
quantity n.
数量;工程量
quantity discount
数量折扣
quantity installation curves
安装工作量曲线
quantity of work
工作量,作业量
quantity pricing
工程量标价
quantity survey
工料测量

quantity surveying
工料测量学
quantity surveyor (QS)
工料测量师,估算师
quantity take-off
工程量计算
quarry n.
采石场
quasi-arbitrator n.
准仲裁员
quasi-judicial a.
准司法的
quasi-official n.
半官方的
quay berth
码头泊位
quay-to-quay transportation
码头至码头运输
queries and replies
质疑与解答
query n. v.
询问;质疑
quick cement
速凝水泥
quick lime
生石灰
quick sand
流沙
quota n.
配额,定额;限额
quotation n.
报价;报价单
quote v.
开价,报价

R

radial gate | 弧形闸门

rail *n.*
铁路；钢轨；栏杆；扶手
rail and air
铁路运输及空运
rail and ocean
铁路运输及海运
rail and water
铁路运输及水运
railway advice
铁路到货通知
railway bill of lading
铁路提货单
railway freight
铁路运费
raise funds
筹措资金
raised check
涂改支票
rammer *n.*
夯，锤体
ramming machine
打夯机
random sample
随机样品
random sampling
随机取样，随机抽样
rate *n.*
比率；费率；单价；速度，速率 *v.* 对…估价
rate of customs duty
海关税率
rate of depreciation charges
折旧费率
rate of discount
贴现率
rate of exchange
兑换率，汇率
rate of interest
利率
rate of margin
毛利率
rate of national taxes
国家税率
rate of operation
开工率
rate of port dues
港口税率
rate of premium
保险费率
rate of progress
施工速度
rate of return
利润率，收益率
rate of return method
（资金）收益率评估法
rate of taxation
税率
ratification *n.*
批准，认可
ratio *n.*
比率
ration *n.*
配额
raw data
原始数据
raw material
原材料
reach an impasse
陷入僵局
read-out bid price
唱标价
ready cash
现金
real account
实账户
real cost
实际成本
real estate
房地产，不动产
real exchange rate
实际汇率
real property
不动产，房地产
real security

实物担保
realizable assets
可变现资产
reasonable *a.*
合理的；适当的
reasonable precautions
合理的预防措施
reasonable price
公平价格
reassemble *v.*
重新组装，重新装配
reassure *v.*
再保险；分保；再次保证
rebate *n. v.*
回扣；退税
rebated acceptance
提前承兑
recall *v.*
撤销，收回
recall an order
撤销订货单
receipt *n.*
收据；[复]进款 *v.* 签收，出具收据
receipt slip
收款便条
received for shipment B/L
待运提单
receiver *n.*
接收人；诉讼财产管理人；破产案产业管理人
receiving order
（法院发出的）接管令
recess *n. v.*
休会
recipient *n.*
接受人；受援国 *a.* 接收的
reciprocal *a.*
互惠的，对等的
reciprocal account
往来账户
reciprocal agreement
互惠协定
reciprocal contract
互惠合同
reciprocal L/C
对开信用证
reciprocal tariff
互惠关税
reciprocal trade
互惠贸易
reciprocal treatment
互惠待遇
reciprocity clause
互惠条款
reckon *v.*
结算，结账；清算
reclamation *n.*
填筑，回填；开垦
recommend *v.*
推荐；建议
recommendation *n.*
推荐；介绍信
recompense *n. v.*
赔偿；补偿
reconciliation *n.*
调解，和解
reconfirm *v.*
重新证实，重新确认
reconstruction *n.*
重建，改建
reconstruction of company
公司重组
record *n. v.*
记录，记载
record drawing
记录图纸；竣工图
recoup *v.*
补偿，赔偿；扣除
recourse *n.*
追索权
recover *v.*
收回，恢复；取得
recoverable *a.*
可回收的；可补偿的；可恢复的
recovery *n.*
恢复；财产收回；追索

recovery of late payment
要求支付拖欠金额
recovery value
回收价值,残值
recruit *v*.
补充;招聘
recruitment *n*.
补充;招聘
rectification *n*.
矫正
rectify *v*.
修补,改正,矫正
red balance
赤字
redeem *v*.
偿还;弥补;赎回
redeemable bond
可赎回债券
redemption price
赎回价格
redress *n*. *v*.
赔偿;补救;纠正
reduce *v*.
减少,降低
reduced price
降低的价格
reducing balance depreciation method
余额递减折旧法
reduction *n*.
减少,降价
re-evaluate *v*.
重新评估
re-exportation *n*.
再出口
refer *v*.
提及;提交;参考
referee *n*.
受委托人;鉴定人;仲裁人
reference *n*.
参考;委托;职权范围;证明;提交仲裁
reference clause
仲裁条款
reference point
参考点
reference price
参考价格
refinance *v*.
重新筹集资金
refractory brick
耐火砖
refractory cement
耐火水泥
refractory concrete
耐火混凝土
refractory material
耐火材料
refrigerating system
制冷系统
refuge *n*.
安全岛
refund *v*. *n*.
退款;偿还,偿还债务
refund of duty
退税
refusal *n*.
拒绝;优先购买权
refuse *v*.
拒绝 *n*. 废料,垃圾
refute *v*.
反驳
regain *v*.
收回
region *n*.
地区,区域;范围
regional planning
地区规划
regional preference
地区性优惠
regional price differential
地区差价
register *v*.
登记,注册;挂号 *n*. 登记簿;记存装置
registered bond
记名债券

registered capital
注册资本
registered company
注册公司
registered design
注册设计
registered letter
挂号信
registered mail
挂号邮件
registered title
注册产权
registered trade mark
注册商标
registration n.
注册
regressive tax
递减税
regular insurance
定期保险
regular meeting
例会
regular payment
定期支付
regular tax
正常税
regulation n.
规章,规定;法规;条例;调节;管理
Rehabilitate-Operate-Transfer (ROT)
修复-运营-移交
rehabilitation n.
修复;重建;改善,更新
reimbursable a.
可偿还的;可补偿的;可报销的
reimburse v.
偿还,补偿
reimbursement n.
补偿;赔偿;报销
re-import v.
再进口
reinforced concrete
钢筋混凝土

reinforced concrete pressure pipe
钢筋混凝土压力水管
reinforcement n.
加强,加固;钢筋;配筋
reinforcement ratio
配筋率
reinstatement n.
恢复原状
reinsurance n.
再保险,分保
reinsurance broker
再保险经纪人
reinsurance contract
再保险合同
reject v.
拒绝,驳回;否决 n. 废品
rejected check
拒付支票
rejected work
拒绝验收的工作
rejection n.
拒绝
rejection of all bids
拒绝全部投标,废标
related agencies
有关机构
relative price
相对价格,比价
release v.
释放;放弃;让与;解除(合同)
release agent
脱模剂
release from
免除
release from obligation
免除义务
release from performance
解除履约
release from the contract
免除合同义务
release of bank guarantee
撤销银行保函
release of mortgage

解除抵押
release pay
遣散费
releasee *n.*
受让人；被免除债务者
releasor *n.*
让与人，放弃权利者
relending *n.*
分贷
relevance *n.*
相关性
relevant cost
相关成本，有关费用
reliability *n.*
可靠性
reliability run
可靠性试运行
relieve from
解除
relieve from obligations
解除义务
relinquish *v.*
放弃；停止；让与（权利、财产等）
relocation settlement costs
搬迁安置费用
remain in force
保持有效
remainder *n.*
剩余物，存货
remaining value
残值，余值
remeasurement *n.*
重新计量
remedial action
补救措施
remedy *n. v.*
修正，修补，补救；赔偿
remedying defects
修补缺陷
remission *n.*
减免；豁免；汇款
remit *v.*
汇款，汇寄；豁免；免除
remittance *n.*
汇款，汇付
remittance against documents
凭单付款
remittance by draft
汇票汇款
remittance settlement
汇款结算
remittance slip
汇款通知单
remittee *n.*
收款人
remitter *n.*
汇款人
remitting bank
汇款银行，托收银行
remote sensing data
遥感数据
removal *n.*
搬迁，迁移；移走
removal cost
拆迁成本
removal expenses
搬运费
removal of defective work
移走有缺陷的工程
remove *v.*
搬迁；移走
remuneration *n.*
报酬，酬劳；补偿
render *v.*
提供，提出；使变为
renew *v.*
修补；补充；准予展期；更新
renew a contract
使合同展期，续订合同
renewal *n.*
更新；修补；展期，延长
renewal of contract
合同续订，合同展期
rent *n.*
租金；租用 *v.* 租用，租赁
rental *n.*

出租,租赁;租金收入
repair *n. v.*
修理;补救;恢复
repair cost
修理费
repair man
修理工
repair outfit
修理工具
repair shop
修配间
reparation *n.*
补偿,赔偿;修理
repatriation *n.*
遣返;汇还本国
repay *v.*
偿还;报答;补偿
repayment *n.*
偿还;报答;补偿
repayment ability
偿还能力
repayment guarantee
偿还保函
repayment of advance
预付款的偿还
repayment of loan
偿还贷款
repayment period
偿还期
repeal *n.v.*
撤销,废止
replacement *n.*
取代;更换;重置
replacement cost
重置成本,更新成本
replacement material
代用材料
repledge *v.*
转抵押
report form of balance sheet
报告式资产负债表
report on bid evaluation
评标报告

representation *n.*
代表;陈述
representative *n.*
代表,代理人;继承人
representative abroad
驻国外代表
representative of contractor
承包商的代表
reproduction cost
再生产成本,重置成本
repudiate *v.*
否认;拒付;拒绝接受
repudiate the contract
否认合同有效
repudiation *n.*
否认;拒付
repugnance *n.*
不一致,矛盾
reputation *n.*
信誉
request *n. v.*
请求,要求,申请
request for bid
邀请投标
request for proposal
(咨询)招标通知,建议书征求函
required rate of return
预期收益率
requirement *n.*
要求;命令;规定;需要
requisite *a.*
需要的,必要的
requisite document
必备文件
requisitioning of land
征用土地
rescission *n.*
解约;取消;废除;解除
research and development cost
研究开发费
reservation *n.*
保留;限制条件;储备;预定
reserve *v.*

保留;准备;储备 *n*. 储备(物,金)
reserve for bad debts
坏账准备,备抵坏账
reserve for depreciation
折旧准备,备抵折旧
reserve for repair
维修费准备
reserve fund
公积金
reserve stock
储备库存量
reservoir *n*.
水库;蓄水池
residence *n*.
居所
residence permit
居住许可证
resident engineer
驻地工程师
residential quarters
住宅区
residual *a*.
残余的,残留的
residual assets
剩余资产
residual income
剩余收益
residual value
残值
resin *n*.
树脂
resolution *n*.
决议;决定;解决;解释
resolutive clause
解除条款
resources *n*.
资源;物力;财力
respondent *n*.
答辩人;被告
responsibility *n*.
责任,职责,任务;偿付能力
responsibility range
职责范围

responsive *a*.
响应的,符合要求的
responsive bid
响应性投标,符合性投标
responsive to bidding documents
符合招标文件要求
rest *n*.
休息;盈余额 *v*. 休息;取决于
restday *n*.
休息日
restitution of advance payment
退还预付款
restitution of the guarantee
归还保函
restoration *n*.
恢复,复原;修复
restraining order
禁止令
restriction *n*.
限制,限定;约束
restriction on eligibility
合格性限制
restrictive clause
限制条款
restrictive element
制约因素
restrictive endorsement
附条件背书
resume of work performed
以往工作的简历
resumption *n*.
恢复;再开始;重新占用
resumption of work
复工
retail *n*. *v*.
零售
retail dealer
零售商
retail price
零售价
retail shipment
零星运输
retailer

零售商
retain v.
保留,保持;聘请
retained profit
待分配利润,留成利润
retainer n.
(律师等的)聘请费
retainer fee
聘请费
retaining wall
挡土墙
retarded cement
缓凝水泥
retarder n.
缓凝剂
retender (rebid)
重新招标,再招标
retention n.
保留;保留金
retention money
保留金,滞付金
retention money guarantee
保留金保函
retirement n.
退休;退职;(固定资产)报废
retiring a bill
赎票,赎单
retrieve v.
挽回,弥补
retroactive a.
有追溯效力的
retroactive pay
补发的工资
return v.
返回;偿还 n.[复]利润,投资报酬率;报表,统计表
return of materials
材料退回
return on investment
投资回报率,投资收益率
return ticket
往返票

returned goods
退回的货物
returns of contractor's equipment
承包商设备报表
returns of labour
劳务统计报表
returns on the investment
投资回报
revaluation n.
重新估价
revenue n.
收入,收益;税收
revenue expenditure
营业支出,经常开支
revenue stamp
印花税票
revest v.
使恢复原状;再归属…
review n. v.
复审,审查
review period
审核期,审查期
review process
审议过程
revise v.
修订,修改
revise a contract
修改合同
revise a schedule
调整进度表
revised programme
修正的计划
revision n.
修改
revocable a.
可撤销的
revocable credit
可撤销的信用证
revocable L/C
可撤销的信用证
revocation n.
撤销

revolving fund
流动资金,循环资金
revolving L/C
循环信用证
reward n.
酬金;奖金;奖励
rework cost
返工成本
right of claim
请求权,索赔权
right of entry
进入权
right of exoneration
免责权,免除权
right of legal representation
法定代表权
right of lien
留置权
right of ownership
所有权
right of patent
专利权
right of possession
占有权
right of priority
优先权
right of property
财产权
right of reimbursement
追偿权
right of rescission
解约权
right of subrogation
代位权
right of way
过境权,道路通行权
right to access
出入权
right to claim
索赔权
right to leased property
财产租赁权
right to the use of a site
现场使用权
rigid foundation
刚性基础
rigid-framed structure
钢架结构
ring beam
圈梁
ripper n.
松土机
risk n.
风险,危险
risk allocation
风险分担
risk allowance
风险准备金
risk analysis
风险分析
risk apportionment
风险分摊
risk avoidance
风险回避
risk contract
风险合同
risk evaluation
风险评价
risk factor
风险因素
risk management
风险管理
risk note
承保证明,暂保单,承保单
risk of contamination
污染险
risk of hook damage
钩损险
risk of leakage
渗漏险
risk of shortage
短量险
risk premium
风险保费
risk rating
风险等级划分,风险评级

risk reduction
风险减少,风险分散
risk retention
风险自留
risk sharing
风险分担
risk speculation
风险利用,风险投机
risk transfer
风险转移
rival *n.*
对手,竞争者
rivet *n.*
铆钉 *v.* 铆接;打铆钉
road accident
车祸,交通事故
road carrier
陆运承运人
road grader
平路机
road roller
压路机
road scraper
刮土机
road way
行车道;路面;道路
rock core sample
岩芯样品
rock stratum
岩层
rock-fill dam
堆石坝
rod spacing
钢筋间距
role *n.*
作用;任务;角色
roller *n.*
碾压机
roof *n.*
屋顶
round trip ticket
往返票
round-the-clock job
昼夜施工
route *n.*
路线,航线 *v.* 为…设计路线
route map
路线图
route survey
路线测量
routine *n.*
常规;惯例;日常工作 *a.* 常规的;日常的
routine inspection
例行检查,定期检查
routine maintenance
日常维修
routine procedure
例行程序
routine test
常规试验
royalty *n.*
产权使用费;矿区使用费
rubber check
空头支票
rubbish disposal
垃圾处理
rubble *n.*
块石,毛石
rubble masonry
毛石砌体
rule *n.*
规则;惯例;裁定
rules and regulations
规章制度
Rules for the International Chamber of Commerce Court of Arbitration
国际商会仲裁法庭仲裁规则
rules of conciliation and arbitration
调解及仲裁规则
rules of conduct
行为守则
ruling *n.*
裁决 *a.* 现行的;主导的
ruling language
主导语言

running days
连续日
rush-repair
抢修
rust-resisting material
防锈材料

S

sabotage n.
破坏行为 v. 进行破坏;怠工
safe a.
安全的 n. 保险箱
safe custody charges
保管费
safe handling
安全装卸
safe working condition
安全工作条件
safeguard clause
保障条款,保护条款
safety n.
安全
safety brake
安全制动器,保险闸
safety controls
安全装置
safety factor
安全系数
safety fence
安全护栏
safety inspection
安全检查
safety installation
安全装置
safety island
安全岛,安全地带
safety measures
安全措施
safety precaution
安全预防措施
salary n.
薪水,薪金
sale n.
销售,卖

sale by inspection
看货买卖
sale by sample
看样出售,凭样品成交
sale by specification, grade or standard
凭规格、等级或标准买卖
sale on account
赊销
sale price
售价;廉价
sales account
销售账
sales agency
代销行
sales commission
销售佣金
sales confirmation
销售确认书
sales contract
销售合同
sales invoice
销售发票
sales manager
营业主任,销售经理
sales margin
销售毛利
sales rebate
销售回扣
sales returns
退货
sales tax
营业税,销售税
sales turnover
销售额
salt v.

(账目、价格等)虚报
salt an account
虚报账目
salvage *n.*
海上救助;救险;残值 *v.*(海上)营救
salvage charges
救助费用
salvage company
打捞公司,海难救援公司
salvage of equipment
设备残值
salvage operation
救助作业
salvage value
残值
sample *n.*
样品;试件;试块;标本
sample bidding documents
招标文件范本
sample inspection
抽样检查
sample room
样品室
sampling *n.*
抽样,取样
sampling inspection
抽样检查
sanction *n.*
认可,批准;处罚;制裁,[复]国际制裁 *v.* 批准;认可
sand and aggregate ratio
砂与骨料比
sand and gravel
砂砾石
sand clay
砂质粘土
sand pile
砂桩
sandstone *n.*
砂岩
sandy gravel
砂砾石
sandy soil
砂土
sanitary facilities
卫生设备
sanitary sewer
污水管道
satisfaction *n.*
满意;赔偿;履行义务
satisfy *v.*
使满意;符合;履行;偿还
satisfy liabilities
清偿债务
satisfy oneself
弄清楚
saving *n.*
搭救;节约;[复]储蓄 *a.* 保留的;节约的;储蓄的
saving account
储蓄账户
saving clause
但书;保留条款
saving deposit
储蓄存款
scaffold *n.*
脚手架
scaffold board
脚手板
scale *n.*
尺度;规模;等级;比例(尺);天平
schedule *n.*
计划表;一览表;进度表
schedule commitment
进度承诺
schedule impact analysis
进度影响分析
schedule of activities
作业进度表
schedule of construction
工程进度表
schedule of earthworks
土方工程进度表
schedule of erection works
安装工程进度表
schedule of freight rates

运费一览表
schedule of inspection and testing
检测计划表
schedule of prices
价格表
schedule of rates
单价表
schedule of requirements
(供货)要求一览表
schedule of supplementary information
补充资料表
schedule of values
(工程分项)价值一览表
schedule of works
工程进度表
scheduled completion date
计划完工日期
scheduled date
计划日期
scheduled output
计划产量
scheduled payment
定期付款
scheduled purchasing
计划采购
scheduling of activities
作业进度安排
schematic design phase
方案设计阶段
schematic drawing
示意图
scheme *n*.
计划;方案;规划
scheme design
方案设计,初步设计
scheme drawing
计划图,方案图
scheme of arrangement
(偿债)安排计划
scope *n*.
范围;可能性

scope for negotiation
谈判范围
scope of agreement
协议范围
scope of cover
保险范围,责任范围
scope of execution
执行范围
scope of liability
责任范围
scope of services
服务范围
scope of supply by contractor
承包商供货范围
scope of supply by owner
业主供货范围
scope of tender designs
招标设计范围
scope of work
工作范围
scope of work claim
工程范围变更索赔
scoring model method
评分比较法
scrap value
残值
scraper *n*.
铲运机;刮泥板
screening *n*.
筛分
screening aggregate
筛分骨料
screening machine
筛分机
screening of projects
项目的筛选
scrip *n*.
凭证,临时单据;手稿;正本
scrutiny *n*.
仔细审查,详尽研究
sea damage
海损

sea damage terms
海损条款
sea freight
海运费
sea insurance
海运保险
seal n.
印章;图章;印记;止水 v. 盖章;密封;止水
sealed bid instruction
密封的投标指令
sealed bid(tender)
密封投标
sealed contract
正式合同,有签署的合同
sealing n.
密封;盖章
sealing and marking of bids
投标的密封和标志
search light
探照灯
seaworthiness n.
适航性
secondary evidence
辅助证据
secondary meaning of words
(法律)词句的引申义
second-hand equipment
二手设备
seconds n.
次品,二流商品
secrecy n.
保密,机密
secret a.
秘密的,机密的,保密的
secret ledger
秘密分类账,内账
secretary n.
秘书
section n.
部分;区段;部门;剖面;节
section foreman
工段长,领班

section line
剖面线
section manager
部门经理
section steel
型钢
sectional drawing
剖面图
sector n.
部门;扇形
secure v.
使安全,保证;为…担保;获得 a. 安全的
secured liabilities
担保负债
secured loan
有担保的贷款,抵押贷款
security n.
保证,担保;安全,治安;[复]债券,证券;抵押物
security holder
证券持有人
security interest
担保权益,抵押权益
security market
证券市场
security measures
安全措施
security of loan
贷款担保
seepage n.
渗流
seepage prevention
防渗
seizure n.
没收,依法占有
selected a.
挑选出来的,精选的
selected bidder(tenderer)
入选的投标人
selected bidding(tendering)
选择性招标,邀请招标
selection criteria

选择标准
selection of a bid（tender）
对投标的选择
selective bidding（tendering）
选择性招标
self-esteem
自尊
self-finance *v.*
自筹资金
self-insurance *n.*
自我保险
seller's market
卖方市场
selling agent
销售代理商
selling agreement
销售协定
selling cost
销售费用
selling price
销售价
semi-finished goods
半成品
semi-skilled labour
半熟练工
sender *n.*
发货人
senior accountant
高级会计师
senior consultant
资深咨询专家
senior creditor
优先债权人
senior development officer
高级项目开发官员
senior engineer
高级工程师
senior partner
主要合伙人；大股东
sense of claims
索赔意识
sense of contract
合同意识
sense of risks
风险意识
sensibility analysis
敏感性分析
sentence *n. v.*
判决，宣判
separate contract
分项发包合同，分段发包合同
separate contractor
独立承包商
separate legal entity
独立法人
separated joint venture
松散型联营体
separation pay
遣散费；离职补偿金
separator *n.*
分选机
sequential construction approach
连续生产方式
sequester *v.*
查封，扣押
serial number
序列号，编号
serial tender
系列招标
servant *n.*
雇工，受雇人
service *n.*
劳务；行政部门；公共设施；维修，保养 *v.* 检修
service agreement
服务协议书
service capacity method of depreciation
定率递减折旧法
service charge
劳务费，服务费
service contract
劳务合同，服务合同
service lease

服务性租赁
service life
(机械等的)使用寿命
service output method of depreciation
生产数量折旧法
set-off *n.*
抵消,冲账
setting out
放样,放线
setting strength
凝固强度
setting time
凝固时间
settle *v.*
决定;解决;支付;结算;沉淀;沉陷
settle a bill
结账
settle day
结算日
settlement *n.*
解决;结算;结账;沉淀;沉陷
settlement accounts
结账
settlement by acceptance
承兑结算
settlement by agreement
协商解决
settlement by arbitration
仲裁解决
settlement by negotiation
议付结算
settlement by payment
付款结算
settlement of claim
理赔
settlement of disputes
争议的解决
settlement of exchange
结汇
settlement price
结算价格
settlement terms
支付条款
setup cost
开办费用,生产准备费用
set-up of a project
项目的开办,项目的准备
severability of the contract
合同条款的可分割性
severable contract
可分的合同
several *a.*
分别的,各自的
several liability
各自责任
severe competition
激烈竞争
sewage disposal
污水处理
sewage drain
排污管
sewerage *n.*
下水道工程;污水工程
shadow price
影子价格
shale *n.*
页岩
share *n.*
份额;股票;分配 *v.* 分担,分配
share risks
分担风险
share the price differences
分担差价
shareholder *n.*
股东
shareholder's agreement
股东协议
shareholder's equity
股东权益
shareholder's meeting
股东大会
sheep-foot roller
羊脚辗
sheet *n.*
表格;单子

sheet pile
板桩
sheet-pile retaining wall
板桩式挡土墙
shift *n.*
班；轮班
shift engineer
值班工程师
shift system
轮班工作制
shipment *n.*
装运；船运；船货
shipment advice
装船通知
shipped B/L
已装船提单
shipping *n.*
海运；发货
shipping advice
装船通知单
shipping bill
船货清单
shipping company
船运公司
shipping conference
航运公会，海运公会
shipping documents
装运单据，货运单据
shipping expenses
运输费用
shipping instructions
装船指示
shipping mark
货物标志，货运唛头
shipping note
装船通知
shipping order
装货单
shipping weight
装货重量
shop drawings
施工图；加工图
shopping *n.*
询价采购，采购
shoring *n.*
临时支撑
short bill
短期期票
short lease
短期租赁
short list
短名单，入选名单
short listed firms
列入短名单的公司，候选公司名单
short of exchange
外汇短缺
shortage *n.*
缺乏；不足
shortage of labour
劳力不足
short-term contract
短期合同
short-term credit
短期信贷
short-term debt
短期债务
short-term insurance
短期保险
short-term investment
短期投资
short-term loan
短期贷款
short-term planning
短期计划
shotcrete *n. v.*
喷(浆)混凝土
shotcrete machine
喷浆机
shrinkage *n.*
收缩；收缩量
shrinkage allowance
收缩容许量；损耗容许量
shrinking *n.*
收缩
shrinking joint
收缩缝

shuttering n.
模板
sick leave
病假
sick leave pay
病假工资
side conditions
附带条件,限制条件
side ditch
边沟
side view
侧视图
side wall
边墙;岸墙
sidewalk n.
人行道
sieving n.
筛分
sight n.
即期 a. 即期的,见票即付的
sight bill
即期汇票,即期票据
sight draft
即期汇票
sight hole
人孔,检查孔
sight L/C
即期信用证
sight payment credit
即期付款信用证
sight rail
视准轨
sight test
当场检查
sign v.
签字;签订 n. 符号,标志
sign a certificate
签署证书
sign a contract
签署合同
sign for
签收;代签
sign on
签字受雇,签字雇用
sign over
签字移交(财产等)
signatory n.
签署人;签署国 a. 签署的;签约的
signature n.
签名,签字
signed check
记名支票
signed declaration
签署的声明
signer n.
签字人
silo n.
筒;仓;罐
silt n.
淤泥
simple contract
口头合同
simple interest
单利
simplicity n.
简明,简单
simply supported beam
简支梁
single case claim
单项索赔,一事一索赔
single liability
单一责任
single payment
整笔支付
single premium policy
一次付清保险费的保单
single shift
一班(制)
single tax system
单一税制
single tender
单项招标
sinking pump
潜水泵
siphon n.
虹吸;虹吸管

siphon culvert
虹吸涵洞
sister company
姊妹公司
site n.
工地,场地,现场
site accommodation
现场生活设施
site arrangement
工地布置
site clearance
现场清理
site data
现场资料
site diary
工地日志
site engineer
现场工程师
site equipment
工地设备
site exploration
现场勘探
site grading
工地平整,场地平整
site hut
工棚
site inspection
现场勘察
site investigation
现场调查
site laboratory
工地实验室
site management
现场管理
site office
工地办公室
site operations
现场作业
site organization
现场施工组织
site overhead cost
现场管理费
site plan
现场平面图
site planning
总平面设计
site reclamation
场地填筑
site selection investigation
选址查勘
siting n.
选址;选线
sizer n.
分选机
sketch n.
草图
skilled labour
熟练工人,技工
skilled worker
熟练工人
slacking at work
怠工
slag cement
矿渣水泥
slaked lime
熟石灰
slice and package
部分与组合(投标)
sliding price
浮动价格
slip n.
单子;承保条;传票
slip form
滑动模板
slip-form construction
滑模施工
slope protection
护坡
slope stability
边坡稳定性
slope stake
边坡桩
slow assets
呆滞资产
slow down
放慢速度

sluice *n.*
泄水道;水闸

slump *n.*
(价格)暴跌;衰退;塌落度

slump test
塌落度试验

smuggle *v.*
走私

snap check
现场抽查

soar *v.*
(价格)猛涨;大幅度上升

soaring prices
飞涨的物价

social benefit
社会福利

social impact assessing
社会影响评价

social insurance
社会保险

social risks
社会风险

social security
社会保障

soft copy
软件副本

soft currency
软通货

soft foundation
软基,软土基础

soft loan
软贷款,优惠贷款,低息贷款

software *n.*
软件

soil compaction
土的压实

soil conditions
土壤条件

soil investigation
土质调查

soil moisture
土壤含水量

soil moisture content
土壤含水量

soil pressure
土压力

soil sample
土样

sole *a.*
单独的,唯一的

sole agent
独家代理人,唯一代理人

sole arbitrator
独任仲裁员

sole discretion
全权处理,单独酌处权

sole distributor
独家经销商

solicited technical alternative
要求的技术备选方案

solicitor *n.*
初级律师

solvency *n.*
偿债能力,支付能力

sound arriving value
到达地完好货价

sound -deadening material
消声材料

sound insulation
隔声

source *n.*
来源,根源

source document
原始凭证

source of funds
资金来源

space frame work
空间框架

space lattice
空间网架

spacing of pile
桩距
span *n*.
跨度
spare parts
备件
special conditions of contract
专用合同条件
special contractor
专业承包商
special discount
特别折扣
Special Drawing Rights (SDRs)
特别提款权
special economic zone
经济特区
special endorsement
记名背书
special inspection
特别检查
special journal
特种日记账
special preference
(关税等)特惠
special provisions
特殊条款,特别规定
special risks
特殊风险
special surtax
特别附加税
specialist *n*.
专家;专门人员
specialist contractor
专业承包商
specialist services
专业服务
specialty *n*.
特长;特殊产品
specific identification method
个别计价法;个别辨认法
specification *n*.
规范,规程;规格;明细单
specification compliance form
规格响应表
specified date
规定日期,指定日期
specified provisional sums
指定的暂定金额
specify *v*.
指定;详细说明;把…列入清单
specimen *n*.
样本,样品;试件
specimen of L/C
信用证样本
specimen of letter of guarantee
保函样本
specimen signature
签字样本
speculation *n*.
投机
speculative risk
投机风险
speculator *n*.
投机商
speed-up construction
加速施工
spending authority
开支权限
spillway *n*.
溢洪道
spoil area
弃土场,废渣厂
spoiled product (goods)
次品,废品
sponsor *n*.
主办人,发起人;出资人;保证人 *v*. 发起;赞助
spot *n*.
现货;地点,场所 *a*. 现付的;现场的
spot cash
现款;货到付款
spot check
现场抽查
spot exchange rate
即期汇率
spot exchange transaction

现汇交易,即期外汇买卖
spot inspection
现场检查
spot payment
现付
spot price
现货价格
spot rate
现汇汇率
spot repair
现场修理
spot test
现场测试,抽查
spot transaction
现货交易,现货业务
spray gun
喷枪
spraying car
洒水车
spreading the risk
分摊风险,分散风险
sprinkler system
喷水消防系统
staff *n*.
职员,工作人员
staff executive
职能部门主管人员,高级职员
staff manager
人事经理
staff regulations
工作人员条例
stage of completion
完工阶段
stage payment
阶段付款
staircase *n*.
楼梯
stale *a*.
过期的;失去时效的
stale B/L
过期提单
stale check
过期支票

stale policy
过期保险单
stamp *n*.
印花;邮票;印章
stamp duty（tax）
印花税
stance *n*.
姿态,立场
standard *n*.
标准;规格;定额 *a*. 标准的
standard agreement
标准协议书
Standard Bidding Documents for Works（SBDW）
（世行的）标准工程招标文件
standard clause
标准条款
standard contract
标准合同
standard cost
标准成本
standard design
标准设计
standard labour hour（time）
标准人工工时,人工工时定额
standard labour rate
标准工资率
standard machine hour（time）
标准机械工时,机械工时定额
standard of conduct
行为准则
standard of construction
施工标准
standard operation procedures（SOP）
标准操作程序
standardization *n*.
标准化
standby *n*.
备用品;后备人员 *a*. 备用的,预备的
standby cost
休闲维持成本,备用成本
standby equipment

备用设备,闲置设备
standby L/C
备用信用证
standby power source
备用电源
standing *a.*
长期的;常设的;不再运转的 *n.* 状况;地位
standing director
常务董事
standing order
长期定单
standing permit
长期许可证
start up
起动,开办
starting date of contract
合同的生效日期
starting-point *n.*
起始点(日),起算日(日)
start-up of a project
项目的开工
state *n.*
状态;情形;国家;政府 *v.* 规定;声明;陈述
state enterprise
国营企业
state investment
政府投资
statement *n.*
财务报表;报表;声明;陈述
statement at completion
竣工报表
statement of account
账单,结算单
statement of assets and liabilities
资产负债表
statement of cash flow
现金流量表
statement of claim
索赔清单;索赔报告
statement of dishonour
拒付声明

statement of expenses
费用清单
statement of financial position
财务状况表
statement of intention
意向书
statement of liquidation
破产清算书
statement of operation
营业报表
statement of profit and loss
损益表
state-owned enterprise
国有企业
statistics *n.*
统计,统计数字;统计资料
status of a project
工程状况
statute *n.*
法令;法定;章程,条例
statutory duty
法定义务
statutory instruments
法定文件
statutory representative
法定代表
statutory right
法定权利
statutory tax rate
法定税率
steam curing
蒸汽养护
steel bender
弯钢筋机
steel pipe pile
钢管桩
steel sheet pile
钢板桩
steel tape
钢卷尺
step *n.*
步骤;措施,手段;台阶
step cost

阶梯成本,步增成本
step-down substation
降压变电站
step-up substation
升压变电站
stilling basin
消力池
stipulate *v.*
规定,预定
stipulated price contract
约定价格合同
stipulated sum
约定金额
stipulated sum contract
约定金额合同
stock *n.*
储备,存货,库存;股票,证券
stock capital
股本,股份
stock exchange index
证券交易所指数
stock in hand
现有存货
stock ledger
存货分类账;股东分户账
stock market
股票市场
stock pile area
堆料场
stock premium
股票溢价
stock requisition
领料单,领货单
stockholder's equity
股东权益
stocking *n.*
库存盘点
stockout *n.*
存货短缺,库存中断
stockout cost
缺料成本;缺货成本
stockpile *n.*
储存,储备;堆料场

stocktaking *n.*
盘存
stone crusher(breaker)
碎石机
stonework *n.*
石方工程;砌石工程
stop clause
终止合同的条款
stoppage *n.*
停止,中止;扣留;罢工
stoppage in transit
(卖方)中途停运权;停止运货
storage *n.*
保管;存储;仓库
storage battery car
电瓶车
storage bin
储料仓
storage charge (cost)
仓储费
storage tank
储水池
storage yard
货场
store *v.*
储存 *n.* 仓库;[复]备用品
store house
仓库,货栈
stores requisition summary
领料汇总单
straight B/L
记名提单,直接提单
straight line method of depreciation
直线折旧法;平均年限法
straight loan
无担保贷款
straight time
正常工作时间
straight unit rate
纯单价(合同)
straightening machine
(钢筋)整直机
strategy *n.*

战略,策略
strategy stage
决策阶段
strictly confidential
绝密
strike *n. v.*
定下(交易等);罢工
strike a bargain
成交定约
strike an agreement
缔结合同
strikes, riots and civil commotions risks
罢工、暴动和民变险
strong box
保险箱
strong currency
硬通货
structural break
结构断裂
sub-assembly *n.*
配件
sub-borrower *n.*
转借人
sub-clause *n.*
款,子条款
subconsultancy *n.*
咨询分包
sub-consultant *n.*
咨询分包人
sub-consulting *n.*
咨询分包
subcontract *n.*
分包合同 *v.* 分包
subcontract package
分包合同包
sub-contracting *n.*
分包
subcontractor *n.*
分包商,分包人
subgrade *n.*
路基
subject *n.*
主题,标题
subject to
受管辖的,受约束的;以…为条件的;以…为准的,依据
subject to change without notice
(条件或规格的)改变不另通知
subject to contract
以合同为准
subject to damage
易受损
subject to final confirmation
以最后确认为准
subject to prior approval
需经事先批准
subject to prior sale
有权先售;以未售出为准
subject to the law
依照法律,受法律管辖
sublease *v.*
分租,转租
sublet *v.*
转包,分包
submission *n.*
提交,呈交;建议
submission of bid (tender)
投标
submit *v.*
提交,呈送;建议
submittal *n.*
建议;提交(文件)
submortgage *n.*
转押;分押;再抵押
sub-project *n.*
子项目,子工程
subrogation *n.*
权利转让;代位权
subscription *n.*
预定;预约金;会费;捐款
subsequent event
随后发生的事项,后续事件
subsidence *n.*
沉陷
subsidiary *n.*

subsidiary 子公司;附属机构 *a.* 附属的;次要的
subsidiary account 辅助账户
subsidiary company 子公司,分公司
subsidiary ledger 明细分类账
subsidiary loan agreement 附属贷款协议
subsidiary record 辅助记录,明细记录
subsidiary work 附属工程
subsidy *n.* 津贴,补助金;奖金
subsistence allowance 生活补贴
sub-stage *n.* 子阶段
substantial *a.* 实际上的,实质的,基本的
substantial completion 实质性竣工,基本完工
substantiate *v.* 证明,证实;(控诉、陈述)有根据
substantiation of claim 索赔证明
substantiator *n.* 证人
substantive provision 实质性规定
substation *n.* 变电站
substitute *n.* 替代人 *v.* 替代
substitution *n.* 替代,替换
substructure *n.* 地下结构
sub-subcontracting *n.* 再次分包,三包
sub-subcontractor *n.* 三包商

sub-supplier *n.* 分包供应商,分包供货人
sub-surface *a.* 地表面下的;水面下的 *n.* 地下部分
sub-surface condition 地表下的条件
subtenant *n.* 转租人
successful bidder (tenderer) 中标者
successor *n.* 继承人,继任者
sue *v.* 起诉
sufficiency *n.* 充足,足量
sufficiency of contract price 合同价格的充分性
sufficiency of tender 投标书的完备性
suggestion *n.* 建议,意见
suit *n.* 控告,诉讼 *v.* 适合
suitability *n.* 适宜性,合适
sulphate cement 硫酸盐水泥
sum *n.* 金额;总和;总数
sum in words 大写金额
sum insured 投保金额
summary of bill of quantities 工程量清单汇总表
summary of tender 投标报价汇总表
summary schedule 简要进度计划
summary sheets of goods 货品说明综合表
summit talk

最高级别会谈
summons *n.*
传票;传唤
sundry *a.*
各种的,杂的 *n.* [复]杂项;杂费;杂物
sundry expenses
杂项开支
sundry revenue
杂项收入
sunk *v.*
沉没
super profit
超额利润
superintendence *n.*
监督;主管;指挥
superintendent *n.*
主管人;指挥者;监督人,监工
superintending staff
管理人员
supersede *v.*
替代,取代;比…优先
supervise *v.*
监督,监理;管理
supervising engineer
监理工程师
supervision *n.*
监督,监理;管理
supervisor *n.*
监督者,监理者;管理者
supervisory personnel
监管人员
supplement *n. v.*
补充,增补,追加
supplementary *a.*
补充的
supplementary agreement
补充协议
supplementary budget
追加预算
supplementary costs
附加成本
supplementary information
补充资料
supplementary tax
附加税
supplier *n.*
供应商,供货商
supplier credit
卖方信贷
supply *v.*
供应,供货,提供 *n.* 供应,供货;[复]供应品
supply bond
供货担保
supply of equipment contract
设备供应合同
supply of equipment with erection contract
设备供应和安装合同
supply of personnel
人员的提供,职员的提供
supply price
供货价格
support *n. v.*
支持;证明;支撑
supporting details
具体证明材料,具体证据人
supporting document
证明文件
supporting particulars
具体证明材料,具体证据
supreme court
最高法院
surety *n.*
保证人;担保人;保证,担保;抵押物
surety bond
保证书;担保书;担保债券
surety commission
保证人佣金
surety company
担保公司
suretyship *n.*
担保人身份(或资格)
surface drainage
地表排水,明沟排水

surface finish 表面装修
surface subsidence 地面沉降
surface treatment 表面处理
surplus *n.* 盈余;顺差 *a.* 剩余的;过剩的
surrender *v.* 放弃;交还;退保
surrogate *n.* 代理人;代替品 *v.* 代理;代替
surroundings *n.* 周围(事物),环境
surtax *n.* 附加税
survey *n. v.* 测量;勘察;调查;检查
survey clause 检验条款
survey report 检验报告
surveyor *n.* 测量员,测量师;商检人
surveyor of customs 海关检验人员
surveyor of port 港口检验人员
surveyor of taxes 税务检查员
suspend *v.* 暂停,中止,停工;悬挂
suspend talks 中止谈判
suspense account 暂记账户;待清理账户
suspension *n.* 暂停,中止,停工;悬挂
suspension bridge 悬索桥,吊桥
suspension of contract 中止合同
suspension of disbursements 暂停拨款
suspension of payment 暂停付款
suspension of work 暂时停工
sustain *v.* 遭受;承受;确认,认可
sustainability *n.* 可持续性
swamp *n.* 沼泽
swap *v.* 交换,互换;易货;换汇
swap credits 互惠信贷;相互赊欠
swing shift 中班
switch trade 转手贸易
syndicated loan 辛迪加贷款,银团贷款
system *n.* 系统,体系;制度
system engineering 系统工程
system management 系统管理
system testing 系统测试
systematic risks 系统风险

T

table *n.* 表格;会议;同席人员

table of adjustment data
数据调整表
table of distribution
发文簿,分布表
tabular ledger
多栏分类账
tabulate v.
把…列表,列表显示
tactics n.
策略
tag n.
标签;签条 v. 加标签于…
take delivery
收货;提货
take over
接收,接管;收货;兼并
take over for use
征用
take proceedings
起诉
take stock
盘货,盘存,清点库存
take up
着手,从事,处理;提出;占(时间);付清
take-and-pay agreement
提货即付款协议
take-home pay
实发工资,实得工资
takeoff n.
估量;权衡
take-or-pay agreement
提货与否均需付款协议
taker n.
接受者;买主
taking-over certificate
接收证书;移交证书
talk v. n.
商谈,会谈
tamper n.
打夯机,击实机
tamping n.
捣固,夯实

tangible assets
实物资产,有形资产
tare n.
皮重
tare weight (gross)
皮重,除皮重量
target n.
目标,指标
target cost
目标成本
target cost contract
目标成本合同
target date
目标日期,预定日期
target list
目标名单
target market
目标市场
target price
目标价格
target profit
计划利润,目标利润
tariff n.
关税;关税率;海关税则;价目表
tariff agreement
关税协议
tariff barrier
关税壁垒
tariff ceiling
关税最高限额
tariff preference
关税优惠
tariff protection
关税保护
tariff quota
关税配额
tariff rate
关税率
tariff schedule
关税率表
tariff value
完税价值
task master

工头,监工
tax *n.*
税,税费,税金 *v.* 征税
tax abatement
减税
tax accrued
应计税金,应征税款
tax assessor
估税员,税收评定员
tax avoidance
避税
tax base
征税依据,课税基础
tax burden
税收负担
tax collector
收税员,税务员
tax court
税务法院
tax credit
抵税,税款减免
tax day
纳税日
tax dodger
偷税人
tax dodging
偷税,逃税,漏税
tax evader
逃税人
tax evasion
偷税,逃税
tax exclusion
课税豁免
tax exemption certification
免税证明
tax haven
低税地区,免税港
tax holidays
免税期
tax items
税目
tax law
税法

tax liability
纳税义务
tax loophole
税法漏洞
tax make-up
补税
tax on business
营业税
tax on income
所得税
tax on property
财产税
tax payer
纳税人
tax rate
税率
tax rebate
退税
tax reduction
减税
tax refund
退税
tax relief
减免税
tax return
纳税申报表
tax withholding certificate
预扣税款凭证
tax year
计税年度
taxable *a.*
应纳税的
taxable goods
应纳税货物
taxable income
应纳税收入
taxable person
应纳税人
taxable profit
应纳税利润
taxable salary
应纳税工资
taxation *n.*

征税;税制;纳税
taxation office
税务局
tax-free *a.*
免税的
tax-free profit
免税利润
T-branch pipe
三通管
team spirit
协作精神,团队精神
team work
协作
technical *a.*
专门的,技术性的,工艺的
technical acceptability
技术上的可接受性
technical analysis
技术分析
technical assessment
技术性鉴定
technical assistance
技术援助
technical assistance credit
技术援助信贷
technical assistance fee
技术援助费
technical characteristics
技术特征,技术性能
technical consultancy firm
技术咨询公司
technical consultant
技术咨询顾问
technical data
技术资料,技术数据
technical degree verification
技术水平的鉴定
technical evaluation
技术评价
technical feasibility
技术可行性
technical measures
技术措施

technical mission
技术代表团
technical performance
技术性能
technical proposal
技术建议书
technical regulations
技术规程
technical responsibility
技术责任
technical review and approval
技术审查与批准
technical scrutiny
技术审核
technical services contract
技术服务合同
technical solution
技术方案
technical specifications
技术规范,技术规程
technical standard
技术标准
technical support
技术支持
technical term
术语
technical terms
术语,专门名词
technical total loss
推定全损
technical transfer
技术转让
technician *n.*
技术员,技师
technique *n.*
技术,技巧,技能
technology *n.*
工艺,技术
technology import
技术引进
technology transfer
技术转让
teething trouble

事情开始时暂时的困难
telegraphic *a.*
电报的;电汇的
telegraphic money order
电汇汇款单
telegraphic transfer(T/T)
电汇
telereply *n.*
电复
telex *n.*
电传
temperament *n.*
气质
temperature cracking
温度裂缝
temperature stress
温度应力
temporary *a.*
临时的,暂时的
temporary account
临时性账户
temporary advance
临时预付款;短期垫款
temporary building
临时建筑物
temporary export
临时出口
temporary facilities
临时设施
temporary import
临时进口
temporary investment
短期投资
temporary loan
短期贷款
temporary payment
暂付款项
temporary receipt
临时收据
temporary support
临时支撑
temporary works
临时工程

tenancy *n.*
租赁;租借权
tenancy at will
意愿租赁,不定期租赁
tenant *n.*
承租人,租赁人
tendency of exchange rate
汇率走势
tendency of market
市场趋势
tender *n.*
投标;投标书;提出 *v.* 投标;提交,提出
tender bond
投标担保
tender documents
招标文件
tender dossiers
招标材料,招标文件
tender evidence
出示证据
tender form
投标书格式
tender guarantee
投标保函,投标保证书
tender price
标底;投标价
tender procedures
投标手续
tenderer *n.*
投标人,投标者
tendering conditions
投标条件
tendering party
投标方
tenor *n.*
票据期限
tensile strength
抗拉强度
tentative plan
初步计划,暂定计划
tentative standard
暂行标准

tenure of use
耐用年限,使用年限
term *n*.
期限;结账期
term bill
期票;定期汇票
term credit
定期信用证;定期信贷
term loan agreement
定期贷款协议
term of contract
合同有效期
term of delivery
交货期限
term of lease
租赁期限
term of loan
贷款期
term of service
使用期;保修期
term of validity
有效期
terminal accounts
终结账户
terminal arbitration
最终仲裁
terminal value
终值
terminate *v*.
终止,结束
terminate a contract
解除合同,终止合同
termination *n*.
终止;解雇;到期
termination at the employer's convenience
业主自便的终止
termination by agreement
协议终止合同
termination by frustration
因合同落空而终止
termination by notice
凭事先通知终止合同

termination for default
由于违约而终止
termination notice
终止通知
termination of contract
合同的终止
termination pay
解雇费
terms *n*.
条款,条件
terms and conditions
条款与条件
terms of appointment
委任条款,委任条件
terms of credit
信用证条件
terms of delivery
交货条件
terms of employment
雇用条件;待遇
terms of insurance
保险条件
terms of payment
支付条件
terms of reference(TOR)
授权范围;工作大纲;咨询范围
terms of sale
销售条件
terms of service
使用条件;维修条件
terms of shipment
装运条件
terms of the contract
合同条款
territorial limitation
地区限制
territory *n*.
地域范围
terrorism *n*.
恐怖活动,恐怖主义
test *n*. *v*.
检验;试验;化验
test certificate

test check
检验证书
test check
抽查
test for suitability
合格性检验
test manual
试验手册
test pile
试桩
test run
试运转,试车
test sample
样品,试样
test specimen(piece)
试件,试样
testimonial n.
证明书;鉴定书
testing certificate
检验证书
testing fee
检验费
testing ground
试验现场
text n.
文本;正本
the British System
英制
the Metric System
公制
the U.S. System
美制
theodolite n.
经纬仪
thermal insulation material
保温材料,隔热材料
things mortgaged
抵押品
things personal
动产
things real
不动产
third party
第三方,第三者

third party insurance
第三方保险,第三者责任险
third party liability
第三方责任
third party motor insurance
机动车第三者责任险
third window loan
(世行)第三类贷款业务
third-country currency
第三国货币
this side up
此端向上
three-way pipe
三通管
threshold n.
界限;最低值
thrift account
储蓄账户
through air waybill
空运直达提单
through B/L
联运提单
through freight
直达货运,联运费
throughout ad.
自始至终
throughout risk
全过程风险
through-put contract
(设施,劳务)使用与否均须付款合同
tick n.
记号;信用;赊购
ticket office
售票处
tied aid
限制性援助
tied loan
限制性贷款,附带条件贷款
tie-in clause
搭卖条款,约束条款
tight money policy
紧缩银根政策
tight standard

严格标准
tile *n.*
瓦；铺地砖
tiling *n.*
贴面砖，铺面砖
till money（cash）
备用现金
timber *n.*
木料，木材
timber form
木模板
timber pile
木桩
timber structure
木结构
time bill
期票，定期汇票
time card
记时卡，工时记录卡
time clerk
考勤员
time cost
时间成本，工时成本
time delay
时间延误
time deposit
定期存款
time difference
时差
time distribution
工时分配
time draft
定期汇票
time for bid submission
投标书提交时间
time for completion
竣工时间
time for payment
支付时间
time for tests
检验时间
time keeping
工时记录

time limit
时间限制，时限
time loan
定期贷款
time of delivery
交货期
time of shipment
装运期，装运时间
time payment
定期付款，分期付款
time rate
计时工资率
time report
工时报告单
time sheet
考勤表
time ticket
考勤卡
time value of money
货币时间价值
time wage
计时工资
time zone
时区
timeliness *n.*
及时性
timely delivery
及时交货
tinned plate
白铁皮，马口铁
tip lorry
自卸卡车
title *n.*
所有权；头衔；标题
title deed
契约；地契
title of account
账户名称
title to property
财产所有权
title transfer
产权转移
tolerance *n.*

公差；溢短装限度
toll *n*.
通行税，通行费
toll road
收费道路
tolling agreement
（设施，劳务）使用与否均须付款合同
tone *n*.
行情
tonnage *n*.
运输吨数；吨位（费）
tonnage duty（tax）
吨位税
top executive
最高级主管人员
top management
最高管理部门
top secret
绝密
top slab
顶板
top soil
表层土
top view
俯视图
topographic map
地形图
topographical survey
地形测量
tort *n*.
侵权行为，违法行为
tortfeasor *n*.
违法行为者，侵权行为人
total *n*.
总计 *a*. 总的，总计的
total amount
总额
total assets
资产总额
total cost
总成本，总费用
total float time
总浮动时间，总时差

total income
总收入
total loss
全损
total price
总价
total quality control（TQC）
全面质量管理
total revenue
营业收入总额
tower crane
塔式起重机
toxic *a*.
有毒的；有害的
tractor *n*.
拖拉机；牵引车
trade *n*.
贸易；商业；商务；行业 *v*. 交换，交易
trade agreement
贸易协定；劳资协议
trade balance
贸易平衡
trade barrier
贸易壁垒
trade bill
商业汇票
trade bill of quantities
工种工程量表
trade company
贸易公司
trade contractor
专业工种承包商
trade credit
商业信贷
trade deficit
贸易逆差
trade directories
商贸行名录
trade discount
贸易折扣，商业折扣
trade fair
商品交易会
trade mark

商标
trade mark infringement
侵犯商标权
trade mission
贸易代表团
trade negotiation
贸易谈判
trade off
物物交换;权衡
trade practice
贸易惯例
trade price
批发价
trade relation
贸易关系
trade representative
商务代表
trade restriction
贸易限制
trade secret
商业秘密
trade surplus
贸易顺差
trade terms
贸易术语,贸易条款
trade union
工会
trade usage
贸易惯例
tradesman *n.*
零售商
trading company's qualification
贸易公司的资格
traffic *n.*
交通,运输;运输量
traffic accident
交通事故
traffic capacity
交通运输能力
traffic expenses
运输费
traffic lights
交通信号灯

traffic management
运输管理
traffic plan
运输计划
traffic safety
交通安全
traffic services
运输服务
traffic signing
交通标志
traffic volume
交通量
trailer *n.*
拖车
train *v.*
培训,训练
trainee *n.*
受训人,学员
trainer *n.*
教员
training centre
培训中心
training of local personnel
培训当地人员
training program
培训计划;培训班
transaction *n.*
生意,交易;处理;事务
transaction tax
交易税
transaction value
成交价值
transborder rate
过境运价
transcript *n.*
副本
transfer *n. v.*
转让;转移;汇兑;过户
transfer of technology
技术转让
transfer price
转移价格
transfer risks

转移风险,转嫁风险
transfer voucher
转账凭证
transferable L/C
可转让信用证
transformer *n*.
变压器
tranship *v*.
转船,转运
transhipment bill of lading
转船提单,转运提单
transhipment surcharge
转船附加费
transit *n*.
经过;通行;运输;中转;经纬仪
transit country
过境国
transit duty(dues)
(货物的)过境税,通行税,转口税
transit letter of credit
转口信用证
transit tax
过境税,通行税
transit trade
转口贸易
transit visa
过境签证
translate *v*.
翻译;折换
translation gain or loss
外汇换算损益
translation risk
外币折算风险
transmission *n*.
传输,传递,传送;转移
transmission line
输电线路
transmit *v*.
传输,传递,传送;转移
transnational company
多国公司,跨国公司
transnational corporation
跨国公司

transport *n. v.*
运输,运送
transport fee
运费
transportation *n*.
交通运输
transportation capacity
运输能力
transportation carrier
运输工具,承运人
transportation carrier's claim
运输承运人的索赔
transportation charges
运费
transportation cost
运输费用,运输成本
transportation equipment
运输设备
transportation firm
运输公司
transportation insurance
运输保险
transportation modes
运输方式
transportation planning
运输计划
transverse *a*.
横向的 *n*. 横梁;横轴
traveling expenses
差旅费
traveller's check
旅行支票
treasurer *n*.
司库;财务主管
treasury *n*.
国库;财政部
treasury bill
国库券
treasury board
财政委员会
treatment *n*.
处理;待遇
treaty *n*.

条约,协议
treaty port
通商口岸
trenching machine
挖沟机
trespass *n. v.*
侵入,侵犯
trial *n.*
试用;审理
tribunal *n.*
法庭
triplicate *n.*
一式三份中的一份 *a.* 三倍的;一式三份的
tripod *n.*
三脚架
truck *n.*
货车,卡车
truck crane
汽车式起重机
truck trailer
卡车拖车
trucking equipment
卡车装运设备
truss *n.*
桁架
trussed bridge
桁架桥
trust *n.*
信任;信托 *v.* 信任,相信
trust bank
信托银行
trust company
信托公司
trust fund
信托基金
trust property
信托财产
trust receipt
信托收据
trustee *n.*
受托人,托管人
trustor *n.*
信托人
tunnel *n.*
隧道
tunnel boring machine
隧洞挖掘机
tunnel drill
隧道凿岩机
tunnel excavation
隧道开挖
tunnel lining
隧道衬砌
tunnel support
隧道支撑
tunneling plant
隧道掘进设备
turn down
拒绝
turnkey contract
交钥匙合同
turnkey project
交钥匙工程,交钥匙项目
turnover *n.*
营业额;周转额
twisted steel bar
螺纹钢筋
two-envelope bid system
双层信封投标方式
two-stage bidding
两阶段招标
two-step loan
两步贷款
tying contract
搭卖合同,附有条件的合同
type *n.*
类型;标志;品种
typical data
典型数据
tyre, tire *n.*
轮胎

U

ultimate *a.*
最终的;极限的;根本的 *n.* 极限;顶点
ultimate beneficiary
最终受益人
ultimate customer
最终用户
ultimate liability
根本责任
ultimate loss
最终损失
ultimatum *n.*
最后通牒
ultimatum commitment
最后承诺
umbrella agreement
总协议
umbrella article
总括条款
umbrella cover
伞括保险
umbrella liability insurance
伞式责任保险
UN Development Forum
联合国发展论坛
unabsorbed cost
待摊成本
unacceptable conditions
不能接受的条件
unacceptable date
不能接受的日期
unamortized cost
未摊销成本
unamortized expenses
未分摊费用
unanimous *a.*
全体的;一致的
un-asserted claim
未确定的索赔
unavoidable cost
不可避免成本,固定成本
unbalanced bidding
不平衡投标
unbinding contract
无约束力的合同
uncashed check
未兑现支票
uncertain factor
不确定因素
uncertain return
不确定利润
uncertainty *n.*
不确定性
unclean B/L
不洁提单
uncollectible account
呆账,坏账
uncollectible notes
坏票(不能收款的票据)
unconditional acceptance
无条件承兑
unconditional bank guarantee
无条件银行保函
unconditional discount
无条件折扣
unconditional L/C
无条件信用证
unconfined *a.*
不受限制的;自由的
unconfirmed *a.*
未确定的;未证实的
unconfirmed L/C
不保兑信用证
uncontrollable cost
不可控制成本
uncrossed check
未划线支票
undepreciated value

未贬值价值;未折旧价值
under construction
正在施工
under contract
受合同的约束,依据合同
underdepreciation
折旧不足,折旧过低
underdrain *n.*
地下排水管
undergo *v.*
经历
underground water
地下水
underground works
地下工程
underlease *n.*
转租,转借
underlying company
附属公司;子公司
underlying document
原始凭证
underlying mortgage
优先抵押权
underpayment *n.*
少付
undersell *v.*
廉价出售
undersigned *n.*
(以下)签字人
understanding *n.*
理解,谅解;达成协议
understatement *n.*
低估,少报
understock *n.*
存货不足
undertaking *n.*
保证,许诺;承担
undervaluation *n.*
低估,计价过低
underwater concreting
水下浇灌混凝土
underwater operation
水下作业

underwriter *n.*
保险人;担保人
underwriting *n.*
承保
undesirable *a.*
不受欢迎的;不需要的
undistributed profit
未分配利润
undivided profit
未分配利润
undue *a.*
未到期的;不恰当的
undue debt
未到期债务
undue delay
不适当延误
undue influence
不适当的影响
undue loss
不当损失
undue note
未到期票据
unearned increment
自然增值
unearned profit
非营业利润
unemployment *n.*
失业
unemployment benefit
失业救济金
unemployment rate
失业率
unentitled *a.*
无权利的;无资格的
unequal terms
不平等条款
unescapable cost
不可避免的成本
unexpected accident
意外事故
unexpected expenses
意外开支
unexpired cost

未耗成本
unexpired insurance
未过期保险
unexpired offer
未过期报盘
unfair competition
不公平竞争,不正当竞争
unfavorable balance
逆差
unfilled order
未发货订单
unfinished work
未完成工作;半成品
unforeseeable *a.*
不可预见的
unforeseeable conditions
难以预见的情况
unforeseeable event
不可预见的事件
unforeseen expenses
意外开支
unforeseen site conditions
未能预见的现场条件
unforeseen work
不可预见的工作
unfulfilled obligation
未履行的义务
uniform *a.*
统一的,一致的;均匀的
uniform customs
统一惯例
uniform invoice
统一发票
unilateral *a.*
单方面的,单边的
unilateral contract
单方合约
unilateral denunciation
单方宣告无效,单方废约
unimpeachable *a.*
无懈可击的
unique method
独特的方法

unit *n.*
单位;单元;机组;部件 *a.* 单位的,单元的
unit cost
单位成本
unit labour cost
单位人工成本
unit method of depreciation
计件折旧法
unit of measurement
计量单位
unit price
单价
unit price contract
单价合同
unit profit
单位利润
unit rate
费率;单价
units-of-production of depreciation method
按产量分摊折旧法
universal currency (money)
世界货币
unlawful *a.*
非法的
unlimited competitive open bidding
无限竞争性公开招标
unlimited duration guarantee
非定期保证
unlimited liability
无限责任
unload *v.*
卸货
unloading port
卸货港
unofficial agreement
非正式协议
unpaid interest
未付利息
unpaid liabilities
未偿债务
unpaid wages and salaries

未付薪金
unpledged assets
未抵押资产
unpredictable element
不可预见因素
unpriced bill of quantities
未标价的工程量表
unprofessional operation
违章操作
unreinforced surface
素混凝土面层
unreserved acceptance
无保留验收
unrestricted *a.*
不受限制的
unsecured *a.*
无担保的,无抵押的
unsecured bid
无担保投标
unsecured creditor
无担保债权人
unsecured debt
无担保债务
unsecured loan
无担保贷款
unsettled account
未结算账户
unsigned *a.*
未签字的
unskilled labour
不熟练工人,普工
unsolicited *a.*
未被要求的,自愿的
unsolicited technical alternative
自愿提出的技术备选方案
unsuccessful bidder (tenderer)
未中标者
untied aid
不附带条件的援助
untied loan
不附带条件的贷款
unusual loss
非常损失

unwarranted *a.*
无保证的;不当的
up to date
最新的
updating *n.*
更新
upkeep *n.*
维修费,养护费
upon sight
见票即付
upset price
拍卖底价
urban facilities
城市设施
urgent document
急件
urgent task
紧急任务
usable floor area
(房屋)使用面积
usage *n.*
用途;习惯;惯例
usage of insurance
保险惯例
usance *n.*
远期汇票的期限
usance bill rate
期票贴现率
usance draft
远期汇票
usance L/C
远期信用证
use before taking over
移交前的使用
use of funds
资金运用
use tax
使用税
useful life
耐用年限,使用寿命
user *n.*
用户,使用者
utility *n.*

公用事业;公用设施;实用性
utilization factor
(设备)利用系数

V

vacancy *n.*
空缺;空房
vacancy rate
闲置率
vague *a.*
含糊的,暧昧的
valid *a.*
有效的;有根据的
valid contract
有效合同
valid period
有效期限
validation *n.*
验证;生效
validity *n.*
有效,有效性;合法性
validity of bid (tender)
投标有效性,投标有效期
validity of contract
合同有效性
valuable *a.*
有价值的,贵重的
valuation *n.*
估价,计价
valuation at cost
按成本计价
valuation at lower of cost or market
按成本或市价孰低计价
valuation clause
估价条款
valuation form
货物估价单
valuation of variation
变更的估价
value *n.*
价值;估价 *v.* 评价;定价;重视
value added
附加价值,增值
value analysis
价值分析
value date
计息日,起息日;生效日
value engineering (VE)
价值工程
value of insurance
保险价值
value of machinery
机械设备价值
value-added tax (VAT)
增值税
vandalism *n.*
故意破坏
variable *a.*
可变的
variable budget
变动预算
variable cost
变动成本
variable costing
变动成本计算(法)
variable levy
差价税
variable rate
可变利率
variance *n.*
差异
variation *n.*
变更,变动;差异
variation of price
价格变动
variation of quantity
工程量变更
variation of work
工程变更

variation order
变更命令
varied work
变更的工作
vehicle *n.*
运载工具；车辆；机动车
vehicle insurance
运输车辆保险
vehicle scheduling
车辆调度
vehicle tax
车辆税
vendee *n.*
受货人，买方
vendor *n.*
发货人；卖方，供货商
vendor-furnished *a.*
卖方提供的，售货商提供的
ventilating exhaust system
排气系统
ventilating shaft
通风井
ventilating system
通风系统
ventilation *n.*
通风
venture *v.*
（商业）冒险，投机
venture capital
投机资本
venture investment
风险投资
venue *n.*
地点，现场
verbal *a.*
口头的；语言的
verbal commitment
口头承诺
verbal contract
口头约定，口头合约
verbal error
用词错误
verbal order
口头命令
verbal promise
口头承诺
verbal request
口头申请
verbal translation
直译
verdict *n.*
裁决
verification *n.*
检查，检验；证实
verification of account
核对账目，对账
verify *v.*
核实，证实
version *n.*
文本
vertical *a.*
垂直的，竖直的
vertical bar chart
直方图
vertical joint
垂直缝
vertical section *n.*
垂直断面，竖截面
vest *v.*
授予；给予；归属
vested *a.*
法律规定的；既得的
vested capital
投入资本
vested interests
既得利益
vesting *n.*
归属，让与 *a.* 授权的
vesting instrument
授权文件
vesting notice
委托通知
vesting order
（法院）财产受托命令
veto *n. v.*
否决；禁止

viable *a.*
可行的，有活力的
vibrating roller
震动辗压机
vibrating sieve
振动筛
vibrating-pile driver
震动打桩机
vibrator *n.*
（混凝土）振捣器
vicarious liability
代偿责任
vicarious performance
代位履行
vice chairman
副董事长；副主席
vice minister
副部长
vice president
副总裁，副总经理；副行长
vice versa
[拉]反过来（也是）
vicious circle
恶性循环
vindicate *v.*
辩护
violate *v.*
违反
violate a law
违反法律
violation of contract
违反合同
visa *n. v.*
签证
visaed passport
已签证的护照
visible means
有形财产
visible trade
有形贸易
vitiate *v.*
使无效
void *a.*
无效的 *v.* 使作废，使无效
void contract
无效合同
voidable contract
可撤销的合同
voided check
作废的支票
voided slab
空心板
voidness *n.*
无效，失效
volatile economic conditions
不稳定的经济情况
voltage regulator
稳压器
volume *n.*
产量；容积；体积
volume discount
多买折扣
volume of business
营业额
volume of earthwork
土方工程量
volume of production
生产量
volume-cost-profit analysis
量本利分析
voluntary bankruptcy
自动申请破产
voluntary deductibles
自愿免赔额
voluntary insurance
自愿保险
voluntary liquidation
自愿清偿
vote *n. v.*
表决，投票
vote down
否决
voting right
表决权
vouchee *n.*
被担保者

voucher *n*.
担保人;证件;凭证;收据
voucher check
凭单支票
vouching *n*.
制单,核单
voyage *n*.
航次,航行;行程
vulnerable *a*.
脆弱的,易受责备的

W

wage *n*.
工资,报酬
wage bill
工资总额单
wage ceiling
工资最高限额
wage garnishment
扣发工资
wage incentive
奖励工资
wage index
工资指数
wage level
工资水平;工资标准
wage per hour
小时工资
wage rate
工资标准,工资率
wages for piece work
计件工资
wages income tax
工资所得税
wages payable
应付工资
wages sheet
工资表,工资单
waive *v*.
放弃,不坚持;不起诉
waive one's right
放弃权利
waive right of claim
放弃索赔权
waiver *n*.
自动放弃,弃权;弃权声明书

waiver clause
放弃条款
wall partition
隔墙
war risk
战争险,兵险
war risk insurance
战争保险
warehouse *n*.
仓库,货栈
warehouse book
仓库账簿
warehouse certificate
栈单,仓库凭证
warehouse charges
仓储费用
warehouse cost
仓储成本
warehouse receipt
仓单,仓库收据
warehouse to warehouse clause
仓至仓条款
warehouse-keeper's order
出库通知单
warning line
警戒线
warning mark
警告性标志
warning signal
警告信号
warrant *n*.
支付款凭单,许可证;保证 *v*. 担保;授权
warrant money

保证金
warrant-check
付款凭单
warranty *n.*
保证(书);担保(书);保修;保单
warranty period
保证期;维修期
wastage *n.*
浪费;废料
waste *v.*
浪费;损耗 *n.* 废料 *a.* 浪费的;多余的;无用的
waste disposal
废料处理
wasting assets
递耗资产,耗减资产
water and soil conservation
水土保持
water conservancy
水利
water cure
混凝土水养护
water discharge
排水量;流量
water level
水平面;水位
water loss and soil erosion
水土流失
water power station
水电站
water reservoir
水库
water service
供水
water stop
止水;止水片
water supply
供水
water treatment
水处理
water way
水路;水运
water-borne *a.*
水路运输的
waterproof *a.*
防水的
water-supply system
供水系统
way of payment
支付方式
waybill *n.*
货运单
wayleaves *n.*
道路通行权,通行权
wear and tear
磨损,损耗
wear cost of tyre
轮胎磨损费
wearing parts
损耗部件
weather forecast
气象预报
weather station
气象台
weather working days (WWD)
晴天工作日;适宜工作日
weekly labour report
每周劳务报告
weekly meeting
每周会议
weekly returns
周报表
weekly scheduling
周计划
weekly time distribution
每周工时分配
weekly wages
周工资
weight *n.*
重量;加权,权重
weight coefficient
加权系数
weighted arithmetic average
加权算术平均数
welfare *n.*
福利

welfare benefits
福利费
welfare expenses
福利费用
welfare funds
福利基金
well drilling
钻井
wet density
湿容重
wharf *n.*
码头
wharfage *n.*
码头费
wheel excavator
轮胎式挖掘机
wheel loader
轮胎式装载机
whereas clause
鉴于条款
white lime
熟石灰
wholesale *n.*
批发
wholesale business
批发业;批发业务
wholesale dealer
批发商
wholesale distributor
批发商
wholesale price
批发价
wholesaler *n.*
批发商
wilful misconduct
故意失职
willingness to pay
乐意支付
win *v.*
成功,胜利;取得
win a contract
赢得合同,中标
winch *n.*
绞车
wind up
结束,停业
windfall *n.*
意外收获;横财
windfall loss
意外损失
windfall profit
意外利益;暴利
wing wall
翼墙
winning bidder
得标人
win-win
对双方有利,双赢
win-win project（scenario）
对双方有利的项目（或方案）
wire rope
钢丝绳
with a view to
为了
with full recourse
享有完全追索权
with intent
蓄意
with particular average（WPA）
水渍险;单独海损赔偿
with reference to
参照;关于
with-and-without
有无对比法
withdraw *v.*
撤回;取消;提取
withdraw an offer
收回报价
withdrawal application
提款申请
withdrawal of bid（tender）
撤销投标
withhold *v.*
扣留,扣压;拒绝;阻止;扣款
withhold payment
止付

withholding n.
扣款;扣交
withholding tax
预扣税款;预提税
without prejudice to
不妨害
without recourse
无追索权,不受追索
witness v.
证明 n. 证人;证据;证言
witness an agreement
在协议上签署作证
wording n.
措词
word-of-mouth a.
口头的,口述的
work n.
工作;工程 v. 工作
work abroad
海外工程
work accident
工伤事故
work capacity
工作能力;工作量
work contracting
工程承包
work defect
工程缺陷
work in mid-air
高空作业
work in progress
正在进行的工作;在建工程
work interruption
工作中断
work item
工作单项,单项工程
work norms
劳动定额
work order
工作通知单;任务单
work overtime
加班
work permit
工作许可证
work plan
工作计划
work program
工作计划,工作方案
work report
工作报告
work sheet
工作底稿
work site
工地
workability of concrete
混凝土和易性
worker's insurance
职工保险
working accident
工伤事故
working assets
流动资产;周转资产
working capital
流动资金,周转资金
working condition
工作条件
working day
工作日
working drawings
施工详图;加工图
working efficiency
工作效率
working expenses
经营费用,工作费用
working fund
周转金
working hours
工作时间;工时
working instruction
工作指令
working liabilities
流动负债;营业负债
working papers
工作文件;就业证件
working rules
操作规程

working years
工龄
workload *n.*
工作负荷,工作量
workman *n.*
工人,工匠
workmanship *n.*
工艺,手艺,工作质量
works *n.*
工程;工厂
works statistics
工程统计
workshop *n.*
车间;工厂;工场
world price
世界市场价格
worth *n.*
价值
writ of detention
扣押令
write off
注销
writing *a.*
书面的 *n.* 书写
written agreement
书面协议
written application
书面申请
written approval
书面批准
written authorization
核准书;授权书
written consent
书面同意
written decision
书面裁决;书面决定
written discharge
书面结清单
written document
书面文件
written evidence
书面证据
written notice
书面通知
written request
书面要求
written statement
书面声明,书面报告
written variation order
书面变更命令
written warning
书面警告

X Y Z

xerox copy
复印件
yard *n.*
码;工厂;场地
year book
年鉴
year-end adjustment
年终调整
year-end audit
年终审计
year-end bonus
年终奖
yearly budget
年度预算
yearly installments
按年分期付款
yearly maintenance
年度维修
yield *n.*
产出;产量;收益 *v.* 生产,产出
yield rate
收益率
yielding *a.*
获利的;出产的
zero *n.*
零

zero balance
余额为零
zero defects management
无缺陷管理
zero salvage value
无残值
zip code
[美]邮政编码

zone *n.*
地带,区域
zone price
区域价格
zoning *n.*
区域规划,市区划分
zoning plan
区域划分图

A

安岸按案暗昂

B

拔坝罢白百败班颁搬板版办半伴拌绑包保报暴爆备背倍被本泵比笔币必避臂边编贬便变辨辩标表兵并病拨波玻剥驳泊薄补不布步部簿

C

猜材财裁采参残仓舱操草侧测策叉查差拆掺产铲闸长偿常厂场唱抄超潮车撤沉陈衬成呈承城乘惩程澄迟持尺赤充冲抽筹酬出初除储处触传船串创吹垂锤纯词此次刺从粗促催脆存磋措错

D

搭达打答大呆代带待怠贷单担但弹淡当挡档导倒捣到道得登等低堤敌底抵地递第缔典电垫吊调跌顶订定东董动冻斗毒渎独镀短断锻堆对兑吨墩趸多

E

讹额恶二

F

发罚法翻繁反返犯范方防妨房放飞非废费分粉份丰风封峰否敷扶服浮符福抚俯辅腐付负附复副覆

G

改盖概干甘赶刚岗钢港杠高告革格隔个各给根跟更工公功供巩拱共贡勾沟钩构购估箍古股骨鼓固故顾雇刮挂关观官管贯惯灌罐光广归规硅贵国过

H

海含涵夯航耗合和核桁横衡红宏洪虹后候呼忽弧互护花滑化划坏还环缓换恢回汇会贿毁混豁活火或货获

J

击机积基激及级即极急集计记纪技既继寄加夹家价假坚间兼监减检简见建健鉴将僵讲奖降交浇胶角绞矫脚搅缴较阶接节结截解介界借金津仅紧尽近进禁经精井警净竞境窘纠酒救就居局举矩巨拒具据聚捐卷决绝君均竣

K

卡开刊勘看抗考苛可客课肯空恐控口扣库夸跨块快宽款旷矿框亏捆困扩

L

垃拉来栏蓝缆滥浪劳乐雷类累冷离礼里理力历立利沥例隶砾连联廉良梁两谅量列劣裂邻临零领流留琉硫龙垄楼漏录陆路旅履律绿卵乱略伦轮论螺裸落

M

麻马码埋买卖满毛矛锚铆冒贸没媒每美门猛弥秘密免面描灭民敏名明命模磨抹默母木目

N

纳耐难内能泥逆年碾捏凝努挪诺

O

欧偶

P

拍排牌派盘判旁抛陪培赔配喷膨碰批皮毗疲匹片偏票频品聘平评
　凭迫破剖铺普

Q

期欺歧企启起气弃汽契砌器千迁牵签前钳潜遣谴欠强抢桥巧切亲
　侵勤清情晴请求区驱渠取圈全权劝缺确群

R

燃壤让扰热人认任日荣容融柔入软润

S

洒三伞散丧扫杀砂筛晒山删扇善膳伤商赏上尚少赊设社涉申伸身
　审渗升生声胜省剩失施湿石时识实使始世市示事视试饰适释誓
　收手首受售授书疏输赎熟署术树竖数衰双水税顺说司私死松诉
　素速塑随碎隧损缩所索

T

塌塔台太贪摊谈探逃陶讨套特梯提体替天添填挑条贴铁听停通同
　统筒偷头投透图涂土团推退托拖脱妥

W

挖蛙瓦歪外弯完玩挽万网往旺危微为围违唯维伪尾纬委卫未位温
　文稳问窝圬污屋诬无舞物误

X

吸息习系细狭下先纤闲现线限宪陷相香箱详享响向项象削消萧销
　小效校协斜泄卸懈辛新薪信兴刑行形型性休修虚需许序叙续蓄
　宣悬选学询循训迅

Y

压押烟延严言岩研掩验堰扬羊养氧样邀遥要野业页夜液一医依仪移遗疑乙已以义议异抑译易意溢翼因银引隐印应英盈营赢影硬佣拥永用优由邮油游友有淤余娱逾与预遇原援远约月越允运

Z

杂灾载再在暂赞遭凿责增赠诈炸摘债粘展占战栈章涨账障招找沼召照折真振震争征蒸整正证政支知执直值职止纸指制治质智滞置中终种仲重周轴昼逐主住助注贮驻筑抓专砖转赚桩装状追准酌着仔咨姿资子姊字自综总纵走租足阻组钻最罪遵作

A

安排
arrange, arrangement, dispose
安排计划
scheme of arrangement
安全
safety, security
安全存货
buffer stock
安全措施
safety measure, protective measure, accident prevention, security measure
安全岛
refuge, safety island
安全的
safe, secure
安全灯
jack lamp
安全工作条件
safe working conditions
安全护栏
safety fence
安全计划费用
cost of safety program
安全检查
safety inspection
安全帽
safety helmet, hardhat
安全门
emergency door
安全系数
safety factor
安全预防措施
safety precaution
安全制动器
safety brake
安全装卸
safe handling
安全装置
safety controls, safety installation
安置
install, installation, establish
安装
install, installation, fix erection, mounting
安装费
installation fee, erection cost
安装工程
erection works
安装工程进度表
schedule of erection works
安装工程一切险
erection all risks (EAR)
安装工作量曲线
quantity installation curves
安装架
mounting rack
安装图
assembly drawing, installation diagram, mounting drawing
安装资料
erection information
岸墙
side wall
按比例的
pro-rate
按比例分摊
prorate distribution
按产量分摊折旧法
units-of-production of depreciation method
按成本或市价孰低计价
at the lower of cost or market
按成本计价
valuation at cost
按成果付酬工资制
payment-by-results
按份额

by share
按固定价格付款
payment on fixed price basis, pay at fixed price
按揭
mortgage
按揭人
mortgagor
按面值
at par
按年分期付款
yearly installments
按年计
per annum
按人计算
capitation
按日计
per diem
按日计息贷款
day loan
按容积配合
proportioning by volume
按市价
at market
按体积
by measurement, by volume
按物价水平调整的报表
price-level-adjusted statement
按预定计划
on a schedule
按月计算的
monthly
按月支付
monthly payment
按照
comply with, in compliance with
按照合同
by contract, in accordance with the contract
按重量配合
proportioning by weight
案例
case
暗管
buried pipe
暗示
imply, implication
昂贵的
dear, expensive

B

拔桩机
pile extractor
坝
dam, barrage
坝顶
crest
罢工
strike, stoppage
罢工、暴动和民变险
strikes, riots and civil commotions risks
白班
day shift
白天
day-time
白铁皮
galvanized iron, tinned plate
百分比
percent
百分率
percentage
败诉
losing a suit, defeated suit
败诉方
defeated party, losing party
班
shift
班轮

liner
班轮公会运价
conference rate
班轮条件租赁
berth charter
班轮运输
liner transport
颁布
publish, issue, issuance
颁发
issue
颁发招标文件
issue bidding documents
搬迁
remove, removal
搬迁安置费用
relocation settlement costs
搬迁费
moving expenses
搬运费
handling charges, handling expenses, removal expenses
板英尺
board foot
板桩
pile sheet, sheet pile
板桩式挡土墙
sheet-pile retaining wall
版权
copyright
办公费
expenses for administration, office expenses
办公时间
office hours
办公室
office
办公室管理费
office overhead costs
办理保险
insure, take out insurance, arrange insurance
办事处

office
办事员
clerk, officer
半成品
half finished goods, semi-finished goods
半官方的
quasi-official
半熟练工
semi-skilled labour
伴随的
incidental
拌合比
mixture ratio
拌合机
mixer
绑扎钢筋
assembling reinforcement
包
bale, package
包干酬金
lump sum remuneration
包干工作
lump work
包干价
lump sum
包干项
lump sum items
包工
lump work
包工包料合同
contract for labour and materials
包工合同
contract for work
包裹
package, parcel
包裹单
bill of parcel
包含
include, contain
包括
comprise, cover
包括的

inclusive
包退包换
caveat venitor
包装
pack, packaging, package
包装不良
bad packing
包装成本
packing cost
包装单
packing slip (sheet)
包装费用
package cost
包装容量
bale capacity
包装须知
packing instructions
包装与标记
packing & marking
保本点
break-even point
保本分析
break-even analysis
保本图
break-even chart
保持
keep, maintain, maintenance, preserve, retain
保持价值
maintenance of value
保持有效
remain in force
保存处
deposit
保单
insurance policy, insurance certificate, warranty
保单持有人
policy holder
保兑
confirm, confirmed
保兑信用证
confirmed letter of credit

保兑银行
confirming bank
保付支票
certified check (cheque)
保管
custody, storage
保管费
safe custody charges
保管人
keeper
保函
guarantee, letter of guarantee (L/G)
保函样本
specimen of letter of guarantee
保护
protect, protection
保护措施
protective measure
保护条款
safeguard clause
保护性关税
protection duty
保护主义
protectionism
保留
reserve, reservation, retain, retention
保留的
reserved
保留金
retention money, retention
保留金保函
retention money guarantee
保留条件
proviso
保留条款
saving clause, proviso clause, reservation clause
保密
confidentiality, secrecy, non-disclosure
保密的
confidential, secret

保密条款
confidential clause
保密性
confidentiality
保赔保险条款
protection and indemnity clause
保释
bail, bailment
保释金
bail
保释金保函
bail bond
保释人
bailer, bailor
保税仓库
bonded warehouse, bonded stores
保税港
bonded port
保税货物
bonded goods
保税区
bonded area, free trade zone
保卫
defend, safeguard
保温材料
thermal insulation material
保险
insure, insurance, cover, assurance,
保险标的
object of insurance
保险储备存量
buffer inventory
保险代理人
insurance agent
保险单
insurance policy, policy, certificate of insurance
保险单的解释
construction of policy
保险单据
insurance documents
保险单转让
assignment of policy

保险担保书
guarantee of insurance
保险的
insured
保险的完备性
adequacy of insurance
保险对象
insured object
保险额
insurance amount, sum insured
保险法
law of insurance, insurance law
保险范围
scope of cover, insurance cover (coverage)
保险费
insurance premium, premium
保险费率
insurance rate, rate of premium, premium rate
保险费总额
gross premium
保险风险
insurance risk
保险公司
insurer, insurance company
保险估价
insurance assessment
保险惯例
usage of insurance
保险合同
contract of insurance, insurance contract
保险基金
insurance fund
保险集团
insurance group
保险价值
value of insurance, insured value
保险鉴定人
insurance surveyor
保险金
insurance premium

保险金额
amount of insurance, amount insured
保险客户
insured, policy holder
保险利益
benefit of insurance, insurance interest
保险赔偿
indemnity of insurance
保险凭证
certificate of insurance, insurance certificate
保险期限
insurance period, period of insurance
保险人
insurer, assurer, underwriter
保险事件
insurance incident
保险受益人
assured
保险条件
terms of insurance
保险条款
insurance clauses
保险箱
strong box, safe
保险要素
essence of insurance
保险责任
insurance liability, insured liability
保险责任开始
commencement of cover
保险闸
safety brake
保险证书
certificate of insurance, insurance certificate
保险总额
insured amount, insurance cover
保修
warranty
保修期
term of service, period of warranty

保养
maintenance, service
保障
indemnify, indemnification, insurance
保障条款
safeguard clause
保证
guarantee, ensure, assure, pledge
保证金
earnest money, deposit, warrant money
保证期
guaranty period, guarantee period, warranty period
保证人
guarantor, surety
保证人佣金
surety commission
保证书
guarantee, letter of guarantee, surety bond
保证条款
engagement clause
保证最大价格
guaranteed maximum price
报表
statement, return
报酬
remuneration, fee, pay
报废
retirement
报告式资产负债表
report form of balance sheet
报告书格式
form of report
报关
declare at the customs, apply to the customs, customs declaration
报关程序
procedure of customs
报关代理人
clearing (clearance) agent, customs

报关代理行
agent customs agency
报关单
customs entry, bill of entry
报关费
customs clearing charges (fee)
报关经纪人
customs broker
报关人
declarant
报关行
customs broker
报价
bid, offer, quote
报价单
quotation
报价人
offerer, offeror
报价有效期
offer period
报价最高的投标人
highest bidder
报销
apply for reimbursement
报销费用账
expense account
保障方
indemnifying party
暴跌
slump, break, crash
暴利
windfall profit
暴露
exposure
爆破
blast, explode
爆破材料
explosive
备案
file
备查资料
backup data

备抵
allowance, provision
备抵坏账
allowance for bad debts, reserve for bad debts, provision for bad debts
备抵销货折扣
allowance for sales discount
备抵折旧
reserve for depreciation, provision for depreciation
备件
spare parts
备忘录
memorandum, protocol, aide-memoire
备选的
alternative
备选方案
alternative
备选方案分析
options analysis
备用成本
standby cost
备用的
standby
备用电源
standby power source
备用金
provisional sums
备用品
stores, standby
备用设备
standby equipment
备用现金
till money (cash)
备用信用证
standby L/C
备用资金
expendable fund
背对背信用证
countervailing credit, back-to-back (letter of) credit
背景

background
背景材料
background material
背面
back
背面的
back
背书
endorse, indorse, endorsement, indorsement, back
背书人
endorser, indorser
背书支票
back a check
倍数
multiple
被保风险
insured perils
被保释人
bailee
被保损失
insured loss
被保险财产
insured property
被保险人
insured, assured, insurant
被背书人
endorsee, indorsee
被查封账户
attached account
被担保者
vouchee
被抵押资产
hypothecated assets
被告
accused person, defendant, respondent
被告承认书
cognovit
被共同保险的
co-insured
被豁免的
exempt
被鉴定为合格的
accredited
被接受的风险
accepted risk
被解雇工人工资
discharged workers payroll
被禁止的
illicit
被控告人
accused person
被扣货物
detained goods
被扣押的财产
arrested property
被免除的
exempt
被免除义务者
exempt
被免除债务者
releasee
被迫终止
frustration
被任命人
nominee
被授权方
authorized party, accredited party
被提名人
nominee
被委任的
accredited
被银行退回的支票
bounced cheque
被指定者
nominee
本地的
native, local
本地区内的
internal
本地人
native, local
本国
home country
本国的

domestic, native
本国人
native
本金
principal, corpus
本金支付
principal payment
本利和
compound amount
本量利分析
cost-volume-profit analysis
本票
promissory note, officer's check
本质
essence
泵站
pump station, lift station
比
supersede
比价
relative price
比较财务报表
comparative financial statement
比较资产负债表
comparative balance sheet
比例
proportion
比例尺
proportion scale, scale
比例附加
add-on
比例税率
flat rate
比例运价
add-on
比率
ratio, proportion, rate
笔误
clerical error
币值
monetary value
币值调整因数
currency adjustment factor

币值稳定
monetary stability
必备文件
requisite document
必须遵守的
binding
必要的
prerequisite, requisite
必要条件
prerequisite
避雷针
lightning rod
避免
avoidance
避免双重征税
avoidance of double taxation
避税
tax avoidance
臂式吊车
boom hoist
边墩
abutment
边沟
side ditch
边际
margin
边际成本
marginal cost
边际利润
marginal profit
边际收入
marginal revenue
边际收益
marginal income
边界
boundary
边境交货
delivered at frontier
边坡稳定性
slope stability
边坡桩
slope stake
边墙

side wall
编标
bid preparation
编号
serial number
编号错误
numerical error
编码
coding
编制
formulate, prepare
编制计划
planning
编制预算
compilation of budget
贬值
devaluation, depreciation, decrement
便利
facility
便条
note
变电站
substation
变动
variation
变动成本
variable cost
变动成本计算
variable costing
变动预算
flexible budget, variable budget
变更
vary, variation, change
变更的工作
varied work
变更的估价
valuation of variation
变更命令
variation order, change order, instruction for variation
变更通知
change notice
变更指令
change order
变现
liquidation
变压器
transformer
变质
deterioration
辨别
discriminate, discrimination
辩护
defence, defense, defend
辩护律师
defence counsel
辩护人
advocate, defender, counsel
标本
sample
标称尺寸
nominal dimension
标的(物)
object
标底
base price, tender price
标高
level
标高金
mark-up
标记
mark, label
标价
bid price, pricing
标价的工程量表
priced bill of quantities
标明的价格
labeled price
标牌
brand name
标签
tag, label
标前会议
pre-bid meeting
标识
indication

标题
subject, title, caption
标志
mark, sign
标准
standard, criteria, norm
标准保险费率
manual rates
标准操作程序
standard operation procedures
标准成本
standard cost
标准的
normal, standard
标准工程招标文件
Standard Bidding Documents for Works (SBDW)
标准工时
normal hour
标准工资率
standard labour rate
标准合同
standard contract
标准化
standardization
标准机械工时
standard machine hour (time)
标准人工工时
standard labour hour (time)
标准设计
standard design
标准条款
standard clause
标准协议书
standard agreement
表层土
top soil
表达
expression
表达方式
expression
表格
table, form, sheet

表决
vote
表决权
voting right
表列的
listed
表面处理
surface treatment
表面的
prima facie
表面装修
surface finish
表明
indicate, indication, show
表现
show, performance, manifestation
兵险
war risk
并发条件
conditions concurrent
并行的
parallel, concurrent
病假
sick leave
病假工资
sick leave pay
拨（款）
allocate
拨给（款项等）
appropriate
拨款
appropriation, allocation, allotment
拨款额
amount allocated
拨款通知
allotment advice
波动
fluctuation
玻璃工
glazier
剥夺
deprive, divestiture
剥夺所有权

expropriation
驳不倒的
irrefutable
驳斥
disproof, confute
驳船
barge
驳回
dismiss, ignore, reject
泊位
berth
泊位包租条款
berth clause
薄利
narrow margin
薄膜
membrane
补偿
compensate, compensation, indemnify, indemnity, reimburse, reimbursement
补偿保险
compensation insurance
补偿贸易
compensation trade
补偿条款
compensation terms
补充
complement, supplement
补充的
complementary, supplementary
补充勘测
additional survey
补充协议
supplementary agreement
补充资料
supplementary information
补充资料表
schedule of supplementary information
补发的工资
retroactive pay
补救
remedy, repair, redress
补救办法
method of redress
补救措施
remedial action
补税
tax make-up
补贴
subsidy, allowance, grant
补遗
addendum
补助费
allowance
补助金
subsidy, benefit
不包括
exclude, except
不保兑信用证
unconfirmed L/C
不保事项
exclusion
不变成本
constant cost
不变承诺
firm commitment
不变的
invariable, constant
不成文法
lex non scripta
不承兑期票
dishonor a bill
不承认
disclaimer
不充分的
inadequate
不出庭
default
不带息票据
no-interest-bearing note
不当的
inappropriate, unwarranted
不当损失
undue loss

不得超过的期限
cut-off period
不定期租赁
tenancy at will
不动产
fixed property, real estate, real property, immovables
不动产抵押贷款
loan on actual estate
不动产清册
cadastre
不动产增值
betterment
不动产债权
encumbrance
不法行为
illegal act, delict, barratry
不妨害
without prejudice to
不符的
inconsistent
不符合
discrepancy, noncompliance
不符合合同条件
non-compliance with contractual conditions
不符合技术规范
non-compliance with specifications
不符合要求的投标
non-responsive bid
不附带条件的贷款
untied loan
不附带条件的援助
untied aid
不公开投标
private bidding (tendering)
不公平
unfair, injustice
不公平竞争
unfair competition
不固定的
unfixed, floating, open-ended
不合法的
illegal
不合格
disqualification
不合格的
non-eligible, improper
不合格的工作
condemned work
不合格货物
disqualified goods
不合格来源国
non-eligible country
不活动的
inactive
不记名背书
blank endorsement, endorsement in blank
不记名的
bearer
不记名提单
bearer B/L, open B/L
不记名债券
bearer bond
不坚持
waive, give up
不接受
non-acceptance
不接受报价
decline an offer
不洁提单
dirty bill of lading, foul B/L, unclean B/L
不景气
depression
不可避免的
inevitable, unavoidable
不可避免的成本
unavoidable cost, unescapable cost
不可剥夺的
inalienable
不可撤销的
irrevocable
不可撤销的保函
irrevocable letter of guarantee

不可撤销的跟单信用证
irrevocable documentary (letter of) credit
不可撤销的信用证
irrevocable L/C, irrevocable credit
不可调解的
irreconcilable
不可兑换
inconvertibility
不可兑换性
inconvertibility
不可分割的
indivisible, inalienable
不可分割协议书
non-separation agreement
不可分债务
indivisible obligation
不可否认的
incontestable
不可抗力
force majeure
不可抗力条款
force majeure clause
不可控制成本
uncontrollable cost
不可能履行
impossibility of performance
不可取消的
irrevocable
不可预见的工作
unforeseen work
不可预见的事件
unforeseeable event
不可预见费
contingency cost
不可预见性评估
contingency evaluation
不可预见因素
unpredictable element
不可原谅的拖期
non-excusable delays
不可争辩的
incontestable

不可转让的
non-assignable, non-negotiable
不可转让信用证
non-transferable credit
不理
ignore
不利的
adverse, unfavourable
不利的天气条件
adverse weather conditions
不利条件
disadvantage
不利自然条件
adverse physical conditions
不利自然条件或障碍
adverse physical conditions or obstructions
不履行
failure, breach
不履行付款义务
default of payment
不履行义务
default
不明确
obscurity
不能接受的日期
unacceptable date
不能接受的条件
unacceptable conditions
不能理解的
baffling, puzzling
不能履行
frustration
不能履行的合同
frustrated contract
不能挽回的
irrecoverable
不能自由兑换的货币
inconvertible currency, irredeemable currency
不偏袒的
impartial
不平等

不平等条款
inequality
不平等条款
unequal terms
不平衡(报价)
unbalanced, front loaded
不平衡投标
unbalanced bidding
不歧视待遇
non-discriminatory treatment
不起诉
non prosecution, waive
不起作用的保证
dead security
不弃权
non-waiver
不恰当的
improper, undue
不确定的
uncertain, indeterminate
不确定利润
uncertain return
不确定性
uncertainty
不确定因素
uncertain factor
不胜任
incapability
不胜任的
incompetent
不使用的
inactive
不适当的
improper, inadequate
不适当的影响
undue influence
不适当延误
undue delay
不适用
inapplicable
不受保资产
non-admitted assets
不受欢迎的
undesirable
不受限制的
free, unconfined, unrestricted
不受益条款
not to insure clause
不受追索
without recourse
不熟练工人
unskilled labour
不索取
disclaim
不停产检修
on-line maintenance
不同的现场条件
differing site conditions (D.S.C)
不同意
disagree, disagreement
不完善的
imperfect
不稳定的经济情况
volatile economic conditions
不相关成本
irrelevant cost
不需要的
undesirable
不一致
discrepancy, repugnance
不一致的
inconsistent, discrepant
不予补偿的延误
non-compensable delay
不正常的
abnormal
不正当竞争
unfair competition
不支付期票
dishonor a bill
不执行
non-execution
不主动信托
inactive trust
不足
short, shortage, inadequate, deficient

不足额
deficiency
不足数
deficiency
不遵守
noncompliance
布告
notice, notification
布局
layout
布置图
layout chart
步增成本
step cost
步骤
approaches, step, procedure
部
ministry
部长
minister
部分
section, proportion, portion
部分保险
partial coverage
部分补偿
partial compensation
部分的
partial
部分废除
derogation
部分赔付
partial coverage
部分损失
partial loss
部分支付
partial payment
部件
component, unit
部门
division, department, sector, section
部门服务经理
division services manager
部门间的事务
inter-sectional matters
部门经理
department manager, section manager
部门主会计师
division controller
簿记
bookkeeping
簿记员
bookkeeper

C

猜测
guesstimate
材料
material
材料采购
procurement of materials
材料成本
material cost
材料出库单
material delivered note
材料短缺
lack of materials
材料发放
material release
材料费
material cost
材料供应
material supply
材料购买
materials purchasing
材料合格证
material certification
材料计划
materials planning

材料明细表
material specification
材料签收报告
material receiving report
材料收据
material receipt
材料说明
description of materials
材料退回
return of materials
材料消耗
consumption of material
材料消耗定额
material consumption norm
材料转运
material handling
财产
property, assets
财产保险
property insurance
财产抵押行为
hypothecation, incumbrance
财产扣押
arrestment
财产权
right of property,. property
财产收回
recovery of property
财产受领人
abandonee
财产受托命令
vesting order
财产税
tax on property, property tax
财产所有权
title to property
财产委托(书)
mandate
财产增益税
accession tax
财产转让
conveyance of estate
财产转让契约
deed of assignment
财产租赁权
right to leased property
财力
resources
财团成员
member of consortium
财务报表
financial report, statement
财务报告
financial statement, financial report
财务比率
financial ratio
财务成本
financial cost
财务代理人
fiscal agent
财务担保
financial guarantee
财务的
fiscal, financial
财务费用
financial expenses
财务分析
financial analysis
财务杠杆
financial leverage
财务顾问
financial counsellor (consultant)
财务管理
financial management
财务会计
financial accounting
财务建议书
financial proposal
财务结算
financial settlement
财务能力
financial capacity
财务审计
financial audit
财务审计报表
audited financial statement

财务数据
financial data
财务预测
financial projection
财务预算
financial budget
财务援助
financial aid
财务账目
financial accounts
财务主管
treasurer
财务专员
financial commissioner
财务状况
financial condition, financial position
财务状况变动
changes in financial position
财务状况表
statement of financial position
财务咨询
financial counselling
财务资产
financial assets
财务租赁
financial lease
财政
finance
财政部
treasury, ministry of finance
财政措施
fiscal measures
财政当局
monetary authorities
财政的
fiscal, financial, monetary
财政年度
fiscal year, financial year
财政收入
fiscal revenue
财政收支平衡
balance of revenue and expenditure
财政危机
fiscal crisis
财政委员会
treasury board
财政政策
fiscal policy
财政资源
financial resources
财政资助
financial aid
裁定
determination, rule, award
裁决
adjudication, arbitration, ruling, verdict
裁决规则
adjudication rule
裁决令
adjudication order
裁决人
arbitrator, adjudicator
裁决书
award, arbitral award
采购
purchase, procure, procurement
采购办法
procurement methods
采购包
procurement packages
采购备忘录
purchase memorandum
采购部
purchasing department
采购代理
purchasing agency
采购工作计划及进度报告
procurement schedule & status report
采购计划
procurement program
采购申请单
purchase requisition
采购限制
procurement restraints

采购员
purchasing clerk
采购指南
guidelines for procurement
采纳
adoption
采暖与通风
heating and ventilating
采取交钥匙的形式
on a turnkey basis
采取行动
take action
采石场
quarry
采用
adopt
采用计量支付
payment by measurement
参加
participate, take part in
参加谈判
enter into negotiation
参考
reference, refer
参考点
reference point
参考价格
reference price, price indication
参数
parameter
参与
involve, enter into, participate
参与投标
participate in a tender
参与者
participant, party
参照
with reference to
残余的
residual
残值
remaining value, salvage value, residual value

仓
silo
仓储成本
warehouse cost
仓储费
storage charge (cost), warehouse charges
仓单
manifest, warehouse receipt
仓库
storehouse, warehouse
仓库交货
ex store
仓库交货价
ex-warehouse
仓库凭证
warehouse certificate
仓库收据
warehouse receipt
仓库账簿
warehouse book
仓至仓条款
warehouse to warehouse clause
舱面货物险
on deck risk
舱面交货提单
on deck B/L
舱位包租
berth charter
舱位损失
broken space
操纵
manipulate
操纵投标
bid-rigging
操作
operation
操作费用
operating cost
操作分析
process analysis
操作工
operator

操作规程
job specification, working rules
操作规范
operational specification
操作和维修费用
operation and maintenance cost
操作和维修手册
operation and maintenance manuals
草案
draft, protocol, outline
草稿
draft
草拟
drawing, draft
草签
initial, initialling
草签合同
initial a contract
草图
draft, layout, sketch
侧石
kerb
侧视图
side view
测定
determine, determination
测量
admeasurement, survey, measure, measurement
测量计
gauge
测量日期
date of survey
测量师
surveyor
测量与成本补偿合同
measurement and cost reimbursement contract
测量员
surveyor
测验
examination
测桩
measuring peg
策划
engineering
策略
tactics, policy, strategy
叉管
branch pipe
查封（财产）
close down, attach, attachment, sequester
查询
inquiry, inquire
查阅
refer to, inspect, consult
查阅权
access right
查账
audit, inspection of accounts
查账人
auditor
查账条款
auditing clauses
查账追踪
audit trail
差别
odds, difference
差额
difference
差价
price difference
差价税
variable levy
差旅费
traveling expenses
差异
difference, discrepancy, variance, variation
拆除
demolish, dismantle, dismantlement, pull down
拆除费
demolition cost
拆除工程

demolition works
拆迁
demolition, disassembly, relocation
拆迁成本
removal cost
掺假
adulterate
掺杂
adulterate
产出
yield
产地检验证书
inspection certificate of origin
产地证书
certificate of origin
产量
output, yield, production volume
产量保证
production quantity guarantee
产量折旧法
production method of depreciation
产品
product
产品成本
production cost
产品返销
buy-back of product
产品鉴定证书
product appraisal certificate
产品寿命
life of product
产品税
product tax
产品责任保险
product liability insurance
产品质量保证
product quality guarantee
产权
equity, property right
产权待定
abeyance
产权归属说明书
abstract of title

产权纠纷
property dispute
产权使用费
royalty
产权式合营
equity joint venture
产权所有权
equity ownership
产权所有人
owner of title
产权要求
property claim
产权转移
alienate, title transfer
产权资本
equity capital
产生
produce, generate, generation
产业
industry
产业税
industry tax
产业所有权
domain
铲斗
bucket
铲运机
scraper
阐明
clarify, expound
长度
length
长名单
long list
长期
long term
长期保单
long-term policy
长期保险协议
long-term agreement
长期贷款
long-term loan
长期的

长期定单
standing, permanent; long-term
长期负债
standing order
长期规划
long-term liabilities
长期投资
long-term planning
长期协议
long-term investment
长期许可证
long-run agreement
长期预测
standing permit
长期债权
long-term forecast
长期债务
long-term claim
长期资产
long-term debt, funded debt
长期租赁
long-lived assets
长期租用
long-term lease
偿付
long-term rental
偿付款
pay back, repay
偿付能力
disbursement
偿还
ability to pay
偿还保函
repay, repayment, pay back, reimburse, satisfy
偿还贷款
repayment guarantee
偿还能力
repayment of loan, loan repayment
偿还期
repayment ability
偿还日
repayment period

偿还债务
maturity date
偿清(债务)
refund, pay back debts, liquidation
偿债能力
pay off, extinguish
偿债能力比率
solvency
偿债协议
liquidity ratio
常规
composition
常规试验
convention, custom
常设的
routine test
常务董事
standing
常用贷款
standing director
厂房
evergreen credit
厂家
plant
厂内生产能力
manufacturer
厂商代理人
in-house capacity
厂商发票
manufacturer's agent
厂商证明书
manufacturer's invoice
场地
manufacturer's certificate
场地平整
field, ground, site, yard
场地填筑
site grading
场内经纪商
site reclamation
场所
floor broker
place, spot

唱标价
announced bid price, read-out bid price
抄件
copy, duplicate
超长附加费
overlength charges, long length charges
超出
exceed, excess
超出额
excess
超出法律范围
outside the law
超出法律范围的
preterlegal, extralegal
超出预算
exceed the budget
超大的
oversize
超大体积
oversize
超额保险
over insurance
超额利润
super profit
超额损失再保险
excess of loss reinsurance
超额条款
excess clause
超过
exceed, overrun, outgo
超过面值
above par
超过票面
above par
超填
overfill
超挖
overexcavation, overbreak
超越合同规定的索赔
ex-contractual claims
超载

overload
超重
overweight
超重的
overweight
潮湿
moist, moisture, damp
车(船)队保险单
fleet policy
车祸
road accident
车间
workshop
车辆
vehicle
车辆调度
vehicle scheduling
车辆税
vehicle tax
撤回
withdraw
撤回投标书
bid withdrawal
撤销
cancel, rescind, revoke, abandon
撤销订货单
recall an order
撤销合同
cancellation of a contract, cancel a contract
撤销诉讼
abatement of action
撤销投标
withdrawal of bid (tender)
撤销银行保函
release of bank guarantee
沉淀
deposit, settlement
沉没
sunk
沉陷
subsidence, settlement
沉箱基础

caisson foundation
沉箱桩
caisson pile
陈述
state, statement, representation
衬垫物
liner
成本
cost
成本、保险费、运费加班轮费用(价)
cost, insurance, freight, liner terms (CIF liner terms)
成本、保险费、运费加船舱底交货(价)
cost, insurance, freight, ex-ships hold (CIF ex-ships hold)
成本、保险费、运费加卸货费(价)
cost, insurance, freight, landed terms (CIF landed terms)
成本、保险费、运费加佣金(价)
cost, insurance, freight and commission (CIF and C.)
成本、保险费加运费(价)
cost, insurance and freight (CIF)
成本、数量、利润分析
cost-volume-profit analysis
成本编码
cost code
成本补偿合同
cost reimbursement contract
成本差异
cost variance
成本超支
cost overrun
成本单
cost sheet
成本定率(折旧)法
fixed-percentage-of-cost method (of depreciation)
成本分类细则
cost breakdown detail
成本分摊
cost contribution, cost allocation

成本分摊公式(或准则)
cost-sharing formula
成本分析
cost analysis
成本工程师
cost engineer
成本估算
estimate of cost
成本固定百分比(折旧)法
method of fixed percentage on cost
成本管理
cost control
成本管理员
cost clerk
成本回收
cost recovery
成本会计
cost accounting
成本计算
costing
成本计算的细则与分配
costing details and allocations
成本加成
mark-up
成本加成合同
cost-plus contract
成本加成计价法
cost-plus pricing
成本加酬金合同
cost-plus-fee contract, cost-and-fee contract
成本加定比酬金合同
cost-plus-percentage-fee contract
成本加浮动酬金合同
cost-plus-fluctuating-fee contract
成本加固定酬金合同
cost-plus-fixed-fee contract
成本加奖金合同
cost-plus-incentive-fee contract, cost-plus-award-fee contract
成本加运费(价)
cost and freight (CFR)
成本控制

cost control
成本明细表
cost schedule
成本目标合同
cost target contract
成本现值
present value of cost
成本项目
cost items
成本削减
cost cutting
成本效益分析
cost-benefit analysis (CBA), cost-effective analysis
成本因素
cost factor
成本影响分析
cost impact analysis
成本与承诺费
cost and commitment
成本与承诺费用计划
cost and commitment program
成本预测
cost forecasting
成本预算
cost budgeting
成本账
cost account
成本直接分摊法
direct method of allocation of cost
成本咨询顾问
cost consultant
成功
succeed, success
成交
strike a bargain, conclude a transaction
成交技巧
closing techniques
成交价值
transaction value
成就
achievement
成立
set up, establish, establishment
成立的
established, tenable
成品
finished goods, completed product
成熟的
mature
成套商业单据
commercial set
成套设备
complex set of equipment, complete plant
成套图纸
complete set of drawings
成文法
formal law, written law, lex scripta
成文合同
literal contract
成员资格
membership
呈交
submit, submission
承按人
mortgagee
承包
contracting, by contract, contract
承包单位
contractor
承包工程
project contracting, construction contracting
承包工程一切险
contractor's all risks insurance (C.A.R)
承包商
contractor
承包商带资承包合同
contractor-financed contract
承包商的酬金
contractor's fee
承包商的代表
contractor's representative, repre-

sentative of contractor
承包商的利润
contractor's profit
承包商的设备
contractor's equipment
承包商的设施
contractor's facilities
承包商的停工权利
contractor's entitlement to suspend work
承包商的图纸
contractor's drawings
承包商的许可证
contractor's license
承包商的许诺
contractor's undertaking
承包商的义务
contractor's obligation
承包商的责任
contractor's liability
承包商的职员
contractor's staff
承包商的资格与能力
contractor's capacity and capability
承包商的最高赔偿额
contractor's total maximum liability
承包商供货范围
scope of supply by contractor
承包商联合体
consortium of contractors
承包商联营体
contractor's joint venture
承包商全险保险
contractor's all risks insurance (C.A.R)
承包商融资
contractor's financing
承包商设备保险单
contractor's equipment floater
承包商设备报表
returns of contractor's equipment
承包商违约
contractor's default, default of contractor, breach of contractor
承包商宣誓书
contractor's affidavit
承包商责任保险
contractor's liability insurance
承保
accept insurance, acceptance, insure, underwriting
承保单
cover note, open cover
承保短量险
insurance against loss in weight
承保人
assurer, insurer
承保条
insurance slip
承保险别
coverage
承保协议
binder
承保证明
risk note
承担
bear, undertake
承担法律责任
bear legal liability
承担费用
bear expenses
承担风险
acceptance of risks
承担赔偿责任
honour one's liability
承担义务
commitment
承担义务的能力
capacity for duties
承兑
acceptance, accept, honour
承兑合同
acceptance contract
承兑汇票
acceptance credit, acceptance bill, D/A draft

承兑汇票手续费
acceptance commission
承兑交单
documents against acceptance (D/A)
承兑交货
delivery against acceptance
承兑结算
settlement by acceptance
承兑金额
acceptance amount
承兑票据
acceptance bill
承兑票据登记簿
acceptance register
承兑人
acceptor
承兑商行
accepting house
承兑提示
presentment for acceptance
承兑信用证
acceptance credit, acceptance L/C
承兑银行
acceptance bank, accepting bank
承兑责任
liability for acceptance
承付人
acceptor
承揽工作
contract work
承诺
accept, acceptance, commit, commitment
承诺的交货日期
promised delivery date
承诺费
commitment charge (fee)
承诺付款额
commitment
承诺价值
commitment value
承诺权
commitment authority

承诺人
accepter, acceptor
承诺时限
commitment time
承诺授权书
commitment authorization
承诺文件
commitment document
承诺信
commitment letter
承诺与授予
commitment and award
承认
admit, acknowledge, acknowledgment, admission
承认及执行外国仲裁裁决公约
Convention on the Recognition and Enforcement of Foreign Arbitration Awards
承受
bear, sustain
承受能力
absorptive capacity
承押人
mortgagee
承运人
carrier, haulier, transportation carrier
承运人留置权
carrier's lien
承运人责任保险
carrier's liability insurance
承运人责任的豁免
immunities of the carrier
承载力
bearing capacity
承重墙
bearing wall
承重桩
bearing pile
承租人
lessee, tenant, leaseholder
诚信

good faith
诚信原则
principle of good faith
城市设施
urban facilities
乘积
product
惩罚条款
penalty clause
惩罚性赔偿费
punitive damages
程序
program(me), procedure, proceeding
程序法
procedural law
程序流程图
program flow chart
程序设计
programming
程序图
flow chart
程租
charter by voyage
澄清
clarification, clarify
迟到的付款
late payment
迟到的投标书
late bid
迟索的赔款
belated claim
迟误
laches
持卡人
card holder
持票人
bearer, holder
持续
last, continue
持续的误期
prolonged delay
持续的暂时停工
prolonged suspension
持续时间
duration
持有
hold
持有人
bearer
持证人
holder
尺寸
dimension
尺度
criteria, scale
赤字
deficit, red balance
赤字财政
deficit financing
赤字开支
deficit spending
赤字预算
deficit budget
充分
adequacy
充分协商
due consultation
充足
abundance, sufficiency
充足的供应
adequate supply
冲击
impact
冲突
conflict
冲突法
conflict of laws
冲突法规
conflict rules
冲销
elimination, abatement, charge off, offset
冲账
set-off, off set
重叠

overlap
重订还债期限
debt rescheduling
重复保险
overlapping insurance
重建
reconstruction, rehabilitation
重新筹集资金
refinance
重新估价
revaluation
重新计量
remeasurement
重新评估
re-evaluate
重新确认
reconfirm
重新招标
retender (rebid)
重新证实
reconfirm
重置
replacement
重置成本
replacement cost, reproduction cost
抽查
spot test, test check
抽象报价
abstract quotation
抽象的
abstract
抽样
sampling
抽样方法
method of sampling
抽样检查
sample inspection, sampling inspection
筹备费
preparation expenses
筹措资金
raise funds
筹资
financing, finance
筹资成本
financing cost
酬金
fee, remuneration, reward
酬劳费
charge for trouble
出差津贴
mission allowance
出厂价
factory price, ex-factory price
出厂税
factory tax
出发
departure, depart
出发港
port of departure
出港
clear a port
出港货物结关(单)
port clearance
出港结关
port clearance
出港手续费
outward port charges
出港许可证
clearance permit
出工
attendance
出借人
lender
出境签证
exit-visa
出具收据
receipt
出口
exportation, export
出口报关
declaration for exportation, declaration outwards
出口报关单
export entry, entry outward
出口补贴

export subsidy	出入权
出口单证	right to access
export documents	出示
出口担保	present, production, produce
export bond	出示证据
出口发票	presentation of evidence, tender evidence
export invoice	
出口港	出售
port of exit	sell, sale, dispose, disposal
出口价	出售价格
export price	offered price
出口检验证	出庭
certificate for export	appear in court, presence
出口免税	出席
free export	attendance, presence, present
出口手续	出席的
process of export	present
出口税	出现
export duty, export tax	occurrence, occur
出口限制	出押人
export restriction	mortgagor
出口信贷	出于无知的错误
export credit	ignorant error
出口信用证	出证方
export letter of credit	licenser, licensor
出口许可证	出资人
export license (permit)	sponsor
出口许可证申请书	出租
application for export licence	lease, rental, let
出口银行保函	出租人
export bank guarantee	lessor
出口装船须知	初步的
export shipping instructions	initial, preliminary, prima facie
出库通知单	初步计划
warehouse-keeper's order	tentative plan
出门不换	初步计算
caveat emptor	preliminary computation
出纳员	初步勘测
cashier	preliminary survey
出票后	初步可行性研究
after date	pre-feasibility study, preliminary feasibility study
出票人	
drawer	初步评价

preliminary evaluation
初步设计
preliminary design, scheme design
初步设计图纸
preliminary drawings
初步验收证书
preliminary acceptance certificate
初步预算
preliminary budget
初步证据
prima facie evidence
初次付款
down payment
初级会计师
junior accountant
初级律师
solicitor
初级市场
primary market
初凝时间
initial setting time
初期价格
initial price
初始强度
initial strength
初始应力
initial stress
初始预算
initial budget
除皮重量
tare weight (gross)
除外
except, exception, exclude, exclusion
除外的
exclusive
除外风险
excepted risk
除外条款
exception clause, exclusion clause
除外责任
excluded liability
除外责任条款

exclusion clause
储备
reserve, reservation, stock, stockpile
储备库存量
reserve stock
储存
store, stockpile
储户
depositor
储料仓
storage bin
储水池
storage tank
储蓄
saving
储蓄存款
saving deposit
储蓄的
saving
储蓄账户
saving account, thrift account
处罚
punish, penalty, sanction
处理
handle, dispose, disposal, take up, treatment
处理不当
misconduct
处理权
discretion
处理数据
process data
处置
disposal
处置能力
disposing capacity
触犯法律
break the law, contravene
传递
convey, conveyance, transmit, transmission
传唤

call, summons
传票
summons, subpoena
传输
transmit, transmission
传送
convey, deliver
传送带
belt conveyor
传送设备
conveyor, conveyer
传送系统
conveying system
传真
facsimile (fax)
传真电报
facsimile telegraph
传真发送
facsimile transmission
传真通知
notice by fax
船
ship, boat, craft
船边交货价
free alongside ship (F.A.S)
船边交货提单
alongside bill of lading
船舶保险
hull insurance
船舶费用保险
disbursement insurance
船舶费用条款
disbursement clause
船东自负风险
owner's risk
船方不负担装卸费用
free in and out
船货
cargo, lading, shipment
船货检查员
jerquer
船货清单
shipping bill, manifest

船级社
bureau of shipping
船龄
age of vessel
船上交货
delivered ex ship (DES)
船上交货价
free on board (FOB)
船体保险单
hull policy
船位
berth
船运
shipment
船运公司
shipping company
串通
collusion
串通投标
collusive bid (tender)
创办人
promoter
创利额
contribution margin
创新
innovation
创业者
enterpriser
吹风机
blower
垂直的
vertical
垂直缝
vertical joint
垂直面
vertical section
锤式打桩机
monkey engine
纯保险费
pure premium
纯粹的
absolute, pure
纯粹风险

pure risk
纯单价合同
straight unit rate contract
纯的
clear, net
纯费率
net rate
纯利
net profit
纯利息
pure interest
纯损失
dead loss
词句的引申义
secondary meaning of words
词首的
initial
此端向上
this side up
次进先出法
next-in-first-out method
次品
spoiled product (goods), seconds
次序
order
次要的
secondary, subsidiary
刺激
incentive
从价关税率
ad valorem tariff
从价进口税
ad valorem import duty
从价税
ad valorem duties, ad valorem tax
从价税率
ad valorem rate of duty
从价提单
ad valorem bill of lading
从价运费
ad valorem freight
从事
take up, engage

从属的
dependent, collateral
从属抵押品
collateral
从属损失
consequential damage (loss)
从属债务人
accessory debtor
粗估
guesstimate
促成
contribute
促进
promote
促凝剂
accelerator
促凝外加剂
accelerating admixture
促销
promotion
催促
prompt
催促交货
expedite deliveries
催付
ask for payment
催缴
call, ask for payment
催款单
prompt
催款信
call letter
催债
dun
脆弱的
vulnerable
存储
storage
存储者
depositor
存放
deposit
存货

goods in stock, inventory, stock
存货不足
understock
存货短缺
stockout
存货分类账
stock ledger
存货估价
inventory valuation
存货管理
inventory control
存货盘点表
inventory sheet
存货数据
inventory data
存货允许限度
inventory allowance
存货周转
inventory turnover
存款
deposit
存款单
deposit slip, certificate of deposit
存款利率
deposit rate
存款银行
bank of deposit
磋商
consult, consultation
措辞
wording, expression
措施
measure, step
错误
error, mistake

D

搭救
saving
搭卖合同
tying contract
搭卖条款
tie-in clause
答辩人
respondent
达成
conclude
达成协议
reach an agreement, agree
达到
achieve, obtain
打包
pack
打夯机
ramming machine, tamper
打捞公司
salvage company
打铆钉
rivet
打算
intend
打印副本
hard-copy
打折后的投标价
discounted bid price
打桩
piling
打桩船
pile driver barge
打桩锤
pile hammer
打桩机
pile driver
打桩者
pile driver
大风
gale
大幅度上升
soar

大副收据 mate's receipt
大纲 brief, outline
大股东 senior partner
大火灾 conflagration
大检修 overhaul
大理石 marble
大梁 girder
大量 bulk
大陆法 civil law, continental law
大陆法系 continental law system
大律师 barrister
大批量的 numerous
大写金额 sum in words
大型工程 heavy construction
大型企业 large-scale enterprise
大修费用 cost of overhaul
大样 detailed drawing
大约的 approximate
呆账 bad debt, bad account, dead account
呆滞存货 inactive stock, dead stock
呆滞资本 dead capital
呆滞资产 slow assets
呆滞资金 inactive money
代办 commission
代办人 attorney
代表 representation, representative, delegate
代表(某人) on behalf of
代表权的授予 grant of representation
代表团 delegation, mission
代偿责任 vicarious liability
代购佣金 purchasing commission
代理 act, agency, surrogate
代理存款 escrow deposit
代理费 agency fee
代理公司 agent firm
代理合同 agency contract
代理机构 agency
代理经理 acting manager
代理权 agency, proxy
代理人 agent
代理人侵权行为 agent's tort
代理融通费 factoring charges
代理融通公司

factoring company
代理商
agent
代理商佣金
factorage
代理手续费
agency commission
代理协议
agency agreement
代理行
correspondent bank
代理业
factorage
代理银行
correspondent bank, agent bank
代理佣金
commission, override
代码
code
代签
sign for
代收人
collecting agent
代收银行
collecting bank
代替
replace, substitute, surrogate
代替品
surrogate
代位履行
vicarious performance
代位权
right of subrogation, subrogation
代销行
sales agency
代用材料
replacement material
代运人
forwarder
带奖励的固定价格合同
fixed price contract with incentives
带式装料机
belt loader

带息票据
interest-bearing note
带薪假日
holiday with pay
带薪休假
leave with pay
带薪休假期
paid holiday
待分配利润
retained profit
待检查物品单
bill of sufferance
待结付的补偿
executory consideration
待履行的合同
executory contract
待清理账户
clearing account, suspense account
待摊成本
unabsorbed cost
待用品
backup
待遇
treatment, terms of employment
待运提单
received for shipment B/L
怠工
slacking at work, idle
贷方
creditor, credit side
贷方栏
credit column
贷方余额
credit balance
贷记
credit
贷款
loan, credit
贷款本金
principal amount
贷款本金偿还额
loan principal repayment
贷款财团

loan consortium
贷款偿还期
loan repayment period
贷款担保
security of loan
贷款额
size of the loan
贷款额度
credit line
贷款方
lender
贷款给
lend
贷款利率
loan interest rate, lending rate
贷款利息
interest on loans
贷款期限
lending term, term of loan
贷款条件
lending terms
贷款委员会
loan committee
贷款文件
loan document
贷款限额
loan ceiling
贷款协议
loan agreement
贷项
credit
贷项通知单
credit memorandum (memo), credit note
单边的
unilateral
单纯背书
absolute endorsement
单独的
individual, sole
单独海损
particular average
单独海损不赔偿
free from particular average (FPA)
单独海损赔偿
with particular average (WPA)
单独事项
particulars
单独折旧
individual depreciation
单独酌处权
sole discretion
单方废约
unilateral denunciation
单方合约
unilateral contract
单方面
ex parte
单方面的
unilateral
单方宣告无效
unilateral denunciation
单价
unit rate, unit price, rate
单价表
schedule of rates
单价分析
breakdown of price
单价合同
contract based on unit price, unit price contract
单据
document, voucher
单利
simple interest
单位成本
unit cost
单位利润
unit profit
单位人工成本
unit labour cost
单位容积土壤含水量
moisture density
单项工程
work item
单项工程量清单

activity bill of quantities
单项工作程序
individual job procedure
单项活动
activity
单项索赔
single case claim
单项招标
single tender
单一税制
single tax system
单一责任
single liability
单元
element, unit
单元工程量清单
elemental bill of quantities
单证
certificate, document
单子
slip, sheet, list
担保
bond, guarantee, security, warrant
担保成本
cost of bond
担保承兑
collateral acceptance
担保代理人
bonding agent
担保额度
bonding capacity
担保费率
bonding rate
担保负债
secured liabilities
担保公司
bonding company, surety company
担保能力
bonding capacity
担保品抵押
collateral mortgage
担保权益
security interest

担保人
surety, guarantor, underwriter
担保人身份
suretyship
担保书
warranty, surety bond
担保债券
collateral bond, surety bond
但书
saving clause
弹劾
impeach
弹性汇率
flexible exchange rate
弹性模量
elastic modulus
弹性预算
flexible budget
淡季
dead season, off season
当班
on duty
当场
on the ground
当场检查
sight test, spot check
当地材料
local material
当地承包商
local contractor
当地代理人
local agent
当地的
local
当地法规
local statute
当地工人
local worker, local labour
当地供应商
local supplier
当地购买
local shopping
当地货币

当地价格
local currency
当地价格
local price, price loco
当地开支
local expenditures
当地利率
local interest rate
当地人员
local personnel
当地政府
local government
当局造成的延误
delays caused by authorities
当面谈判
face to face negotiation
当期营业收入
current revenue
当前的
current
当前工资简报
current wage bulletin
当事人
principal, client concerned, client
当事人对当事人
principal to principal
当事人间的相互关系
privity
挡水建筑物
barrage
挡土墙
retaining wall
档案
file
档案资料
file data
导洞
pilot tunnel
导流
diversion
导流渠
diversion channel
倒涵管
dive culvert

倒虹吸管
dive culvert, inverted siphon
倒填日期
antedate, foredate, backdate
倒填日期支票
antedated check
捣固
tamping
到岸成本
landed cost
到岸价格
cost, insurance and freight (CIF)
到岸价格加班轮条件(价)
cost, insurance, freight, liner terms (CIF liner terms)
到岸价格加卸货费(价)
cost, insurance, freight, landed terms (CIF landed terms)
到岸价格加佣金
cost, insurance, freight and commission (CIF and C.)
到岸轮船舱底交货(价)
cost, insurance, freight, ex-ship's hold (CIF ex-ship's hold)
到岸品质
landed quality
到达
arrival, arrive
到达地完好货价
sound arriving value
到达日
date of arrival
到港日期
date of arrival
到货合同
arrival contract
到货品质
arrival quality
到货条件
arrival terms
到货通知
arrival notice, advice of arrival
到货质量

arrival quality
到期
fall due, at maturity
到期的
become (fall) due, due
到期清单
due date checklist
到期日
expiration date, date due
到期未付款
overdue payment
到期应付
due
到期支付
payment in due course
到期值
maturity value
道·琼斯指数
Dow-Jones Index
道德标准
ethical standard
道德风险
moral risk
道德准则
ethics, moral standard
道路
road, way
道路通行权
right of way, wayleaves
道义上的支付
ex gratia payment
道义索赔
ex gratia claim
得标人
winning bidder
登记
register, enter
登记簿
register
登陆
landing
等高线
contour line

等级
classification, grade, scale
等价
par
等同性
equivalency
等效的
equivalent
等值货币
money equivalent
等值货币价值
money's worth
低档的
inferior
低估
underestimate, undervalue, undervaluation
低税地区
tax haven
低息贷款
easy money, cheap credit, soft loan
低息借款
cheap money
低效的
inefficient
低于票面价值
at a discount
堤
dyke
敌对行为
hostilities
底价
bottom price, floor price, base price
底线
base line
抵岸价
landed price
抵补支付款
cover of payment
抵埠通知
arrival notice
抵偿
compensate, cover

抵税
tax credit
抵消
offset, set-off
抵消税
countervailing duty
抵销账户
contra account, offset account
抵押
mortgage, hypothecate, pledge
抵押贷款
mortgage loan, collateral loan, secured loan
抵押贷款人
mortgagee
抵押单
mortgage
抵押借款人
mortgagor
抵押款
mortgage
抵押品
pledge, things mortgaged
抵押凭证
pawn ticket
抵押契约
deed of mortgage
抵押权
lien, mortgage
抵押权益
security interest
抵押人
pledger, mortgagor
抵押条款
mortgage clause
抵押物
pledge, things mortgaged
抵押债券
mortgage bond
抵押证书
memorandum of deposit, letter of hypothecation
抵押资产
hypothecated assets
抵制
boycott, resist, curb
地板
floor
地表排水
surface drainage
地产
landed property, estate
地产信托证
land trust certificate
地带
zone
地点
location
地方长官
commissioner
地方当局
local authority
地方法规
by-law
地方法院
local court
地方税
local tax
地方性的
local
地方杂税
miscellaneous local taxes
地基沉降
foundation settlement
地基处理
ground improvement
地基加固
ground improvement
地脚螺栓
ground bolt, anchor bolt
地理位置
geographic(al) position
地面
ground surface, floor
地面沉降
surface subsidence

地面沉陷
land subsidence
地面高程
ground elevation
地契
land certificate, title deed
地区
area, locality, region
地区差价
regional price differential
地区规划
regional planning
地区限制
territorial limitation
地区性优惠
regional preference
地位
standing position, status
地下工程
underground works
地下结构
substructure
地下排水管
underdrain
地下水
underground water, groundwater
地下水位
groundwater level
地形测量
topographical survey
地形图
topographic map
地役权
easement
地域范围
territory
地震
earthquake
地址
address
地址变更
address modification
地址更正
address correction
地质勘探
geological investigation
地质剖面图
geological profile
地质条件
geological condition
递耗资产
diminishing assets, wasting assets
递减
decrease
递减税
regressive tax
递减折旧
degressive depreciation
递交
deliver, forward
递延保险金
deferred premium
递延成本
deferred cost
递延贷项
deferred credits
递延费用
deferred charges (expenses)
递延负债
deferred liabilities
递延股权
deferred equity
递延借项
deferred debits
递延收入
deferred revenue
递延收益
deferred income
递延资产
deferred assets
递增成本
increasing cost
递增的
progressive
第三方
third party

第三方保险
third party insurance
第三方托管账户
escrow account
第三方责任
third party liability
第三国货币
third-country currency
第三类贷款业务
third window loan
第三者责任险
third party insurance
第一抵押权
first mortgage
第一流的
first-rate
第一手资料
first-hand information
第一损失保险
first loss insurance
第一优先权
first priority
缔结
enter into, conclude, conclusion
缔结和约
conclude a contract
缔结协议
strike an agreement
缔约
conclude a treaty
缔约能力
capacity to contract, competency
典当
pawn
典型数据
typical data
典质
hypothecate
电报
cable
电报的
telegraphic
电厂
power station
电传
telex
电动机
electric motor
电复
telereply
电焊
electric welding
电弧焊机
electric arc welder
电汇
telegraphic transfer(T/T)
电汇的
telegraphic
电汇费率
cable rate
电汇汇款单
telegraphic money order
电力
power
电力工程
power project
电力资源
power resources
电瓶车
storage battery car
电气安装
electrical installation
电气工程师
electrical engineer
电梯
lift, elevator
电梯责任保险
elevator liability insurance
电站
power station
垫付
make advance
垫款
advance
吊车
crane

吊罐
bucket
吊桥
suspension bridge
吊销执照
cancellation of licence
调查
investigation, survey
调查人
inquirer, surveyor
调度
despatch, dispatch
调价公式
price adjustment formula
调价价格
escalation price
调价条款
escalation clause
调节
regulate, regulation
调解
conciliate, conciliation, mediate, mediation, intermediation, reconciliation
调解程序
conciliation procedure
调解及仲裁规则
rules of conciliation and arbitration
调解人
conciliator, mediator
调解委员会
conciliation committee, commission of conciliation
调试
commissioning
调试前的准备
precommissioning
调停
mediate, mediation
调整
adjust, adjustment, consolidate
调整后价格
adjusted price
调整后试算表
adjusted trial balance
调整后银行余额
adjusted bank balance
调整后账面余额
adjusted book balance
调整进度表
revise a schedule
调值总价合同
escalation lump sum contract
跌价
beat down
顶板
top slab
顶管法
pipe jacking method
订购
place an order
订合同
enter into a contract
订货
order, place an order, indent
订货单
order, order sheet, indent
订货单格式
order form
订货档案
order file
订货费用
ordering cost
订货付现
cash with order
订货合同
purchase contract, ordering contract, contract for goods
订货卷宗
order file
订货量
order quantity
订货人
orderer
订立合同
conclude a contract, enter into a con-

tract with
订约人
contractor, promisor, contracting party
定单
purchase order
定单积压
backlog
定额
quota, standard, norm
定额备用金
imprest fund
定额备用现金
imprest cash
定额备用制
imprest system
定额拨款
definite appropriation
定额投资基金
closed-end investment fund
定价
pricing, price, value
定金
down payment, earnest money, purchase money
定金保函
down payment guarantee
定量
quantification
定量分析
quantitative analysis
定律
law
定率递减折旧法
fixed-percentage-on-declining-balance method, service capacity method of depreciation
定期保函
limited duration guarantee
定期保险
regular insurance
定期报告
periodic report
定期测量
periodic measurement
定期存款
time deposit, term deposit
定期贷款
time loan, term loan
定期贷款协议
term loan agreement
定期付款
scheduledpayment, time payment, periodic payment
定期合同
fixed-term contract
定期汇票
date draft, time draft, time bill, term bill
定期会议
periodic meeting
定期检查
routine inspection, periodic inspection
定期交付的利息
gale
定期交付的租金
gale
定期盘存
periodic inventory
定期票据
day bill
定期信贷
term credit
定期信用证
term credit
定期支付
regular payment
定线
alignment
定义
definition
东道国
host country
东道国政府
host government

董事
director
董事长
chairman, chairman of the board
董事会
board of directors, board
董事会会议
board meeting
董事会主席
board chairman
动产
movable property, chattel, personal property
动产抵押
chattel mortgage
动机
motive, intention
动力车间
power house (plant)
动力电缆
power cable
动力切断
power cut
动员
mobilize, mobilization
动员费
mobilization charges
动员预付款
mobilization advance
冻结
freeze
冻结存款
blocked deposit
冻结货币
blocked currency
冻结账户
blocked account, frozen account
冻结资产
frozen assets
冻结资金
blocked fund
斗式提升机
belt-bucket elevator

斗式装载机
bucket loader
毒品
drug
渎职
malfeasance, dereliction of duty
渎职罪
offence of dereliction of duty, misconduct offense
独家代理
exclusive agency, sole agency
独家代理人
exclusive agent, sole agent
独家经销
exclusive distribution
独家经销商
exclusive dealer, sole distributor
独家销售代理商
exclusive selling agent
独家专利权
exclusive patent right
独立保险人
independent insurer
独立承包商
independent contractor, separate contractor
独立代理人
independent agent
独立的
independent
独立订约人
independent contractor
独立法人
separate legal entity
独立工程师
independent engineer
独立会计师
independent accountant
独立理赔人
independent claim settling clerk
独立一方
independent party
独任仲裁员

sole arbitrator
独特的方法
unique method
独销市场
exclusive market
独有的
exclusive
独占许可证
exclusive licence
独资
individual proprietorship
独资企业
solely foreign-owned enterprise, enterprise owned by sole investor
镀锌铁皮
galvanized iron
镀锌铁丝
galvanized iron wire
短量险
risk of shortage
短名单
short list
短期保险
short-term insurance
短期贷款
short-term loan, temporary loan
短期垫款
temporary advance
短期放款
money at call
短期合同
short-term contract
短期计划
short-term planning
短期流动资金
hot money
短期期票
short bill
短期同行拆借
money at call, call loan
短期投资
short-term investment, temporary investment, current investment
短期信贷
short-term credit
短期银行贷款
current loan
短期债务
current debt, current liabilities, floating debt, short-term debt
短期租赁
short lease
短溢装条款
allowance clause, more or less clause (M/L clause)
断层
fault
断流器
circuit breaker
断路开关
circuit breaker
断面
cross section
断言
assertion
锻造
forge
堆料场
stock pile area, stockpile
堆石坝
rock-fill dam
对比
contrast
对策
countermeasure
对承包商违约的反索赔
counterclaim for contractor's defaults
对等的
reciprocal
对等贸易
countertrade
对工程的损害
damage to works
对国内承包商的优惠
preference for domestic contractors
对国内制造商的优惠

preference for domestic manufacturers
对价
consideration
对开信用证
reciprocal L/C
对开账户
back-to-back account
对立
antagonism, opposition
对立的
opposed, opposite
对施工缺陷的反索赔
counterclaim for remedying defaults
对手
opponent, rival
对双方有利的方案
win-win scenario
对投标的选择
selection of a bid (tender)
对外的
external, foreign
对外贸易
foreign trade
对外事务
external affairs
对物税
objective tax
对象
object
对业主的合同承诺
contractual commitments with the client
对账
verification of account
对账单
bank statement
兑换
exchange, convert, conversion
兑换价格
conversion price
兑换率
conversion rate, exchange rate, rate of exchange
兑现
cash
吨位（费）
tonnage
吨位税
tonnage duty (tax)
墩
pier
趸船
warfboat, pontoon, landing stage
多倍的
multiple
多边的
multilateral
多边合同
multilateral contract
多边合作
multilateral cooperation
多边结算
multilateral settlement
多边贸易
multilateral trade
多边清算
multilateral clearing
多边税收协定
multilateral tariff treaty
多边协定
multilateral agreement
多边援助
multilateral aid
多方仲裁
multi-party arbitration
多国参加的
multilateral
多国的
multinational
多国公司
multinational company (MNC), transnational company
多国企业
multinational enterprises (MNE)
多栏分类账

tabular ledger
多买折扣
volume discount
多数裁定原则
majority rule
多险种保险
multiple line insurance
多项的
multiple

多选择的融资安排
multiple options funding facility
多余的
surplus, unnecessary
多种风险保险
multiple perils insurance
多重关税制
multiple tariff system

E

讹传
misrepresentation
额定的
nominal
额定利率
nominal interest rate
额外成本
extra cost
额外的
extra, additional
额外费用
extra cost
额外费用索赔
claim for extra cost
额外服务
exceptional service
额外付款
additional payment
额外工作
extra work
额外津贴
extra allowance, bonus
额外开支

extra charges (expenses)
额外利润
extra profit, premium returns
恶化
deteriorate, deterioration, exacerbate
恶劣天气
inclement weather, adverse weather
恶劣天气损失
heavy weather damage
恶性通货膨胀
galloping inflation
恶性循环
vicious circle
恶意破坏
malicious damage
二流商品
seconds
二手设备
second-hand equipment
二元的
dual

F

发布
issue, issuance

发电
power generation

发电厂
power house (plant)
发电机
electric generator
发电站
power station
发放工薪额
payroll
发函日期
date of letter
发货
shipping, shipment
发货单
shipping document, bill of sale
发货国
country of dispatch
发货清单
shipping list, invoice
发货人
consignor, consigner, vendor, sender
发件人
addresser
发盘
offer, make an offer
发盘人
offerer, offeror
发票
invoice
发票副本
duplicate invoice
发票价值
invoice value
发起
sponsor, promote, promotion
发起人
sponsor, promoter
发生
occur, occurrence, happen
发送
forward, dispatch
发文簿
table of distribution

发薪日
payday
发信人
addresser
发行
issue, publish
发展
develop, development, expand, grow
发展基金
development fund
发展银行
development bank
罚金
fine, forfeit, penal sum
罚金条款
penalty clause
罚款
financial penalty, penalty
法案
act, bill
法典
code
法定
statute
法定保险
legal insurance
法定代表
statutory representative, legal representative
法定代表权
right of legal representation
法定代理人
legal representative, legal agent
法定单位
legal entity
法定的
lawful, legal
法定股本
authorized capital stock
法定货币
lawful money, legal tender
法定假日

legal holiday, official holiday
法定赔偿
legal compensation
法定清算
legal liquidation
法定权利
statutory right, legal right
法定身份
legal capacity
法定税率
statutory tax rate
法定所有权
legal title
法定文件
statutory instruments
法定义务
statutory duty
法定重量
legal weight
法定资本
legal capital (value)
法定资产
legal assets
法定资格
legal title
法官
judge
法规
code, statute, legislation
法规要求
code requirement
法规与标准
codes and standards
法规允许的
code-allowable
法令
act, decree, statute, ordinance
法律
law
法律冲突
conflict of laws
法律的
legal

法律的解释
interpretation of law
法律的选择
choice of law
法律的字面意思
letters of the law
法律顾问
counselor, legal adviser
法律规定
legal provisions, legal rules
法律界
law circle
法律确认的占有
constructive possession
法律上的推定
presumption of law
法律事实
legal fact
法律释义
legal construction
法律诉讼程序
legal proceedings
法律文件
legal document
法律效力
force of law
法律行为
legal act
法律依据
legal basis, merit
法律用语的解释
interpretation of statutory language
法律责任
legal liability
法律制裁
legal sanction
法律仲裁
legal arbitration
法律咨询
legal consultation
法人
artificial person, legal person, judicial person

法人单位
legal entity, impersonal entity
法人实体
legal entity
法人业主
corporate owner
法人资格
legal personality
法人组织的
corporate
法庭
court, tribunal
法庭费用
court fee, adjudication fee
法系
legal system
法院
court, law court
翻斗车
dumper
翻译
translate, translation, translator, interpretation, interpreter
繁荣
boom
繁杂的
onerous
反避税措施
anti-avoidance measures
反驳
refute, contradict, disproof, contravene
反补贴税
countervailing duty
反铲挖土机
backhoe excavator
反担保函
counter guarantee
反对
object, objection
反对的理由
reason for objection
反购
counterpurchase
反控诉
countercharge
反馈
feedback
反滤层
inverted filter
反面证据
proof to the contrary
反倾销税
anti-dumping duty, countervailing duty
反诉
counterclaim
反索赔
counterclaim
反逃税措施
anti-evasion measures
反托拉斯法
anti-trust law
反向贸易
countertrade
反证
proof to the contrary
反之亦然
vice versa
返工成本
rework cost
返回
return
返销
buy-back
返销协议
buy-back agreement
犯法
offend, offence
犯罪
convict, crime, commit a crime
范例
example
范围
scope, limit, range
方案

scheme, plan, program(me), project
方案设计
engineering, scheme design
方案设计阶段
schematic design phase
方案图
scheme drawing
方便
convenience, facility, amenity
方程式
equation
方法
method, means, way, approaches
方面
aspect
方式
means, manner, mode
方位
locality, direction
方向
direction
防波堤
breakwater
防潮
keep dry
防潮层
damp-proof coating
防尘的
dust-proof
防范索赔
defence against claim
防腐
anticorrosive
防腐剂
preservative substance
防护工程
protection works
防火
fire prevention
防火的
fireproof
防火费用
cost of fire protection

防渗
seepage prevention, antiseepage
防渗护面
membrane
防渗墙
cut-off, diaphragm
防水的
waterproof
防锈材料
rust-resisting material
防锈的
antirust
防锈漆
anticorrosive paint
防御
defend, defence
防止
prevent
妨碍
interfere, interference, obstruct, objection, impede
妨害
nuisance
房产税
building tax
房产主
building owner
房地产
real estate, real property, property assets
房地产公司
property company
房屋
house
房屋建造规章
building regulations
房屋建筑
construction of buildings
放款
lending
放慢速度
slow down
放弃

give up, abandon, disclaim, waive
放弃合同
abandonment of contract
放弃权利
abandonment of right, waive one's right
放弃权利者
releasor
放弃上诉
abandonment of appeal
放弃索赔权
waive right of claim, abandonment of claim
放弃条款
waiver clause
放弃责任
disclaimer of responsibility
放弃者
disclaimer
放线
setting out
放样
setting out
放置
lay
飞涨的物价
soaring prices
非比例再保险
non-proportional reinsurance
非标准期限
broken period
非常的
extraordinary, unusual
非常损失
unusual loss
非常损益
extraordinary gains and losses
非常折旧
abnormal depreciation
非承重墙
non-bearing wall
非定期保证
unlimited duration guarantee

非法的
illegal, unlawful
非法合同
illegal contract
非法利润
illegal profit
非法途径
back door
非法行为
illegality
非法支付
illegal payment
非分期还款信贷
non-installment credit
非根本性违约
non-fundamental breach
非公开招标
closed bidding
非关税壁垒
non-tariff barrier
非合同规定的索赔
non-contractual claim, ex-contractual claims
非货币性负债
non-monetary liabilities
非货币性资产
non-monetary assets
非经常性项目
extraordinary item
非竞争性报价
non-competitive bid
非贸易收入
non-trade receipt
非美元国家
non-dollar countries
非契约性文件
non-contractual document
非贴现票据
non-discountable bill
非物质资本
immaterial capital
非物主占有
adverse possession

非现金支出
non-cash charges
非限定的
open-ended
非营业费用
non-operating expenses
非营业利润
unearned profit
非营业收入
non-operating income, non-operating revenue
非正常成本
abnormal cost
非正常利润
abnormal profit
非正常收益
abnormal gains
非正常损失
abnormal loss
非正式草拟合同
open contract
非正式的
informal, unofficial
非正式合同
informal contract
非正式记录
informal record, memorandum
非正式协定
informal agreement
非正式协议
unofficial agreement, agreement of understanding
非政府机构
non-governmental institution
非自愿的
involuntary
废标
rejection of all bids
废除
abate, abolish, annul, rescind
废除条款
denunciation clause
废除原合同
abrogate the original contract
废料
wastage, refuse, waste
废料处理
waste disposal
废品
waste product (goods), reject, spoiled product (goods)
废弃
abandon
废弃财产
abandoned property
废弃物
debris, rubbish, garbage
废弃物的处理
disposal of surplus
废弃资产
abandoned assets
废约
invalidate the contract
废渣厂
spoil area
废止
abate, avoid, repeal
废止合同
avoid a contract
费
fee
费率
rate, unit rate
费用
cost, charge, expense
费用超支
cost overrun
费用的减少
decrease in cost
费用的增加
increase in cost
费用分摊
expense allocation
费用估算
cost estimate
费用率

expense ratio
费用清单
statement of expenses
费用上涨
cost escalation
费用要素
elements of cost
费用指数
cost index
分包
subcontract, subcontracting, sublet
分包出去
job out
分包供货商
sub-supplier
分包合同
subcontract
分包合同包
subcontract package
分包商
subcontractor
分包商的误期
delays by subcontractor
分保
reassurance, reinsurance
分保公司
ceded company
分保明细表
bordereau
分别的
several, respective
分布表
table of distribution
分步成本计算法
process costing
分步收益表
multiple-step income statement
分贷
relending
分担
share, contribution
分担差价
absorb the price difference, share the price differences
分担风险
share risks
分公司
branch, division, affiliate, subsidiary company
分户账
ledger
分级费率
class rate
分阶段
sub-stage
分界
demarcation
分界线
boundary
分类
classify, categorize
分类日记账
ledger journal
分类账
ledger
分类账表格
ledger form
分类账科目
account as recorded in a ledger
分类折旧
classified depreciation
分类折旧法
group method of depreciation
分录
journal entry
分录簿
journal
分录凭单
journal voucher
分派
allocate
分配
allot, distribute, allocate, assign, apportion
分配额
amount allocated

分批成本单
job cost sheet
分批成本预算法
batch costing
分批法
job lot method
分批预算
batch budgeting
分批装船
installment shipment, partial shipment
分批装运
installment shipment, partial shipment
分期偿还
amortization
分期偿还抵押贷款
amortized mortgage loan
分期偿还率
amortization rate
分期分批
installment
分期付款
installment, pay by installments
分期付款购买
installment buying, hire purchase
分期付款合同
installment contract
分期付款汇票
bill payable by installments
分期付款销售
installment sale
分散风险
spreading the risk
分摊
apportion, allocate, distribute
分摊保险
contributing insurance
分摊成本
allocate cost
分摊风险
spreading the risk
分摊价值
contribution value
分摊数额
apportionment
分析
analyze, analysis, breakdown
分析和评估方法
analysis and evaluation methodology
分析行情
analyze a market
分项的说明
description of items
分项发包合同
separate contract
分项价格
itemized price, breakdown price
分销
distribution
分销网
distribution network
分选机
separator, sizer, grader
分押
submortgage
分支道路
diversion road
分支机构
branch, affiliate
分租
sublease
粉煤灰
fly ash
份额
share
丰富
abundance
风道
air flue
风俗习惯
custom, manners and customs
风险
risk, hazard, peril, exposure
风险保费
risk premium

风险辨识
identification of risks
风险的分离
isolation of risk
风险等级划分
risk rating
风险度
degree of risk
风险分担
allocation of risks, risk allocation, risk sharing
风险分散
distribution of risks, risk reduction
风险分摊
risk apportionment
风险分析
risk analysis
风险管理
risk management
风险合同
risk contract
风险回避
risk avoidance
风险减少
risk reduction
风险利用
risk speculation
风险评级
risk rating
风险评价
risk evaluation
风险事故
peril
风险投机
risk speculation
风险投资
venture investment
风险意识
sense of risks
风险因素
hazard, risk factor
风险责任的起期
attachment of risk

风险转移
risk transfer
风险准备金
risk allowance
风险自留
risk retention
风钻工
drifter
封闭式市场
closed market
封入
enclosure
峰值
crest
否定的
negative
否决
reject, veto, vote down
否认
contradict, disclaim, repudiate
否认合同有效
repudiate the contract
敷设
lay
扶手
hand rail, rail
服从
obey
服务范围
scope of services
服务费
service charge
服务合同
contract for service, service contract
服务小费
courior charges
服务协议书
service agreement
服务性租赁
service lease
浮吊
pontoon crane
浮动

float
浮动的
floating
浮动汇率
floating exchange rate
浮动价格
sliding price
浮动价格合同
fluctuating price contract
浮动利率
floating interest rate
浮动利率票据
floating rate note (FRN)
浮码头
landing stage
浮桥
float bridge
浮时
float
符号
character, sign
符合
comply with, conform, conformity
符合的
correspondent, responsive
符合计划
compliance with a schedule
符合进度表
compliance with a schedule
符合性投标
responsive bid
符合要求的
responsive
符合招标文件要求
responsive to bidding documents
符合资助条件
eligible for financing
福利
welfare
福利费
welfare benefits
福利费用
welfare expenses
福利基金
welfare funds
抚恤金
pension
俯视图
top view
辅助记录
subsidiary record
辅助账簿
auxiliary book
辅助账户
subsidiary account
辅助证据
secondary evidence
腐化
corruption
腐化的
corrupt
付给持票人
pay to bearer
付给指定人
pay to the order of ...
付还
pay back
付款
payment
付款保函
payment guarantee
付款程序
disbursement procedure
付款代理人
paying agent
付款地点
place of payment
付款国
country of payment
付款交货
cash and delivery, delivery against payment
付款结算
settlement by payment
付款期
payable period, payment term

付款期限
prompt
付款清单
bill of payment, paying list
付款人
drawee, payer
付款日
payday
付款申请
application for payment
付款提示
presentment for payment
付款条件
terms of payment, credit terms
付款通知
advice of payment, payment order
付款通知书
bill of credit
付款信用证
payment credit
付款银行
paying bank
付款证书
certificate for payment
付讫
paid off
付讫支票
canceled check, paid check
付清
pay off, take up
付清本息
pay off the principal and interest
付清的
paid-off
付现
pay cash
付现成本
out-of-pocket cost
付现费用
out-of-pocket expenses
负担
burden
负担损失
bear a loss
负的
negative
负荷
burden
负现金流量
negative cash flow
负有义务
incur obligation
负有义务的
incumbent
负有责任
accountability
负责
in charge of
负责人
person in charge
负增长
negative growth
负债
liability
负债净额
net liabilities
负债人
debtor
负债与资产比
debt to equity ratio
负债账户
negative assets account, liabilities account
负债者
obligor
负债准备金
liability reserves
负资产账户
negative assets account
附表
attached list
附带担保
collateral warranty
附带费用
incidental expenses
附带服务

incidental service
附带事件
incidental
附带收入
incidental revenue
附带条件
side conditions
附带条件贷款
tied loan
附加
affix, add, annex
附加保险费
additional premium, extra premium
附加成本
supplementary costs
附加的
additional, cumulative, accessory
附加费率
additional rate
附加费用
additional charge, additional cost
附加费用的补偿
compensation of additional cost
附加风险
accessory risk, extraneous risks
附加服务
additional service
附加福利
fringe benefits
附加工作
additional work
附加合同
accessory contract
附加价值
value added
附加税
additional tax, supplementary tax, surtax
附加条款
attached clause, additional clause, additional provision
附加物
addendum
附加险
additional risk
附加限制
ancillary restrictions
附加运费
additional freight
附加装置
attachment
附件
appendix, annex, attachment, enclosure, exhibit
附录
appendix, annex
附批注提货单
claused bill of lading
附上
attach, enclose
附条件背书
restrictive endorsement
附条件承兑
qualified acceptance
附有单证的发票
invoice with document attached
附有条件的合同
tying contract
附约
accessory contract
附则
additional contract clauses
附属
affiliation
附属贷款协议
subsidiary loan agreement
附属担保品
collateral
附属的
collateral, subsidiary
附属工程
subsidiary work
附属公司
affiliate, underlying company
附属合同
collateral contract

附属机构
subsidiary
附属建筑物
easement, auxiliary structures
附属企业
auxiliary enterprise
附属物
accessory, ancillary
附属装置
fixture
附注
foot-note, marginal note
复工
resumption of work
复合保险
multiple line insurance
复合的
composite, compound, multiple
复合关税
compound duties, compound tariff
复利
compound interest
复利计算
compounding
复利率
compound rate
复审
review
复式税则
complex tariff, multiple tariff system
复式账户制
double-account system
复税制
multiple taxation
复印件
copy, xerox copy
复原
restore, restoration
复杂的
complex, complicated
复制
duplicate
复制品
duplicate
副本
copy, duplicate
副部长
vice minister
副担保书
collateral warranty
副的
associate
副董事长
vice chairman
副经理
deputy manager
副手
deputy
副行长
vice president
副主席
vice chairman
副总裁
vice president
副总经理
deputy general manager, vice president
覆盖
cover

G

改变不另通知
subject to change without notice
改变订单程序
change order procedure
改变订单日志
change order log

改动
change, alter, alteration
改建
reconstruct, reconstruction
改建费用
improvement cost
改进
improve, improvement
改进成本
improvement cost
改良
betterment
改善
improve, rehabilitation
改正
amend, rectify
盖章
seal, imprint, affix
盖章合同
contract under seal
概况
profile
概率
probability
概念估算
conceptual estimate
概念设计
conceptual design
概算
budget estimate, budget proposal, preliminary computation
概算书的检查
checking of estimate
干砌石圬工
dry-stone masonry
干扰
interruption, interference
干容重
dry density
干涉
interference
干缩裂缝
desiccation fissure

甘特图
Gantt chart
赶工
expedite
刚性基础
rigid foundation
岗上培训
on-the-job training
钢板桩
steel sheet pile
钢管桩
steel pipe pile
钢轨
rail
钢架结构
rigid-framed structure
钢筋
reinforcement
钢筋布置
arrangement of reinforcement
钢筋混凝土
reinforced concrete
钢筋混凝土压力水管
reinforced concrete pressure pipe
钢筋间距
rod spacing, bar spacing
钢筋截断机
bar cutter
钢筋网配筋
bar-mat reinforcement
钢卷尺
steel tape
钢丝绳
wire rope
港口
port
港口费用
port charge, port dues, groundage
港口附加费
port surcharge
港口工程
port works
港口惯例

custom of the port
港口检验人员
surveyor of port
港口税
harbor duty, port dues
港口税率
rate of port dues
港口条例
harbor regulation
港口拥挤附加费
port congestion surcharge
港湾工程
harbor works
港湾项目
harbor project
港务费
harbor dues
港务局
port authority
杠杆比率
leverage ratio
杠杆作用
leverage
高标号水泥
high-quality cement
高标价投标
high priced bid
高层建筑
high-rise building
高层谈判
high-level talks
高程
elevation
高程控制点
level-control point
高额关税
prohibitive duty
高峰交通量
peak traffic flow
高估
overestimate, overstate
高级工程师
senior engineer
高级管理人员
executive
高级会计师
senior accountant
高级项目开发官员
senior development officer
高级职员
staff executive
高价
high price, long price
高价的
dear
高架公路
high-flying highway
高空作业
work in mid-air
高强度钢筋
high-tensile steel bar
高强水泥
high-strength cement
高速公路
expressway
高速轨道方式
fast track method
高息贷款
dear money
高压泵
high pressure pump
告贷
ask for loan
革新
innovation
格式
form
隔墙
wall partition
隔热材料
thermal insulation material, heat-insulating material
隔声
sound insulation
隔音板
acoustical board

个别辨认法
specific identification method
个别的
individual, particular
个别计价法
specific identification method
个人
individual
个人财产
personal property
个人的
individual, private, personal
个人侵权行为
personal tort
个人所得
individual income
个人所得税
individual income tax, personal income tax
个人责任
personal liability
个人咨询专家
individual consultant
个人咨询专家注册资料
data on individual consultant (DICON)
个人资产
personal assets
个体
entity, individual
个体企业
individual enterprise
个体业主
individual owner
各方
all parties
各国货币比值手册
cambist
各种的
sundry, miscellaneous
各自的
several, respective
各自负有连带和单独责任

joint and several liability
各自责任
several liability
给承包商的指示
instruction to contractor
给予
extend, vest
给予权利
entitle
给予特许
franchise
根本性变更
cardinal changes
根本性违约
fundamental breach
根本责任
ultimate liability
根据
pursuant to, in accordance with
根源
source
跟不上进度
behind schedule
跟单汇票
documentary bill (draft)
跟单汇票托收委托书
advice for collection of documentary bill
跟单托收
collection on documents, documentary collection
跟单信用证
documentary letter of credit
更改
alter, alteration, modify, modification
更换
replace, replacement, substitute
更新
renew, renewal, updating
更新成本
replacement cost
更正

amend, amendment
工长
foreman
工厂
plant, works, workshop
工厂交货(价)
ex works (EXW), ex-factory
工厂交货价
ex-works price, price of ex-factory
工厂生产能力
plant capacity
工场
workshop, yard
工潮
labour disturbance
工程
works, engineering, project, work
工程保险
insurance of works, project insurance
工程报表
bill of works
工程变更
alteration of works, job changes, variation of work
工程变更单
bill of variations
工程采购
procurement of works
工程成本分类账
job cost ledger
工程成本记录
job cost record
工程成本日记账
job cost journal
工程承包
project contracting, work contracting
工程范围变更索赔
scope of work claim
工程范围数据库
engineering scope database
工程风险
project risk

工程服务贷款
engineering service loan
工程管理费
job overhead cost
工程管理员
clerk of the works
工程合同
project contract, engineering contract
工程计划
project program
工程计划概要
outline programme
工程检查报告
project inspection reports
工程进度
progress of project, progress of works, job progress
工程进度表
schedule of construction, schedule of works
工程进展与执行报告
project progress and performance report
工程竣工
completion of works, job completion
工程扩建
extension of works
工程蓝图
blueprint of the project
工程量
quantity
工程量变更
variation of quantity
工程量标价
quantity pricing
工程量表
bill of quantities
工程量表合同
bill of quantities contract
工程量计算
quantity take-off
工程量清单

bill of quantities
工程量清单汇总表
summary of bill of quantities
工程描述
description of works
工程期限
period of construction
工程缺陷
work defect
工程设计
project design
工程设计方案
project design plan
工程师
engineer
工程师代表
engineer's representative
工程师的(复审)决定
Engineer's decision
工程师的期中支付证书
engineer's interim certificate
工程施工一切险
construction's all risks insurance
工程说明书
description of project
工程统计
works statistics
工程维修
maintenance of works
工程详细报告
detailed project report
工程项目实施的决定
decision to proceed with the project
工程性质
nature of works
工程延期
deferment of a project
工程验收
acceptance of works, acceptance of a project
工程造价
cost of works, project cost
工程专用
exclusive use for the works
工程状况
status of a project
工程咨询公司
engineering consultancy firm
工程咨询合同
engineering consulting contract
工程组织机构
job organization
工地
site, construction site, job site, work site, field
工地办公室
site office
工地报告
field reporting
工地布置
site arrangement
工地记录本
field book
工地勘察
job site survey
工地平整
site grading
工地清理
job site cleanup
工地日志
site diary
工地设备
site equipment
工地设施
job site facilities
工地实验室
site laboratory
工地视察
field inspection
工地试验室
field laboratory
工地照明
lighting of the site
工段长
section foreman
工会

labour union, trade union
工匠
craftsman, workman
工具
tool, instrument, facility
工料测量
quantity survey
工料测量师
quantity surveyor (QS)
工料测量学
quantity surveying
工龄
working years
工棚
site hut
工期
construction period
工期拖延
construction delay
工期延长
extension of time
工人
labour, workman
工日
man day
工伤
industrial injury, injury on job
工伤事故
accident work injury, work accident, working accident
工伤事故保险
insurance against accident to workmen
工商企业
business
工商所得税
industrial and commercial income tax
工时
working hours, man hour
工时报告单
time report
工时成本
time cost

工时分配
time distribution
工时记录
time keeping
工时记录卡
time card
工时率
labour hour rate
工头
leading hand, task master
工薪税
payroll tax
工序
process
工序分析
process analysis
工序控制
process control
工业
industry
工业产权
industrial property right
工业建筑
industrial architecture
工业所有权
industrial property right
工艺
workmanship, technology, craft
工艺的
technological, technical
工艺工程师
process engineer
工艺流程图
process chart, process flow chart, process diagram
工艺设计
process design
工种工程量表
trade bill of quantities
工资
pay, wage
工资标准
wage level, wage rate

工资表
payroll, wages sheet
工资表格
payroll form
工资单
payroll, wages sheet
工资汇总表
payroll recapitulation
工资记录
payroll records
工资率
wage rate
工资水平
wage level
工资所得税
wages income tax
工资支票
pay cheque, payroll check
工资指数
index of wage, wage index
工资总额
gross pay
工资总额单
wage bill
工资最高限额
wage ceiling
工字钢
I-steel(bar)
工字梁
I-beam
工作
work, occupation, job
工作报告
work report
工作变动
job changes
工作大纲
terms of reference(TOR)
工作单项
work item
工作底稿
work sheet
工作范围
scope of work
工作方案
work program, work plan
工作费用
working expenses
工作负荷
workload
工作规范
job specification
工作计划
work plan, work program
工作量
quantity of work, work capacity, workload
工作能力
ability to work, work capacity
工作缺陷
faulty work
工作人员
staff
工作人员条例
staff regulations
工作日
working day
工作时间
working hours
工作台
mounting rack
工作条件
working condition
工作通知单
work order
工作完成
job completion
工作文件
working papers
工作效率
labour efficiency, working efficiency
工作协调
coordination of work
工作许可证
work permit
工作业绩

job performance
工作指令
working instruction
工作质量
workmanship
工作中断
work interruption
公布
announce, publish
公布账目
accounting released
公差
tolerance
公断人
arbitrator, arbiter
公断书
arbitration award
公吨
metric ton (MT)
公法
public law
公告
announcement, proclamation
公共当局
public authority
公共的
public
公共福利
public welfare
公共工程
public works
公共关系
public relation
公共基础设施
institutional infrastructure
公共假日
public holiday
公共设施
public facilities, common facilities, service
公共责任
public liability
公害
hazard
公函
official letter
公积金
reserve fund
公开的
public, open
公开发行股份有限公司
public company
公开投标
open bid (tender)
公开有限公司
Public Limited Company (PLC)
公开招标
public bidding, open bid (tender)
公款
public money
公路
highway
公路工程
highway engineering
公路运输
carriage by road
公民的
civil
公民地位
civil status
公平的
fair
公平工资
fair wages
公平价格
fair price, reasonable price
公平交易
fair dealing, arm's length transaction
公平交易法
fair trading act
公平竞争
fair competition
公平市价
fair market price
公认的国际惯例
established international practice

公认会计原则
acceptable accounting principle
公式
formula
公式调价法
formula price adjustment
公司
corporation, firm, incorporation, company, enterprise
公司本部费用
home office cost
公司财产
company property
公司创办人
incorporator
公司的
corporate
公司法
corporation act (law), company act, company law, law of company
公司合并
corporate merger
公司汇票
house bill
公司间贷款
inter-company loan
公司间往来抵销账项
inter-company elimination
公司间往来业务
inter-company transactions
公司收购
corporate acquisition
公司税
corporation tax (CT), corporate tax
公司税法
corporation tax act (CTA)
公司所得税
corporate income tax
公司条例
company act, corporation regulation
公司印章
corporation seal
公司债券
corporate bond, debenture
公司章程
charter of company, corporation by-laws, memorandum of association
公司执照
corporate charter, charter
公司重组
reconstruction of company
公私合营企业
joint state and private enterprise
公务员
officer
公营公司
public company
公营企业
public enterprise
公用工程
public works
公用设施
public utility
公用事业
utility, public utility
公约
convention, pact
公允表达
fair presentation
公债
government bond, bond
公正的
fair, just, impartial, equitable
公正无偏的态度
impartial and unbiased manner
公正性
impartiality
公证
notarize, notarization
公证的
notarial
公证人
public notary, notary
公证手续
notarial act
公证文件

notarial document
公证证书
notarial certificate
公职
office
公制
Metric system
公制的
metric
公制换算
metric conversion
公制计量
metric measure
公众
public
功能
function
功效
efficiency
供不应求
in short supply
供电线路
charging line
供给
provide
供货
supply
供货担保
supply bond
供货价格
supply price
供货商
vendor, supplier
供料斗
feed hopper
供料线
charging line
供暖系统
heating system
供水
water supply, water service
供水管
feed pipe, charging line

供水系统
water-supply system
供选择的货物
alternative goods
供应
supply, furnish, furnishings, provision
供应品
supply
供应商
supplier, materialman
巩固
consolidate
拱坝
arch dam
拱桥
arch bridge
拱座
abutment
共保交叉责任条款
joint insured cross liability clause
共同保险
co-insurance
共同承保人
co-assurer
共同承兑人
co-acceptor
共同错误
common mistake
共同贷款
participating loan
共同担保人
co-guarantor
共同的
mutual, joint
共同的和各自的责任
joint and several liability
共同管理人
co-manager
共同海损
general average (G.A.)
共同海损保函
letter of general average guarantee

共同海损保证金
general average deposit
共同海损保证书
average bond
共同海损补偿
make good on general average
共同海损担保
general average security
共同海损担保书
general average guarantee
共同海损费用保险
general average disbursement insurance
共同海损分摊
general average contribution
共同海损基金
general average fund
共同海损理算
general average adjustment, adjustment of general average
共同海损理算书
general average statement
共同海损赔偿理算
adjustment of claim for general average
共同海损损失
general average loss
共同海损条款
general average clause
共同海损行为
general average act
共同基金
mutual funds
共同借款人
co-borrower
共同市场
common market
共同受益人
co-beneficiary
共同诉讼
joinder
共同所有权
joint ownership
共同行为
joint act
共同延误
concurrent delay
共同义务
joint liability
共同债权人
joint creditor
共同债务人
co-debtor
共同资助
cofinancing
共同租赁人
joint tenant
共有的
joint
贡献
contribute, contribution
贡献毛利
contribution margin
勾结投标
collusive bid (tender), level tendering
勾结性协议
collusive agreement
沟
ditch, trench, dike
钩损险
risk of hook damage
构成
composition, constitute, form
构架
frame
构件
component
购方企业
acquiring enterprise
购货成本
cost of goods purchased, purchasing cost
购货代理人
purchasing agent
购货单

buying order, purchase order
购货发盘
buying offer
购货发票
purchase invoice
购货确认书
purchase note
购货日记账
purchase journal
购货样品
purchase sample
购货约定
purchase commitment
购买
buy, purchase
购买地价格
price loco
购买方
acquiring party
购买力
purchasing power, ability to pay
购买要约
buying offer
购置
procurement, purchase
购置财产
acquisition of property
购置成本
acquisition cost
估定价值
assessed value, constructed value
估计残值
estimated residual value, estimated salvage value
估计负债
estimated liabilities
估计工程量单价合同
bill of approximate quantity contract
估计价格
estimated price
估价
assess, assessment, estimate, value, valuation

估价财产人
assessor
估价人
appraiser, estimater
估价条款
valuation clause
估价文件
estimate documentation
估量
takeoff
估税员
tax assessor
估算
estimate, assess
估算成本
estimated cost
估算师
estimator
箍筋
hoop reinforcement
古董
antiquities
股本
capital stock
股本持有者
equity holder
股东
shareholder, stockholder
股东大会
shareholder's meeting
股东分户账
stock ledger
股东权益
shareholder's equity, proprietary equity, stockholder's equity
股东协议
shareholder's agreement
股份
stock capital
股份公司
incorporated companies
股份有限公司
company limited by shares, limited li-

ability company, corporation
股份有限责任公司
proprietary limited (Pty Ltd)
股利收入
dividend earned
股利支付率
dividend payout ratio
股票
stock, share, equity
股票股利
capital bonus
股票基金
equity fund
股票市场
equity market, stock market
股票溢价
stock premium
股权
equity, interest
股息
dividend
骨料
aggregate
骨料仓
aggregate bin
骨料级配
aggregate gradation
骨料水泥比
aggregate-cement ratio
鼓风机
fan blower, blower
鼓励
incentive
固定
fix
固定成本
fixed cost, constant cost, unavoidable cost
固定单价合同
fixed unit price contract
固定的
permanent
固定费率
par exchange rate
固定费用
fixed cost, fixed charges
固定分保
obligatory reinsurance
固定工程量总价合同
lump sum on firm bill of quantities
固定工资
fixed wages
固定管理费
fixed overhead
固定汇率
fixed exchange rate, fixed rate
固定价格
fixed price, definite price
固定价格合同
fixed price contract
固定开支
fixed expenses
固定劳工工资等级
fixed labour rates
固定利率
fixed exchange rate, fixed rate
固定利率贷款
fixed rate loan
固定设备
fixed equipment
固定提成
fixed royalty
固定投资总额
gross fixed investment
固定信贷额
fixed credit line
固定资本
fixed capital
固定资产
fixed property, fixed assets, capital assets, permanent assets
固定资产残值
fixed assets salvage value
固定资产的处置
disposal of fixed assets
固定资产净值

fixed assets net value
固定资产税
fixed assets tax
固定资产统计师
actuary
固定资产账户
capital account
固定总价合同
firm lump sum contract
固结灌浆
consolidation grouting
固结试验
consolidation test
故意破坏
vandalism
故意侵权行为
intentional tort
故意失职
wilful misconduct
故意行为
intentional act
故障
fault
顾客
client, customer
顾问
adviser, advisor, consultant, counselor
顾问的
advisory
顾问律师
office lawyer
顾问委员会
advisory committee
雇工
hired labour
雇工合同
contract of hire of labour
雇用
employ, hire
雇用合同
contract of employment
雇用条件
conditions for employment, conditions of engagement, terms of employment
雇员
employee
雇员履历表
employee experience profile
雇主
employer, hirer
雇主的风险
employer's risks
雇主的义务
employer's obligation
雇主的责任
employer's liability
雇主的责任保险
employer's liability insurance
雇主提供的保障
indemnity by employer
雇主违约
employer's default
刮泥板
scraper
刮土机
road scraper
挂号
register
挂号信
registered letter
挂号邮件
registered mail
关键
key
关键的
critical
关键点
critical point
关键路径方法
critical path method (CPM)
关键人员
key personnel
关键项目清单
critical items list

关境
customs territory
关税
customs duty, duty, tariff
关税保护
tariff protection
关税壁垒
customs barrier, tariff barrier
关税减让
concession of tariff
关税率
tariff, tariff rate
关税率表
tariff schedule
关税配额
tariff quota
关税同盟
custom union
关税未付
duty unpaid
关税协议
tariff agreement
关税已付
duty paid
关税优惠
tariff preference
关税最高限额
tariff ceiling
关于
with reference to
观测站
observation station
观察
observe, observation
观点
point of view, view point
官方当局
authority
官方兑换率
official rate
官方公报
official gazette
官方价格
official price
官员
officer
管道
pipeline, pipe, conduit, pipe run
管道安装
piping erection
管道工程
pipe work, plumbing
管理
manage, management, administer, administration, supervise, supervision
管理部门
management
管理成本
administration cost
管理承包
management contracting
管理承包商
management contractor
管理费
administration fee, administration expenses, overhead, management fee
管理费分配
overhead allocation
管理费用
overhead charges (cost)
管理费账户
administration expense account
管理顾问
management consultant
管理规定
administration rules, administration practice
管理合同
management contract
管理会计
managerial accounting, management accounting
管理机构
government
管理技巧

management techniques
管理局
board of control
管理控制系统
management control system
管理人员
superintending staff, manager
管理协定
management agreement
管理信息系统
management information system (MIS)
管理员
clerk
管理者
supervisor
管理职能
management function
管网
network
管辖的法律
governing law
管辖权
jurisdiction
管线
line, pipeline, pipe run
管线工程项目
pipeline project
管押
custody
管制价格
controlled price
管柱桩
caisson pile
管桩
pipe pile
贯彻
enforce, enforcement
惯例
convention, custom, practice, usage
惯例法
customary law
灌溉渠
irrigation channel
灌浆
grouting
灌浆机
grouting machine
灌注桩
filling pile
罐
silo
光船租赁
bareboat charter
光明正大的
fair
光票
clean bill, clean draft
光票托收
clean (bill for) collection, collection on clean bill
光票信用证
clean (letter of) credit
广告
advertisement
归还
return, release
归还保函
restitution of the guarantee, release of the guarantee
归属
vesting, vest
规程
specification
规定
specify, stipulate, prescribe, provide
规定日期
specified date
规范
specification, code, norm
规格
specification, standard
规格响应表
specification compliance form
规划
blue print, project, planning, scheme

规划同意书
planning consent
规律
law
规模
scale
规则
rule
规章
regulation, articles
规章制度
rules and regulations
硅酸盐矿渣水泥
portland slag cement
硅酸盐水泥
portland cement
贵重的
valuable
国别配额
country quota
国产的
domestic
国产品
domestic product
国货
domestic product
国际避税
international tax avoidance
国际博览会
international fair
国际部
international division
国际财团
consortium
国际的
international
国际法
international law, law of nations
国际工程
international project
国际公司
international corporation
国际公约
international convention
国际惯例
international customs, international practice, international convention
国际货物运输保险
international cargo transportation insurance
国际价格
international price
国际借贷差额
balance of international indebtedness
国际金融
international finance
国际竞争性招标
international competitive bidding (ICB)
国际开发协会信贷
IDA credit
国际贸易
international trade
国际贸易法
law of international trade
国际贸易货币
international trading currency
国际贸易逆差
adverse balance of international trade
国际贸易术语
International Commercial Terms (Incoterms)
国际贸易术语解释通则
International Rules for the Interpretation of Trade Terms (Incoterms)
国际商会仲裁法庭仲裁规则
Rules for the International Chamber of Commerce Court of Arbitration
国际双重征税
international double taxation, international double tax imposition
国际税收协定
international taxation agreement
国际私法
private international law
国际逃税

international tax evasion
国际通行货币
international currency
国际效力
international validity
国际行为准则
code of international conduct
国际性协议
consortium
国际询价采购
international shopping
国际银团贷款
international syndicated loan
国际制裁
international sanction, sanctions
国际仲裁裁决书
international arbitral award
国际仲裁法庭
international arbitral tribunal
国家
nation, country, state
国家保险
national insurance
国家标准
national standard
国家财政
national finance
国家的
national
国家公债
national bond
国家海关辖区
national customs territory
国家税率
rate of national taxes
国家税收
national revenue
国家岁入
national revenue
国库
treasury
国库券
treasury bill

国民
nationals
国民产值
national product
国民待遇
national treatment
国民的
national
国民生产净值
net national product (NNP)
国民生产总值
gross national product (GNP)
国民收入
national dividend
国民收入总值
gross national income (GNI)
国民所得
national dividend
国内财务
domestic finance
国内财政
domestic finance
国内的
national, local, civil, domestic, internal
国内费用
domestic cost
国内费用筹措
local cost financing
国内工程项目
domestic project
国内合同
domestic contract
国内汇兑
domestic remittance, domestic exchange
国内货运保险
domestic cargo transportation insurance
国内竞争性招标
local competitive bidding (LCB), national competitive bidding
国内贸易

domestic trade
国内生产总值
gross domestic product (GDP)
国内市场
national market
国内市场价格
domestic market price
国内税
domestic tax, internal tax
国内提单
inland bill of lading
国内提单条款
inland bill of lading clause
国内通货膨胀率
domestic inflation rate
国内消费
home consumption
国内消费品进口报关单
entry for home use
国内销售额
domestic turnover
国内询价采购
national shopping
国内优惠
domestic preference
国内优先
domestic preference
国内制造
home made
国内资源成本
domestic resources cost
国内总产值
gross domestic product (GDP)
国税
national tax
国外
abroad
国外分部
overseas branch
国外分行
overseas branch
国外分支机构
foreign branch

国外工程
overseas works
国外汇票
foreign draft
国外培训
overseas training
国外市场
foreign market
国外投资
foreign investment
国外项目
overseas project
国营公司
public corporation
国营企业
government enterprise, state enterprise, national enterprise
国有公司
state-owned corporation
国有化
nationalization
国有企业
state-owned enterprise
国债
national debt
过程
process
过错
default
过渡贷款
bridge loan
过渡性融资
bridge financing
过户
transfer
过户结账日
pay day, account day
过境国
transit country
过境签证
transit visa
过境权
right of way

过境税
transit tax, transit duty(dues)
过境运价
transborder rate
过量的
excess
过期
past-due
过期保险单
stale policy
过期的
back, stale
过期的索赔
belated claim
过期利息
over interest
过期票据
past-due bill (note)
过期提单
stale B/L
过期未付的
overdue
过期未付款
back money, overdue payment
过期支票
out-of-date check, stale check
过去成本
historical cost
过剩的
surplus
过失
negligence
过失行为
negligent act
过失责任
liability for fault
过失罪
error of omission, negligent crime
过时的设备
out-of-date equipment
过账
post, posting

H

海关
customs, customs house, maritime customs
海关保税保证书
customs bond
海关登记
customs entry
海关发票
customs invoice
海关法
customs law
海关放行证
customs clearance
海关估价
customs appraised value, customs valuation
海关官员
customs house officer
海关检查证
jerque note
海关检验
customs examination
海关检验人员
surveyor of customs
海关进口手续
customs entry
海关进口税则
customs import tariff
海关境域
customs territory
海关收据
customs receipt
海关手续
customs procedures, customs formalities
海关税率

rate of customs duty
海关税则
customs tariff, tariff
海关条例
customs regulations
海关通行证
customs pass
海关退税单
debenture
海关委托人
customs consignee
海关许可证
customs permit
海关验货单
customs examination list
海关佣金
customs brokerage
海陆联运
ocean and rail (O. & R.)
海难
perils of the sea
海难救援公司
salvage company
海商法
marine law, maritime law
海上保险契约
contract of marine insurance
海上的
marine
海上风险
perils of the sea, maritime perils
海上火灾
fire on the sea
海上建筑物
marine structure
海上救助
salvage
海上综合保险
all risks marine insurance
海事的
maritime
海事法
marine law, maritime law

海事法庭
maritime court
海事索赔
maritime claim
海事仲裁委员会
maritime arbitration commission
海损
average, sea damage, maritime loss
海损保险单
average policy
海损代理人
average agent
海损分摊
average contribution
海损精算书
adjustment letter
海损理算
adjustment of average
海损理算人
average taker, adjuster
海损理算书
average statement, adjustment letter
海损条款
sea damage terms
海损协议
average agreement
海图
chart, marine chart
海外
overseas, abroad
海外办事处
offshore office
海外的
overseas
海外工程
overseas project, work abroad
海外津贴
overseas allowance
海外市场
overseas market
海外投资
overseas investment
海险

maritime perils
海洋货运保险
cargo marine insurance
海洋运输保险
maritime transportation insurance
海洋运输货物保险
ocean marine cargo (transportation) insurance
海运
ocean carriage, shipping
海运保险
marine insurance, sea insurance
海运保险单
marine insurance policy
海运保险费
marine premium
海运承运人
ocean carrier
海运的
maritime
海运费
sea freight
海运公会
shipping conference
海运公会运价
conference rate
海运公司
ocean carrier
海运合同
contract of carriage by sea
海运提单
ocean waybill, ocean bill of lading, marine bill of lading
海运运费
ocean freight
含糊的
vague
含水量
moisture capacity (content)
含义
intendment, implication
含义不明确
ambiguity

涵洞
culvert
夯
rammer
夯具
compactor
夯实
tamping, compaction, ramming
行规
professional etiquette
行话
jargon
行情
conjuncture, tone
行业
craft, calling, line, trade
行业工资
craft wage
行长
president
航次
voyage
航次租船
charter by voyage
航海的
marine
航空货运
air freight
航空托运单
air consignment note (ACN)
航空运费
air freight
航空运输货物保险
Air Transportation Cargo Insurance
航线
line, route
航行
voyage
航运公会
shipping conference
耗减准备
depletion reserve
耗减资产

wasting assets
耗尽
deplete, exhaust
合并
merge, amalgamation, combination
合并报价（单）
combined quotation
合并财务报表
consolidated financial statement, combined financial statement
合并发盘
combined offer
合并资产负债表
consolidated balance sheet, amalgamated balance sheet
合法
legality
合法持票人
bona-fide holder
合法当局
constituted authority
合法的
legal, lawful
合法的请求
legitimate claim
合法的中止付款
eligible termination payment (ETP)
合法抵押
legal mortgage
合法继承人
legitimate heir
合法权利
legitimate right
合法收入
legitimate income
合法授权
legal authorization
合法性
legality
合格材料
acceptable material
合格承兑票据
eligible acceptance

合格程度
accredited degree
合格的
eligible, acceptable, qualified
合格来源国
eligible source country
合格票据
eligible bill
合格投标者
eligible bidders
合格性
eligibility
合格性检验
test for suitability
合格性限制
restriction on eligibility
合股人
partner
合伙
partnership
合伙关系
partnership
合伙企业
partnership
合伙契约
deed of partnership
合伙人
associate, partner
合伙受让人
coassignee
合伙受托人
coassignee
合计
total, aggregate
合理驳回
fair dismissal
合理的
reasonable
合理的预防措施
reasonable precautions
合理索赔
legitimate claim
合适

suitability
合同
contract
合同安排
contractual arrangement
合同包
contract package
合同保险单
contract policy
合同变更
contract variation
合同补充条款
additional contract clauses
合同草稿
contract draft
合同担保
contract bond
合同当事人间的相互关系
privity of contract
合同到期
expiration of contract
合同的
contractual
合同的不履行
non-implementation of contract
合同的解除
contractual release, discharge of contract
合同的解释
interpretation of contract
合同的履行
implementation of contract, performance of contract
合同的签署
signing the contract, execution of contract
合同的生效日期
starting date of contract, effective date of contract
合同的一般责任
general contractual liabilities
合同的约束
contractual restrictions
合同的终止
termination of contract
合同的准据法
proper law of the contract
合同缔结
conclusion of contract
合同法
contract law, law of contract
合同范围
contract package scope
合同范围变更
contract scope changes
合同分类账
contract ledger
合同风险
contract risks
合同附件
appendix to contract
合同格式
contract form
合同各方
parties to a contract
合同工
contract labour (worker), bound labour
合同工程师
contract engineer
合同构成
contract formation
合同关系
contractual relationship
合同管理
contract administration
合同管辖法
proper law of the contract, law governing the contract
合同惯例
contractual practice
合同规定
contract provisions, provisions of contract
合同规定的货币
currency of contract, contract curren-

cy
合同货物验收证书
acceptance certificate of the contract goods
合同记录
contract records
合同价格
contract price, contract amount, contract sum
合同价格的充分性
sufficiency of contract price
合同价格调整公式指数
indices for contract price adjustment formula
合同价值
contract value
合同接口
contract interface
合同卷宗
contract files
合同落空
frustration of contract
合同批准通知
approval notice of the contract
合同期
contract period
合同期满
contract expiry, expiration of contract
合同期限
duration of contract
合同签署日期
contract signature date
合同前的程序
pre-contract procedures
合同权利
contractual right
合同上的相互关系
mutuality of contract
合同涉及的索赔
contractual claims
合同生效
entry of contract into force, execution of contract
合同生效日期
effective date of contract
合同实施
performance of contract
合同授权
contract authorization
合同谈判
contract negotiation
合同条件
conditions of contract
合同条款
contract clause, provisions of contract
合同条款的可分割性
severability of the contract
合同文本
contract version
合同文件
contract documents
合同文件的优先次序
priority of contract documents
合同文件的准备
preparation of contract documents
合同文件分析
contract document analysis
合同项目
contract project
合同项下的投入
contractual input
合同协议书
contract agreement
合同序号
contract serial number
合同续订
contract renewal, renewal of contract
合同要点
point of contract
合同义务
contract duty, contract obligation, contractual obligation
合同意识
sense of contract

合同有效期
contract period, term of contract
合同有效性
validity of contract
合同语言
contract language, language of contract
合同预付款
advance payment for contract
合同暂停
contract suspension
合同责任
contractual liabilities
合同债务
contract debt
合同展期
renewal of contract
合同争端
contract dispute
合同终止
contract termination
合同转让
assignment of contract
合同综述
contract general
合约正本
original of the contract
合资公司
joint venture company
合资企业
joint venture, joint adventure
合资企业协议
joint venture agreement
合资银行
joint venture bank
合作
collaboration, cooperation
合作生产
co-production
和解
conciliate, conciliation, compromise, reconciliation
和解和清偿
accord and satisfaction
核查
review, examine
核单
vouching
核定股本
authorized capital stock
核对符号
check mark
核对清单
checklist
核对账目
verification of account
核实
verify
核算
accounting, computation
核准
authorize, authorization
核准的
authorized
核准书
written authorization
核准资本
authorized capital
桁架
truss
桁架桥
trussed bridge
横财
windfall
横道图
Gantt chart
横断面
cross section
横杆
beam
横截面
cross section
横梁
transverse
横线支票
cross (crossed) check (cheque)

横向的
transverse
横向钢筋
lateral reinforcement
横向协议
horizontal agreement
横轴
transverse
衡量
measurement
衡平法按揭
equitable mortgage
红利
bonus, dividend
红利股
bonus share (stock)
宏观分析
general equilibrium analysis
宏观结构
macrostructure
宏观进度计划
overview schedule
宏观预测
macro-forecast
洪峰
flood peak
洪峰流量
peak flow, peak discharge
洪水
flood
洪水流量
flood discharge
洪水位
flood level
虹吸
siphon
虹吸管
siphon
虹吸涵洞
siphon culvert
后备计划
program backup
后备人员
backup, standby
后果
consequence
后继条件
condition subsequent
后进先出法
last-in first-out (LIFO)
后门
back door
后评价
post evaluation
后勤
logistics
后审查
post review
后续事件
subsequent event
后续投资
follow-up investment
后张法预加应力
post-tensioned prestressing
后照管工程师
aftercare engineer
候选公司名单
short listed firms
呼吁
appeal
忽略
omit, omission, neglect
忽视
ignore, neglect
弧形闸门
radial gate
互购
counterpurchase
互换
exchange, swap
互换许可证
cross license
互惠
mutual benefit
互惠待遇
reciprocal treatment

互惠的
reciprocal
互惠关税
reciprocal tariff
互惠合同
reciprocal contract
互惠基金
mutual funds
互惠贸易
reciprocal trade
互惠条款
reciprocity clause
互惠协定
reciprocal agreement
互惠信贷
swap credits
互利
mutual benefit
互让的
give-and-take
互相谅解
mutual understanding
互助保险公司
mutual insurance company
护岸工程
bank protection work
护坡
slope protection
护照
passport
花费
cost, expense
花岗岩
granite
滑动模板
slip form
滑模施工
slip-form construction
滑坡塌方
landslide
化验
test
划分
demarcation, dividing
划线支票
cross (crossed) check (cheque)
坏账
bad debt, bad account, uncollectible account
坏账准备
reserve for bad debts
还本付息
debt service
还价
counter offer, abate a price
还盘
counter offer
还债
money returned, pay a debt
环筋
hoop reinforcement
环境
environment, surroundings
环境保护
environment protection, protection of environment
环境保护费
pollution prevention cost
环境工程
environment engineering
环境监测系统
environmental monitoring system
环境污染
environmental pollution, environment contamination
环境影响评价
environmental impact assessment
环氧树脂涂料
epoxide-resin paint
缓冲基金
buffer fund
缓冲库存
buffer inventory
缓凝剂
retarder
缓凝水泥

retarded cement
换汇
exchange, swap
恢复
restore, restoration, recover, recovery
恢复原状
reinstatement
回程运费
back freight
回购
buy-back
回购产品
buy-back of product
回函
reply (to a letter), letter of acknowledgement
回扣
brokerage, kickback, rebate
回收价值
recovery value
回收期评估法
payback method
回填
backfill, reclamation
回填料
backfill
回执
acknowledgment of receipt
回租
leaseback
汇编
proceedings
汇兑
remittance, transfer
汇兑风险
exchange risk
汇兑商
cambist
汇兑损益
foreign exchange gains and losses
汇付
remittance

汇还本国
repatriation
汇寄
remit
汇价
exchange rate
汇款
remit, make remittance, remittance
汇款单
money order
汇款结算
remittance settlement
汇款人
remitter
汇款通知单
remittance slip
汇款银行
remitting bank
汇率
exchange rate, rate of exchange
汇率走势
tendency of exchange rate
汇票
bill of exchange (B/E.), draft
汇票汇款
remittance by draft
汇票金额
amount of a draft
汇票贴现
discount of draft
汇票正本
original bill
汇票支付
payment by draft
汇票支付日期
maturity of a draft
会长
president
会费
subscription
会见
interview
会所

chamber
会谈
conference, talk
会谈纪要
minutes of meeting
会议
conference, meeting, convention
会议记录
meeting notes, minutes of meeting, minutes
会议记录本
minute book
会议厅
chamber
会议召集人
convener
会员
member
会员费
membership fee (due)
会员证
membership card
会员资格
membership
贿赂
corrupt, bribe
贿赂费
hush money
贿赂物
bribe
贿赂罪
offence of bribery
毁坏
destroy, collapse
毁灭
destroy, destruction
混合
amalgamation, mix
混合比
mixture ratio
混合成本
mixed cost
混合关税
compound tariff
混合税
mixed duties
混合税率
mixed tariff
混凝土
concrete
混凝土拌和
mixing of concrete
混凝土拌和厂
batching plant
混凝土拌和楼
concrete mixing plant, batching plant
混凝土保护层
concrete cover
混凝土泵
concrete pump
混凝土打毛机
chipping machine
混凝土骨料
concrete aggregate
混凝土和易性
workability of concrete
混凝土缓凝剂
concrete retarder
混凝土浇筑
concrete placement
混凝土浇筑设备
placing plant
混凝土搅拌机
concrete mixer
混凝土块
concrete block, concrete brick
混凝土快速养护
accelerated curing of concrete
混凝土路面
concrete pavement
混凝土模板
concrete formwork
混凝土配筋
concrete reinforcement
混凝土强度
concrete strength

混凝土试件
concrete sample
混凝土试块
concrete test cube
混凝土摊铺机
concrete paver
混凝土外加剂
concrete admixture(additive)
混凝土心墙
concrete core wall
混凝土养护
concrete curing
混凝土震捣器
concrete vibrator
混凝土砖
concrete brick
豁免
exempt,exemption,immunity,remit
活期存款
demand deposit,current deposit
活期贷款
demand loan,call loan,call money
活期账户
current account,checking account
活跃账户
active account
火
fire,disaster
火灾
fire
火灾保险
fire insurance
火灾风险事故
fire perils
或有费用
contingent expenses
或有负债
contingent liabilities
或有利润
contingent profit
或有权益
contingent interest
货币
currency,money
货币比例
currency proportion
货币贬值
currency depreciation, currency devaluation
货币贬值调整
devaluation adjustment
货币储备
currency reserve
货币单位
monetary unit
货币的
monetary
货币的可获得性
currency availability
货币兑换
conversion of currency, currency conversion
货币兑换性
convertibility
货币风险
currency risk
货币互换
currency swap
货币汇率
monetary exchange rate
货币计价
money measurement
货币计量
money measurement
货币可兑换性
currency convertibility
货币利率
money interest rate
货币期货合同
currency futures contract
货币期权
currency option
货币升值
currency appreciation, currency revaluation
货币时间价值

time value of money
货币市场
money market
货币市场存单
money market certificate
货币市场存款账户
money market deposit account
货币市场互助基金
money market mutual funds
货币损益
monetary gain or loss
货币套期保值
currency hedge
货币限制
currency restriction, monetary restraint
货币性项目
monetary item
货币性与非货币性方法
monetary-nonmonetary method
货币性资产
monetary assets
货币性资产或负债
money assets or liabilities
货币债务
monetary liabilities
货币政策
monetary policy
货币周转
money turnover
货币自由兑换性
currency convertibility
货场
storage yard
货车
truck
货到付款
cash on delivery, payment on arrival, pay on delivery, spot cash
货交承运人(指定地点)(价)
free carrier…(named point) (FCA)
货名
name of commodity

货盘
pallet
货品说明综合表
summary sheets of goods
货损理算
cargo damage adjustment
货物
goods, commodity, cargo, merchandise
货物保险
insurance of goods
货物保险单
cargo policy
货物标志
cargo mark, shipping mark
货物采购
procurement of goods
货物发运费用
freight forward cost
货物估价单
valuation form
货物检查
cargo inspection
货物进口完税单
import duty memo
货物品质证书
certificate of quality
货物申报单
merchandise declaration
货物实行禁运
put an embargo on
货物税
excise
货物说明书
description of goods
货物运输保险
cargo transportation insurance
货物账款通知单
cargo accounting advice
货运
freight, carriage
货运保险
cargo insurance

货运代理行
forwarder
货运单
waybill
货运单据
shipping documents
货运单证
cargo paper
货运合同
contract of carriage
货运唛头
cargo mark, shipping mark
货运提单
cargo document
货运条件
conditions of carriage
货栈
warehouse, store house
货值提单
ad valorem bill of lading
货主负担风险
owner's risk
获得
acquire, acquisition, gain, obtain, secure, procure
获得方
acquiring party
获得技术
acquisition of technology
获得新市场
acquire a new market
获得用地
land acquisition
获利
earn, gain, make profit
获利能力
profitability

J

击实机
tamper
机场税
airport tax
机动车
vehicle
机动车第三者责任险
third party motor insurance
机动车辆税
motor vehicle tax
机动车责任险
motor car liability insurance
机构
machine, organization, institution
机构的
institutional
机构内部的
in-house
机构内部能力
in-house capabilities
机构自身能力
in-house capabilities
机会
chance, occasion, opportunity
机会成本
opportunity cost
机会研究
opportunity study
机密
confidential, confidentiality, secrecy
机密的
confidential, secret
机密的细节
confidential details
机密分类账
private ledger
机密文件
confidential document
机器
machine, machinery

机器损坏保险
machinery breakdown insurance
机损条款
break down clause
机械
machine, plant, machinery
机械的
mechanical
机械工时定额
standard machine hour (time)
机械故障保险单
machinery breakdown policy
机械加工
machining
机械间接损失保险
machinery consequential loss (interruption) insurance
机械设备安装工程
mechanical equipment installation works
机械设备价值
value of machinery
机械设备折旧
depreciation of machinery
机械寿命
machine life
机组
unit
积累
accrual, accumulate
积累资金
accumulated funds
积压的工作
backlog
积载空隙
broken stowage
基本成本估计
base cost estimate
基本贷款汇率
base lending rate
基本的
basic, fundamental, substantial
基本费率

基本费用估计
base cost estimate
基本分项工作
basic item
基本风险
prime risk
基本工资
basic salary, basic wages
基本合同责任
basic contractual responsibilities
基本价格
basic price
基本价格指数
base price index
基本建设
capital construction
基本建设费用
capital cost
基本库存
base stock
基本利率
basic interest rate
基本设计
basic design
基本事实
primary fact
基本完工
substantial completion
基本文件
keystone document
基本运费
base freight rate
基本证据
primary evidence
基础
basis, foundation
基础工程
foundation works, foundation work
基础设施
infrastructure, macrostructure
基础设施项目
infrastructure project

基价
base price, base value
基建投资
capital outlay
基建预算
construction budget
基建资金
capital fund
基金
fund
基面
base level
基线
base line
基线费用
base line cost
基线预算
base line budget
基准
datum
基准点
datum point
基准利率
benchmark rate
基准面
datum level, base level
基准年
base year
基准日期
base date
基准线
datum line
激励
motivation
激烈竞争
severe competition
及时到达
due arrival
及时交货
timely delivery
及时性
timeliness
级别
grade
级配骨料
graded aggregate
即付保函
demand guarantee
即付的
prompt
即刻装运
prompt shipment
即期
demand, sight
即期存款
demand deposit
即期的
sight
即期付款交单
documents against payment at sight
即期付款信用证
sight payment credit
即期汇率
spot exchange rate
即期汇票
demand bill, demand draft, bill payable on demand, sight draft, sight bill
即期交货
prompt delivery
即期票据
demand note, note on demand, sight bill
即期外汇买卖
spot exchange transaction
即期信用证
sight L/C
即期债务
debt at call
即时的
immediate
极端的
extreme
极限
limit
急件

urgent document, dispatch
急救
first aid
集水
catchment
集水坑
catch pit
集体抵制
group boycotts
集体行为
group action
集团
aggregation
集装箱
container
集装箱船
container ship
集装箱堆场
container yard
集装箱货物集散站
container freight station
集资
call for funds, raise funds
计划
plan, program, scheme
计划编制方法
method of programming
计划表
schedule
计划采购
scheduled purchasing
计划产量
scheduled output
计划的修改
modification of planning
计划的依据
programming frameworks
计划费用
planned cost
计划风险
calculated risk
计划工期
as-planned schedule

计划利润
target profit
计划拟定
programming
计划评审技术
program evaluation and reviews technique (PERT)
计划期限
planned period
计划日期
scheduled date
计划图
scheme drawing
计划完工日期
scheduled completion date
计划委员会
planning commission
计划中的项目
planned project
计价
valuation, pricing
计价过低
undervaluation
计件工资
wages for piece work, piece wages
计件工资率
piece-work rate, piece rate
计件工作
piece work system
计件折旧法
unit method of depreciation
计量
admeasurement, measurement
计量单位
unit of measurement
计量合同
measurement contract
计量型合同
admeasurement type of contract
计量原则
principle of measurement
计日工
daywork

计日工资
daywork rate, day wage
计日工资率
day rate
计时工资
time wage
计时工资率
time rate
计税年度
tax year
计算
compute, count, calculate
计算机辅助设计
computer aided design(CAD)
计算价值
computed value
计算式
formula
计算书
calculations
计息日
value date
记存装置
register
记号
mark, sign, tick
记录
record, note-taking, mark
记录错误
clerical error
记录图纸
record drawing
记名背书
special endorsement
记名提单
named bill of lading, straight B/L
记名债券
registered bond
记名支票
order check, signed check
记入借方
debit
记时卡
time card
记载
record
记账
keep account, book, on account
记账单位
accounting unit
记账货币
currency of account, money of account
记账卡
debit card
记账员
bookkeeper
纪律
discipline
技工
skilled labour
技能
skill, technique
技巧
technique, skill
技师
technician
技术
technique, technology
技术标准
technical standard
技术措施
technical measures
技术代表团
technical mission
技术方案
technical solution
技术分析
technical analysis
技术服务合同
technical services contract
技术规程
technical specifications, technical regulations
技术规范
technical specifications

技术建议书
technical proposal
技术诀窍
know-how
技术可行性
technical feasibility
技术秘密
know-how
技术评价
technical evaluation
技术上的可接受性
technical acceptability
技术审查与批准
technical review and approval
技术审核
technical scrutiny
技术数据
technical data
技术水平的鉴定
technical degree verification
技术特征
technical characteristics
技术性的
technical
技术性鉴定
technical assessment
技术性能
technical performance, technical characteristics
技术引进
technology import, acquisition of technology
技术员
technician
技术援助
technical assistance
技术援助费
technical assistance fee
技术援助信贷
technical assistance credit
技术责任
technical responsibility
技术支持
technical support
技术转让
transfer of technology, technology transfer
技术咨询公司
technical consultancy firm
技术咨询顾问
technical consultant
技术资料
technical data
既得的
vested
既得利益
vested interests
继承
inherit, succeed
继承的财产
inherited property
继承人
heir, inheritor, successor
继任者
successor
继续
continuation
寄存
lodge
寄售
consignment
寄宿
lodge
寄托
bailment
寄销品
consigned goods
加班
work overtime, overhours, overtime
加班的
overtime
加班费
overtime pay, overtime, overhours
加班工时
overtime workhour
加班工资

overtime wages, premium pay
加班工作
overtime work
加班奖金
overtime premium (bonus)
加班津贴
overtime allowance
加班时间
overtime, overhours
加保费
additional premium
加标签于
tag
加工
process, manufacture
加工成本
processing cost
加工费
processing cost
加工能力
process capability
加工时间
processing time
加工图
working drawings, shop drawings
加工制造的检验点
fabrication check points
加固
reinforce, reinforcement
加价
price mark up
加快速度
expedite, accelerate
加气混凝土
aeroconcrete
加气剂
air entrained agent
加强
reinforcement
加权
weighting
加权百分数
percent weighting

加权法
method of weighting
加权算术平均数
weighted arithmetic average
加权系数
weight coefficient
加速
accelerate
加速偿还条款
acceleration clause
加速成本回收制度
accelerated cost recovery system
加速竣工
accelerated completion
加速施工
acceleration, speed-up construction
加速施工费
acceleration cost
加速施工指令
acceleration order
加速折旧
accelerated depreciation
加速折旧法
accelerated method of depreciation
加载试验
loading test
夹具
fixture
家具及办公用具
furniture and office appliances
价格
price
价格变动
variation of price
价格表
schedule of prices
价格波动
fluctuation of price
价格波动因子
price fluctuation factor
价格不变性
invariability in price
价格单

price list
价格的接受者
price taker
价格的决定者
price maker
价格低廉的
keen, cheap, low
价格调整
price adjustment
价格调整合同
price adjustment contract
价格调整条款
price adjustment clause
价格调整系数
price adjustment factor
价格幅度
price range
价格监督
price control
价格控制
price control
价格敏感性
price sensitivity
价格上涨
advancing, price escalation
价格谈判
price bargaining
价格谈判的地位
bargaining position
价格条件
price terms
价格贴现
discount for price
价格修正条款
price revision clause
价格指数
price index
价格组成的各部分
components of price
价目表
price list, tariff
价值
value, worth, price

价值分析
value analysis
价值工程
value engineering (VE)
价值检验证书
inspection certificate of value
价值一览表
schedule of values
价值重估
revaluation
假报告
false report
假定
presumption
假冒
counterfeit
假期
holiday
假日工资
premium pay, holiday pay
假设价格
notional price
假账
false entry
坚持
abide, adhere
间接标价法
indirect quotation
间接材料费用
indirect material cost
间接成本
indirect cost, oncost
间接费
indirect costs, overhead charges
间接费分配
overhead allocation
间接开支
indirect expenses
间接贸易
indirect trade
间接人工成本
indirect labour cost
间接融资

indirect financing
间接税
indirect tax
间接损害
indirect damage
间接损失
consequential damage (loss), indirect loss
间接损失保险
indirect loss insurance
间接责任
indirect liability
兼并
merge, merger, take over
监督
monitor, supervise, supervision, superintendence
监督合同能力
ability to monitor contract
监督人
superintendent, supervisor
监工
ganger, superintendent, overseer, task master
监管人员
supervisory personnel, job supervisor
监控
monitor
监控工作
monitor work
监理
supervise, supervision
监理工程师
consulting engineer, supervising engineer
监理者
supervisor
监视
monitor, observe, oversee
监视人
overseer
减除的
deductible

减价
reduce the price, mark down, price cutting
减量
decrement
减免
mitigation, remission
减免税
tax relief
减轻
mitigate, mitigation
减轻债务
abatement of debt
减去
deduct
减少
decrease, diminish, diminution, reduce, reduction
减税
abatement of tax, tax abatement, tax reduction
检测计划表
schedule of inspection and testing
检查
inspect, inspection, check, verification, examination
检查工作
inspection of works
检查井
inspection well
检查孔
sight hole
检查日期
date of survey, date for inspection
检查员
inspector
检举人
plaintiff
检修
service
检验
test, verification
检验报告

survey report
检验费
fee for inspection, testing fee
检验合格证书
inspection certificate
检验日期
date for testing, date of survey
检验时间
time for tests, proving time
检验条款
survey clause
检验通知
notice of test
检验证书
certificate of inspection, testing certificate, test certificate
简单
simplicity
简介
introduction, profile
简明
simplicity
简明的
concise, brief
简述
introduction
简图
diagram, sketch
简要进度计划
summary schedule
简支梁
simply supported beam
见票后(若干天)付款期票
after sight bill
见票后定期付款汇票
bill payable at fixed date after sight
见票即付
payable at sight, payable on demand
见票即付的
sight
见票即付汇票
bill at sight
见票即付汇票
bill payable at sight
见票即付票据
demand bill
见习期
period of probation
建立
establish, establishment
建立联络关系
liaise
建立营地
encamp
建设
construction
建设-出租-移交
Build-Rent-Transfer (BRT)
建设单位
organization of construction
建设性的
constructive
建设许可证
building permit
建设-移交-运营
Build-Transfer-Operate (BTO)
建设-拥有-运营
Build-Own-Operate (BOO)
建设-拥有-运营-补贴-移交
Build-Own-Operate-Subsidize-Transfer (BOOST)
建设-拥有-运营-移交
Build-Own-Operate-Transfer (BOOT)
建设-拥有-运营-维护
Build-Own-Operate-Maintain (BOOM)
建设-拥有-出售
Build-Own-Sell (BOS)
建设-运营-出售
Build-Operate-Sell (BOS)
建设-运营-移交(或转让)
Build-Operate-Transfer (BOT)
建议
advice, proposal, suggestion, recommend

建议书
proposal
建议书大纲
outline proposal
建议书提交前预备会
pre-proposal conference
建议书征求函
request for proposal
建造
construct
建造阶段
construction stage
建造商
builder
建造师
builder, constructor
建造者
constructor, builder
建造周期
construction cycle
建筑
construction
建筑材料
construction material, building material
建筑贷款
building loan
建筑费用指数
index of construction costs
建筑缝
construction joint
建筑工程
construction works
建筑工程保险单
construction work policy
建筑工程公司
construction engineering corporation
建筑工程师
architectural engineer
建筑工程造价
cost of building works
建筑工地
construction site

建筑管理方式
construction management (CM)
建筑合同
construction contract
建筑和扩建
construction and addition
建筑会计
construction accounting
建筑设计
architecture, architectural design
建筑师
architect
建筑施工图
architectural working drawing
建筑透视图
architectural perspective
建筑物税
building tax
建筑许可
construction concession
建筑学
architecture
建筑业
construction business, construction industry
建筑账户
construction account
建筑执照
building permit
建筑综合体
complex
建筑资产负债表
construction balance sheet
健康保险
health insurance
健康证明
medical certificate, health certificate
鉴别
identify, identification
鉴定
appraise, appraisal, identify
鉴定人
appraiser, expert witness, referee

鉴定书
testimonial
鉴定意见
expert opinion
鉴于
considering, in view of
鉴于条款
whereas clause
将来交货
forward delivery
僵局
impasse, deadlock
讲究实际的
business-like
奖金
bonus, reward, premium
奖励
incentive, award, reward
奖励工资
wage incentive
奖励条款
bonus clause
降低
reduce, diminish
降低成本
cost reduction
降低的价格
reduced price
降价
reduce the price, price reduction, price cutting, mark down
降压变电站
step-down substation
降雨强度
intensity of rainfall
交叉过失
cross-default
交叉过失条款
cross-default clause
交叉汇兑
cross exchange
交叉路
cross road

交叉折扣
cross discounts
交错
overlap
交单
presentation
交单付款
cash against document
交到船上
delivered on board the ship
交付
delivery, deliver
交付材料
delivery of materials
交还
surrender
交换
exchange, swap, trade
交货
delivery of goods
交货承运人
delivering carrier
交货地点
delivery point
交货付款
cash against delivery, payment on delivery
交货港
port of delivery
交货价格
delivered price
交货期
delivery period, time of delivery
交货期限
term of delivery
交货清单
delivery order
交货日期
date of delivery, delivery date
交货时间表
delivery schedule
交货条件
delivery terms, terms of delivery, de-

livered terms
交货通知
delivery advice
交货证明
proof of delivery
交际费
expenses for social intercourse, entertaining expenses
交流发电机
alternator
交涉
negotiate, negotiation
交税
payment of tax, payment of duties
交替的
alternate
交通
communication, traffic
交通安全
traffic safety
交通标志
traffic signing
交通量
traffic volume
交通事故
traffic accident, road accident
交通信号灯
traffic lights
交通运输
transportation
交通运输能力
traffic capacity
交往
contact, associate with
交易
deal, transaction, trade
交易价格
price of transacting
交易税
transaction tax
交易所
exchange
交钥匙工程
turnkey project
交钥匙合同
turnkey contract
交钥匙项目
turnkey project
浇注
cast, pour, place
胶带
adhesive tape
胶合板
plywood, glued board
胶合板混凝土模板
plywood concrete forms
角钢
angle steel
角色
role
绞车
winch, cable hoist
矫正
rectify, rectification
脚手板
scaffold board
脚手架
scaffold
脚注
foot-note
搅拌机
mixer
搅拌运料车
mixer truck, agitating truck
缴款通知
memorandum of payment
缴清股本
paid-up capital, paid-in capital
较小的工程变更
minor change in the work
较小的工程变更命令
order for minor change in the work
校正
adjust, adjustment
校正后的投标价
corrected bid price

校准
correct, alignment
阶段
phase, stage
阶段发包方式
phased construction method
阶段付款
stage payment
阶梯成本
step cost
接触
contact
接触器
contactor
接缝
joint
接缝填料
joint filler
接管
take over
接管令
receiving order
接近
access
接口
interface
接收
receive, accept
接收人
receiver
接收投标的截止时间
deadline for receipt of tenders
接受
accept, acceptance, take over
接受报价
acceptance of offer, accept a quotation, accept an offer
接受报价者
offeree
接受报盘
entertain an offer
接受承兑
acceptance for honor
接受的合同款额
accepted contract amount
接受抵押人
pledgee
接受订单
accept an order
接受订货
entertain an order
接受发盘
accept an offer
接受人
recipient, taker
接受声明
declaration of acceptance
接受索赔
accept a claim, entertain a claim
接受投标
accept the bid (tender)
接受投标书
acceptance of the bid (tender)
接受邀请
accept an invitation
接头
joint
节假日
holiday
节日
festival
节约
economy, saving
节约的
economical, frugal, saving
节约时间奖
premium bonus
结构
frame, structure
结构断裂
structural break
结构加工
fabricate
结关
customs clearance, clearance, clear a port

结关单
jerque note
结关手续
clearance procedure
结关文件
document on customs clearance
结关证明书
clear certificate
结合
merge, incorporate, combine
结汇
settlement of exchange
结论
conclusion
结欠余额
balance due
结清
discharge
结清单
discharge
结实的
compact
结束
finish, conclude, wind up, terminate
结算
clearing, reckon, settle
结算单
statement of account
结算价格
settlement price
结算日
account day
结算协定
clearing agreement
结余
balance
结账
settle accounts, close an account
结账分录
closing entry
结账后试算表
closing trial balance
结账日期
closing date
结转
carry down
结转价格
transfer price
截断
cutting
截水坑
catch pit
截水墙
cut-off
截止日期
deadline, date of expiration (expiry), closing date, lastest date, cut-off date
截止时间
deadline
解除
release, relieve from, get rid of
解除抵押
release of mortgage
解除合同
terminate a contract
解除合同补偿费
compensation for cancellation of contract
解除履约
release from performance
解除条款
resolutive clause
解除义务
relieve from obligations
解雇
dismiss, fire, discharge
解雇费
termination pay
解决
settle, settlement, resolve, resolution
解决差价
bridge the price gap
解决索赔案件
administer claim
解散

dissolve, dissolution
解释
interpretation, explain, explanation, construe, construction
解释权
power of interpretation
解说
comment
解体
dissolution
解约
rescission of a contract, cancel a contract, terminate a contract
解约权
right of rescission
介绍
introduce, introduction
介绍信
letter of recommendation, letter of introduction
界线
demarcation line, boundary line
界限
threshold, boundary
借出
loan, lend
借贷
debit and credit, borrowing
借贷成本
borrowing cost
借贷信用
creditworthiness
借方
debtor, debit
借方卡
debit card
借方栏
debit column
借方余额
debit balance
借记
debit
借据
note of hand, IOU (I Owe You), note
借款
borrow
借款保函
letter of guarantee for loan
借款单证
loan note
借款国
borrowing country
借款人
borrower
借款银行
borrowing bank
借入
borrow
借项
debit entry, debit item, debit
借项通知单
debit memorandum (note)
借用人
borrower
借债
ask for loan
金额
amount, figure, sum
金钱
money
金融
finance
金融偿付能力
financial viability
金融的
financial, monetary
金融风险
financial risk
金融工具
financial instrument
金融公司
finance company, moneyed corporation
金融机构
financial institution, financier

金融家
financier
金融界
financial community
金融票据
financial instrument
金融期货
financial futures
金融市场
financial market
金融性资产
financial assets
金融中介
financial intermediation
金融中心
financial center
金融咨询
financial counselling
津贴
subsidy, allowance
仅供参考
for reference only
紧急的
urgent, emergency, critical
紧急法令
emergency act
紧急情况
emergency, emergency circumstances
紧急任务
urgent task
紧急行为
emergency action
紧缩银根政策
tight money policy
尽管
notwithstanding
近海的
maritime
近似的
approximate
近似工程量清单
approximate bill of quantities
进程
progress
进出口许可证
import and export license
进度
progress
进度报告
progress report
进度表
progress chart, schedule
进度承诺
schedule commitment
进度分析
progress analysis
进度付款
progress payment
进度控制
progress control
进度影响分析
schedule impact analysis
进风口
air inlet
进货成本
prime cost
进货费用
buying expenses
进货运费
freight-in
进货折扣
discount on purchases
进口
import
进口报关单
declaration for importation, declaration inwards, import entry
进口材料
import material
进口代理商
import agent
进口附加税
import surtax (surcharge)
进口港
port of entry
进口国货币

importer's currency
进口合同
import contract
进口禁令
import ban
进口贸易
import trade
进口免税
free import
进口配额
import quota
进口批件
import license (permit)
进口申报单
import declaration
进口手续
import procedure, process of import
进口税
customs, import tax, impost, import duty
进口通知
import announcement
进口限额
import limit
进口限制
import restraint
进口许可
import permit, import admission
进口许可证
import license (permit)
进口许可制
import licensing
进库材料
incoming material
进款
incoming payment, receipt
进料斗
feed hopper
进入
enter, entry
进入工程现场
access to works
进入权
access right, access
进入现场
access to site
进水口
inlet, intake
进退两难
dilemma
进行
carry out, proceed
进行保险
assure, insure, take out insurance
进行破坏
sabotage
进行谈判
conduct negotiations
进展
advancement, progress
禁令
ban, prohibition
禁运
embargo
禁止
embargo, ban, prohibit, prohibition
禁止出口
ban on export
禁止翻供
estoppel
禁止进口
ban on import, import prohibition
禁止令
injunction, restraining order
禁止输入
import ban
经常费用
overhead expenses
经常开支
revenue expenditure
经常项目差额
balance of current account
经常性修理
current repair
经度
longitude

经法庭判定
awarded by court
经过
pass, transit
经纪人
broker, middleman, operator
经纪人佣金
brokerage
经纪行
broker, finder
经纪业
broking, brokerage
经济
economy
经济补偿
financial compensation
经济成本
economic cost
经济单位
economic unit
经济担保
financial security
经济的
economic
经济法
economic law
经济风险
economic risk
经济封锁
economic blockade
经济规律
economic law
经济合同
economic contract
经济核算
economic reckoning
经济净现值
economic net present value (ENPV)
经济内部收益率
economic internal return rate (EIRR)
经济批量
economic lot size

经济评估
economic appraisal
经济权益
economic interest
经济上的
economic
经济师
economist
经济实体
economic entity
经济寿命
economic life
经济寿命与残值
economic life and salvage value
经济索赔
financial claim
经济特区
special economic zone
经济危机
economic crisis
经济效益
economic benefit
经济学家
economist
经济援助
economic aid
经济周期
economic cycle
经理
manager
经历
experience, undergo
经授权的
authorized
经纬仪
theodolite, transit
经销商
dealer, distributor
经协商的合同
negotiated contract
经验
experience
经营

经营
manage, run, operate
经营报表
operation statement, operating statement
经营场所
business location, establishment
经营费用
working expenses, operating expenses
经营风险
operating risk
经营利润盈余
operating surplus
经营人
keeper, dealer
经营业绩
operating performance
经营中断保险
business interruption insurance
经营周(转)期
operating cycle
经正式授权的
duly authorized
精加工
finishing
精确的
exact, precise
精确度
precision
精算师
actuary
精通
proficiency
精选的
selected
井点排水
drainage by well point
警察
police
警告
warn, admonish, admonition
警告信号
warning signal

警告性标志
warning mark
警戒线
warning line
净保险费
net premium
净残值
net salvage
净的
net
净吨位
net tonnage
净额
net amount
净发票价格
net invoice price
净费率
net rate
净加价百分率
net markup percentage
净价
net price
净利
net profit
净利润
clear profit, pure profit, net profit
净皮重
net tare
净收入
clear income, net income
净收入损失
loss of net income
净收益
net earnings, net income, net yield
净数
net
净损失
net loss
净投资收入
net investment income
净息
net interest
净现金流量

net cash flow
净现值
net present value (NPV)
净现值法
net present value method (NPV method)
净销售额
net sales
净效益
net benefit
净营业损失
net loss from operation
净运费
net freight
净值
net worth
净重
net weight
净资产
net assets
净租赁
net lease
竞争
competition, compete
竞争对手
competitor
竞争能力
competitiveness
竞争性价格
competitive price
竞争性招标
competitive bidding
竞争者
competitor, rival
境外第三方账户
offshore escrow account
境外利率
external interest rate
境外银行
offshore bank
窘境
dilemma
纠正
correct, redress
纠正措施
corrective action
纠正延误
correct delays
酒精
alcohol
救险
salvage
救助费用
salvage charges
救助作业
salvage operation
就地浇灌地下连续墙
cast-in-place diaphragm wall
就业保障
employment security
就业法
employment act
就业证件
working papers
居所
residence
居住面积
floor space
居住区
dwelling district
居住许可证
residence permit
居住者
occupant
局面
conjuncture
举例说明
illustrate, illustration
举起
hold
举债经营
financial leverage, leverage
举债经营比率
leverage ratio
矩阵式机构
matrix style organization

巨灾损失
catastrophe loss
拒付
dishonor, repudiate, repudiation
拒付的票据
dishonored notes (bill)
拒付声明
statement of dishonour
拒付通知
notice of dishonour
拒付通知单
protest jacket
拒付证书
certificate of dishonour, protest
拒付支票
rejected check
拒绝
refuse, refusal, reject, rejection, turn down
拒绝承兑
dishonor, non-acceptance
拒绝接受
repudiate
拒绝全部投标
rejection of all bids
拒绝验收的工作
rejected work
具体证据
supporting details, supporting particulars
具体证明材料
supporting details, supporting particulars
具有法律地位的
legal
具有竞争力的
competitive
具有吸引力的价格
attractive price
据此
hereby
聚集
gather, assemble, aggregation

捐款
contribution, donation, subscription
捐献
contribute, donate
捐赠
contribute, donate
捐赠人
donor
捐赠资本
contributed capital, donated capital
捐赠资产
donated assets
捐助
contribute
卷扬机
hoist, cable hoist
决策
make policy
决策错误
mistake of decision-making
决策阶段
strategy stage
决策树
decision tree
决策者
policy maker
决定
decide, decision, determine, determination, resolution
决定性的
decisive, material
决定性的一票
casting vote
决算
final settlement of account, audit
决算表
final account, final statement
决算后诸项费用
back charges
决算日
date of balance sheet
决议
resolution, decision

绝对产权
absolute title
绝对承担
absolute acceptance
绝对的
absolute
绝对免赔额
deductible average
绝对配额
absolute quota
绝对全损
actual total loss
绝对权益
absolute interest
绝对所有权
absolute title
绝对条件
absolute condition
绝对优势
absolute advantage
绝对优先权
first priority
绝密
strictly confidential, top secret
绝热材料
heat-insulating material
绝缘
insulation
绝缘体
insulation
君子协定
gentleman's agreement
均匀的
uniform
竣工
completion
竣工报表
statement at completion
竣工报告
completion report
竣工奖金
bonus for completion
竣工期限的延长
extension of time for completion
竣工时间
time for completion
竣工图纸
as-built drawing, record drawing, completion drawing
竣工拖延
delay in completion
竣工文件
as-built documents
竣工验收证书
final acceptance certificate
竣工证明
certificate of completion
竣工证书
certificate of completion, certificate for completion, completion certificate

K

卡车
truck, lorry
卡车拖车
truck trailer
卡车装运设备
trucking equipment
卡片
card
开办
start up
开办费
setup cost, initial costs (expenses), establishment charges, preliminary expenses
开办项目
preliminary items

开标
bid opening
开标程序
bid opening procedure
开标纪要
bid opening minutes
开采
exploitation
开出提单
issue a bill of lading
开除
dismiss, discharge, fire
开发
develop, development, exploitation
开发成本
development cost
开发公司
development corporation
开发规划
developmental program
开发商
developer
开发信贷协议
development credit agreement
开发银行
development bank
开发资本
development capital
开放政策
open door policy
开工
commencement of work, commence
开工的先决条件
conditions precedent to commencement
开工令
order of commencement of work
开工率
rate of operation, operating rate
开工日期
commencement date, date of commencement
开工通知
notice to commence
开航日期
date of departure
开户
opening an account
开价
quote, price asked
开具发票
invoicing
开垦
reclamation
开空头支票
kiting
开空头支票者
kite-flier
开口保单
open policy
开口定货单
open-end orders
开口合同
open contract, open-end contract
开口信用证
open credit
开盘价
opening price
开票人
drawer
开始
start, commence, proceed
开始采购
initiate procurement
开始记录
opening entry
开始阶段
inception stage
开脱性条款
exculpatory clause
开脱罪责的
exculpatory
开业会计师
independent accountant, public accountant
开证银行

issuing bank, opening bank
开支
expenses, expenditure, outlay
开支票
write a check
开支权限
spending authority
开支项目
outgo
开支账
expense account
刊出
publish, list
刊登
publish, appear
刊明
list
勘测设计费
expenses for survey & design
勘查
investigation
勘察
exploration, survey, prospect
勘探
exploration, explore, prospect
勘误
erratum
看法
points of view
看货买卖
sale by inspection
看样成交
conclude business after viewing samples
看样出售
sale by sample
抗辩
contradict, confute, counterplead
抗地震的
antiseismic
抗冻混凝土
frost-resisting concrete
抗拉强度
tensile strength
抗诉
counterappeal, protest
抗压模量
compressive modulus
抗压强度
compressive strength
抗议
protest
考察
inspect, explore, exploration, observation
考级
merit-rating
考虑
consider, consideration
考虑到
considering
考勤表
time sheet
考勤卡
time ticket
考勤员
time clerk
苛捐杂税
harsh duties
可保财产
insurable property
可保风险
insurable risks
可保价值
insurable value
可保权益
insurable interest
可保险的
insurable
可报销的
reimbursable
可比成本
comparable cost
可比的
comparable
可比性

comparability
可避免成本
avoidable cost, escapable cost
可避免的事故
avoidable accident
可变的
variable
可变利率
variable rate
可变现价值
cash realizable value
可变现净值
net realizable value
可变现资产
realizable assets
可辨认的
discernible, decipherable
可补偿的
recoverable, reimbursable
可偿还的
reimbursable
可撤销的信用证
revocable L/C, revocable credit
可撤销的
revocable
可撤销的合同
voidable contract
可持续性
sustainability
可得的
available
可得性
availability
可调单价
adjustable unit price
可调价的包干
lump sum with fluctuations
可调价的固定价格合同
fixed price contract with adjustments
可调利率抵押贷款
adjustable-rate mortgage
可动用结余
available balance

可兑换的
convertible
可分的合同
severable contract
可分割的信用证
divisible L/C
可分割合同
divisible contract
可分摊的成本
distributable cost
可管理风险
administrative risk
可归因于
attributable to
可恢复的
recoverable
可回收的
recoverable
可获得的
obtainable, available
可计量性
quantification
可接受的
acceptable
可接受的变更
acceptable variation
可接受的当地程序
acceptable local procedures
可接受的偏离
acceptable deviation
可接受价格
acceptable price
可接受日期
acceptable date
可接受证据
admissible evidence
可靠的
reliable, authenticated, bona fide
可靠性
reliability, authenticity
可靠性试运行
reliability run
可控成本

controllable cost
可量化
quantification
可流通的
negotiable
可流通性
negotiability
可买到的
obtainable
可能性
possibility, probability, chance
可强制履行的合同
enforceable contract
可驱逐的
expellable
可取得专利权的
patentable
可赎回的
callable
可赎回公司债券
callable bond
可赎回债券
redeemable bond
可随时支取的
callable
可谈判的
negotiable
可推定的工程变更
constructive change, constructive variation
可推定的工程变更指令
constructive change order
可推定的加速施工
constructive acceleration
可推定的暂停施工
constructive suspension
可为银行所接受的
acceptable to the bank
可协商的
negotiable
可信的
authenticated, trustworthy
可行的
viable, feasible
可行性
feasibility, practicability
可行性研究
feasibility study
可延期债券
extendible bond
可以忽略的
negligible
可译出的
decipherable
可用的
available
可用性
availability
可用支票付款的
checkable
可预见的损失
foreseeable losses
可原谅并应给予补偿的拖期
excusable and compensable delays
可原谅但不给予补偿的拖期
excusable but not compensable delays
可原谅的拖期
excusable delays
可在银行贴现的票据
bankable bill
可转换的
convertible
可转换债券
convertible bond
可转让的
assignable, negotiable
可转让定期存单
negotiable certificate of deposit
可转让票据
negotiable paper, negotiable instrument
可转让信用证
transferable L/C, negotiable credit
可转让性
negotiability

可转让证券
marketable securities
可转让支票
negotiable check
可资本化成本
capitalizable cost
可自由兑换的货币
convertible currency
可自由兑换的纸币
convertible money (paper)
可自由支配的基金
discretionary funds
可作证据文件
admissible document
客观的
objective
客观事实
objective fact
客观性
objectivity
客观原因
objective cause
客观证据
objective evidence
客户
customer, client
客户定金
customer's deposit
客户账
customer's account
课税
imposition
课税对象
object of taxation
课税豁免
tax exclusion
课税基础
tax base
肯定的
definite, positive
空白背书
endorsement in blank, blank endorsement, open endorsement

空白背书汇票
bill endorsed in blank
空白的
blank
空白票据
blank bill
空白提单
blank bill of lading
空白信用汇票
blank (letter of) credit
空白支票
blank check, blank note
空舱费
dead freight
空额信用证
blank (letter of) credit
空房
vacant room, vacancy
空间框架
space frame work
空间网架
space lattice
空气调节器
air conditioner
空气压缩机
air compressor
空缺
vacancy
空头
bear
空头支票
bouncer, bad cheque, kite, rubber check
空心板
voided slab
空心砖
H-brick, hollow brick, air brick
空余舱位
broken space
空运
carriage by air
空运保险
aerial insurance

空运承运人
air carrier
空运单条款
conditions of contract of air waybill
空运发货单
air consignment note (ACN)
空运货物
air freight
空运收据
air receipt
空运提单
airway bill (AWB), airway bill of lading
空运险
air risk
空运直达提单
through air waybill
空转的
idle
恐怖活动
terrorism
恐怖主义
terrorism
控告
accuse, accusation, charge, impeach, suit
控告方
accusing party
控告人
accusing person
控股公司
holding company, proprietary company
控股股东
majority stockholder
控股人
majority stockholder
控股有限公司
proprietary limited (Pty Ltd)
控诉
accuse, denounce, complain
控制
control

控制权
control
控制账户
control (controlling) account
口岸
port
口述的
word-of-mouth
口头变更指令
oral instruction of variation
口头承诺
verbal commitment, verbal promise
口头的
verbal, word-of-mouth, oral
口头合同
simple contract, oral contract
口头合约
verbal contract
口头命令
verbal order
口头申请
verbal request
口头通知
oral notice
口头协议
oral agreement
口头形式
oral form
口头约定
verbal contract
口头证据
oral evidence
口头指令确认书
confirmation of oral instruction
口头指示
oral instruction
口译
interpretation
扣除
deduct, deduction, recoup
扣除的
deductible

扣除额
deduction
扣发工资
wage garnishment
扣发支付款
payment withheld
扣减
abatement
扣交
withholding
扣款
withhold, withholding
扣留
detain, detainment, stoppage, withhold, arrest
扣押
detain, distrain, impound, levy, sequester
扣押财产
levy on property
扣押财物
distraint
扣押令
garnishee order, writ of detention
扣押权
lien
库存
stock, inventory
库存储备量
inventory reserve
库存盘点
stocking
库存清单
inventory
库存现金
cash on hand, cash in treasury
库存中断
stockout
夸大
overstate, exaggerate
夸大的索赔
exaggerated claim
跨部门影响
cross-sectoral effect
跨度
span
跨国的
multinational
跨国公司
multinational company, transnational company, transnational corporation
块石
rubble
快递
express delivery
快件
express
快捷的
express
快信
dispatch
快运物品
express
会计
accounting
会计报表
accounting statement, accounts
会计变更
accounting changes
会计程序
accounting procedure
会计单位
accounting unit, accounting entity
会计的
fiscal
会计等式
accounting equation
会计法
fiscal law, account law
会计方法
accounting method
会计分录
accounting entry
会计分期
accounting period

会计工作
accounting, accountancy
会计惯例
accounting convention
会计恒等式
accounting equation
会计计价
accounting valuation
会计记录
accounting records
会计监督
accounting control
会计科目
caption of account, account title, account
会计科目表
chart of accounts
会计科目一览表
account chart
会计控制
accounting control
会计年度
fiscal year, account year, financial year
会计凭证
accounting evidence, accounting document
会计期间
accounting period
会计人员
accountant
会计师
accountant
会计事务所
accounting firm
会计原理
accounting principles
会计账簿
accountant book, accounts, book of account
会计账册
account books
会计主管
account officer
会计主体
accounting entity
宽容
forbearance
宽容条款
allowance clause
宽限期
grace period, period of grace
宽限日期
days of grace
款项
money
款项余额
balance of amount
旷工
absent, absence
矿区使用费
royalty, override
矿渣水泥
slag cement
框架结构
framed structure
亏舱
broken stowage
亏空
deficit
亏损
loss, deficit
亏损账户
deficit account
捆
bale
困惑的
baffling
扩大
growth, extend
扩建
extension
扩展
extension

L

垃圾
refuse, rubbish, garbage
垃圾处理
rubbish disposal
拉平的价格
leveled price
来样加工
manufacturing with orderer's sample
来源
source
栏杆
hand rail, rail
蓝图
blueprint
缆索起重机
cable crane
滥用
abuse
滥用法律
abuse of law
滥用权力
abuse of power
滥用信用
abuse of trust
滥用职权
abuse of authority
浪费
waste, wastage
浪费的
waste
劳埃德保险公司
Lloyd's (Llds)
劳动保护
labour protection
劳动保护费
expenses for labour protection
劳动报酬
labour due
劳动定额
work norms, labour norms
劳动法
labour law
劳动纪律
job discipline, labour discipline
劳动力
labour force
劳动力充裕
abundance of labour
劳动力过剩
labour surplus
劳动密集型的
labour-intensive
劳动生产率
labour productivity
劳动生产能力
labour capacity
劳动条件
conditions of labour
劳动效率
labour efficiency
劳工保险
insurance of workmen
劳工法
industrial act, labour law
劳工工资
labour wage
劳工监督
labour monitoring
劳工许可证
labour permit
劳合社
Lloyd's (Llds)
劳合社保险单
Lloyd's policy
劳累
fatigue
劳力
work force, labour

劳力不足
shortage of labour
劳务
labour, service
劳务成本计算
costing of labour
劳务费
service charge
劳务费率
labour rate
劳务合同
labour contract, contract of services, service contract
劳务计划
labour planning
劳务收入
labour income
劳务统计报表
returns of labour
劳务协议
labour agreement
劳资关系
labour relations
劳资集体谈判协议
collective bargaining agreement
劳资纠纷
labour dispute, labour disturbance, labour trouble
劳资双方
capital and labour
劳资协议
labour agreement, trade agreement
劳资争端
labour dispute, industrial dispute
劳资争议
labour dispute, labour unrest
乐意支付
willingness to pay
雷管
detonator
类别
classification
类目
category
类型
pattern, type, category
累计
accumulate
累计成本
accumulation cost
累计的
cumulative
累计结算
accumulation settlement
累计金额
accruing amount
累计利息
accrual of interest
累计损失
accumulated loss
累计盈余
accumulated earnings, accumulated surplus
累计折耗
accumulated depletion
累计折旧
accumulated depreciation
累计总额
progressive total
累进偿付
graduated payment
累进的
progressive
累进付款
progressive payment
累进税
progressive tax
冷拉钢筋
cold-drawn bar
离岸成本加保险费(价)
cost and insurance (C&I)
离岸成本加运费(价)
cost and freight (CFR)
离岸价格
free on board (FOB)
离开

departure
离去
leave
离心泵
centrifugal pump
离职补偿金
separation pay
礼品
gift
里程碑
milestone
里程碑进度表
milestone schedule
里程碑日期
milestone dates
理财
financing
理解
understanding, knowledge
理论价格
notional price
理赔
claim settlement, settlement of claim
理赔代理人
claim settling agent, average agent
理事会
board of governors
理算
adjust, adjustment
理由
reason, ground, justification
力量
force
历法
calendar
历史成本
historical cost
历月
calendar month
立场
stance
立法
legislation

立法的变动
changes in legislation
立法机构
legislature
立方的
cubic
立方度量
cubic measure
立方厘米
cubic centimeter (cu. cm)
立方码
cubic yard (cu. yd)
立方米
cubic meter (cu. m)
立方体
cube
立方英尺
cubic foot (cu. ft)
立方英寸
cubic inch (cu. in)
立即的
immediate, prompt
立即付款
immediate payment, prompt cash
立即交货
immediate delivery
立即赔偿
immediate compensation
立即装运
immediate shipment
立交桥
grade separation bridge
立面图
elevation, elevation drawing
立约人
promisor
利率
rate of interest, interest rate
利率调整
interest rate adjustment
利率套购
interest rate arbitrage
利润

利润,收益,盈余
profit, gain, earnings
利润表
earnings report
利润额
profit margin
利润分配
profit distribution
利润估算
profit estimating
利润汇总
profit pooling
利润加成
profit mark-up
利润率
profit rate, rate of return, profit margin
利润税
profit tax
利润损失
loss of profit
利润损失保险
loss of profit insurance
利润预测
profit forecast
利息
interest
利息差额
interest margin
利益
benefit, interests
利益的冲突
conflict of interests
利用系数
utilization factor
沥青
asphalt, bitumen
沥青层
bituminous layer
沥青防水层
bituminous water-proof coating
沥青灌浆
bituminous grouting
沥青混凝土
bituminous concrete, asphalt concrete
沥青混凝土路面
asphalt concrete pavement
沥青搅拌设备
asphalt mixing unit
例会
regular meeting
例外
exception
例外的
exceptional, excepted
例外管理
management by exception
例行程序
routine procedure
例行检查
routine inspection
例证
example
隶属于
affiliate
砾石
gravel
砾石路
gravel road
连带保证人
joint sureties
连带责任
joint liability, joint and several liability
连接
interface
连锁风险
chain risks
连续的
continuous, consecutive
连续合同
continuing contract
连续日
consecutive days, running days
连续生产方式
sequential construction approach
联邦预算

federal budget
联邦政府
federal government, federation
联合
associate, join, combine, combination, joinder
联合保险
co-insurance
联合保险单
combined policy
联合财团保函
consortium guarantee
联合筹资
joint financing
联合贷款
joint loan
联合担保
joint guarantee
联合的
joint
联合抵押
joint mortgage
联合抵制
boycott
联合股份公司
joint-stock company
联合国发展论坛
UN Development Forum
联合合同
contract of association
联合会
federation
联合集团
consortium
联合监督
joint supervision
联合经理
co-manager
联合凭证
combined certificate
联合融资
cofinancing
联合体

consortium
联合体成员
member of consortium
联合投标
joint tendering, joint bid
联合运货
combined carriage of goods
联合运输人
intermodal carrier
联合账户
joint account
联机的
on-line
联络
liaise
联络办事处
liaison office
联络官
liaison officer
联盟
federation, confederation, alignment
联名保证
joint guarantee
联营
affiliate, affiliation, pooling
联营承包商
co-contractor
联营公司
affiliate company, allied company
联营体
joint venture (JV), joint adventure
联营体负责人
partner in charge
联运承运人
intermodal carrier
联运费率
joint rate
联运集装箱
intermodal container
联运提单
combined transport bill of lading (C. T. B/L), through B/L
联运运费

through freight
廉价
sale price
廉价出售
undersell
廉价的
cheap, inexpensive
廉价劳动力
cheap labour force
良好平均品质
fair average quality (FAQ)
良好信誉
good faith
梁
beam
梁板结构
beam and slab structure
两班制
double shift
两步贷款
two-step loan
两阶段招标
two-stage bidding
两讫
on the balance
两者挑一的
alternative
谅解
understanding
谅解备忘录
memorandum of understanding
量本利分析
volume-cost-profit analysis
量测仪器
measuring instrument
量度
measure
量具
measuring instrument
列表
tabulate
列表显示
tabulate

列出的
listed
列入短名单的公司
short listed firms
列入清单的
listed
劣等的
inferior
裂缝
crack
邻近地域
adjacent
临界的
critical
临时成本
provisional cost
临时出口
temporary export
临时单据
scrip
临时的
interim, temporary, provisional
临时发票
provisional invoice
临时分录账
blotter
临时付款
interim payment, provisional payment
临时工
casual worker, jobber
临时工程
temporary works
临时工程用地
land for temporary works
临时工作
odd job
临时估价
provisional assessment
临时雇工
odd hand
临时建筑物
temporary buildings

临时解雇
lay off
临时进口
temporary import
临时设施
temporary facilities
临时收据
temporary receipt
临时协议
binder, provisional agreement
临时性的
temporary, provisional, interim
临时性收支
non-recurring incomes and expenses
临时性账户
temporary account
临时延期决定
interim determination of extension
临时验收
provisional acceptance
临时预付款
temporary advance
临时再保险
facultative reinsurance
临时证书
provisional certificate
临时支撑
shoring, temporary support
临时仲裁
ad hoc arbitration
零活
odd job
零配件
spare parts, parts
零钱
change, odd money
零售
retail
零售价
retail price
零售商
tradesman, merchant, retailer, retail dealer
零星用料
miscellaneous material
零星运输
retail shipment
零用现金
petty cash
领班
ganger, foreman, section foreman, leading hand
领班人员
operator in charge
领导
leader, lead
领导能力
leadership
领导艺术
leadership
领货单
stock requisition
领料单
material requisition note, stock requisition
领料汇总单
stores requisition summary
领事发票
consular invoice
领事馆
consulate
领土
domain
领先
precede, precedence
领有执照者
licencee, licensee
领域
field, domain
流程图
flow chart, flow diagram
流出
outflow
流动
flow
流动比率

liquid ratio
流动财产
floating property
流动的
floating, current, fluid, liquid
流动负债
circulating liabilities, current liabilities, working liabilities
流动债务
current debt, floating debt
流动资本
floating capital, current capital, fluid capital
流动资产
fluid assets, floating assets, current assets, liquid assets
流动资金
working capital, fluid capital, liquid fund
流量
water discharge, flow
流量计
flow meter
流沙
quick sand
流水生产法
line production method
流水账
blotter
流体的
fluid
流通
circulate
流通存单
negotiable certificate of deposit
流通的
current
流通票据
negotiable instrument
流通税
circulation tax
流通信用证
circular credit
流通支票
negotiable check
流行
prevail
流域
catchment
留成利润
retained profit
留存收益
earning surplus
留有余地
leave some leeway
留置权
right of lien, lien
留置权书
letter of lien, letter of trust
琉璃瓦
enameled tile
硫酸盐水泥
sulphate cement
龙门吊
frame crane, gantry crane
垄断
monopoly
垄断价格
monopoly price
楼梯
staircase
漏洞
loophole
漏税
tax dodging
陆路的
overland
陆路共通地点
overland common point
陆上的
overland
陆运
carriage by land
陆运承运人
road carrier
陆运可到达的地点

overland common point
陆运提单
inland bill of lading
录用
admission
路货
afloat goods, afloat cargo
路基
subgrade
路基标高
grading elevation
路面
road way, pavement
路面结构
pavement structure
路面破碎机
pavement breaker
路线
route
路线测量
route survey
路线图
route map
路缘石
kerb
旅行信用证
circular credit
旅行支票
traveller's check
履带式起重机
crawler crane, caterpillar crane
履带式挖掘机
caterpillar excavator
履带式装载机
caterpillar loader
履历表
curriculum vitae (CV)
履行
perform, performance, execute, execution, discharge, fulfill
履行合同
carry out a contract, perform a contract

履行义务
fulfill an obligation, satisfaction
履行职责
discharge of duty
履约
perform, performance
履约保函
performance guarantee
履约保证
performance security
履约保证书
performance guarantee
履约担保
performance bond
履约信用证
performance letter of credit
律师
lawyer, counselor, attorney
律师服务费
legal charges
律师事务所
law office
律师委员会
bar council
律师协会
bar association
律师业
bar
绿化
landscaping
卵石
gravel
乱石
free-stone
略图
outline
伦敦保险协会罢工、暴动及民变险条款
Institute Strikes, Riots, and Civil Commotions Clauses
伦敦保险协会货物保险条款(A)(一切险)
Institute Cargo Clauses (A)

伦敦保险协会货物保险条款(B)(水渍险)
Institute Cargo Clauses (B)
伦敦保险协会货物保险条款(C)(平安险)
Institute Cargo Clauses (C)
伦敦保险协会货物条款
Institute Cargo Clauses (ICC)
伦敦保险协会战争险条款
Institute War Clauses
伦敦银行同业拆放利率
London Inter-Bank Offered Rate (LIBOR)
轮班
shift
轮班工作制
shift system
轮廓
profile
轮廓线
contour line
轮流的
alternate
轮胎
tyre, tire
轮胎磨损费
wear cost of tyre
轮胎式挖掘机
wheel excavator
轮胎式装载机
wheel loader
论点
argument, contention
螺母
nut
螺栓
bolt
螺纹钢筋
twisted steel bar
裸装货
nude cargo
落后
lag
落空
frustration
落空的合同
frustrated contract
落实
implement

M

麻烦的
onerous
马口铁
tinned plate
马力
horse power
码
yard
码头
wharf
码头泊位
quay berth
码头费
wharfage
码头至码头运输
quay-to-quay transportation
埋管机
pipe layer
买方
buyer, vendee, purchaser
买方递盘
buying offer, bid
买方发价
buying offer
买方负责
caveat emptor
买方市场
buyer's market

买方信贷
buyer credit

买价
buying price, purchase price, purchase money

买卖
deal, market

买卖合同
bargain

买入的汇票
bill purchased

买入价值
entry value

买通
buy off

买主
buyer, customer, purchaser, taker

买主垄断价格
oligopsony price

卖方
vendor, seller

卖方负责
caveat venitor

卖方市场
seller's market

卖方提供的
vendor-furnished

卖方信贷
supplier credit

卖据
bill of sale

卖空
bear

卖主垄断价格
oligopoly price

满意
satisfaction

毛的
gross

毛费率
gross rate

毛价
gross price

毛利
gross margin (profit), gross earnings, margin

毛利率
gross profit ratio, rate of margin

毛利润
gross profit

毛石
free-stone, rubble

毛石砌体
rubble masonry

毛值
gross value

毛重
gross weight

矛盾
contradiction, repugnance

矛盾的
contradictory, contrary

锚杆
anchor bar, anchor

锚固
anchorage, anchor

锚筋
anchor, anchor bar

锚具
anchorage

锚栓
anchor bolt

锚座
anchorage

铆钉
rivet

铆接
rivet

冒犯
offence

冒牌商标
imitation trade mark

冒险
venture, adventure

贸易
commerce, trade

贸易壁垒
trade barrier
贸易代表团
trade mission
贸易代理合同
commission contract
贸易的
commercial
贸易公司
commercial company, trade company
贸易公司的资格
trading company's qualification
贸易关系
trade relation
贸易惯例
custom of trade, trade usage, trade practice
贸易逆差
trade deficit
贸易平衡
trade balance
贸易入超
import surplus
贸易手续的简化
facilitation of trade procedures
贸易术语
trade terms
贸易顺差
favourable balance of trade, trade surplus
贸易谈判
trade negotiation
贸易条款
trade terms
贸易条约
commercial treaty
贸易限制
trade restriction
贸易协定
trade agreement
贸易协会
chamber of trade
贸易折扣
trade discount
没收
confiscate, confiscation, seizure
没收条款
forfeiture clause
没收物
forfeit, forfeiture
媒介
intermediation, medium
每股收益
earnings per share(EPS)
每年
per annum
每年的
annual
每人平均值
per capita
每日保险费
daily premium
每日单价
daywork rate
每日的
daily
每日津贴
day allowances, per diem allowance
每日施工作业
day to day construction activities
每日贴(或升)水
daily premium
每天一次的
daily
每月的
monthly
每月付款
monthly payment
每月期中付款证书
monthly interim payment certificate
每月详细进度表
monthly detailed schedule
每周工时分配
weekly time distribution
每周会议
weekly meeting

每周劳务报告
weekly labour report
美元信贷
dollar credit
美制
the U.S. System
门路
contact
门式起重机
gantry crane, portal crane
猛涨
soar
弥补
cover, remedy, retrieve, redeem
秘密的
secret
秘密分类账
secret ledger
秘书
secretary, clerk
密封
sealing, seal
密封的投标指令
sealed bid instruction
密封投标
sealed bid (tender)
免除
exempt, exemption, release from
免除合同义务
release from the contract
免除权
right of exoneration
免除双重税收
double taxation relief
免除义务
release from obligation
免除责任
exemption from liability, hold harmless
免除债务
abatement of debt, debt relief
免费
free of charge

免费的
free, gratuitous
免费医疗
free medical treatment
免关税
free of duty
免赔额
deductible, excess
免赔条款
deductible clause, franchise clause
免税
tax exemption, free of tax, exemption from duty
免税单
bill of sufferance
免税的
duty-free, tax-free
免税港
tax haven
免税货进口报关单
entry for free goods
免税货物
duty-free goods
免税进口
duty-free importation
免税利润
tax-free profit
免税期
tax holidays
免税区
free trade area, duty-free zone
免税人
exempt
免税商店
duty-free shop
免税条款
exemption clause
免税证明
tax exemption certification
免责权
right of exoneration
免责条款
escape clause, exemption clause, ex-

ception clause
面积
area
面洽
face to face negotiation
面值
face amount (value)
面砖
face brick
描述
describe, description, depict
灭火器
fire extinguisher
民法
civil law
民法典
civil code
民间骚乱
civil commotion
民事的
civil
民事诉讼
civil action
民事损害赔偿
civil damages
民事责任
civil liability, civil responsibility
民事责任险
civil liability insurance
民用的
civil
民用建筑
civil architecture
民用建筑师
civil architect
民族的
national
民族习惯
national customs
敏感性分析
sensitivity analysis, sensibility analysis
名片

name card, business card
名义成本
nominal cost
名义尺寸
nominal dimension
名义代理人
ostensible agent
名义工程量
nominal quantity
名义合伙人
nominal partner, ostensible partner
名义汇率
nominal exchange rate
名义价值
nominal value
名义金额
nominal amount
名义利率
nominal interest rate
名义上的
nominal
名义数量
nominal quantity
名义账户
nominal account
名义资本
nominal capital
明沟排水
surface drainage
明渠
open channel
明确表达
express
明确的
definite, express
明示承诺
express undertaking
明示放弃
express waiver
明示规定
express provision
明示弃权书
express waiver

明示条款
express terms
明示同意
express consent
明示协议
express agreement
明示转让
express assignment
明细表
breakdown
明细单
specification
明细分类账
detailed ledger, subsidiary ledger
明细记录
itemized record, subsidiary record
明细账目
detailed account
明显的
obvious, evident
明显的缺陷
obvious defect
命令
order, command, requirement
命令的
mandatory
命令者
mandator
模板
formwork, shuttering, form
模板拆除
form removal
模板工程
formwork
模板支撑
form support
模糊
ambiguity, obscurity
模糊的
ambiguous, vague
模棱两可
ambiguity
模式
mode
模型
pattern
模型试验
model test
磨损
wear and tear
抹灰工
plasterer
抹面
finishing
抹面机
finishing-machine
默契
privity
默认的
implied
默示
imply
默示保证
implied warranty
默示的
implied
默示工作
implied work
默示合同
implied contract
默示权力
implied power
默示条件
implied terms
默示异议
implied objection
母公司
parent company, mother company
木板桩
plank pile
木材
lumber, timber
木工
carpenter
木结构
timber structure

木料
lumber, timber
木模板
timber form
木桩
timber pile
目标
goal, target, objective
目标成本
object cost, target cost
目标成本合同
target cost contract
目标的
objective
目标管理
objective management, management by objective
目标价格
target price
目标利润
target profit
目标名单
target list
目标日期
target date
目标市场
target market

目的
goal, object, purpose, objective
目的地
destination, place of destination
目的地国家
country of destination
目的地交货价
price of delivery to destination
目的地交货价的
franco
目的地码头交货(价)
ex dock (EXD)
目的港
destination port, port of destination
目的港船上交货(价)
ex-ship (EXS)
目的港码头交货
delivered ex quay (duty paid) (DEQ)
目的港码头交货(价)(关税已付)
ex-quay (EXQ) (duty paid)
目的税
objective tax
目录
catalogue, list
目录与摘要
catalogue and summary

N

纳入
incorporate
纳税
taxation, payment of duties
纳税后净收益
net income after tax
纳税能力
ability to pay
纳税人
tax payer
纳税日
tax day

纳税申报表
declaration, tax return
纳税义务
tax liability
耐火材料
refractory material
耐火的
fireproof
耐火混凝土
fire-resisting concrete, refractory concrete
耐火水泥

耐火砖
refractory cement
refractory brick, fire brick
耐久性
durability
耐酸材料
acid-proof material
耐酸混凝土
acid-resisting concrete
耐用年限
useful life, tenure of use
耐用消费品
consumer durable
难以确定的情况
borderline cases
难以预见的情况
unforeseeable conditions
内部成本
internal cost
内部的
internal
内部风险
internal risk
内部回收率
internal rate of return (IRR)
内部会计
internal accounting
内部控制
internal control
内部审计
internal auditing
内部收益率
internal rate of return (IRR)
内部效益
internal benefits
内部装修
interior decoration
内地的
inland
内河运输保险
inland marine insurance
内陆
inland
内陆运输
inland transportation
内陆运输保险单
inland transit policy
内容
content
内向型的人
introvert
内向型性格的
introvert
内销
domestic sales
内行
expert
内债
internal debt
内账
private ledger, secret ledger
能力
ability, capability, capacity, competence
能源
power resources, power
泥瓦工
mason
逆差
adverse balance, unfavorable balance
逆的
adverse
逆向占有
adverse possession
年度
calendar year
年度报告
annual report
年度的
annual
年度费用
annual costs
年度结算
annual closing
年度决算
annual accounts

年度决算书
annual statement
年度审计报告
audited annual report
年度维修
yearly maintenance
年度休假
annual leave
年度预算
annual budget, yearly budget
年度支付额
annual disbursements
年度支付最高限额
annual cash ceiling
年鉴
year book
年降水量
annual precipitation
年金
annuity
年金金额
amount of an annuity
年利率
annual interest rate
年生产能力
annual production capacity (APC)
年收入
annual income
年通货膨胀率
annual inflation rate

年息
interest per annum
年销售额
annual sales volume
年销售量
annual sales
年终调整
year-end adjustment
年终奖
year-end bonus
年终审计
year-end audit
年资较浅的
junior
年租
annual rental
碾压机
roller
捏造
fabricate, fake
凝固强度
setting strength
凝固时间
setting time
努力
diligence, effort
挪用
misappropriate, divert
诺言
promise

O

欧洲货币
Eurocurrency
欧洲货币单位
European Currency Unit (ECU)
欧洲美元
Eurodollar
欧洲商业票据
Eurocommercial paper
欧洲市场
Euromarket
欧洲银团贷款
Eurosyndicated loans
欧洲银行
Eurobank
偶发事故条款
contingency clause
偶然的
occasional, fortuitous

偶然事件
accident, contingency
偶因

偶有的
contingent
occasion

P

拍卖
auction, public sale
拍卖底价
upset price
排除
eliminate
排除在外
exclude
排气管道
discharge duct
排气系统
ventilating exhaust system
排水
drainage, drain
排水泵
discharge pump
排水干沟
main drain
排水沟
drain, gully, ditch
排水管
drainage conduit, drain pipe
排水管道
discharge duct
排水涵洞
drainage culvert
排水量
water discharge, displacement
排水渠
drainage channel, discharge canal
排水系统
drainage
排水总管
main drain
排污管
sewage drain

牌价
list price
牌照
licence plate
牌照费
fee for permit, licence fee
牌照税
licence duty, licence tax
派发红股
bonus issue
派遣
dispatch
盘存
stocktaking, take stock
盘存单
inventory sheet
盘存截止日
inventory cut-off date
盘存折旧法
inventory method of depreciation
盘货
take stock
判案要点陈述
case stated
判断
judge, judgment, discretion
判给
award
判决
verdict, decide, judge, judgment
判例
legal, precedent
判例法
case law, common law
旁证
collateral evidence

旁注
marginal note
抛弃
abandon
陪审团
jury
培训
train
培训班
training program
培训当地人员
training of local personnel
培训计划
training program
培训中心
training centre
赔偿
indemnify, indemnification, compensate, compensation, reimburse, reimbursement
赔偿保证书
letter of indemnity
赔偿的限额
limit of compensation
赔偿理算
adjustment of claim
赔偿契约
deed of indemnity
赔偿限度
measure of indemnity
赔偿限额
limits of indemnity
赔偿责任
indemnity liability
赔付率
claim ratio, loss ratio
赔款
damages
配电网
distribution network
配额
quota, ration
配件
parts, accessory
配筋
reinforcement
配筋率
reinforcement ratio
配料
batch
配料仓
batch bin
喷混凝土
shotcrete
喷浆
guniting
喷浆机
shotcrete machine
喷枪
spray gun
喷水消防系统
sprinkler system
膨胀水泥
expansive cement
碰撞
collide, collision
碰撞险
collision insurance
批单
endorsement, indorsement
批发
wholesale
批发价
wholesale price, trade price
批发商
distributor, wholesaler, wholesale dealer
批发业务
wholesale business
批量生产
batch production
批注
indorse, endorse
批准
approve, approval, ratify, ratification, sanction

批准程序
procedure of approval
批准的
approved
批准的变更命令
approved change order
批准的供货商名单
approved vendors list
批准的投标人名单
approved bidders list
批准合同
affirmation of contract
批准通知
notification of approval
皮带运输机
belt conveyor
皮重
tare, tare weight (gross)
毗邻产业主
adjoining owner
疲劳
fatigue
疲劳裂缝
fatigue crack
疲劳试验
fatigue test
匹配
matching
片面
one-sided, ex parte
偏爱
partiality, preference
偏差
deviation
偏差折价
priced deviations
偏见
prejudice
偏离
deviate, deviation
偏离折价
priced deviation
偏袒的
partial
票据
document, bill, paper, note, instrument
票据迟到拒绝承兑
dishonor by non-acceptance
票据迟到拒绝付款
dishonor by non-payment
票据拒付证明
protest of bill
票据期限
tenor
票据贴现率
bill rate, acceptance rate
票面价值
par, par value, nominal value
票面金额
face amount (value)
票面上的
nominal
票证
coupon
频率
frequency
品牌
brand
品行证明书
character reference
品质
quality
品质检验证书
inspection certificate of quality
品质证明
certificate of quality, hallmark
品种
type
聘请
engage, employ, retain
聘请费
retainer fee
聘用
employ, engage
平安险

free from particular average (FPA)
平板
plane-table
平板车
flat truck(lorry)
平板大卡车
platform truck
平板仪
plane-table
平等对待投标者
equal treatment of bidders
平等互利
equality and mutual benefit
平等交换
give-and-take
平等原则
principle of equality
平底船
barge
平地机
blade machine
平衡
balance
平衡表
balance sheet
平衡账户
balancing account
平价
par
平价汇率
par exchange rate
平均保险费
level premium
平均单位成本
average cost per unit
平均的
average
平均价格
average price
平均年限法
straight line method of depreciation
平均皮重
average tare
平均使用年限
average life
平均数
average, mean
平均停工时间
mean down time
平均停机时间
mean down time
平均折旧法
composite depreciation method, depreciation-straight line method
平路机
leveling machine, road grader
平面
plane
平面布置图
layout
平面图
plan
平土机
leveling machine, grader
平行贷款
parallel loans
平行的
parallel
平行工序
parallel process
平行市场
parallel market
平行作业
parallel operation
平整度
evenness
评标
evaluation of bids, bid evaluation
评标报告
report on bid evaluation
评标价
evaluated bid price
评定价值
appraised value
评分比较法
scoring model method

评估
assess, assessment, appraise, appraisal, evaluate, evaluation
评估过程
evaluation process
评估确认价值
appraised value
评价
evaluate, evaluation, appraise, appraisal, assess, assessment
评价标准
evaluation criteria
评价人
appraiser
评价书
appraisal
评论
comment, observation
评审委员会
board of review
评算
evaluation
凭单
indenture, document
凭单付款
remittance against documents
凭单支票
voucher check
凭发票付款
payment on invoice
凭规格、等级或标准买卖
sale by specification, grade or standard
凭事先通知终止合同
termination by notice
凭样品成交
sale by sample
凭账单付款
payment on statement
凭证
document, voucher, scrip
迫使
force

破产
bankruptcy, bankrupt, insolvency, insolvent
破产案产业管理人
receiver
破产产业管理人
administrator in a bankrupt estate
破产倒闭
bankruptcy
破产的
broke, bankrupt
破产法
act of insolvency, act of bankruptcy, insolvent law
破产法案
bankruptcy act
破产管理人
bankruptcy administrator
破产清算人
insolvency assignee, liquidator
破产清算书
statement of liquidation
破产人的债权人
creditor of bankruptcy
破产债务人
insolvent debtor
破产者
bankrupt, insolvent
破产资产管理人
assignee in bankruptcy
破坏
damage, destroy, destruction, sabotage
破坏试验
break-down test
破坏行为
sabotage
剖面
section
剖面图
sectional drawing, sectional drawing, profile
剖面线

section line
铺地砖
tile
铺管
piping
铺管机
pipe layer
铺路机
paving machine
铺面
paving
铺面砖
tiling
铺砌
paving
铺设
pave
铺设机
laydown machine
铺筑
lay
普遍的
general
普遍优惠制
generalized system of preferences (GSP)
普工
general labour, unskilled labour
普惠制
generalized system of preferences (GSP)
普惠制单据
generalized system of preferences documents
普通承兑
general acceptance
普通法
common law
普通法系
common law system
普通股
equity share
普通合伙
general partnership
普通汇票
clean draft
普通集装箱
general container
普通年金
ordinary annuity
普通日记簿
general journal
普通日记账
general journal
普通事故保险
ordinary accident insurance
普通支票
open cheque

Q

期初余额
initial balance, beginning balance, opening balance
期汇
forward exchange
期货
forward, futures
期货差价
forward margin
期货的
forward
期货抵补
forward cover
期货定单
order for future delivery
期货汇率
forward exchange rate
期货价格
forward price, futures price
期货交易

期货贸易
forward dealings, futures
期货市场
futures trading
期间
futures market
期间成本
duration, period
期间的
period cost
期刊
interim
期满
journal
期满日
expire, expiration, expiry
期末存货
date of expiration (expiry)
期末余额
ending inventory, closing stock
期票
ending balance, closing balance
期权
promissory note, term bill
期权的买方
option
期权购买价
option buyer
期权交易定金
option purchase price
期权卖方
option money
期望
option seller
期限
expectancy, prospect
期中(付款)证书
period, term
期中财务报表
interim certificate
期中的
interim financial statement
interim

期中付款
interim payment
期中审计
interim audit
期中验收证书
interim acceptance certificate
期中业绩
interim results
欺骗
fraud, cheat, deceive
欺骗性的不正确陈述
fraudulent misrepresentation
欺诈行为
barratry, fraudulent act
歧视
discrimination, prejudice
企业
enterprise
企业财产保险
enterprise property insurance
企业法
law of enterprises
企业国有化
nationalization of enterprise
企业环境风险指数
business environmental risk index
企业机构
establishment
企业家
enterpriser, entrepreneur
企业业主
corporate owner
企业一般管理费
overhead
启动费
mobilization fee
启运港
port of departure
起草
draft, draw
起草合同
draft a contract, draw up a contract
起动

起
start up
起伏
fluctuation
起始点（日）
starting-point
起诉
sue, charge, accuse, take legal action, prosecution
起诉人
suitor, complainant
起诉书
bill of complaint
起算点（日）
starting-point
起息日
date of value, value date
起因
cause, origin
起源
origin
起重机
crane
起重机船
crane barge
气锤
air hammer
气焊
acetylene welding
气候
climate
气候异常情况
climate extremes
气象台
weather station
气象条件
meteorological conditions
气象预报
weather forecast
气压表
barometer
气压灌浆泵
boojee pump
气质
temperament
弃权
waiver, disclaimer
弃权声明书
waiver
弃权条款
disclaimer clause
弃土场
spoil area
汽车保险
motor car insurance
汽车式起重机
truck crane
汽油
petrol, gasoline
契约
covenant, deed, indenture, contract
契约废除证明
acquittance
契约式合营
contractual joint venture
砌石工程
stonework
砌筑墙体
masonry wall
砌筑体
masonry
器材
equipment, material
千斤顶
jack
迁移
remove, removal, relocation
迁移费
compensation for removal
牵头方
leading partner
牵头公司
leading company
牵引车
tractor
签订
sign, conclude

签订合同策略
contracting strategy
签订合同的程序
procedure for concluding a contract
签订合同方法
contracting approach
签订合同各方
contracting parties
签订协议
conclude an agreement
签订协议各方
parties to an agreement
签发
issue
签发证书
grant a certificate, issue a certificate
签护照
endorse a passport
签名
signature
签收
sign for, receipt
签署
sign, affix, execute
签署的
signatory
签署的声明
signed declaration
签署国
signatory
签署合同
execute a contract, sign a contract
签署人
signatory
签署证书
sign a certificate
签约的
signatory
签约日期
date of contract
签证
visa
签证费
certificate fee
签注
endorse, indorse, indorsement, endorsement
签字
signature, sign
签字权
power to sign
签字人
signer, signatory, undersigned
签字受雇
sign on
签字样本
specimen signature
签字移交
sign over
前述条款
preceding clause
前提
precondition
前线经理
line manager
前重后轻的报价
front loaded
钳工
benchworker
潜水泵
sinking pump
潜在的
potential
潜在风险
potential risk
潜在客户
prospective client
潜在缺陷
latent defect
潜在市场
potential market
遣返
repatriation
遣散
demobilize, demobilization
遣散费

cost of repatriation, compensation for removal, release pay, separation pay
谴责
condemnation
欠
owe
欠据
debit instrument
欠款
debt, arrears, outstanding amount
欠条
credit note, IOU (I Owe You)
欠薪
back pay
欠债
debt, owe
强加
impose, imposition
强迫的
involuntary
强制
force, constrain, constraint
强制保险
forced insurance, compulsory insurance
强制的
mandatory, compulsory
强制令
injunction
强制破产
involuntary bankruptcy
强制清理
compulsory liquidation
强制清算
forced liquidation
强制条款
compulsory clause
强制性保险
legal insurance
强制执行
enforce, enforcement
抢修
rush-repair
桥墩
bridge pier
桥栏杆
bridge rail
桥面板
bridge deck
桥式吊车
bridge crane, overhead crane
桥式起重机
overhead crane, bridge crane
桥台
abutment
巧合
coincide, coincidence
切削加工
machining
亲笔签名
autograph
侵犯
infringe, infringement, disturbance, contravene
侵犯商标权
trade mark infringement
侵犯专利权
infringement of patent, patent infringement
侵权行为
infringement, tort
侵权行为人
tortfeasor, infringer
侵权性质
nature of tort
侵入
trespass
侵吞公款
defalcation
侵占
encroach
勤奋
diligence
清偿
clear off, liquidate, satisfy

清偿不足额判决
deficiency judgement
清偿能力
liquidity
清偿责任
liability for satisfaction
清偿债务
discharge of debt, satisfy liabilities
清除
clearing, clear away
清楚的
clear
清单
bill
清点库存
take stock
清关
customs clearance, clearance
清关代理人
customs clearing agent
清关费
charges for customs clearance
清关证书
certificate of clearance
清还债务
liquidation of debt
清洁提单
clean bill of lading
清理
clearance, disentangle, liquidate, liquidation
清理费用
disposal cost
清理现场
clean up the site
清算
liquidation, clear an account, audit
清算代理人
clearing (clearance) agent
清算管理人
equity receiver
清算价值
liquidation value

清算银行
clearing bank
情报
intelligence
情况
circumstances, information
情况说明书
fact sheet
情形
situation, circumstances
晴天工作日
weather working days (WWD)
请求
demand, petition, request
请求权
right of claim
请求人
claimant, claimer
求职申请
application for employment
区别
difference, discrimination, differentiation
区段
section
区域
zone, region, area
区域规划
zoning
区域划分图
zoning plan
区域价格
zone price
驱逐
expel
驱逐出境
deportation
渠首
head
取代
replace, replacement, substitute, supersede
取得

acquire, acquisition, win, recover
取得控制权
acquiring of control
取决于
rest with, depend on
取款凭单
bill of credit
取消
revoke, cancel, rescind, withdraw, abrogate
取消的工作
deleted work
取消付款
forfeiture of payment
取消合同
contract cancellation
取消赎回权
foreclosure
取消资格
disqualification
取样
sampling
圈梁
ring beam
全部成本
full cost, complete cost
全部的
complete
全部费用在内价的发票
franco invoice
全部费用在内价格的
franco
全部付讫
payment in full
全部接收
blanket acceptance
全部认可
blanket approval
全部同意
blanket approval
全部预期费用
all expected costs
全部预期效益
all expected benefits
全部重置成本
full replacement cost
全断面掘进机
moling machine
全额保险
full insurance
全额支付
payment in full
全过程风险
throughout risk
全面检修
overhaul
全面均衡分析
general equilibrium analysis
全面质量管理
total quality control (TQC)
全球公司
global corporations
全球配额
global quota
全权处理
sole discretion
全权代表
plenipotentiary
全权委托客户
discretionary client
全权信托
discretionary trust
全损
total loss
全套清洁已装船提单
full set of clean on board bills of lading
全套提单
full set of bills of lading, complete set of bills of lading
全套文件
full set of documents
全体的
unanimous
全体人员
personnel

全险
all risks (a/r, A.R.)
全新的
brand-new
权衡
trade off, takeoff
权力
power, authority
权力范围
authority limits
权力机构
authority
权力失效
lapse
权力委托
authority to delegate
权利的丧失
forfeiture
权利能力
legal capacity
权利人
obligee
权利要求书
affidavit of claim
权利转让
subrogation
权威性的
authoritative, authenticated
权威性解释
authoritative interpretation
权威性判例
authoritative precedent
权限
extent of power, limits of authority
权限的解释
construction of references
权限委托
delegation of power
权益
equity, benefited interest, interest
权益比率
equity ratio
权益转让
assignment of interests
权益资本
equity capital
权责发生制
accrual system
权责发生制会计
accrual basis accounting
权重
weight
劝告
advice, admonition
缺点
weakness, defect, drawback
缺乏
absence, shortage, lack
缺乏经验的
inexperienced
缺乏证据
absence of proof, lack of evidence
缺货成本
stockout cost
缺料成本
stockout cost
缺勤的
absent
缺少
lack
缺席
absence
缺陷
defect
缺陷改正期
defects correction period
缺陷改正证书
defects correction certificate
缺陷通知
notice of defect
缺陷通知期
defects notification period
缺陷修补
defect repair
缺陷责任期
defects liability period

缺陷责任期的延长
extension of defects liability period
缺陷责任证书
defects liability certificate
确保
ensure
确定
determine, determination, decide, confirm
确定的
firm, established
确定授标
confirmation of award
确定税款的人
assessor
确定损害赔偿额
assess the damages
确定性的
conclusive
确定性负债
determinable liability
确认
acknowledge, acknowledgment, confirm
确认保证
affirmative warranty
确认函
letter of acknowledgement
确认书
confirmation, letter of confirmation
确认样品
confirmation sample
确认银行
confirming bank
确凿事实
absolute fact
群体意识
group sense
群桩
group of piles

R

燃料
fuel
燃料费
fuel cost
燃油附加调整率
bunker adjustment factor
壤土
loamy soil
让步
concession
让步的
concessional
让价
price concession
让位
demise
让与
cede to, transfer
让与人
releasor
让与条件
conditions of grant
扰动土
disturbed soil
扰乱
disturbance
扰乱进度
disruption of progress
热轧
hot-rolling
热轧钢筋
hot-rolled bar
人工费用
labour cost
人工工时定额
standard labour hour (time)
人工周转率
labour turnover rate

人均小时产量
output per man-hour
人孔
sight hole, man hole
人力曲线
manpower curves
人力资源
human resources, labour resources
人力资源管理
management of human resources
人身保险
personal insurance
人身的
personal
人身伤害
bodily injury, personal injury
人身事故
accident to workmen
人身意外保险
personal accident insurance
人身意外伤害险
personal accident insurance
人身与财产损害
damage to persons and property
人事部门
personnel department
人事经理
staff manager, personnel manager
人头税
head tax
人为风险
artificial risk
人为拖延手段
artificial obstruction
人为障碍
artificial obstruction
人行道
sidewalk, pavement
人行横道
cross walk
人行桥
pedestrian bridge, foot bridge
人员的更换
changes in personnel
人员的提供
supply of personnel
人造的
artificial
认可
accept, endorse, endorsement, ratify, ratification, sanction, approbate
认为
deem, hold
认真的
earnest
任命
appoint, designate, nominate, admission
任命机构
appointing authority
任命证书
deed of appointment
任务
task, mission, role
任务单
work order
任务进度表
objective schedule
任选目的港
optional port of discharge
任选卸货港
optional port of discharge
任意
at discretion
任意成本
discretionary cost
任意的
optional, facultative
任用
engage
日报表
daily statement
日常费用
general expenses
日常开支

overhead expenses
日常通讯
day to day communication
日常维修
routine maintenance, operational maintenance
日常咨询
on-going consulting
日程表
schedule, agenda, itinerary
日工资
day rate, daily pay (wage)
日记簿
diurnal
日记账
journal
日技术服务费
daily technical service fee
日降雨量
daily rainfall
日历
calendar
日历年
calendar year
日历日
calendar day
日历月
calendar month
日息
daily interest, interest per diem
日志
diurnal, journal
荣誉
honor
荣誉的
honored
荣誉证书
honorary certificate
容积
volume
容量
capacity
容纳
contain
容器
container
容许荷载
allowable load, admissible load
容许土压力
allowable soil pressure
融通
accommodation
融通背书
accommodation endorsement
融通背书人
accommodation endorser
融通票据
accommodation paper, accommodation bill, accommodation note
融通支票
accommodation check
融资
finance, financing
融资费
financing charges
融资计划
financing plan
融资结构
financing structure
融资利率
financing interest rates
融资条件
financing terms
融资租赁
finance lease
柔性路面
flexible pavement
入档备案文件
file copy
入港费用
inward charges
入港申报
entry declaration
入港税
harbor dues, keelage, port charge
入境

entrance
入境报关单
declaration inwards
入境签证
entrance visa, entry visa
入境证书
entry certificate
入口
entrance
入库单
godown entry
入选的投标人
selected bidder(tenderer)
入选名单
short list
入账
enter up an account

入账价格
entry price
软贷款
soft loan
软基
soft foundation
软件
software
软件副本
soft copy
软通货
soft currency
软土基础
soft foundation
润滑油
lubricant

S

洒水车
motor flusher, spraying car
三包
sub-subcontracting
三包商
sub-subcontractor
三倍的
triplicate
三脚架
tripod
三通管
three-way pipe, T-branch pipe
伞括保险
umbrella cover
伞式责任保险
umbrella liability insurance
散工
day work
散装的
bulk, laden in bulk
散装货船
bulk cargo carrier

散装货物
bulk
散装水泥
bulk cement
丧失
forfeit, forfeiture
扫尾工作
outstanding work
杀价
beat down
砂浆搅拌器
grout mixer
砂砾石
sandy gravel, sand and gravel
砂土
sandy soil
砂岩
sandstone
砂与骨料比
sand and aggregate ratio
砂质粘土
sand clay

砂桩
sand pile
筛分
sieving, screening
筛分骨料
screening aggregate
筛分机
screening machine
晒图机
blueprinter
山坡
hillside
删除
delete, eliminate, elimination
删除的工作
omitted work
删去
cancel, cancellation, omit, omission
扇形
sector
善意
good faith
善意被背书人
bona-fide endorsee
善意持有人
bona-fide holder
善意的
bona fide
善意过失
error in good faith
善意投标人
bona-fide bidder
膳食供应
accommodation
伤害
injure, injury
伤害保险
injury insurance
伤害工人的事故
accident to workmen
伤亡人员
casualty
商标
brand, trade mark, merchandise mark
商标所有权
ownership of trade marks
商定
agree, bargain
商定的补偿
agreed compensation
商定金额
agreed sum
商定条件
agreed terms
商法
law of merchant, commercial law
商号
firm, house, company
商号票据
house bill
商会
chamber of commerce
商检人
surveyor
商贸行名录
trade directories
商品
commodity, goods, merchandise
商品价格
commodity price
商品检验
commodity inspection
商品交易会
trade fair
商品名称
name of commodity
商品目录
catalogue
商品盘存
merchandise inventory
商品注册
commercial registration
商人
merchant
商事法庭

commercial court
商谈
negotiate, talk
商务
commerce, commercial affairs, trade
商务备选方案
alternative of financial nature
商务参赞
commercial counselor
商务代表
commercial representative, trade representative
商务索赔
commercial claim
商务条款
commercial articles
商务选择性报价
alternative of financial nature
商务专员
commercial attaché
商行
business, firm
商业
commerce, business, trade
商业保险
commercial insurance
商业承兑汇票
commercial acceptance
商业代理行
commercial agency
商业贷款
commercial loan
商业单据
commercial paper
商业的
commercial, merchant
商业发票
commercial invoice
商业法规
commercial code
商业公司
commercial company
商业广告
commercial
商业合同
merchant contract
商业汇票
commercial bill, commercial draft, trade bill
商业机构
business organization
商业交易
business transaction
商业秘密
trade secret
商业票据
commercial paper
商业信贷
trade credit
商业信函
commercial correspondence
商业信用证
commercial letter of credit
商业银行
commercial bank, merchant bank
商业折扣
commercial discount, trade discount
商业周期
business cycle
商誉
commercial, goodwill
赏钱
gratuity
上岸
landing
上班
on duty
上等品
prime quality
上级管理费
management overheads
上升
escalation
上市的
listed
上市公司

listed company
上市证券
listed securities
上诉
appeal
上诉保证书
appeal bond
上诉委员会
appeal board, board of review
上限
top-limit, upper limit
上一个的
last
上涨
escalate
上涨的价格
escalating price
上涨费用
escalation charges
尚好的
fair
少报
understatement
少付
underpayment
少量的
nominal, marginal
少数制造商对市场的控制
oligopoly
赊购
account purchase, credit purchase, tick
赊买
account purchase
赊售
charge sales
赊销
charge sales, credit sale, sale on account
赊账
open account, on account
赊账支付
payment on account

设备
facility, equipment, plant
设备安装
erection of plant, erection of equipment, mounting of equipment
设备保养
equipment maintenance, maintenance of plant
设备采购
equipment procurement
设备残值
salvage of equipment
设备成本计算
costing of plant
设备的拆除
dismantling of plant
设备的记录
plant records
设备的维护
maintenance of plant
设备供货贷款
equipment supply loan
设备供应合同
supply of equipment contract
设备供应和安装合同
supply of equipment with erection contract
设备利用率
capacity operating rate
设备能力
machine capability
设备清单
equipment list
设备维修
equipment maintenance
设备闲置时间
machine idle time
设备再出口保函
guarantee for re-export of equipment
设备折旧
equipment depreciation, depreciation of equipment
设备租赁

equipment leasing
设备租用费
equipment rental
设定价值
declared value
设计
design, engineer, layout
设计、采购与施工合同
Engineering, Procurement and Construction Contract (EPC Contract)
设计单位
design unit, designer
设计方案
design approach, design proposal
设计分包者
design subcontractor
设计负荷
design load
设计工程师
design engineer
设计工程一切险
engineering all risks (E.A.R)
设计工作量
design quantities
设计规范
design code
设计合同
contract of design
设计和规划
design and engineering
设计和建造
design and build
设计—建设—运营—移交
Design-Build-Operate-Transfer (DBOT)
设计经理
engineering manager
设计目标
design objective
设计能力
design capacity
设计审查
design audit, design review

设计师
designer
设计师的估价
designer's estimate
设计师的顾问
designer's consultant
设计数据
design data
设计数据包
package of engineered data
设计图样
design draft
设计图纸
design drawing
设计文件
design documentation
设计细则
design details
设计延误
delays in engineering
设计要求
design requirement
设计—建造合同
design-build contract
设计准则
design criteria
设计组
design team
设立
establish, set up
设施
installation, facility
设施供应
installation supplying
设置
install
社会保险
social insurance
社会保障
social security
社会风险
social risks
社会福利

social benefit
社会影响评价
social impact assessing
社团
association, incorporation, community
社团成员
incorporator
社团的
corporate
涉及
involve
涉外民事法律关系
civil legal relation with foreign element
申报
declare
申报保险单
declaration policy
申报表
declaration form
申报出口
entry of goods outward
申报货物
declare goods
申报价值
declared value
申报进口
entry of goods inward
申请
apply, application, petition, request
申请表
application form
申请撤回
application for withdrawal
申请方法
method of application
申请费
application fee
申请人
applicant, declarant
申请书
letter of application

申请特别承诺
application for special commitment
申诉
complaint, complain
申诉人
complainant, declarant
伸缩缝
expansion joint
伸缩接头
expansion joint
身份
identity, identification
身份证
identification card
身体伤害
bodily injury
审查
review
审查期
review period
审定
authorize, examine and approve
审核结果
audit findings
审核期
review period
审核人
auditor
审计
audit
审计师
auditor, controller
审计条款
auditing clauses
审计线索
audit trail
审计员
auditor
审理
try, trial, hear, hearing
审理辩护费用
costs
审判记录

minutes
审判庭
adjudication division
审判员
judge
审批过程
approval process
审议过程
review process
渗流
seepage
渗漏险
risk of leakage
升降机
lift (elevator)
升水
premium
升水率
premium rate
升压变电站
step-up substation
升值
appreciation
生产
produce, production, yield
生产报表
manufacturing statement
生产成本
cost of production, production cost
生产定额
job rate, output quota, production quota
生产管理
production control
生产管理制度
management operating system (MOS)
生产计划
production plan
生产奖金
production bonus
生产经理
line manager, production manager

生产量
volume of production
生产流程
line of production
生产率
productivity, production rate
生产能力
productivity, output capacity, production capacity
生产期
production term
生产数据
production data
生产数量折旧法
service output method of depreciation
生产通知单
factory order
生产污水
production waste
生产线
assembly line, production line
生产线性能考核
production line performance test
生产许可证
production license
生产指标
production quota, production target
生产准备费用
setup cost
生活补贴
subsistence allowance
生活费
cost of living
生活垃圾
domestic waste
生活设施
accommodation
生活污水
domestic waste
生石灰
quick lime, calcium lime
生效

come into force, enter into effect, go into force, validation
生效的保险单
insurance policy in force
生效日期
effective date
生意
business, transaction
声明
declare, declaration, state, statement
胜过
prevail
胜利
win
胜诉的一方
prevailing party, winning party
省略
omit, omission
剩余的
surplus
剩余收益
residual income
剩余物
remainder
剩余物的处理
disposal of surplus
剩余现金的汇出
export of cash surpluses
剩余资产
residual assets
失败
fail, failure
失策
mistake, inexpedience
失去
lose, forfeit
失去的
lost
失去时效的
stale
失去时效的债权
barred claim

失效
losing effect, voidness
失效法律
expiring laws
失效支票
out-of-date check
失业
unemployment
失业救济金
unemployment benefit
失业率
unemployment rate
失职
breach of duty, omission, official misconduct, neglect of duty
失踪的
missing
施工
construct, construction, execution
施工报告
construction report
施工变更指示
construction change directive
施工标准
standard of construction
施工布置图
construction layout
施工场地图
construction map
施工成本
construction cost
施工成本控制
construction cost control
施工成本预算
construction cost estimating
施工程序
construction procedure
施工单位
construction organization
施工导流
construction diversion
施工队
construction team, gang

施工方法
construction method, construction means, method of construction
施工分包合同
construction subcontract
施工缝
construction joint
施工服务
construction service
施工管理承包
construction management contracting
施工管理合同
construction management contract
施工管理员
construction superintendent
施工规范
code of practice
施工规划
construction planning
施工合同
construction contract
施工合同管理
construction contract management
施工划拨用地
area allotted for the construction
施工机械
constructional mechanism, construction plant, constructional plant
施工机械费预算
equipment cost estimating
施工机械台时费
equipment charge out rates
施工计划
construction program
施工技术
construction technique
施工技术规范
construction specifications
施工监督
construction supervision
施工检查
construction inspection
施工阶段
construction phase
施工进场道路
construction access road
施工进度
construction progress
施工进度核查单
construction schedule check list
施工进度汇总表
construction summary schedule
施工进度控制
construction progress control
施工经理
construction manager
施工流程图
layout chart
施工平面布置图
construction plan
施工期限
construction period, period of construction
施工桥
construction bridge
施工日报表
daily construction report
施工日历
construction calendar
施工日志
daily record of construction, construction diary
施工设备
construction plant, construction equipment, constructional equipment
施工设备情况报告
construction equipment status report
施工设计
construction design
施工剩余物资
construction surpluses
施工手段
construction way, construction method
施工顺序

construction sequence
施工速度
rate of progress
施工索赔
construction claims
施工索赔管理
construction claim management
施工图
construction drawings, shop drawings
施工文件
construction document
施工现场
job location, job site
施工详图
working drawings
施工详细情况
particulars of construction
施工协调员
construction coordinator
施工协议书
construction agreement
施工与安装
construction and installation
施工中间进度表
construction intermediate schedule
施工装备
construction facilities
施工总平面图
overall construction plan
施工组织
organization of construction
施工作业
construction activities
施惠人
obliger
湿度
moisture capacity (content), moisture
湿容重
wet density
石方工程
stonework

石膏
gypsum
石灰砂浆
lime mortar
石灰岩
limestone
石棉
asbestos
石棉瓦
asbestos tile
石油
petroleum
时差
time difference
时价
current price, prevailing price
时间成本
time cost
时间限制
time limit
时间延误
time delay
时区
time zone
时限
time limit
时效
limitation, prescription
时效期限
limitation period
时效终止
lapse of time
识别
identify, identification
实得工资
take-home pay
实地调查
field inspection
实发工资
take-home pay
实付工资
net pay
实际成本

actual cost, real cost
实际成本法
actual cost method
实际的
actual, practical
实际附加成本
actual additional cost
实际工期
as-built schedule
实际购货定单价格
actual purchase order price
实际汇率
real exchange rate
实际价格
actual price
实际价值
actual value
实际建成的
as constructed
实际交货
actual delivery
实际进度
physical progress, actual progress
实际进度与计划进度对比
progress—actual vs scheduled
实际竣工日期
physical completion date
实际开支成本
out-of-pocket cost
实际利率
effective interest rate
实际量
physical volume
实际皮重
actual tare
实际全损
actual total loss
实际容积
physical volume
实际损失
actual loss
实际损失率
actual loss ratio

实际违约
actual breach
实际现金价值
actual cash value
实际延误的工期
effective duration of delay
实价
net price
实缴股本
contributed capital
实盘
firm offer
实施
execute, execution, implement, implementation, enforce, enforcement
实施方法
manner of execution, means of execution
实体
entity
实物担保
real security
实物盘存法
physical inventory method
实物证据
physical evidence
实物支付
in-kind payment, payment in kind, pay in kind
实物资本
physical capital
实物资产
tangible assets
实行
effect, exercise
实验
experiment
实验的
pilot
实验室
laboratory
实用的

practical
实用性
utility, practicability
实账户
real account
实质的
substantial
实质性规定
substantive provision
实质性竣工
substantial completion
实质性条款
material terms
实质性证据
material evidence
使安全
secure
使变为
render
使不合格
disqualify
使成为必需
necessitate
使承担
charge
使从事
engage
使合格
qualify
使合同展期
renew a contract
使缓和
mitigate
使恢复原状
revest
使加剧
exacerbate
使减到最少
minimize
使结实
compact
使满意
satisfy

使免于受罚
indemnify
使命
mission
使能够
enable
使偏离
deviate
使人承担
entail
使上升
escalate
使生效
effect, enforce
使缩到最小
minimize
使无效
annul, vitiate, invalidate
使用费
occupancy expenses
使用率
occupancy rate
使用面积
usable floor area, floorage
使用年限
tenure of use, life expectancy
使用期
term of service
使用寿命
service life, useful life
使用税
use tax
使用条件
operating condition, terms of service
使用与否均须付款合同
tolling agreement, through-put contract
使用者
user
使用周期成本
life-cycle cost
使转向
divert

使作废
void
始发地
place of departure
世界货币
universal currency (money)
世界市场价格
world price
市场
market
市场崩溃
crash
市场波动
market fluctuation
市场分配
market allocation
市场分析
market analysis
市场份额
market share
市场划分
market allocation
市场价格
market price
市场价值
market value
市场利率
market rate
市场趋势
tendency of market
市场信息
market intelligence
市场需求
market demand
市价
market
市区划分
zoning
市政当局
municipality
市政府
municipality
市政工程
public works, municipal engineering, municipal works
示范协议
model agreement
示意图
schematic drawing
事故
accident
事故保险
accident insurance
事故报告
accident report
事故预防
accident prevention
事件
occurrence, event
事情
business
事实真相
merits
事实证明
proof by facts
事务
transaction
事先审查
prior review
事先协商
prior consultation
事业
career, enterprise
视察
inspect, inspection
视察员
inspector
视准轨
sight rail
试车
commissioning, test run
试车组
commissioning team
试件
test specimen (piece), specimen, sample

试块
sample
试验
experiment, test
试验日期
date for testing
试验手册
test manual
试验现场
testing ground
试样
test specimen(piece), test sample
试用
trial, probation
试用期
probationary period, period of probation
试运行
commissioning
试运行期
commissioning period
试运转
test run
试桩
test pile
饰面石
facing stone
适当的
appropriate, due, reasonable
适当降价
modest price reduction
适当涨价
modest price increase
适度价格
moderate price
适航性
seaworthiness
适航证明书
certificate of seaworthiness
适合
suit, fit
适宜的
proper, appropriate

适宜工作日
weather working days
适宜性
suitability
适应性规划
adaptive planning
适用的
applicable
适用的法律
applicable law, governing law
适用于
be suitable for, apply
释放
acquit, release
誓约
pledge
收电人
addressee
收费
charge
收费道路
toll road
收费过高
overcharge
收工
cease work
收购
purchase, buy
收回
recover, recall, regain
收回报价
withdraw an offer
收回贷款
call in a loan
收货
take over, take delivery
收货单
mate's receipt
收货回单
acknowledgment
收货人
consignee
收集资料

collect data
收件人
addressee
收据
receipt
收款便条
receipt slip
收款人
remittee, payee
收买
bribe
收盘
closing
收盘汇率
closing rate
收盘价
closing price
收讫通知书
acknowledgment
收取
collect
收入
income, revenue, proceeds
收入保险
income insurance
收市
closing
收税员
tax collector
收缩
shrink, shrinkage
收缩缝
shrinking joint, contraction joint
收缩容许量
shrinkage allowance
收益
income, gain, earnings, revenue
收益表
income sheet, earning statement
收益分配
income distribution
收益汇总账户
income summary account
收益扣除额
income deduction
收益率
earning rate, yield rate, rate of return
收益率评估法
rate of return method
收益账户
income account
收债公司
factoring company
收账
collections
收账代理人
collecting agent
收支表
account of receipts and payments
收支差额
balance of payment
收支赤字
deficit balance
收支两讫
account balanced
收支逆差
balance of payments deficit
收支平衡
balance, on the balance
收支顺差
balance of payments surplus
手册
handbook, manual
手段
device, means
手稿
script, manuscript
手工的
manual
手工工人
handworker
手头现金
cash on hand
手续
formalities, process, procedure

手续费
commission, charge for trouble, fee, handling charge
手艺
workmanship
首次要求即付
payable upon first demand
首次要求即付保函
guarantee on the first demand
首期付款
initial payment
首期建筑
priority construction
首席承保人
leading underwriter
首席代表
chief delegate
首席的
chief
首席仲裁员
chief arbitrator
首要的
prime, prerequisite
受保护的持票人
protected holder
受挫
frustration
受法律管辖
subject to the law
受雇者
employee
受管辖的
subject to
受合同的约束
under contract
受贿
acceptance of bribes, corruption
受惠人
obligee
受货人
vendee
受控公司
controlled company

受款人
payee
受理申诉
hearing
受盘人
offeree
受票人
drawee
受权人
attorney
受让人
assignee, endorsee, indorsee, assigns
受时效限制的债务
barred debt, barred obligation
受托人
attorney, consignee, trustee, bailee
受委付人
abandonee
受委托人
referee
受训人
trainee
受押人
mortgagee
受益的
beneficial
受益方
benefited party
受益权
beneficial interest
受益人
beneficiary
受益业主
beneficial owner
受援国
recipient
受约人
offeree, promisee
受约束的
bound, subject to
售后服务
after-sales service

售后回租
leaseback
售价
sale price
售票处
ticket office
授标
contract award, award of contract
授标函
letter of award
授标后会议
post-award meeting
授标决定
award decision
授标前会议
pre-award meeting
授标通知
award notification
授标准则
award criteria
授权
authorize, authorization, delegate, delegation
授权代表
authorized representative
授权的权力
authority to delegate
授权范围
terms of reference(TOR)
授权付款
authority to pay
授权付款通知书
advice of authority to pay
授权进行
authorization to proceed
授权人签名
authorized signature
授权书
power of attorney, letter of attorney, written authorization
授权文件
vesting instrument
授权银行
authorized bank
授予
award, grant, vest, confer
授予合同
award of contract
书面报告
written statement
书面变更命令
written variation order
书面裁决
written decision
书面的
writing, written
书面合同
literal contract
书面结清单
written discharge
书面警告
written warning
书面决定
written decision
书面批准
written approval
书面确认
confirmation in writing
书面申请
written application
书面声明
written statement
书面通知
written notice, notice in writing
书面同意
written consent
书面文件
written document
书面协议
written agreement
书面要求
written request
书面证据
documentary evidence, written evidence
书写

书写错误
clerical error
疏忽
negligence, laches
疏忽性的误述
negligent misrepresentation
输出
output
输电线路
transmission line
输入
input
输水道
conduit
输送带
conveyer belt
赎单
retiring a bill
赎回
redeem
赎回价格
call price, redemption price
赎票
retiring a bill
熟练
proficiency
熟练的
expert, skilled
熟练工人
skilled worker, skilled labour, journeyman
熟人
contact
熟石灰
white lime, slaked lime, drowned lime
署名的委托人
named principal
术语
technical term, jargon
树脂
resin

竖截面
vertical section
竖起
erection
竖直的
vertical
数额
amount
数据
data
数据处理
data processing
数据库
database
数据调整表
table of adjustment data
数量
quantity
数量检验证书
inspection certificate of quantity
数量折扣
quantity discount
数目
number
数字
figure, number
数字错误
numerical error
衰退
decline, decay, slump
双边合同
bilateral contract
双边文件
bilateral document
双边协议
bilateral agreement
双层信封投标方式
two-envelope bid system
双方
both parties
双方同意
mutual consent
双重保险

double insurance
双重的
dual
双重关税
dual tariff
双重货币记录
dual currency record
双重货币债券
dual currency bond
双重税收
double taxation
水泵站
pump station
水处理
water treatment
水电站
hydraulic power station, water power station
水工建筑
hydraulic structure
水工结构
hydraulic structure
水管
water pipe
水库
reservoir, water reservoir
水利
water conservancy
水利工程
hydraulic engineering, hydraulic works
水利资源
hydraulic resources
水陆联运提单
overland bill of landing
水路
water way
水路运输的
water-borne
水泥仓
cement bunker
水泥浆
cement grout

水泥牌号
cement brand
水泥喷浆
cement injection
水泥砂浆
cement mortar
水平面
water level, level
水上起重机
pontoon crane
水桶
bucket
水头
head
水土保持
water and soil conservation
水土流失
water loss and soil erosion
水位
level, water level
水位计
nilometer
水文的
hydrological
水文地质资料
hydrological and geological data
水文站
hydrological station
水下浇灌混凝土
underwater concreting
水下作业
underwater operation
水险
marine insurance
水养护
water cure
水运
water way
水灾
flood
水灾险
flood insurance
水闸

sluice
水准点
benchmark
水准投标
level tendering
水准仪
level
水渍险
with particular average (WPA)
税
tax
税法
tax law
税法漏洞
tax loophole
税费
tax
税后价格
price after tax
税后利润
after-tax profit, profit after tax
税后收益
earnings after tax (EAT)
税金
tax
税款
imposition, dues
税款减免
tax credit
税款专用
earmarking of taxes
税率
rate of taxation, tax rate
税目
tax items
税前利润
profit before tax, before tax profit
税前收益
before tax income
税收
revenue, tax
税收负担
tax burden

税收评定员
tax assessor
税务法院
tax court
税务检查员
surveyor of taxes
税务局
taxation office
税务员
tax collector
税制
taxation
顺差
active balance, surplus
说明
describe, description
说明书
instructions
司法的
judicial
司法权
jurisdiction
司法委员会
bar council
司法协助
judicial assistance
司库
treasurer
私法
private law
私人财产(尤指动产)
personal property, personal estate
私人的
personal, private
私人支票
individual check
私人助理
personal assistant
私下接触
private contact
私营的
private
私营工程合同

contract of privately performed work
私营公司
private company
私营企业
private enterprise
私有的
private
死胡同
impasse
死亡事故
fatal accident
松散型联营体
separated joint venture
松土机
ripper
诉讼
proceedings, litigation, suit, legal action, lawsuit
诉讼标的
object of action
诉讼财产管理人
receiver
诉讼程序
litigation procedure
诉讼当事人
litigant
诉讼的
litigant
诉讼法
procedural law
诉讼费
legal costs, costs
诉讼费加损害赔偿费
costs and damages
诉讼理由
count of lawsuit
诉讼人席位
floor of the court
诉讼项目
action item
诉讼中止令
prohibition
诉因
cause
诉诸法律
litigate
诉诸仲裁
appeal to arbitration
诉状
petition, pleadings
素混凝土面层
unreinforced surface
速度
velocity, speed, rate
速率
rate, speed, velocity
速凝混凝土
fast-setting concrete
速凝水泥
fast-setting cement, quick cement
速遣费
dispatch money
塑料薄膜
plastic film
塑料管
plastic pipe
塑料制品
plastics
塑性土
plastic soil
随后发生的事项
subsequent event
随机抽样
random sampling
随机取样
random sampling
随机样品
random sample
随意
at discretion
碎砾石
crushed gravel
碎石
crushed stone
碎石机
crusher, stone crusher (breaker),

knapping machine
隧道
tunnel
隧道衬砌
tunnel lining
隧道掘进设备
tunneling plant
隧道开挖
tunnel excavation
隧道凿岩机
tunnel drill
隧道支撑
tunnel support
隧洞挖掘机
tunnel boring machine
损害
damage, prejudice, nuisance
损害保险
insurance of damage
损害程度
extent of damage
损害赔偿
compensation for damage
损害赔偿的分担
apportionment of damages
损害赔偿的减轻
mitigation of damages
损害赔偿金
damages
损害索赔
damage claim
损害责任
liability for damage
损耗
depletion, waste, loss, wear and tear
损耗部件
wearing parts
损耗量
breakage
损耗容许量
shrinkage allowance
损坏
deterioration
损坏赔偿
indemnity for damage
损坏赔偿条款
ad damnum clause
损失
loss, damage
损失舱位
broken stowage
损失的
lost
损失的减少
loss abatement
损失机会
chance of loss
损失控制
loss control
损失率
loss ratio
损失频率
loss frequency
损失条款
loss clause
损失通知
notice of loss
损失与花费
loss and expenses
损失与开支索赔
claim for loss and expenses
损失预防
loss prevention
损失证明
proof of loss
损蚀
deterioration
损益
gain and loss, loss and gain, profit and loss, break-even
损益报表
operation statement
损益表
income sheet (statement), profit and loss statement, statement of profit

and loss
损益平衡分析
break-even analysis
损益平衡图
break-even chart
损益账
profit and loss account
缩小
deflation, narrow
缩写的签名
initialling
所得
income
所得税
income tax, tax on income
所得税申报表
income tax return
所得税预扣法
pay-as-you-earn (PAYE)
所欠余额
balance due
所有权
proprietary, ownership, title, right of ownership, possession, proprietary right
所有权凭证
document of title
所有权证据
evidence of title
所有权转移
ownership transfer, passage of title
所有人
proprietary, owner
所有人的
proprietary
所有制
ownership
所在地
locality
索价
asked (asking) price
索赔
claim

索赔报告
statement of claim
索赔补偿费
claim for compensation
索赔程序
procedure for claims
索赔的支付
payment for claims
索赔额
amount of claim
索赔款
claim money
索赔款的组成部分
claim cost components
索赔理算
adjustment of claim
索赔率
claim ratio
索赔清单
statement of claim
索赔权
right of claim, right to claim
索赔人
claimant, claimer
索赔事件
claim event
索赔书
affidavit of claim
索赔损害赔偿费
claim for damages
索赔通知书
notice of claim
索赔文件
document for claim
索赔悬案
outstanding claim
索赔意识
claim consciousness, sense of claims
索赔证明
substantiation of claim
索取
claim
索引

index

T

塌方
cave-in, collapse
塌落度
slump
塌落度试验
slump test
塌陷
collapse
塔式起重机
tower crane
台阶
step
台时
machine hour
太平门
emergency door
贪污
corruption, embezzlement, peculation
贪污行为
corrupt practice
摊销
amortization
谈判
negotiate, negotiation
谈判策略和技巧
negotiating tactics and skills
谈判程序
negotiating procedure
谈判范围
scope for negotiation
谈判失败
fail in negotiation
谈判心理学
psychology of negotiating
谈判艺术
art of negotiation
谈判招标
negotiated bidding
探井
exploratory shaft
探亲假
home leave
探伤仪
fault detector, flaw detector
探照灯
search light
逃避
dodge, evade, avoid
逃税
evade taxes, tax evasion, tax dodging
逃税人
tax evader
陶粒混凝土
ceramsite concrete
讨价还价
price bargaining
套汇
cross exchange, arbitrage
套利
arbitrage
套利率
interest rate arbitrage
套期保值
hedging
套算汇率
cross rate
特别
ad hoc
特别成本
abnormal cost
特别的
extraordinary, special
特别恶劣的天气
exceptionally inclement weather

特别附加税
special surtax
特别规定
special provisions
特别检查
special inspection
特别利润
abnormal profit
特别提款权
Special Drawing Rights (SDRs)
特别折旧
abnormal depreciation
特别折扣
special discount
特长
specialty
特此
hereby
特点
characteristics
特定的
specific, particular, ad hoc, given
特惠
special preference
特惠关税
preferential duties
特惠税率
preferential tariff
特权
privilege
特设仲裁
ad hoc arbitration
特殊补救办法
exceptional remedy
特殊产品
specialty
特殊的
exceptional, particular
特殊风险
special risks, abnormal risk
特殊紧急事件
exceptional urgency
特殊条款
special provisions
特殊应用条件
conditions of particular application
特性
quality
特许
concession, franchise, charter
特许的
concessionary, concessional, patent
特许公司
concessionary
特许会计师
chartered accountant (CA)
特许经营税
franchise taxes
特许期
concessionary period
特许权
franchise, concession
特许权出让人
franchiser
特许权受让人
franchisee
特许使用费
override
特许协议
franchise agreement, concession agreement
特种日记账
special journal
梯子
ladder
提倡
advocate
提出
put forward, propose
提出索赔
file a claim
提出者
presenter
提存账户
drawing account
提单

bill of lading (B/L.)
提单运费
bill-of-lading freight
提供
furnish, supply, provide, render
提供方便
accommodation
提供劳务合同
contract for the supply of labour
提供资金
fund
提货
take delivery
提货单
delivery order, bill of lading (B/L.)
提货即付款协议
take-and-pay agreement
提货通知
cargo delivery notice
提货与否均需付款协议
take-or-pay agreement
提及
refer to, mention
提价
price mark up
提交
submit, submission, produce, presentation
提交董事会
board presentation
提交仲裁
refer to arbitration, reference to arbitration, reference
提款
draw, drawing, withdraw
提款申请
application for withdrawal, withdrawal application
提款账户
drawing account
提名
nomination, nominate
提起诉讼
lawsuit
提前偿付
anticipate, anticipation
提前偿付条款
acceleration clause
提前承兑
rebated acceptance
提前竣工
earlier completion
提前竣工奖励
bonus for early completion
提前取款罚金
early withdrawal penalty
提前完成计划
ahead of schedule
提前完工
accelerated completion
提前完工的奖励
incentives for early completion
提前支付的承兑汇票
anticipated acceptance
提取
withdraw, collect
提升
promote, promotion
提示
presentment
提示人
presenter
提要
brief, outline
提议
offer, propose, proposal
体格检查
medical examination
体积
cubic measure, volume
体检证明
medical certificate
体力的
manual
体力劳动者
manual labour

体谅
consideration
体系
system
替代
substitute, substitution, supersede
替代材料与设备
alternative material and equipment
替代方案
alternative, alternative solution
替代进口
import substitution
替代人
substitute
替代条款
alternative provisions
替换
substitution
天花板
ceiling
天平
scale
天然资源
natural resources
天灾
Act of God
添加
add
添加剂
agent, additive
填迟日期
postdate
填方
embankment, fill
填料
filler
填土
earth fill, embankment
填早日期
backdate, foredate, antedate
填筑
reclamation
挑选出来的
selected
条件
condition, terms
条件苛刻的贷款
hard loan
条款
article, clause, terms
条款与条件
terms and conditions
条例
regulation, rule, ordinance, act
条目
entry
条目的说明
description of items
条约
pact, treaty
贴面砖
tiling
贴水
at a discount, premium, agio
贴现
discount
贴现的现金流量
discounted cash flow (DCF)
贴现经纪人
discount broker
贴现率
discount rate, rate of discount
贴现票据
note on discount
贴现期
discount period
贴现系数
discount factor
贴现银行
discount bank
贴现值
discounted value
铁路
rail, railway
铁路到货通知
railway advice

铁路交货
on rail
铁路交货价
free on rail (FOR)
铁路提货单
railway bill of lading
铁路运费
railway freight
铁路运输
carriage by rail
铁路运输及海运
rail and ocean
铁路运输及空运
rail and air
铁路运输及水运
rail and water
铁面无私的
inexorable
听证会
hearing
停泊地
anchorage
停泊费
groundage, harbor dues, port dues
停泊税
anchorage
停车场
parking lot
停电
power cut
停港费
keelage
停工
cessation of work, cease work, suspend, suspension
停工时间
idle time, downtime
停机时间
downtime
停靠港
port of call
停业
closing, wind up
停止
cease, cessation, stop, stoppage
停止诉讼申请
caveat
停止运货
stoppage in transit
停止支付通知
caveat
通道
access, passage
通风
ventilation
通风管
draft tube, pipe vents
通风井
ventilating shaft
通风系统
ventilating system
通告
advertisement, announcement
通过
pass, pass through
通货
currency
通货紧缩
deflation
通货膨胀
inflation, currency inflation
通货膨胀调整
inflation adjustment
通融索赔
ex gratia claim
通商口岸
treaty port
通行
prevail, transit
通行费
toll
通行汇率
prevailing rate
通行权
wayleaves, passage
通行税

transit tax, transit duty(dues), toll
通讯
communication
通讯录
address book
通讯社
news agency
通讯系统
communication
通用财务报表
all-purpose financial statement
通用的
general, universal
通用合同条件
general conditions of contract
通用条件
general conditions
通用要求条款
common requirement clause
通知
advise, inform, notify, notification, notice
通知偿还
call, notice of payment
通知存款
call deposit
通知贷款
call loan
通知单
advice note
通知交货
delivery on call
通知期限
notice period
通知手续费
advising charges
通知书
letter of advise, letter of notice, notification, note
通知行
advising bank, notifying bank
同等的
equivalent, equal

同等机会
equal opportunity
同等机会条款
equal opportunity clause
同盟
confederation
同盟费率
conference rate
同期记录
contemporary records
同时发生的延误
concurrent delay
同事
associate
同席人员
table
同业
profession
同业工会
craft union, trade association
同意
agree, consent, grant, accede
统筹法
program evaluation and reviews technique (PERT)
统计
statistics
统计表
returns, statistical chart
统计数字
statistics
统计资料
statistics
统一的
uniform
统一发票
uniform invoice
统一费率
flat rate
统一惯例
uniform customs
统一税率
flat rate

统驭账户
control (controlling) account
筒
silo
筒式搅拌机
drum mixer
偷工减料的
jerry
偷工减料的建筑商
jerry builder
偷工减料的施工
jerry construction
偷税
evasion of tax, evade taxes, tax evasion, tax dodging
偷税人
tax dodger
头等风险
primary risk
头衔
title
投保
effect insurance, insure against
投保单
application for insurance, proposal form
投保方
insuring party
投保金额
insurance amount, sum insured, insured amount
投保人
assured, applicant for insurance, policy holder, insurant, insured
投保书
proposal, proposal of insurance
投保项目
insured item
投标
bid, bidding, submission of bid (tender), tender, tendering
投标包干价格分解
breakdown of lump sum bid price

投标保函
bid bond, bid guarantee, letter of guarantee for bid, tender guarantee
投标保证
bid security
投标保证书
bid guarantee, tender guarantee
投标报价
bidding price
投标报价汇总表
summary of tender
投标表册
bid tabulations
投标步骤
bid process
投标程序
bid procedure
投标澄清会议
bid clarification meeting
投标单价
bid unit price
投标担保
bid bond, tender bond
投标的密封和标志
sealing and marking of bids
投标方
tendering party
投标费用
cost of tendering, bid cost
投标格式
bid form
投标核查
bid examination
投标候选人
candidate for tendering
投标汇总
bid summary
投标货币
bid currencies
投标价
bid price, tender price, price tendered

投标价目表
bid schedule of prices
投标阶段
bid phase
投标期
bid period
投标前现场调查
pre-bid site visit
投标人
bidder, tenderer
投标人的义务
bidder's obligation
投标人退还文件
bidder's return of documents
投标人须知
instructions to bidders
投标人资格
bidder's qualification
投标人资格预审
bidder's prequalification
投标日期
bid due date
投标时间
bidding time
投标实质内容
bid substance
投标手续
tender procedures
投标书
tender
投标书补遗
bid addenda
投标书的审查与评估
bid review and evaluation
投标书的完备性
sufficiency of tender
投标书附录
appendix to bid
投标书格式
form of tender, tender form
投标书签收
bid receipt
投标书提交时间
time for bid submission
投标书中问题的澄清
bid clarifications
投标条件
tendering conditions
投标通知
bidding advice
投标文件包
bid package
投标文件的修改
modification of bid, modification of tender
投标文件内容
bid package contents
投标压价
bid shopping
投标邀请函
bid invitation letter
投标要求
bid requirement
投标有效期
bid validity period, validity of bid (tender)
投标有效性
validity of bid (tender)
投标与授标
bidding and award
投标语言
bid language
投标预备会
pre-bid meeting
投标者
bidder, tenderer
投标准备
bid preparation, preparation of bid
投标总报价
bid price
投产
put into production
投机
venture, speculation
投机风险
speculative risk

投机商
speculator, profiteer
投机资本
venture capital
投料试生产
commissioning test run
投票
vote
投入
input, invest
投入运营
go into operation
投入资本
vested capital
投诉
complain
投资
invest, investment
投资补贴额
investment allowance
投资回报
returns on the investment, investment return
投资回报率
rate of return on investment
投资回收期
investment recovery period, payback period
投资评价
investment appraisal
投资前研究
preinvestment studies
投资入股型联营体
equity joint venture
投资收益率
return on investment
投资信托
investment trust
投资银行
investment bank
投资预算
investment budget
投资者

investor
投资证券
investment securities
投资周转
investment turnover
透视图
perspective
透水层
pervious bed
透水性
perviousness
透支
overdraft, overdraw
透支保函
overdraft guarantee
图表
graph, chart, diagram
图解
graph, diagram
图解的
graphic(al)
图例
legend
图示的
graphic(al)
图形
figure
图样
pattern
图章
seal
图纸
drawing
图纸目录
drawing list
涂改的支票
altered check, raised check
涂改支票
raise a check
土坝
earth dam
土的压实
soil compaction

土堤
embankment
土地
land
土地改良
land improvement
土地税
land tax
土地所有权
property in land
土地通行权
easement
土地征用
expropriation of land
土地征用权
domain
土地证
land certificate
土地转让证
land patent
土地租约
ground lease
土方工程
ground works, earthwork
土方工程进度表
schedule of earthwork
土方工程量
volume of earthwork
土工织物
geotextile fabrics
土建
civil work
土建公司
civil engineering firm
土木工程
civil work, civil engineering
土木工程程序
civil engineering procedure
土木工程工程量计算规则
civil engineering standard method of measurement
土木工程师
civil engineer

土木工程师学会调解程序
Institution of Civil Engineers' Conciliation Procedure
土木工程造价
cost of civil engineering works
土壤含水量
soil moisture content, soil moisture
土壤条件
soil conditions
土石坝
earth-rock dam
土压力
earth pressure, soil pressure
土样
soil sample, soil sample
土质调查
soil investigation, soil investigation
团体
corporation
推测
presumption
推迟
defer, postpone, postponement
推定的
constructive
推定价值
constructed value
推定全损
constructive total loss, technical total loss
推定条款
constructive clause
推定占有
constructive possession
推荐
recommend, recommendation, nomination, nominate
推荐信
letter of recommendation
推土机
bulldozer
推销商
promoter

推销商品的信件
call letter
退保
surrender
退还保险费
premium returns
退还担保
back bond
退还预付款
restitution of advance payment
退回的货物
returned goods
退货
sales returns
退货凭单
merchandise credit slip
退货运费
back freight
退款
draw-back, refund
退料单
materials return report
退票
dishonored notes (bill)
退票通知单
protest jacket
退税
tax refund, refund of duty, tax rebate
退休
retirement
退休金
pension
退约条款
denunciation clause
退职
retirement
托付
consignment
托管人
trustee
托盘
pallet

托收
collect, collection
托收单
order for collection
托收汇票
bill for collection, collect a bill, collection bill
托收票据
bills for collection (BC)
托收委托书
collection order
托收银行
collecting bank, remitting bank
托运
consignment, consign
托运人
consignor, consigner
拖车
trailer
拖拉机
tractor
拖期
behind schedule
拖期付款
delayed payment
拖期交付的施工图
delayed shop drawings
拖期竣工
delayed completion
拖欠风险
default risk
拖欠款
back money
拖延
delay, prolong
拖延策略
delaying tactics
脱模
demoulding
脱模剂
release agent
脱手价值
exit value

妥协 | compromise

W

挖沟
trench
挖沟机
trenching machine, ditcher, channeller
挖掘
excavation, cutting
挖掘机
excavator
挖泥船
dredger
蛙式打夯机
frog rammer
瓦
tile
瓦工
bricklayer
歪曲
misrepresentation
外币
foreign currency
外币需求
foreign currency requirements
外币折算风险
translation risk
外币支付
payment in foreign currencies
外部障碍
physical obstruction
外埠付款汇票
domiciled bill (draft)
外国代理机构
foreign agency
外国的
alien, overseas, foreign
外国公司
foreign corporation
外国技工
expatriate craftsmen
外国投资
foreign investment
外国银行
foreign bank
外汇
foreign exchange
外汇短缺
short of exchange
外汇额度
exchange quota
外汇风险
foreign exchange risk, foreign exchange exposure, exchange risk
外汇管理规定
exchange control regulations
外汇管制
exchange control, foreign exchange control
外汇换算损益
translation gain or loss
外汇汇率
currency rate
外汇交易
foreign exchange transaction, exchange dealings
外汇税
exchange tax
外汇限制
exchange restriction
外汇赢利
foreign exchange earning
外籍劳工
expatriate labour
外加的
extra
外加费用
extra cost, extras

外加剂
agent, additive
外界的
external
外界条件
environmental conditions
外来风险
extraneous risks
外商
alien merchant
外向型的人
extrovert
外向型性格的
extrovert
外形图与装配图
outline and assembly drawings
外在缺陷
patent defects
外债
foreign debt, external debt
弯板机
plate bender
弯钢筋机
steel bender
弯管机
pipe bender
弯筋机
bender
弯头
elbow
完成
complete, completion, finish, achieve
完成的工程
completed project
完成合同
completion of contract
完成进度计划
fulfillment of schedule
完工成本
finished cost
完工阶段
stage of completion

完工日期
completion date
完全成本
full cost, absorption cost
完全承保
full coverage
完全的
absolute, complete
完全信托
complete trust
完全责任
full liability
完税后交货(价)
delivered duty paid(DDP)
完税货价
price duty paid
完税价值
duty-paying value, dutiable value, tariff value
完整的合同
entire contract
玩忽
neglect, negligence
玩忽职守
dereliction, neglect of duty, misconduct in office
挽回
retrieve
万国公法
law of nations
网络
network
网络分析
network analysis
网络计划
network program
网络进度计划法
network scheduling technique
网络图
network chart (diagram)
网状系统
network
往返票

round trip ticket, return ticket
往来银行
correspondent bank
往来账户
current account, reciprocal account
往来账结余
balance of current account
旺季
peak season
危险
danger, hazard, risk, peril
危险的
dangerous
危险工作津贴
danger money
危险建筑物
dangerous building
危险品
dangerous goods (articles)
危险区
danger area
危险信号
danger signal
微小的
marginal, minute
为了
with a view to
为某目的而安排的
ad hoc
为其他承包商提供方便
facilities for other contractors
为支付进行的计量
measurement for payment
为准的
subject to
围墙
enclosure
围堰
cofferdam
违背
break, breach, default
违法
breach of law, illegality

违法的
illicit
违法乱纪
malfeasance
违法行为
illegal act, tort
违法行为者
tortfeasor
违反
contravene, breach, violate
违反法律
violate a law
违反合同
break a contract, breach of contract, violation of contract
违反合同的诉讼
covenant
违反义务行为
act against duty
违犯
violate, infringe
违禁品
contraband, prohibited articles (goods)
违约
fail, default, breach of contract, non-performance
违约罚款
contractual fines, penalty of breach of contract
违约方
default party, party in breach
违约风险
default risk
违约赔偿金
damages for default
违约通知
notice of default
违章操作
unprofessional operation
唯一代理
exclusive agency
唯一代理人

sole agent
唯一的
sole, only
维持关税
preserving duty
维护
maintain, maintenance
维护费用
cost of upkeep
维修
maintain, maintenance, service
维修保函
maintenance guarantee
维修担保
maintenance bond
维修费
maintenance cost, upkeep
维修费准备
reserve for repair
维修期
maintenance period, warranty period
维修手册
maintenance manual
维修条件
terms of service
维修证书
maintenance certificate
伪造
fabricate, forge, counterfeit
伪造的文书
false document
伪造记录
false entry
伪造签字
forged signature
伪造文件
forged document
尾水管
draft tube
纬度
latitude
委付通知
notice of abandonment
委派
delegate, delegation, appoint
委派管理
administration of assignment
委弃通知
notice of abandonment
委任
appoint
委任书
letter of attorney
委任条款
terms of appointment
委任者
mandator
委托
entrust, authorize
委托代理人
entrusted agent
委托的
mandatory
委托加工
manufacturing consignment
委托贸易
commission trade
委托人
client, principal, entruster, consignor, consigner
委托人的责任
liability of the client
委托收债费
factoring charges
委托书
certificate of entrustment, power of attorney, commission
委托书格式
form of proxy
委托通知
vesting notice
委员会
council, committee, board, commission
卫生设备
sanitary facilities

未被要求的
unsolicited
未贬值价值
undepreciated value
未标价的工程量表
unpriced bill of quantities
未偿本金
outstanding principal
未偿清货款
outstandings
未偿损失
outstanding losses
未偿债务
debt outstanding, unpaid liabilities
未到期的
undue
未到期汇票
bill undue
未到期票据
undue note
未到期债务
undue debt
未抵押资产
unpledged assets
未定数量的契约
open-end contract
未兑现支票
outstanding check, uncashed check
未发货订单
unfilled order
未分配利润
undistributed profit, undivided profit
未付的
unpaid, outstanding
未付的应付款
outstanding dues
未付利息
unpaid interest
未付赔款
outstanding losses
未付薪金
unpaid wages and salaries
未耗成本
unexpired cost
未划线支票
uncrossed check, open cheque
未交定货
outstanding order
未交付订单
back order
未交货
non-delivery
未结清账户
open account
未结算账户
unsettled account
未经检验的
off-test
未决赔款
outstanding claim
未决问题
pending question
未来价值
future value
未履行的义务
unfulfilled obligation, outstanding obligation
未履约
non-performance
未能交货
failure to deliver
未能收回的金额
amount not recovered
未能送达
non-delivery
未能预见的现场条件
unforeseen site conditions
未签字的
unsigned
未清偿的债务
outstanding debt
未清算账目
outstandings
未清余额
outstanding balance
未清账款

outstanding account
未确定的索赔
un-asserted claim
未摊销成本
unamortized cost
未填写的
blank
未通过检验
fail the test
未完成的
outstanding
未完成的工作
outstanding work, unfinished work
未完工程
construction in progress
未完税后交货(价)
delivered duty unpaid (DDU)
未折旧价值
undepreciated value
未中标者
unsuccessful bidder (tenderer)
位移
displacement
位于
locate
位置
location, locality
温度裂缝
temperature cracking
温度应力
temperature stress
文本
version, text
文件
file, document, present
文件查阅
inspection of documents
文件审查
inspection of documents
文件证明书
affidavit of document
文书工作
paper work
文书工作的
clerical
文物
culture relics
文摘
abstract
稳压器
voltage regulator
问询
inquire
窝工的
idle
窝工费用
idle cost
窝工时间
downtime, idle time
圬工
masonry
污染
contaminate, contamination, pollute, pollution
污染物
contamination
污染险
risk of contamination
污水处理
sewage disposal
污水工程
sewerage
污水管
pipe sewer
污水管道
sanitary sewer
屋顶
roof
诬告
accuse falsely, malicious prosecution
无保留验收
unreserved acceptance
无保证的
unwarranted
无残值
zero salvage value

无差别待遇
non-discriminatory treatment
无偿的
free, gratuitous
无偿付能力的
insolvent
无偿付能力者
insolvent
无担保贷款
unsecured loan, straight loan, open credit
无担保的
unsecured
无担保合同
naked contract
无担保投标
unsecured bid
无担保债权人
unsecured creditor
无担保债券
debenture
无担保债务
unsecured debt
无抵押的
unsecured
无调价规定
no price fluctuation provisions
无法律根据的
preterlegal
无法实行
impracticability
无跟单信用证
clean (letter of) credit
无价值担保
dead security
无力偿付债务
insolvency
无利息
ex-interest
无论灭失与否条款
lost or not lost clause
无论损失如何全部赔偿
irrespective of percentage (I.O.P)

无能力的
incompetent
无赔款奖金
no-claim bonus
无赔款退费
no-claim return
无赔款折扣
no-claim discount
无权利的
unentitled
无缺陷管理
zero defects management
无人继承权
bona vacantia
无条件保函
guarantee on the first demand, unconditional guarantee
无条件背书
absolute endorsement
无条件承兑
unconditional acceptance
无条件接受
absolute acceptance
无条件信用证
unconditional L/C
无条件银行保函
unconditional bank guarantee
无条件账户
discretionary account
无条件折扣
unconditional discount
无拖期赔偿条款
no damages for delay clause
无息贷款
free loan, interest-free credit, passive loan
无息信贷
interest-free credit
无息债券
passive bond
无暇疵提单
clean bill of lading
无限竞争性公开招标

unlimited competitive open bidding
无限责任
unlimited liability
无效的
invalid, inefficient, ineffective, void, null
无效合同
contract void, void contract
无效诺言
naked promise
无效性
invalidity
无懈可击的
unimpeachable
无薪休假
leave without pay
无形财产
intangible property
无形的
intangible
无形动产
intangible movables
无形固定资产
fixed intangible assets, intangible fixed assets
无形价值
intangible value
无形贸易
invisible trade
无形商品
intangible goods
无形资本
immaterial capital
无形资产
intangible assets, intangible property
无用的
useless, waste
无约束力的合同
unbinding contract
无责任的
exculpatory
无证据的
naked

无支付能力
failure
无主物
bona vacantia
无追索权
non-recourse, without recourse
无资格
disqualification, incapability
无资格的
unentitled
舞弊
fraud, collusion
物价
commodity price
物价暴涨
inflation
物价变化系数
price fluctuation factor
物价加权指数
price-weighted index
物价上涨
price escalation
物价上涨指数
escalation index
物价稳定
price stability
物价指数
commodity price index, index of prices
物力
resources
物力资源
physical resources, material resources
物品
goods, article
物权
property
物物交换
barter, trade off
物证
exhibit, material evidence, proof
物质的

material
物质损失
material damage
物资部
purchasing department
物资储运费
charge for storage & freight of goods
物资所有权
ownership of goods and materials
误差
error
误差范围
error range

误解
misunderstanding, mistake
误期的
belated
误期罚款
penalty for delay
误期费用
cost of delay
误期损害赔偿费
liquidated damages for delay
误期责任
liability for delay

X

吸声板
acoustical board
吸收
absorption, absorb
吸收能力
absorptive capacity
息差
margin
息票
coupon
息前税前收益
earnings before interest and tax (EBIT)
习惯
custom, usage
习惯法
customary law, common law
习惯皮重
customary tare
系数
factor
系统
system
系统测试
system testing
系统的阐述

formulate
系统风险
systematic risks
系统工程
system engineering
系统管理
system management
细节
detail, detailed particulars
细目
particular
细微的
fine, subtle
细则
abstract of particulars, by-law, details
狭窄的
narrow
下班
off-duty
下水道工程
sewerage
下游的
downstream
先决条件
condition precedent, prerequisite,

precondition
先例
precedent
先期违约
anticipatory breach
先张法预加应力
pre-tensioned prestressing
纤维板
fiber board
闲人莫入
off limits, no attendance
闲置的
inactive, idle
闲置率
vacancy rate
闲置设备
idle equipment, standby equipment
闲置生产能力
idle capacity
闲置资金
dead money, idle money
现场
field, site
现场安全费用
cost of site security
现场安装
erection on site, field erection
现场搬运
handling in field
现场采购主管
field procurement supervisor
现场测试
spot test
现场抽查
spot check, snap check
现场代表
field representative
现场的
in-situ, spot
现场的占有
possession of site
现场调查
field survey, site investigation

现场服务
field service
现场工程师
site engineer
现场工作
field work
现场管理
site management
现场管理费
site overhead cost
现场检查
spot inspection, on-site inspection
现场检查人员
field inspection staff
现场检验
on-site inspection
现场浇筑的混凝土
cast-in-situ concrete
现场勘察
field investigation, site inspection
现场勘探
site exploration
现场量测
field measurement
现场培训
on-site training
现场平面图
site plan
现场清理
site clearance
现场审计
on-the-spot audit
现场生活设施
site accommodation
现场施工经理
field construction manager
现场施工组织
site organization
现场使用权
right to the use of a site
现场视察
inspection of site
现场试验

现场试验
field test
现场条件变化
differing site conditions (D.S.C)
现场项目人员
field project staff
现场销售
field sales
现场修理
spot repair
现场营地与住房
camps and housing
现场杂费
oncost
现场整洁状况
cleanliness of site
现场资料
site data
现场作业
site operations
现代化
modernization
现付
spot payment
现付的
spot
现购
cash purchase
现汇
spot exchange
现汇汇率
spot rate
现汇交易
spot exchange transaction
现货
goods in stock, spot
现货供应的
off-the-shelf
现货价格
spot price
现货交易
spot transaction
现货业务
spot transaction

现浇混凝土
poured concrete
现浇混凝土桩
in-situ concrete pile
现金
cash, ready cash
现金簿
cash book
现金出纳机
cash register
现金存款
cash deposit, primary deposit
现金贷方
cash credit
现金担保
cash guarantee
现金额度
cash allowance
现金购买
cash purchase
现金股息
cash dividend
现金管理账户
cash management account (CMA)
现金红利
cash bonus
现金基金
cash fund
现金奖金
cash bonus
现金交易
money transaction, on cash
现金交易市场
cash market
现金结算
cash settlement
现金流出量
cash outflows
现金流估计
cash flow estimate
现金流量
cash flow
现金流量表

cash flow statement, statement of cashflow
现金流入量
cash inflows
现金流图
cash flow diagram
现金赔款
cash losses
现金日报表
daily cash report
现金收入日记账
cash receipts journal
现金销售
cash sales
现金溢缺
cash over and short
现金账
cash account, cash book
现金账户
cash account
现金折扣
cash discount
现金支出
cash credit
现金支出日记账
cash disbursement journal
现金支付
cash payment, payment in cash
现金支付费用
out-of-pocket expenses
现金资产
cash assets
现款
spot cash
现时的
current
现时工资
current labour rates
现行成本
current cost
现行的
current, prevailing
现行的进度计划

current programme
现行法令
current decrees
现行费率
prevailing rate
现行价格
current price, prevailing price
现行价格指数
current price index
现行市价
current market value
现行重置成本
current replacement cost
现有存货
stock in hand
现在的
present
现值
present value
线路图
layout chart
线条
bar
线条图
bar chart, Gantt chart
线性荷载
linear load
限定
definition, restriction
限度
limitation
限额
limit, quota
限额保函
limited amount guarantee
限制
confine, constrain, restriction, limit
限制索赔条款
disclaimer clause
限制条件
reservation, side conditions, qualification
限制性贷款

tied loan
限制性契约
negative covenant
限制性条件
proviso
限制性条款
proviso clause, qualifying clause, restrictive clause
限制性援助
tied aid
宪法
constitution
陷阱
pitfall
陷入僵局
reach an impasse
相等物
equivalent
相对价格
relative price
相反的
contrary, counter
相关
pursuant to, related to
相关成本
relevant cost
相关服务
incidental service
相关性
relevance
相互补偿
mutual indemnification
相互的
mutual
相互理解
mutual understanding
相互矛盾
contradict, contradiction
相互赊欠
swap credits
相互协作的
cooperative
相互影响

interplay
相互影响的
interactive
相信
believe, trust
相撞
come into collision with
香港银行同业拆放利率
Hongkong Interbank Offered Rate (HIBOR)
箱
case
箱型大梁
box girder
详尽阐述
elaborate
详尽研究
scrutiny
详图
details, detailed drawing
详细报表
detailed account
详细的施工进度表
detailed construction schedule
详细费用
detailed cost
详细概算
detailed estimation
详细估计
detailed take-off
详细计划
detailed program
详细计划表
detailed schedule
详细目录
inventory
详细设计
detailed design, detailed engineering
详细设计法
detailed design approach
详细申述
detailed particulars
详细审计

detailed audit
详细说明
specify
详细预算
detailed budget
详细装箱单
detailed packing list
享有完全追索权
with full recourse
响应的
responsive
响应性投标
responsive bid
向承运人索赔
claim against carrier
向银行下达通知
instruct a bank
项
item
项目
project, item
项目报告
project report
项目备选方案
project alternative
项目参与者
project participant
项目程序手册
project procedure manual
项目持续性评价
project sustainability assessing
项目筹备
project startup
项目筹资
project funding
项目代表
project representative
项目的开办
set-up of a project
项目的开工
start-up of a project, commencement of a project
项目的扩建
project extension
项目的起始
project inception
项目的筛选
screening of projects
项目的执行
project performance
项目的执行与监督
project execution and supervision
项目的准备
set-up of a project
项目范围
project scope
项目分析
project analysis
项目负责机构
project entity
项目概要
project brief
项目工程师
project engineer
项目官员
project officer
项目管理
project management
项目合同
contract for project
项目后评价
project post-evaluation
项目机构
project organization
项目机会
project opportunities
项目计划
project planning
项目监督人员
project superintendent
项目监督员
project monitor
项目监控
project monitoring
项目建议书
project proposal

项目进度计划 project schedule
项目经理 project manager
项目经理助理 assistant project manager
项目竣工报告 project completion report
项目控制 project control
项目联营体 joint venture for project
项目描述 project description
项目目标 project objective, project goal
项目内容确定 project definition
项目评估 project appraisal, project evaluation
项目期末评估 end-of-project evaluation
项目日志 project diary
项目融资 project financing
项目审批过程 project approval process
项目实施计划 plan of operations
项目实体 project entity
项目手册 project manual
项目说明 project description
项目谈判 project negotiation
项目停止使用日期 date off-project
项目投入使用日期 date on-project
项目协调 project coordination
项目协调员 project coordinator
项目协议 project agreement
项目选定 project identification
项目选择 project selection
项目循环 project cycle
项目要求 project demands
项目业务 activities of project
项目影响评估 ex-post evaluation
项目有关各方 parties to a project
项目预测 project forecast
项目预评估 project pre-appraisal
项目预算 project budget
项目运营 project operation
项目暂停 project suspension
项目执行计划 project implementation schedule
项目执行评估报告 project performance assessment report (PPAR)
项目执行审计报告 project performance audit report (PPAR)
项目职员 project staff
项目质量考核 project quality test
项目周期 project cycle

项目主办者
project sponsor
项目准备
project preparation
项目组
project team
项目组成部分
project components
项目作业
project activities
象征性的
nominal
削价
price cutting
削减
cutback
消除
eliminate
消毒检验证书
disinfection inspection certificate
消防栓
fire hydrant
消费
consume, consumption, expenditure
消费贷款
consumer loan
消费品
consumer goods
消费品价格指数
consumer price index
消费品进口报关单
entry for consumption
消费税
excise, consumption tax
消费信贷
consumer credit
消耗
consume, use up, expend
消耗品
consumables
消极的
negative
消极因素
negative factor
消力池
stilling basin, plunge pool
消声材料
sound-deadening material
消息
message, news
萧条
depression
销货成本
cost of goods sold
销货毛利
gross profit on sales
销路
marketing outlet
销售
sale, market
销售代理商
selling agent
销售额
sales turnover
销售发票
sales invoice
销售费用
marketing expenses, selling cost
销售合同
contract of sales, sales contract
销售回扣
sales rebate
销售价
selling price
销售经理
sales manager
销售毛利
sales margin
销售渠道
distribution outlet, market channel
销售权
power of sale
销售确认书
sales confirmation
销售税
sales tax

销售条件
conditions of sale, terms of sale
销售协定
selling agreement
销售佣金
sales commission
销售账
sales account
销售折扣
discount on sales
销售组合
marketing mix
销账
charge off
小费
tip, gratuity
小签
initial
小石子
handstone
小时工资
hourly wage rate, wage per hour
小心轻放
handle with care
小型交易会
minifair
小修
current repair
小组
gang, team, crew
效果
effect
效力
force, effect
效率
efficiency
效率降低
loss of efficiency
效益
benefit, profitability
效益成本比率
benefit-cost ratio (BCR)
协调
coordinate, coordination
协调人
coordinator
协调中心
coordination center
协定
agreement, convention
协定的损害赔偿费
liquidated damages
协定价格
conventional price
协定运费率
agreed rate
协会
association, institute, institution
协商
consult, consultation, negotiate, negotiation
协商合同
negotiation contract
协商解决
settlement by agreement, negotiated settlement
协商一致的利率
consensus rate
协议
agreement, arrangement, treaty
协议的性质
nature of agreement
协议范围
extent of agreement, scope of agreement
协议利益
benefit of agreement
协议书格式
form of agreement, agreement form
协议书规定的货币
currency of agreement
协议书语言
language of agreement
协议条文
articles of agreement
协议终止合同

termination by agreement
协助
assistance
协作
cooperation, collaboration, team work
协作合同
contract of association
协作精神
team spirit
协作型联营体
cooperative joint venture
斜拉桥
cable-stayed bridge
泄漏
leak, divulge
泄露
disclose, disclosure, reveal
泄水道
sluice
卸岸日期
date of landing
卸货
discharge, clear a ship, unload
卸货地点
landing place
卸货费
landing charges
卸货港
discharging port, port of discharge, unloading port
卸货记录
landing account
卸货价格
landed price
卸货日期
date of discharge
卸货通知单
landing order
卸货重量
landed weight
卸料斗
discharge hopper

懈怠行为
act of omission
辛迪加贷款
syndicated loan
新方法
innovation
新增成本
additional cost
新增工作
additional work
薪金
salary
信贷
credit
信贷保函
credit guarantee
信贷额度
lines of credit
信贷公司
finance company
信贷市场
credit market
信贷条件
credit terms
信贷协议
credit agreement
信贷银行
credit bank
信贷政策
credit policy
信函
letter, communication
信汇
mail transfer (M/T)
信汇通知书
mail transfer advice
信任
confidence, trust
信守合同
honour the contract
信托
entrust, trust
信托财产

trust property
信托服务
fiduciary service
信托公司
trust company
信托基金
trust fund
信托契约
deed of trust
信托人
trustor
信托收据
trust receipt
信托受益人
cestui que trust
信托书
declaration of trust, letter of trust
信托银行
trust bank
信托账户
account in trust
信息
information, message
信息管理系统
information management system (IMS)
信息数据库
information data bank
信用
credit, honour
信用保险
credit insurance
信用保险单
credit policy
信用贷款
fiduciary loan
信用分析
credit analysis
信用卡
credit card, card
信用赊账
on credit
信用债券
debenture
信用证
letter of credit (L/C)
信用证金额
amount of the credit
信用证申请书
application for letter of credit
信用证条件
terms of credit
信用证修改书
amendment of letter of credit
信用证样本
specimen of L/C
信用证总限额
aggregate amount of letter of credit
信誉
reputation
兴趣
interest
刑法
criminal law
刑事责任
criminal liability, criminal responsibility
行车道
road way
行程
voyage
行动
act, action, conduct, deed
行动纲领
action programme
行贿
bribery, bribe
行使
exercise
行使权力
exercise power
行使权利
exercise right
行使职权
exercise of authority
行使职权能力

capacity for right
行使职务
officiate
行为
action, behavior, conduct
行为标准
behavior criterion, behavioural characteristics criteria
行为能力
disposing capacity
行为守则
rules of conduct
行为准则
standard of conduct
行政部门
administrative department, administration
行政措施
administration measure
行政当局
administering authority
行政的
executive, administrative
行政法
administration law
行政法庭
administrative tribunal
行政费
overhead
行政管理
administration
行政管理费
expenditure on administration
行政管理费用
administrative overhead
行政管理人员
administrative personnel, administrative staff
行政管理员
administrator
行政惯例
administration practice
形式的
formal
形式发票
proforma invoice
型钢
section steel
性能
performance, characteristics
性能标准
performance criteria
性能检验
performance test
性能指标
performance criteria
性质
nature, property, character
休会
recess
休假
leave, off-duty
休息
rest
休息日
off-day, restday
休闲维持成本
standby cost
休止
cease, cessation
修补
repair, rectify, remedy, patch
修补缺陷
remedying defects
修订
amend, amendment, revise
修复
make good, restore, restoration, rehabilitation
修复－运营－移交
Rehabilitate-Operate-Transfer (ROT)
修改
amend, amendment, revise, revision, modify, modification
修改合同

revise a contract
修改书
addendum
修改通知单
amendment advice
修改信用证金额
amend the amount of L/C
修改信用证条款
amend the terms of L/C
修理
fix, repair, mend
修理费
repair cost
修理工
repair man
修理工具
repair outfit
修配间
repair shop
修缮和扩建
betterment and extension
修缮经费
betterment
修整
fitting
修正
correct, modify, remedy
修正的计划
revised programme
修正合同
amendment of contract
虚报
salt, misrepresent, misstatement
虚报账目
salt an account
虚构的索赔
fabricated claim
虚假的
artificial, false
虚假利润
false profit
虚盈实亏
false profit

虚账户
nominal account
需经事先批准
subject to prior approval
需求
demand
需求预测
demand forecast
需要
require, requirement
需要的
requisite
许可
approve, permit, consent
许可证
permit, licence, license, letters
许可证颁发人
licenser, licensor
许可证法
licensing law
许可证交易
licensing
许可证接受人
licencee, licensee
许可证协议
licence agreement
许诺
promise, undertaking
序列号
serial number
序时账簿
chronological books
叙述
depict
叙述情况
depicting progress
续订合同
renew a contract
蓄水池
reservoir
蓄意
with intent, intention
宣布

announce
宣传
advertisement
宣告
notify
宣告不适用
condemnation
宣告破产
adjudication of bankruptcy
宣判
sentence
宣判某人无罪
acquit sb. of a crime
宣誓
attestation
宣誓书
affidavit
悬臂梁
cantilever beam, overhanging beam
悬而未决的
pending, outstanding
悬索桥
suspension bridge, cable suspension bridge
选派
designate
选线
siting
选择(权)
option
选择标准
selection criteria
选择目的港附加费
optional destination additional
选择税
alternative duty
选择条款
optional clause
选择投标人
bidder selection
选择投标人准则
bidder selection criteria
选择项目
optional items
选择性招标
selected bidding (tendering), selective bidding (tendering)
选址
siting
选址查勘
site selection investigation
学会
institute, institution, society
学科
discipline
学员
trainee
学院
institute
询价
enquire, enquiry, inquire, inquiry
询价采购
shopping
询价文件
enquiry documents
询盘
enquiry, inquiry
询问
query
询问者
inquirer
循环信用证
revolving L/C
循环资金
revolving fund
训练
train
迅速处理
despatch, dispatch
迅速地
expeditiously, prompt

Y

压价
beat down price, force down prices
压力灌浆
pressure grouting
压力涵洞
pressure culvert
压力喷浆
pneumatic mortar
压力隧道
pressure tunnel
压路机
pavement roller, road roller
压实
compact, compaction
压实工具
compactor
压缩机
compressor
压缩空气管道
pneumatic tube
压土机
compactor
押汇银行
negotiating bank
押金
deposit, cash deposit as collateral
烟道
air flue
延长
extend, extension, prolong, renewal
延长工期索赔
claim for extension of time
延长合同
extend a contract
延长合同有效期
prolong a contract period
延长有效期
prolong the period of validity

延迟
defer, delay, postpone
延迟付款利息
interest for delayed payment
延迟交货
late delivery
延迟接受
late acceptance
延迟装运
late shipment
延缓偿付期
moratorium
延交定货
back order
延米
linear metre
延期
extend, extension, defer, delay, postpone
延期偿付权
moratorium
延期费用
extension fee, deferment charge
延期付款
defer payment, deferred payment, payment deferred
延期付款保函
deferred payment guarantee
延期付款销售
deferred payment sale, installment sale
延期付款信用证
deferred payment credit
延期交货
deferred delivery
延期利息
deferred interest
延期年金
deferred annuity

延期支付
postponed payment
延误
delay
延误船期保险
overdue risk
延误的
delayed
严格标准
tight standard
严格的
exact, strict
严重渎职
gross misconduct
严重违约
material breach of contract
严重遗漏
material omission
言外之意
implication
岩层
rock stratum
岩芯样品
rock core sample
研究开发费
research and development cost
研究所
institute
掩护性投标
cover bid (tender)
掩饰
dodge
验关
customs examination, customs inspection
验明
identify
验收
check and accept, acceptance
验收规范
acceptance specification
验收试验
acceptance test

验收证书
acceptance certificate, taking-over certificate
验收准则
acceptance criteria
验证
verify, verification, validation
验证方法
means of verification
堰
barrage
扬水站
lift station
羊脚辗
sheep-foot roller
养护费
upkeep
养护覆盖物
curing mat
养老基金
pension fund
氧气切割器
oxygen lance
样板房
model house
样本
specimen
样品
specimen, sample, pattern, test sample
样品室
sample room
邀请
invite
邀请函
letter of invitation (LOI)
邀请谈判
invitation to negotiate
邀请投标
request for bid, invitation to bid (tender)
邀请招标
selected bidding

遥感数据
remote sensing data
要点
key point
要价
asked (asking) price, charge, price asked
要求
claim, request, requirement
要求的技术备选方案
solicited technical alternative
要求调整合同价
claim for adjustment of price
要求权
claim
要求提出建议书
calling for proposals
要求一览表
schedule of requirements
要求支付拖欠金额
recovery of late payment
要样
ask for samples
要约
offer
要约人
offerer, offeror
野外作业
field work
业绩
performance
业绩评价
performance evaluation
业务代表团
operational mission
业务开发
business development
业务开支
operating expenses
业主
client, employer, owner, proprietary
业主财产保险
insurance of client's property
业主产权
proprietary equity
业主的
proprietary
业主的财产
client's property
业主的代表
client's representative
业主的代理人
agent for owner
业主的风险
owner's risk
业主的批准
client's approval
业主的权利
owner's right
业主的权益
owner's equity
业主的设备
employer's equipment
业主的义务
owner's obligation, owner's duty
业主的责任
liability of the client
业主的职员
client's personnel
业主的咨询顾问
owner's consultant
业主供货范围
scope of supply by owner
业主顾问
client adviser
业主权益
proprietary interest, proprietary equity
业主认可
acceptance by owner
业主索赔
claim by owner
业主违约
default of employer, default of owner
业主自便的终止

termination at employer's convenience

页岩
shale

夜班
night shift

液体的
liquid

液压式挖土机
hydraulic excavator

一班(制)
single shift

一般代理
general agency

一般的
general, average

一般抵押
general mortgage

一般留置权
general lien

一般侵权行为
general tort

一般权利
general right

一般使用条件
average service conditions

一般条件
general conditions

一般条件
general terms and conditions

一般物价水准
general price level

一般义务
general obligation, general responsibilities

一般责任
general responsibilities

一次付清保险费的保单
single premium policy

一次还款式贷款
bullet loan

一次性采购
one-stop shopping

一次性付清债务
compounding a debt

一次性支出
lump sum cost

一定的
definite

一贯方针
consistent policy

一惯性
consistency

一级风险
primary risk

一览表
schedule, list

一揽子
package

一揽子采购
procurement packages

一揽子采购合同
blanket purchase contract

一揽子抵押
package mortgage

一揽子合同
blanket contract, package contract

一揽子交易
package deal

一揽子索赔
compound claim

一揽子投标
package bid

一揽子项目
all-in-one program

一批
batch

一切险
all risks (a/r, A.R.)

一切险保险
all risks insurance

一切险保险单
all-risk policy

一时疏忽
lapse of attention

一式三份的

triplicate
一事一索赔
single case claim
一致
conformity
一致的
consistent, uniform, unanimous
一致性
identity, consistency
医疗
medical treatment
医疗保险
health insurance
医疗费
medical fee
医疗费用保险
medical expense insurance
医疗证明
medical certificate
依从
compliance
依法的
lawful
依法定程序
in a manner prescribed by law
依法占有
seizure
依据
subject to
依据合同
under contract
依赖的
dependent
依照
in accordance with
依照法律
subject to the law
仪器
apparatus, instrument
移动式搅拌机
portable agitator
移交的
hand-over

移交前的使用
use before taking over
移交证书
taking-over certificate, handing-over certificate
移居国外者
expatriate
移走
removal
移走有缺陷的工程
removal of defective work
遗产管理人
administrator
遗产管理诉讼
administration suit
遗产管理委任书
letter of administration
遗漏
omit, omission
遗漏错误
error of omission
遗失的
missing
遗赠
demise
遗嘱执行人
executor
疑难的
problematical
乙醇
alcohol
乙炔焊接
acetylene welding
已背书债券
backed bond
已变更的条件
changed conditions
已拆除的分项工程
items dismantled
已承兑汇票
accepted bill
已承兑信用证
accepted letter of credit

已承诺数量
committed amount
已兑现支票
cashed check
已分摊成本
allocated cost
已付的
paid
已付合同保证金
contract deposit paid
已付金额
disbursements to date (DTD)
已付款的
paid, honored
已耗成本
expired cost
已获收益
earned income
已获营业收入
earned revenue
已缴许可证费
paid-up licence fee
已缴资本
paid-up capital, paid-in capital
已结清账户
closed account
已签证的护照
visaed passport
已上涨的价格
advanced price
已收合同保证金
contract deposit received
已提货提单
accomplished bill of lading
已贴现票据
bill discounted, discounted notes
已完成的工时
earned man-hours
已有初步证据的案件
prima facie case
已知损失
known loss
已知危险
known danger
已赚保险费
earned premium
已装船
on board
已装船货物
afloat cargo, afloat goods
已装船清洁提单
clean-on-board bill of lading
已装船提单
shipped B/L
以复利计算
compound
以合同为准
subject to contract
以货代款
in-kind
以毛重作净重
gross for net
以未售出为准
subject to prior sale
以月复利计算的
compounded monthly
以最后确认为准
subject to final confirmation
义不容辞的
incumbent
义务
duty, obligation, liability
义务人
obligor
议标
negotiated bidding
议标合同
negotiation contract
议定
negotiate
议定书
protocol
议付
negotiation
议付结算
settlement by negotiation

议付手续费
negotiation commission
议付银行
negotiating bank
议价
bargain, negotiated price
议价能力
bargaining position
议价条件
negotiating condition
议事记录
minutes of proceedings
议院
chamber
异常的
abnormal, exceptional
异常恶劣的气候条件
exceptionally adverse climatic conditions
异议
disagreement
抑制性关税
prohibitive duty
译员
interpreter
易变为现金的
liquid
易货
barter, swap
易货贸易
barter trade
易燃材料
inflammable material
易燃的
inflammable
易燃品
inflammable
易受损
subject to damage
易损坏的
fragile
意见
opinion, suggestion

意见一致
meeting of minds
意外
chance
意外的
contingent, unexpected
意外开支
contingent expenses, contingency, unforeseen expenses, unexpected expenses
意外利益
windfall profit
意外事故
unexpected accident, accident, contingency, casualty
意外事故保险
contingency insurance
意外事故赔偿
accident compensation
意外事故险
casualty insurance
意外事件
fortuitous event
意外收获
windfall
意外损害
accident damage
意外损失
casualty loss, windfall loss
意外损失基金
contingency fund
意向
intent, intention
意向书
letter of intent
意向协定
intention agreement
意愿租赁
tenancy at will
意旨
intendment
溢短装限度
tolerance

溢洪道
spillway, overflow
溢价
at a premium, above par, premium
溢流
overflow
翼墙
wing wall
因合同落空而终止
termination by frustration
因素
element, factor
银行
bank
银行保函
bank guarantee
银行保证书
bank guarantee
银行本票
cashier's check (cheque), bank's order, cashier's order
银行承兑票据
banker's acceptance, bank acceptance
银行承兑信用证
banker's acceptance credit
银行存款
bank deposit
银行存款余额
bank balance
银行存折
bank book, pass book
银行贷款
bank financing, bank loan
银行贷款项目
bank-financed project
银行电汇
bank cable transfer
银行发票
banker's invoice
银行汇款
bank transfer
银行汇款手续费
bank remittance fee
银行汇票
bank's draft
银行活期存款
cash at bank
银行间贷款
inter-bank loan
银行间的转账
bank transfer
银行控股公司
bank holding company
银行利率
bank rate
银行留置权
banker's lien
银行票据
bank bill
银行手续费
bank charge, agio
银行贴现
bank discount
银行贴现率
bank rate
银行透支
bank overdraft
银行信贷
bank credit
银行优惠利率
bank prime rate
银行愿担保的项目
bankable project
银行账户
bank account
银行支票
bank check
银行资金融通
bank accommodation
银行资助
bank financing
银行资助的咨询服务
bank financed consulting services
银货两讫
both sides clear

银团贷款
syndicated loan
引进方
acquiring party
引进方企业
acquiring enterprise
引起
cause, give rise to, occasion
引水
diversion
隐蔽损失
hidden loss
隐含
imply, implication
隐含的
implied
隐含的工作
implied work
隐含的意思
implied meaning
隐患
pitfall
隐瞒
conceal
隐瞒情况不报
non-disclosure
印花
stamp
印花税
stamp duty, stamp tax
印花税票
revenue stamp
印记
imprint, seal
印章
stamp, seal
应得的权利
entitlement
应得权益
due
应付承兑票据
acceptance payable
应付的
become due, fall due, due, owing
应付工资
accrued payroll, wages payable
应付股利
dividend payable
应付款
payment due, dues
应付款凭单
warrant payable
应付利息
accrual of interest, interest payable
应付票据
bill payable, note payable
应付期
payable period
应付所得税
income tax payable
应付债券
bond payable
应付账款
account payable
应付账款登记簿
account payable register
应付账款分类账
accounts payable ledger
应付账款明细账
account payable ledger
应急储备金
contingency reserve
应急费
contingency cost
应急基金
contingency fund
应急计划
contingency plan
应急用款
contingency allowance
应计的
accrual
应计和递延账户
accrued and deferred accounts
应计税金
tax accrued

应计账户
accrued account
应计折旧资产
depreciable assets
应加说明的文件
accountable document
应纳税的
taxable
应纳税工资
taxable salary
应纳税货物
taxable goods
应纳税利润
taxable profit
应纳税人
taxable person
应纳税收入
taxable income
应收
due from, accrue
应收承兑汇票
acceptance receivable
应收分期账款
installment accounts receivable
应收合同款
contract price receivable
应收票据
bill receivable, note receivable
应收账款
account receivable, collections
应收账款回收期
accounts receivable collection period
应收账款明细账
account receivable ledger
应收账款融资
account receivable financing
应收账款账户
customer's account
应收账款周转率
accounts receivable turnover
应收账款周转天数
accounts receivable collection period
应要求即付的
callable
应用
application
应有的小心和注意
due care and attention
应予赔偿的损失
compensatory damages
应征税款
tax accrued
英寸
inch
英美法系
common law system, Anglo-American Law System
英制
The British System
盈亏
gain and loss
盈亏平衡点
break-even point
盈亏平衡分析
break-even analysis
盈利
earnings
盈利能力
earnings power
盈利能力分析
profitability analysis
盈余
gain, margin, surplus
营地
camp
营房设备
camp equipment
营救
salvage
营销
marketing
营业报表
business report, statement of operation
营业地点
business place

营业额 turnover, volume of business
营业负债 working liabilities
营业利润 operating profit, operation profit
营业利润分摊 allocation of business profits
营业毛利 gross operating spread
营业申请 application for business
营业时间 office hours
营业收入 operation revenue, operating revenue
营业收入总额 total revenue
营业税 tax on business, sales tax
营业损失 operating loss
营业循环 operating cycle
营业盈余 earned surplus, earning surplus
营业账户 operating account
营业支出 revenue expenditure
营业执照 business license
营业主任 sales manager
营业资本 operating capital
营业租赁 operating lease
营造师 builder
赢得合同 win a contract
影响 affect, impact, force, effect
影响力 impact
影响评价报告 impact evaluation report
影子价格 shadow price
硬币 hard currency
硬副本 hard-copy
硬件 hardware
硬通货 hard currency, strong currency
硬通货贷款 hard loan
佣金 commission, commission charges
佣金经纪人 commission broker
拥护 advocate
拥有过半数股权的附属公司 majority-owned subsidiary
永久的 permanent
永久工程 permanent works
永久性投资 permanent investment
永久债券 perpetual bond
永久资产 permanent assets
用本国货币支付的费用 expenses in local currency
用词错误 verbal error
用公式表示 formulate
用户 user

用具
implement, appliance, tool
用料清单
bill of materials
用数量表示
quantify
用图表说明
illustration
用途
function, use, usage, purpose
优点
merit, advantage
优惠
concession, favour, privilege
优惠差额
margin of preference
优惠待遇
favourable treatment
优惠贷款
concessional loan, soft loan
优惠贷款利率
prime interest rate
优惠贷款限额
concessional line of credit
优惠的
concessionary, favourable, concessional
优惠关税
concessional tariff
优惠价
favourable price
优惠利率
favourable interest rate, concessional rate, preferential rate of interest
优惠贸易协定
preferential trade agreement
优惠期
days of grace
优惠税则
preferential tariff
优惠条件
easy terms, favourable condition, favourable terms
优惠支付
exgratia payment
优良的
fine
优势
advantage
优先
supersede, precede, preference
优先次序
order of precedence
优先的
precedent, prior
优先抵押权
underlying mortgage
优先购买权
refusal
优先购置权
preemptive right
优先股
preferred stock
优先权
preference, priority, option, right of priority, precedence
优先权利要求
prior claims
优先顺序
priority
优先索赔
prior claims
优先于
prevail, override, precede
优先债权人
senior creditor
优秀的
outstanding
优于
superior to
优质
quality
优质标记
hallmark
由买方选择

at buyer's option
由卖方选择
at seller's option
由于
due to, as a result of, because of
由于违约而终止
termination for default
邮戳日期
date of postmark
邮寄
post, mail
邮件
post, mail
邮票
stamp
邮政编码
post code, zip code
邮政信箱
post office box
油毛毡
asphalt felt
油漆
paint
油压千斤顶
oil jack
游资
hot money
友好
goodwill
友好的
amicable, friendly
友好合作
friendly cooperation
友好解决
amicable settlement
有保留接受
acceptance with reservation
有待完成契据
escrow
有担保的贷款
secured loan
有担保债券
backed bond

有抵押品的贷款
collateralized loan
有毒的
toxic
有法定资格的
competent
有法律效力的协议
legally-binding agreement
有分歧
at odds
有风险
at risk
有根据
substantiate
有根据的
valid
有关当局
authorities concerned
有关的
concerned
有关费用
relevant cost
有关机构
related agencies
有过错
in fault
有害的
adverse, toxic
有活力的
viable
有价值的
valuable
有经营权的信托
active trust
有竞争力的
keen, competitive
有竞争力的价格
keen price
有竞争性的计日工
competitive daywork
有理由的
justifiable, reasonable
有利的

有利于
in the interests of, favourable
有利于
in favour of, favour
有矛盾
at odds
有面值股票
par value stock
有名无实的条款
nominal terms
有能力的
competent
有全权的
plenipotentiary
有权
at liberty
有权先售
subject to prior sale
有权益的
beneficial
有缺陷的材料
defective material
有缺陷的工作
defective work
有条件的贷款
conditional loan
有无对比法
with-and-without
有息债务
active debt
有限的
limited, narrow
有限的追索
limited recourse
有限公司
limited company
有限合伙公司
limited partnership
有限竞争性选择招标
limited competitive selected bidding
有限责任的
limited
有限责任公司
limited liability company

有效
in force, validity
有效保证
effective guarantee
有效程度
effectiveness
有效的
effective, efficient, valid
有效合同
valid contract
有效合同价
effective contract price
有效期
valid period, period of validity, term of validity
有效日期
date of validity
有效条款
effective terms
有效性
effectiveness, availability, validity
有形财产
visible means
有形固定资产
fixed tangible assets
有形贸易
visible trade
有形资产
material assets, tangible assets
有义务
accountability
有义务的
bound, liable
有意投标者
prospective bidder(tenderer)
有约束力的
binding
有约束力的合同
binding contract
有约束力的签字
binding signature
有责任
be liable

有责任的
liable
有争议的事项
controversial issue
有追溯效力的
retroactive
淤泥
silt
余地
leeway
余额
balance
余额递减折旧法
declining balance method of depreciation, reducing balance depreciation method
余额为零
zero balance
余值
remaining value
娱乐
amusement
逾期未交货物
overdue delivery
逾越
overstep
与原本一致的文本
conformed copies
预报
forecast
预备
prepare, get ready for
预备的
standby, preliminary
预备工程
preliminary works
预备进口报关单
preliminary entry
预备诉讼行为
preliminary act
预测
forecast, projection, prediction
预垫款

advance call
预调试
precommissioning
预订
book, reserve
预定日期
target date
预定损失率
assumed loss ratio
预定违约金
liquidated damages
预防
prevent, prevention
预防性索赔管理
preventive claims management
预付
pay in advance, advancement
预付保险费
deposit premium
预付费用
prepaid expenses
预付分包商款
advances to subcontractor
预付汇款
advance remittance
预付款
advance payment, advance, payment in advance, prepayment
预付款保函
advance payment guarantee, prepayment guarantee
预付款的偿还
repayment of advance
预付款的支付
payment of advance
预付款条款
prepayment clause
预付运费
advance freight, prepaid freight
预计财务报表
projected financial statement
预计成本
predicated cost, projected cost

预计到达时间
estimated time of arrival (ETA)
预计的合同支付
estimated contract payment
预计费用
estimated cost
预计风险
calculated risk
预计离港时间
estimated time of departure (ETD)
预计使用年限
expected life, estimated physical life
预计卸货完成时间
estimated time of finishing discharging (ETFD)
预见
foresee
预见到的损害赔偿费
foreseen damages
预见性
foreseeability
预开发票
proforma invoice
预可行性研究
pre-feasibility study, preliminary feasibility study
预扣税款
withholding tax
预扣税款凭证
tax withholding certificate
预料
anticipate, predict
预评估
preappraisal
预期
anticipate, anticipation, prospect
预期成本
anticipated cost
预期的市场
prospective market
预期价格
anticipated price
预期利润
anticipated profit
预期利润损失保险
loss of advanced profits insurance
预期利息
anticipated interest
预期收益
anticipated gain, prospective yield
预期收益率
required rate of return
预期投标者
prospective bidder (tenderer)
预收合同款
contract price received in advance
预收款项
advance collections
预算
budget, estimate
预算拨款
budget allocation
预算成本
estimated cost, budgeted cost
预算导则
estimate guideline
预算费
budget
预算工时
budgeted man-hour
预算和成本核算
estimating and costing
预算汇总
budget summary
预算控制
budget control
预算书
budget document
预算与成本控制
budget and cost control
预算与进度的依据
basis for budget and schedule
预提税
withholding tax
预投资研究
preinvestment studies

预先报关单
preentry
预先承兑
anticipated acceptance
预先的
advance, prior
预先规定的
pre-defined
预先计划
advanced planning
预先申报
preentry
预应力混凝土
prestressed concrete
预约保单
open policy
预约保险
open cover
预约的
forward
预约金
subscription
预支
make advance
预支付
pay in advance
预制
prefabricate
预制构件
prefabricated unit
预制混凝土
precast concrete
预制混凝土空心块
precast hollow concrete block
预制混凝土楼板
precast concrete floor
预制水泥块
cement block
预制桩
premoulded pile
遇险
emergency
原案

original bill
原保险
original insurance
原本的
naked
原材料
raw material
原产地
origin, country of origin
原产地标志
origin marking
原产地证明书
certificate of origin (C/O)
原稿
manuscript
原告
claimant (claimer), complainant, plaintiff
原合同
original contract
原件
original
原理
principle
原料
feedstock
原始成本
original cost
原始成本加成
original mark-up
原始单据
original document
原始的
original, prime
原始发票
original invoice
原始费用
base line cost
原始记录
primary record
原始价值
original value
原始凭单

原始凭证
source document, underlying document
原始数据
first-hand data, initial data, raw data, primary data
原始文件
original document
原始账
blotter
原始证据
primary evidence
原始资本
original capital
原始资料
primary data, original data
原型
original, prototype
原型试验
prototype testing
原样品
original sample
原因
cause
原则
principle
援助
assistance
远期差价
forward margin
远期的
forward
远期付款交单
documents against payment after sight
远期合同
forward contract
远期汇率
forward rate, forward exchange rate
远期交货
forward delivery
远期外汇
forward exchange
远期信用证
usance L/C
远洋班轮
ocean liner
远洋船舶
ocean vessel
远洋运输
ocean carriage
约定
appoint, engage, commitment
约定价格合同
stipulated price contract
约定金额
stipulated sum
约定金额合同
stipulated sum contract
约定目的港
agreed port of destination
约定皮重
computed tare
约定时间
commitment time
约束
bind, hold, restrict
约束力
force of bind, binding power
约束条件
constraint
约束条款
tie-in clause
月报表
monthly statement, monthly returns
月报告
monthly report
月工资
monthly wages
月汇总表
monthly summary
月结算报告
monthly settlement report
月结算单
monthly statement

月津贴
monthly allowance
月历
calendar
月息
interest per mensem
月薪
monthly wages, monthly pay
越权行为
act in excess of authority
越野车
off-highway vehicle
允许
allow, allowance, permit, permission
允许成本
allowable cost
允许利润
allowance for profit
运费
freight cost, freight, transportation charges
运费、保险费付至
carriage and insurance paid to (CIP)
运费保险
freight insurance
运费保险单
freight policy
运费待付
carriage forward
运费单
freight note, freight bill
运费到付
freight to collect, freight to be paid, express collect
运费付至
carriage paid to (CPT)
运费率
freight rate
运费审查
freight audit
运费条款
freight clause

运费一览表
schedule of freight rates
运费已付
freight paid, carriage paid
运费已预付
freight prepaid
运费由收货人付
carriage forward, freight collect, freight forward
运货费
cartage
运价表
freight list (F/L)
运距
haul distance
运输
carriage, transport, traffic
运输保险
insurance in transit, transportation insurance
运输车辆保险
vehicle insurance
运输成本
transportation cost
运输承运人的索赔
transportation carrier's claim
运输代理行
freight forwarder
运输单据
documentary of carriage
运输吨数
tonnage
运输方式
transportation modes
运输费
transportation cost, forwarding charges, shipping expenses
运输服务
traffic services
运输工
haulier
运输工具
carrier, conveyance, transportation

carrier
运输工具保险
conveyance insurance
运输公司
carrier, transportation firm
运输管理
traffic management
运输合同
contract of carriage
运输计划
transportation planning, traffic plan
运输距离
haul distance
运输量
traffic volume
运输能力
transportation capacity
运输设备
hauling equipment, transportation equipment
运送
deliver, transport
运送材料
delivery of materials
运送的货物
delivered goods, freight
运行检验
performance test
运营
operation
运营成本
operation cost, operating cost
运营条件
operating condition
运营维修合同
operation and maintenance contract
运用
apply, use, utilize, exercise, operate
运载
carry
运载工具
vehicle
运转
operation

Z

杂的
sundry
杂费
incidental, sundry
杂税
irregular tax
杂物
sundry
杂项
incidental, sundry
杂项的
miscellaneous
杂项开支
miscellaneous expenses, sundry expenses
杂项收入
sundry revenue
灾害
calamity
灾荒
calamity
灾难
casualty
载荷
load
载重
burden
载重量
loading capacity
再保险

reassure, reinsurance
再保险分出公司
ceding company
再保险公司
ceded company
再保险合同
reinsurance contract
再保险经纪人
reinsurance broker
再出口
re-export
再出口证书
certificate of re-export
再次保证
reassure
再次分包
sub-subcontracting
再抵押
submortgage
再归属
revest
再进口
re-import
再开始
resumption
再生产成本
reproduction cost
再招标
retender (rebid)
在场的
present
在船上
on board
在国外居住的
expatriate
在建工程
construction in progress, work in progress
在票据上背书
back a bill
在前的
precedent
在途货物
goods in transit
在途账
account in transit
在下游
downstream
在协议上签署作证
witness an agreement
在有效期中
in force
暂保单
binder, cover note (C/N), risk note
暂保收据
binding receipt
暂定计划
tentative plan
暂定价格指数
provisional index
暂定金额
provisional sums
暂定金额的支付
payment against provisional sums
暂定项目
optional items
暂付
payment on account
暂付款项
temporary payment
暂缓
abeyance
暂记账户
clearing account, suspense account
暂时的
provisional, temporary, interim
暂时停工
suspension of work
暂时停工费用
cost of suspension
暂时停工命令
order to suspend
暂时停工情况下的支付
payment in event of suspension
暂停
suspend, suspension

暂停拨款
suspension of disbursements
暂停付款
suspension of payment
暂行办法
interim procedures
暂行标准
tentative standard
暂行规定
interim provisions
暂行条例
interim regulations
赞成
approve, agree, consent
赞同
approve, approval, in favour of, favour
赞助
sponsor, support
遭受
sustain, suffer
凿岩机
drifter
责任
liability, responsibility
责任保险
insurance for liability, liability insurance
责任范围
extent of liability, scope of cover, scope of liability, limitation of liability
责任分担
apportionment of liability, allocation of responsibility
责任分担条款
contribution clause
责任分界线
interface of responsibilities
责任风险
liability risk
责任期限
duration of liability

责任条款
liability clause
责任限度
limitation of liability
责任证明
accountability verification
增补
supplement, augment
增长
increase, grow, growth, accrue, accrual
增长率
growth rate
增额
increment, addition
增股筹资
equity financing
增加
increase, add, addition
增加的费用
increased cost
增加人工投入
additional input of labour
增添
addition
增值
added value, increment, appreciation, value added
增值保险
increased value insurance
增值税
value-added tax (VAT), added-value tax
增值条款
increased value clause
赠款
endowment, grant
赠品
gift, present
赠券
coupon
赠送人
presenter

赠与
present, gift
诈骗
deceit
炸药
explosive, dynamite
摘要
brief, abstract
债款
debt, liability
债权
financial claim
债权人
creditor, claimant (claimer), obligee
债权人从破产人处得到的赔偿金
dividend
债权受益人
creditor beneficiary
债券
bond, security
债券利率
bonding rate
债券市场
bond market
债务
liability, debt
债务-产权比率
debt-equity ratio
债务偿还的优先次序
priority of debts
债务偿还期的延展
forbearance
债务和解
composition
债务解除证书
certificate of release
债务清偿收据
acquittance
债务确认书
cognovit
债务人
debtor, obligor
债务危机
debt crisis
债务与股本比率
debt to equity ratio
债务证明书
debt certificate
债务转让
assignment of debt
债息
debt service
债主
obligee
粘结
adhesion
粘土
clay
展期
continuation, renewal
展期条款
continuation clause
展示件
exhibit
展望
prospect
占用费
occupancy expenses
占用率
occupancy rate
占用权
occupancy right
占用许可证
occupancy permit
占优势的意见
prevailing opinion
占有
occupation, possession
占有留置权
possessory lien
占有权
right of possession
占有人
occupant, occupier
占有诉讼
action for possession

占有证明书
certificate of occupancy
战略
strategy
战胜
defeat
战争保险
war risk insurance
战争险
war risk
栈单
warehouse certificate, landing account
章程
charter, constitution, articles, statute
涨价
escalation, appreciation
涨价公式
escalation formula
涨价后的费用
escalation cost
涨落
fluctuation
账
account
账簿
account book
账单
bill, check
账号
account number
账户
account
账户分类
account classification
账户结平
account balanced
账户名称
account title, title of account
账户式资产负债表
account form of balance sheet
账户一览表
chart of accounts
账户余额
account balance
账户转换
account conversion, account transfer
账款回收期
collection period
账面
book
账面成本
book cost
账面价值
carrying value, book value
账面利润
book profit, paper profit
账面盘存
book inventory
账面收益
accounting income
账面损失
book loss, paper loss
账面盈余
book surplus, paper profit
账面余额
balance of account, book balance
账目
account
账目编号
code of accounts
账目摘要
abstract of account
障碍
bar, obstacle
障碍物
obstruction
招标
bid invitation, call for bids (tenders), invitation to bid (tender)
招标内容
bid invitation contents
招标设计范围
scope of tender designs

招标通知
bid invitation, request for proposal
招标文件
bidding documents, tender documents
招标文件的澄清
clarification of bidding (tender) documents
招标文件的修改
amendment of bidding (tender) documents
招标文件范本
sample bidding documents
招工
job opening
招聘
recruit, recruitment
招致重大损失
incur a heavy loss
找出
find out, locate
沼泽
swamp
沼泽地区
marshy area
召集会议
convene
照做
comply with
折耗备抵
depletion allowance
折换
translate, convert
折旧
depreciate, depreciation
折旧不足
underdepreciation
折旧成本
depreciation cost
折旧方法
depreciation method
折旧费
amortization cost, depreciation charge
折旧费率
rate of depreciation charges
折旧过低
underdepreciation
折旧后净收益
net income after depreciation
折旧基金
depreciation fund
折旧基数
depreciation base
折旧率
depreciation rate
折旧年限
period of depreciation
折旧期
period of depreciation
折旧准备
depreciation reserve, reserve for depreciation
折扣
discount, rebate
折扣率
discount rate
折扣期限
discount period
折扣系数
discount factor
折损
depletion
折余成本
depreciated cost
折余价值
depreciated value
真诚的
sincere, bona fide
真实的
true, authentic, objective
真实记录
factual record
真实性
authenticity
真相

naked truth
振捣器
vibrator
振动筛
vibrating sieve
震动打桩机
vibrating-pile driver
震动辗压机
vibrating roller
争辩者
contestant
争端
dispute
争端裁决委员会
dispute adjudication board (DAB)
争端的友好解决
amicable settlement of dispute
争端解决
dispute settlement
争端审议委员会
disputes review board (DRB)
争端审议专家
disputes review expert
争端事宜
matters in dispute
争端仲裁
arbitration of disputes
争论
contention, controversy, dispute, argument
争议
dispute
争议的解决
settlement of disputes
争执
dispute
争执点
point in dispute
争执方
contestant
征收
impose, demand
征收税款

levy
征税
collect duties, levy duties on, taxation, tax, levy
征税依据
tax base
征用
requisition, expropriation, take over for use
征用土地
requisitioning of land
蒸汽养护
steam curing
整笔支付
single payment
整理资料
process data
整套承包制合同
all-in contract
整套服务
integrated service
整套购买
basket purchase
整体的
integrated
整体浇灌混凝土
monolithic concrete
整直机
straightening machine
正本
original, text
正常报价
arm's length quotation
正常的
natural, normal
正常的服务
normal services
正常的收缩
normal shrinkage
正常费用
normal cost
正常工作时间
straight time

正常情况
normal condition
正常使用条件
average service conditions
正常税
regular tax
正常损耗
normal loss
正常条件
normal condition
正当持票人
holder in due course
正当的
justifiable
正当解雇
fair dismissal
正断面图
normal section
正面条款
face clause
正式承兑
formal acceptance
正式代表
official representative
正式的
formal, official
正式发票
formal invoice, official invoice
正式合同
contract under seal, formal contract, sealed contract, official contract
正式价格
official price
正式确认
formal confirmation
正式条款
formal clause
正式通知
formal notice
正式协定
formal agreement
正式验收
formal acceptance

正式要求
formal request, demand
正式语言
official language
正态的
normal
正现金流量
positive cash flow
正在进行的工作
work in progress
正在施工
under construction
正在实施的项目
on-going project
正直
integrity
证词
attestation, evidence, proof
证件
evidence, instrument, voucher
证据
evidence, attestation, proof
证明
certify, certificate, attestation, support, witness, substantiate, proof
证明拒付
protest
证明书
testimonial
证明文件
supporting document
证明有罪
convict
证券
security, stock, paper
证券持有人
security holder
证券交易所指数
stock exchange index
证券市场
security market
证人
witness, evidence, substantiator

证实
verify, verification, substantiate, justification
证书
certificate, letters
证言
witness
政策
policy
政府
government, state
政府部门
government department
政府采购政策
government procurement policy
政府的承诺
government commitment
政府干预
government intervention
政府税收
government revenue
政府特派员
commissioner
政府投资
government investment, state investment
政府信贷
government credit
政府业主
government owner
政府预算
government budget
政府债券
government bond
政令
government decree, decree
政治风险
political risk
支撑
support
支承桩
bearing pile
支持
favour, support
支出
expenditure, outgo
支出费用
disbursement
支出预算
budget of expenditure
支出证明书
certificate of expenditure
支付
pay, payment, disburse, defray
支付百分比
disbursement percentage
支付保险费
premium payment
支付担保
payment bond
支付的款项
payment
支付方式
method of payment, mode of payment, way of payment
支付货币
currency of payment
支付计划
payment schedule
支付进度表
payment schedule
支付宽限
grace of payment
支付里程碑
payment milestone
支付能力
ability to pay, solvency
支付凭单
disbursement voucher, warrant
支付期票
honour a bill
支付日期
due date
支付申请
application for payment
支付时间

time for payment
支付手段
means of payment
支付条件
payment terms, terms of payment
支付条款
settlement terms, payment provisions
支付协议
payment agreement
支管
branch pipe
支架
fixture
支票
check, cheque
支票簿
check book
支票簿存根
check book stubs
支票登记簿
check register
支票兑现
cash a cheque
支票账户
checking account
支柱
pier
支座
abutment
知识
knowledge
知识产权
intellectual property right
执行
implement, carry out, execute, perform
执行的
executive
执行董事
executive director, managing director
执行董事会
board of executive directors
执行范围
scope of execution
执行合同
contract performance
执行机构
executing agency
执行进度
implementation schedule
执行人
executor
执行委员会
executive committee, executing agency
执行中的项目
operational project
执业会计师
public accountant
执照
licence, license, permit
执照费
fee for permit
执照税
excise, licence duty
执照有效期
duration of licence
直达港
direct port
直达货运
through freight
直达提单
direct B/L
直达运输
direct shipment
直方图
vertical bar chart
直接报价
direct quotation
直接比价
direct quotation
直接材料
direct material
直接裁决

direct verdict
直接采购
direct purchase
直接成本
direct cost, prime cost
直接成本计算法
direct costing
直接的
direct, immediate
直接费用
direct cost
直接付款
direct payment, direct debit
直接管理费
direct overhead
直接管理费账户
direct overhead account
直接借记
direct debit
直接贸易
direct trade
直接人工费
direct labour cost
直接融资
direct financing
直接受益人
immediate beneficiary
直接税
direct tax
直接损害
direct damage
直接损失
direct loss
直接提单
straight B/L
直接销售
direct sale
直接原因
immediate cause
直接支付
direct payment
直接装运
direct shipment

直流电
direct current
直线折旧法
average method of depreciation, straight line method of depreciation
直译
literal translation
值班
on duty
值班工程师
shift engineer
职称
job title
职工保险
worker's insurance
职工养老金
employee's pension fund
职工忠诚保险
fidelity bond (insurance)
职能
function
职能部门主管人员
staff executive
职权
authority
职权范围
reference
职位
position, capacity, post
职位空额
job vacancy
职业
occupation, profession, calling
职业保障保险
professional indemnity insurance
职业道德
professional ethics
职业的
professional
职业责任
professional responsibility
职业责任保险

professional liability insurance
职员
clerk, employee, staff, personnel
职员的
clerical
职员的变更
changes in personnel
职员的提供
supply of personnel
职责
duty, obligation, responsibility
职责范围
responsibility range
职责委托
delegation of duties
止付
withhold payment
止水
water stop, seal
止水片
water stop
纸币
paper
纸黄金
paper gold
指标
index, indicator, target
指导
guide, direct, direction, instruct, instruction
指定
designate, nominate, nomination
指定船名的保险单
named policy
指定的代表
designated representative
指定的银行
appointed bank
指定的暂定金额
specified provisional sums
指定分包商
nominated subcontractor
指定目的地

named place of destination
指定启运地
named departure point
指定人提单
order bill of lading
指定人支票
order check
指定日期
specified date
指定银行
authorized bank
指定装船港
named port of shipment
指挥
command, superintendence
指挥系统
chain of command
指挥者
superintendent
指控
charge, accuse
指控某人有罪
accuse sb. of a crime
指令
direction, mandate
指南
guideline, manual
指示
indicate, indication, instruct, instruction
指示提单
order bill of lading
指示物
indicator
指示性标志
indicative mark
指数
index
制裁
sanction
制单
vouching
制定

work out, formulate, institution
制定决策
decision-making
制度
system
制冷系统
refrigerating system
制约因素
restrictive element
制造
produce, manufacture
制造厂家的授权书
letter of authority from manufacturer
制造成本
factory cost, manufacturing cost
制造费用
overhead charges (cost), manufacturing expenses
制造间接费用
factory expenses
制造商
manufacturer
制造图
manufacturing drawing
制造证明书
certificate of manufacture
制止
check, correct
制作
produce, production, fabricate, fabrication
治安
security
质量
quality
质量保证
quality assurance
质量保证期
period of quality guarantee
质量保证书
quality guarantee
质量成本
quality cost

质量监察
quality audit
质量监督
quality surveillance
质量控制
quality control
质量审查
quality review
质量维修保函
letter of guarantee for maintenance
质量以买方样品为准
quality as per buyer's sample
质量以卖方样品为准
quality as per seller's sample
质量证明
quality certificate
质量追踪系统
quality tracking system
质疑
query
质疑与解答
queries and replies
智力
intelligence
滞付金
retention money
滞后
lag
滞留
demurrage
滞纳税款
delinquent tax
滞期费
demurrage
滞销货
dead stock
置存成本
carrying cost
置存价值
carrying value
中班
swing shift
中标

award of contract, win a contract
中标函
letter of acceptance
中标合同
contract awarded
中标合同价
awarded contract price
中标通知书
letter of acceptance
中标者
successful bidder (tenderer)
中长期
medium long-term
中等的
medium
中等价格
moderate price
中等品质
fair average quality (FAQ)
中断
interruption, discontinue
中间的
medium, intermediate, intermediary
中间调解
mediation
中间人
intermediary, intermediate, middleman
中间商
middleman, broker
中介
intermediation
中介人
finder, broker, intermediate
中介人佣金
finder's fee
中介物
intermediary
中介业务
intermediary business
中立的
neutral
中立国

neutral state
中立国的
neutral
中立性
impartiality
中立者
neutral
中期
medium term, intermediate term
中期评估
mid-term evaluation
中途停运权
stoppage in transit
中心文件
keystone document
中央银行
central bank
中止
suspend, suspension, stoppage
中止合同
suspension of contract
中止谈判
suspend talks
中止条款
cesser clause
中转
transit
终结
terminate, termination, determinate, determination
终结账户
terminal accounts
终值
final value, maturity value, terminal value
终止
terminate, termination, cease, cessation, expire, expiration
终止合同
terminate a contract
终止合同的条款
stop clause
终止后的付款

payment after termination
终止日期
date of termination
终止时的付款
payment on termination
终止通知
termination notice
终止责任
cessation of liability
种类
category, kind, sort
仲裁
arbitrate, arbitration
仲裁裁决
arbitral decision, arbitration award
仲裁程序
arbitral procedure, arbitration procedure, procedure of arbitration
仲裁的
arbitral
仲裁地点
place of arbitration
仲裁法
arbitration law
仲裁法案
arbitration act
仲裁法庭
court of arbitration, arbitration tribunal
仲裁费
arbitration fee
仲裁规则
arbitration rules
仲裁解决
settlement by arbitration
仲裁人
referee
仲裁人员
arbitration panel
仲裁申请
application for arbitration
仲裁使用的程序法
procedural law for arbitration

仲裁条款
arbitration clause, reference clause
仲裁庭
arbitral tribunal, arbitration tribunal
仲裁委员会
arbitration board
仲裁小组
arbitration panel
仲裁协议
arbitration agreement
仲裁语言
language of arbitration
仲裁员
arbitrator, arbiter
仲裁争端
arbitrate a dispute
重大的
material
重大偏离
material deviation
重大事件
milestone, major event
重大修改
material alteration
重点
key
重合同、守信誉
honouring contract and acting in good faith
重力坝
gravity dam
重量
weight
重量检验证书
inspection certificate of weight
重视
value
重型卡车
heavy-duty truck
重型起重机
heavy lift
重要部分
chief

重要的
important, earnest, leading
重要性
importance, materiality
重粘土
heavy clay
周报表
weekly returns
周工资
weekly wages
周计划
weekly scheduling
周期
period, cycle
周围
surroundings
周围情况
environmental conditions
周转额
turnover
周转金
working fund
周转账户
account turnover
周转资产
working assets
周转资金
working capital
轴
axis
轴线
axis
昼夜施工
round-the-clock job
逐条记载
itemize
逐字译出
construe, literal translation
主办人
sponsor
主包工程
main works
主厂房
power house (plant)
主承包商
principal contractor
主持会议
officiate, chair the meeting
主持人
host
主导的
ruling
主导语言
ruling language
主干线路
main circuit
主管
superintendence
主管当局
competent authorities
主管的
competent
主管法庭
competent court
主管工程师
engineer in charge
主管人
controller, person in charge, superintendent
主合同
main contract, prime contract
主合同条款
main contract clauses
主梁
girder
主人
host
主任
director
主题
subject
主体
entity
主席
chairman
主信用证

overriding credit
主要备选方案
major alternative
主要成本
prime cost, first cost
主要成本加定比酬金
prime cost plus percentage fee
主要成本加固定酬金
prime cost plus fixed fee
主要的
chief, main, prime, principal
主要公司
leading company
主要合伙人
senior partner
主要人员
key personnel
主要施工设备
major items of construction plant
主要市场
primary market
主要事实
primary fact
主要营业地
principal place of business
主要预算
main budget
主要债务人
principal debtor
主要证据
evidence in chief
主张
claim, assertion
主租约
master lease
住房
housing, lodging quarters
住宅
house
住宅建设
housing development
住宅建设基金
housing fund

住宅区
residential quarters
助理
assistant
助理工程师
assistant engineer
助理监理员
assistant superintendent
助手
assistant
注册
register, registration
注册产权
registered title
注册成本工程师
certified cost engineer
注册承包商
licensed contractor
注册工程师
chartered engineer
注册工料测量师
chartered quantity surveyor
注册公司
registered company
注册会计师
chartered accountant (CA), certified accountant
注册建筑师
licensed architect
注册商标
registered trade mark
注册设计
registered design
注册证书
certificate of registry
注册资本
registered capital
注释
comment
注销
cancel, cancellation, write off
注销的支票
canceled check

注意
attention, notice
贮存备用
backup
驻地工程师
resident engineer
驻地首席工程师
chief resident engineer
驻国外代表
representative abroad
筑堤
dyke
筑路
road building, pave
抓斗式起重机
clamshell crane
专家
expert, specialist
专家评价
expertise
专家委员会
expert committee (council)
专家意见
expert opinion
专利
patent
专利保护
patent protection
专利产品
proprietary product
专利持有人
patent holder
专利代理人
patent agent
专利的
patent
专利法
patent law
专利费
patent fee
专利局
patent office
专利品
proprietary articles
专利权
patent, patent right
专利权使用费
patent royalty
专利许可证
patent license
专利证书
letter of patent
专卖
monopoly
专卖价格
monopoly, price
专卖品
proprietary articles
专卖权
monopoly right
专门的
technical, expert
专门技术
know-how
专门律师
barrister
专门名词
technical terms
专门人员
specialist
专业
profession
专业承包商
special contractor, specialist contractor
专业的
professional
专业服务
specialist services, professional service
专业服务费
professional fee
专业工种承包商
trade contractor
专业技能
expertise

专业人员
professional
专业设计师
design professional
专业证人
professional witness
专一的
exclusive
专营合同
exclusive contract
专营权
franchise
专用
earmark
专用合同条件
special conditions of contract
专用税
objective tax
专用条件
conditions of particular application
专有的
proprietary
专有技术许可证
know-how license
专员
commissioner
专制行为
autocratic acts
砖
brick
砖石结构
brick masonry structure
转包
sublet, subcontract
转船
tranship
转船附加费
transhipment surcharge
转船提单
transhipment bill of lading
转贷
on lending
转抵押
repledge
转换
conversion
转嫁风险
transfer risks
转交
forward, transfer
转借
underlease
转借人
sub-borrower
转开信用证
back-to-back (letter of) credit
转口贸易
transit trade
转口税
transit duty(dues)
转口信用证
transit letter of credit
转让
transfer, assign, assignment
转让财产
assign
转让契据
deed of transfer
转让人
assigner, assignor, indorser, endorser
转让手续费
negotiation commission
转让书
letter of assignment
转让证书
deed of conveyance, assignment
转手贸易
switch trade
转押
submortgage
转移
transfer, transmit, transmission
转移风险
transfer risks
转移价格

transfer price
转移责任
hold harmless
转运
tranship, transhipment
转运公司
forwarder
转运提单
transhipment bill of lading
转账凭证
transfer voucher, journal voucher
转租
assignment of lease, sublease
转租人
subtenant
赚得
earn, gain
赚钱
make money
赚取的保险费
earned premium
桩
pile
桩锤
rammer
桩基
pile foundation
桩距
spacing of pile
桩帽
pile cap, head of pile
桩身
pile shaft
桩头
head of pile
装备
equipment, furnishings
装船
loading on board
装船付现
cash on shipment (COS)
装船期
period for shipment

装船日期
date of shipment
装船通知
shipment advice, notice of shipment, shipping note
装船通知单
shipping advice
装船许可证
lading permit
装船指示
shipping instructions
装货
loading
装货单
shipping order
装货地
place of loading
装货港
loading port, lading port
装货国
country of embarkation
装货日期
date of loading
装货重量
shipping weight
装配
assemble, assembly, fabricate, fitting
装配场
fabricating yard
装配车间
fitting shop, assembly shop
装配件
fittings
装配图
erection diagram, assembly drawing, mounting drawing
装配线
assembly line
装填
load
装箱单
packing list, packing slip (sheet)

装卸费
handling charge, handling cost
装卸费用
discharge cost
装卸期限
lay days
装卸时间
lay time
装修
finishing
装修工程
finishing work
装运
shipment
装运单据
shipping documents
装运付款
cash on shipment (COS)
装运港
port of shipment
装运期
time of shipment
装运申请
application for shipment
装运时间
time of shipment
装运条件
terms of shipment
装运误期费
demurrage
装载
load, loading, lading
装载过多
overcharge
装置
device, apparatus, mounting, fitting, fixtures
状况
condition, standing
状态
state
追偿权
right of reimbursement

追加
supplement
追加保证金的通知
margin call (notice)
追加的
additional, cumulative
追加订货
additional order
追加定单
additional order
追加利息
add-on interest
追加预算
supplementary budget
追溯
backdate
追索
recovery
追索权
recourse
准备
prepare, reserve
准备费
mobilization fee
准备工作
preliminaries
准备就绪通知
notice of readiness
准会员
associate member
准据法
proper law
准确性
accuracy
准司法的
quasi-judicial
准线
alignment
准许
permit, permission, empower
准许进入
admission
准予

准
grand, permit, approve
准则
code, criteria, principle
准仲裁员
quasi-arbitrator
酌处权
discretion
着手
proceed, take up
仔细调查
explore
仔细审查
scrutiny
咨询
consult, consultation
咨询的
advisory
咨询范围
terms of reference (TOR)
咨询费
consultant's fee
咨询分包
sub-consultancy
咨询分包人
sub-consultant
咨询服务
consulting service, adviser service
咨询服务采购
procurement of consulting services
咨询服务合同
contract for consulting services
咨询服务用户手册
handbook of users of consulting services
咨询工程师
consulting engineer
咨询公司
consulting firm, consultant company (corporation)
咨询人员
consultant
咨询委员会
consultative committee, board of reference, advisory committee
咨询协议
consulting agreement
咨询专家
expert consultant, consultant
咨询专家的责任
liability of the consultant
姿态
stance
资本
capital, principal
资本成本
cost of capital
资本红利
capital bonus
资本基金
capital fund
资本结构
capital composition structure
资本净收益
net capital gains
资本市场
capital market
资本收益率
capital return
资本投资
capital investment
资本形成
capital formation
资本性账户
capital account
资本性资产
capital assets
资本盈利
capital surplus
资本盈余
capital surplus
资本预算
capital budget
资本折旧
depreciation of capital
资本支出
capital expenditure, capital charges,

capital outlay
资本周转率
capital turnover rate
资本转移税
capital transfer tax
资产
assets
资产担保
assets cover
资产抵偿
assets cover
资产负债表
balance sheet, statement of assets and liabilities
资产负债表日期
date of balance sheet
资产负债数据
balance sheet data
资产估价
assets valuation
资产计价
assets valuation
资产净额
net assets
资产留置权
encumbrance
资产评估
property valuation
资产清算人
liquidator
资产与负债
assets and liabilities
资产账户
assets account
资产折旧
assets depreciation
资产周转率
assets turnover
资产总额
total assets
资方
capital
资格
eligibility, capacity, qualification
资格后审
post qualification
资格预审
prequalification
资格预审申请
prequalification application
资格预审文件
prequalification documents
资格证书
qualification certificate
资金
finance, financial resources, capital, fund
资金充足
abundance of capital
资金分配
allocation of funds
资金来源
source of funds
资金流动
cash flow
资金流动折现评估法
discounted cash flow method
资金流分析
cash flow analysis
资金流转
fund flow, flow of funds
资金密集项目
capital intensive project
资金缺额担保
deficiency guarantee
资金外逃
capital flight
资金运用
use of funds
资金支出
expenditure of fund
资料
information, data
资料查阅
access to data
资深咨询专家

senior consultant
资信证明
certificate of credit standing
资信状况
credit standing (status)
资源
resources
资助
fund, subsidize
资助费用
back-stopping cost
资助计划
financing plan
子工程
sub-project
子公司
daughter company, subsidiary company, subsidiary
子条款
sub-clause
子项目
sub-project
姊妹公司
sister company
字面解释
literal interpretation
自筹资金
self-finance
自定成本
discretionary cost
自动放弃
waiver
自动分保
obligatory reinsurance
自动取款机
cash dispenser
自动申请破产
voluntary bankruptcy
自动转账服务
automatic transfer service
自负额
deductible
自负额条款
excess clause
自负风险
own risk
自负损害
own damage
自负责任
own risk
自负责任条款
deductible clause
自留部分
priority
自然保护区
natural reserve
自然的
natural
自然风险
natural risk, physical risk
自然风险因素
physical hazard
自然人
natural person
自然损耗
natural wastage, ordinary wear and tear
自然条件
natural conditions
自然灾害
natural disaster, natural calamity
自然增长
accrue
自然增值
accretion, unearned increment
自然障碍
physical obstruction
自然资源
natural resources
自始至终
throughout
自我保险
self-insurance
自卸车
dumper
自卸卡车

dump truck, tip lorry
自行决定权
discretionary power
自营工程
force account
自由
liberty
自由处置权
disposal
自由的
free
自由兑换货币
free convertible currency
自由港
free port
自由货币
free currency
自由竞争
free competition
自由贸易区
free trade area
自有资金
own fund
自愿保险
voluntary insurance
自愿的
unsolicited, voluntary
自愿免赔额
voluntary deductibles
自愿清偿
voluntary liquidation
自愿提出的技术备选方案
unsolicited technical alternative
自重
deadweight
自主税率
autonomous tariff
自主税则
autonomous tariff system
自尊
self-esteem
综合单价
all-in rate

综合的
comprehensive, composite, complex, integrated
综合分析
comprehensive analysis
综合价格
composite price
综合解决办法
compound settlement
综合企业
complex
综合收益表
consolidated income statement
综合税率
composite rate of tax
综合索赔
compound claim
综合物价指数
overall price index
综合险
all risks (A.R.)
综合招标文件
comprehensive tender documents
综合指数
composite index
综述
overview
总包合同
main contract
总包价格
lump sum price
总包商
general contractor
总布置图
general arrangements
总部
headquarters, head office, principal office
总部费用
head office cost
总部管理费
general overhead, head office overhead

总裁
president
总采购通告
general procurement notice
总成本
complete cost, total cost
总承包合同
general contract, main contract
总承包商
general contractor, prime contractor, main contractor
总代理
general agency
总代理人
general agent
总的
general, gross, total, main
总抵押
general mortgage
总额
total amount
总费用
total cost
总分类账
key ledger
总分类账户
general ledger account
总浮动时间
total float time
总工程师
chief engineer, engineer in chief
总公司
head office, parent company, main office
总顾问
principal consultant
总和
sum
总会计师
accountant general, controller
总计
aggregate, total
总计的
total
总价
gross price, total price, lump sum
总价付款
lump sum payment
总价格
all-in price
总价合同
lump sum contract
总监工
general foreman
总建筑面积
gross floor area, overall floorage
总建筑师
chief architect
总进度计划
master programme, master schedule
总经理
general manager, managing director, president
总经销
exclusive distribution
总控制账户
master control account
总括保证
blanket bond
总括条款
umbrella article
总括性利率
all-in rate
总贸易体系
general trade system
总平面布置图
general layout
总平面设计
site planning
总清单
master list
总设计师
chief designer
总时差
total float time
总收入

gross income, total income
总收益
gross earnings
总数
amount, sum
总体布置图
general plan, general arrangement drawings
总体规定
general specification
总体规划
general plan
总体要求
general requirements
总体预测
macro-forecast
总协议
umbrella agreement
总行
main office
总预算
main budget, overall budget, master budget
总账
general account, ledger
总值
gross value
总重
gross weight
总咨询师
principal consultant
纵断面
profile
纵梁
longitudinal beam
纵向钢筋
longitudinal reinforcement
纵向接缝
longitudinal joint
走私
smuggle
走私货
contraband

租船
charter
租船方
charter party
租船合同
charter contract, charter party
租船运费
chartered freight
租购
hire purchase, installment buying
租借
hire
租借期
leasehold
租借期限
lease
租借权
tenancy
租借人
leaseholder, lessee
租借物
leasehold
租借者
hirer
租金
rent, rental
租金收入
rental
租赁
lease, hire, rent
租赁保函
leasing guarantee
租赁公司
leasing company
租赁购买
lease purchase
租赁合同
contract of lease
租赁期限
term of lease
租赁权
leasehold
租赁人

租赁融资
lease financing
租期
chartered period
租让协议
concession agreement
租用
hire, rent
租用的设备
leased equipment
租用条件
conditions of hire
租约
lease, lease agreement
足够
adequacy
足量
sufficiency
阻碍
encumbrance, impediment, obstruction
阻止
bar, prohibit, prevent
组成
form, compound, consist of
组成部分
component
组成公司
incorporate
组成投标的文件
documents comprising the bid
组合
alignment
组合投标
combination of bids, package bid
组织的
institutional
组装
assembly, erection
钻机
drilling machine, boring rig
钻架
boring rig
钻井
drilled well, well drilling
钻孔
bore hole, drill-hole
钻孔桩
bored pile
钻探设备
boring rig
最初成本
first cost
最初的
prime, original
最大的
maximum
最大金额
maximum amount
最大可能损失
maximum possible loss
最大量
maximum amount
最大赔偿额
maximum liability, maximum compensation
最大限度的责任
maximum liability
最低保险费
minimum premium
最低报价
lowest offer
最低标
lowest bid (tender)
最低的
minimum
最低额
minimum amount
最低罚款
minimum fine
最低风险
prime risk
最低价格
floor price, bottom price, minimum price

最低价投标人
lowest bidder(tenderer)
最低评标价投标
lowest evaluated bid
最低限度
minimum
最低限价
price floor
最低支付限额
minimum amount of payment
最低值
threshold, minimum
最多
maximum, at most
最高保证价格
maximum guaranteed price
最高成本
cost ceiling
最高成本限价合同
guaranteed maximum cost contracts
最高的
maximum, highest, summit, supreme
最高法院
supreme court
最高管理部门
top management
最高级别会谈
summit talk
最高级主管人员
top executive
最高价格
price ceiling
最高限额
ceiling amount, maximum limit
最高限价
ceiling price
最后成本
final cost
最后承诺
ultimatum commitment
最后的
final, conclusive, last

最后的支付
final payment, complete payment
最后检查
final inspection
最后进价法
last invoice price method
最后决策人
final decision maker
最后通牒
ultimatum
最惠国待遇
most-favoured-nation treatment
最惠国关税率
most-favoured-nation tariff rates
最惠国条款
most-favoured-nation clause (MFN cl.)
最少的
minimum
最晚开工日期
late start date
最晚日期
latest date
最先的
leading
最小的
minimum
最小金额
minimum amount
最小量
minimum amount
最新出品的
brand-new
最新的
up to date
最优更新周期
optimal replacement cycle
最优化
optimization
最优批量
economic lot size, optimum lot size
最早开工日期
early start date

最终报表
final statement
最终报表草稿
draft final statement
最终裁决
final verdict
最终产品
end-product
最终的
final, last, ultimate
最终发票
final invoice
最终付款
final payment
最终进度
definitive schedule
最终设计
final design
最终审查与评定
final review and assessment
最终受益人
ultimate beneficiary
最终损失
ultimate loss
最终验收
final acceptance
最终验收证书
final acceptance certificate
最终用户
ultimate customer
最终账目
final account
最终证书
final certificate
最终支付证书
final certificate of payment
最终仲裁
terminal arbitration
最重要的
main, principal
罪行
crime
遵从
conform
遵守
comply with, compliance, observe, observance, abide by
遵守法律
obey the law
遵守国际惯例
follow the international practice
遵守合同
compliance with the contract, abide by the contract
遵守协议
abide by the agreement
作抵押
on mortgage
作废
cancel, cancellation, become null and void
作废的支票
voided check
作记号
mark
作业
activity, operation
作业次序网络图
precedence network
作业工程量表
operational bill of quantities
作业计划
plan of operations
作业进度安排
scheduling of activities
作业进度表
schedule of activities
作业量
quantity of work
作业区
operation area
作业循环
job cycle
作用
function, effect, role, operation

附录一 有关中外机构团体名称表

机构团体外文名称	外文缩写	机构团体中文名称
African Development Bank	AFDB	非洲开发银行
Agency for International Development	AID	[联合国]国际开发署
American Arbitration Association	AAA	美国仲裁协会
American Association of Cost Engineers	AACE	美国成本工程师协会
American Bankers' Associations	ABA	美国银行家协会
American Bar Association	ABA	美国律师协会
American Bureau of Standards	ABS	美国标准局
American Concrete Institute	ACI	美国混凝土学会
American Consulting Engineers Council	ACEC	美国咨询工程师理事会
American Engineering Standards Committee	AESC	美国工程标准委员会
American Institute of Architects	AIA	美国建筑师学会
American Institute of Electrical Engineers	AIEE	美国电气工程学会
American Institute of Steel Construction	AISC	美国钢结构学会
American Society for Civil Engineers	ASCE	美国土木工程师协会
American Society for Testing and Materials	ASTM	美国材料试验协会
American Standard Association	ASA	美国标准协会
Asia Development Bank	ADB	亚洲开发银行
Asian Development Fund	ADF	亚洲开发基金
Asian Pacific Economic Cooperation	APEC	亚太经济合作组织
Asian Reinsurance Corporation		亚洲再保险公司
Associated General Contractors of America	AGC	美国总承包商协会
Association of Caribbean States		加勒比海国家联盟
Association of Consulting Architects	ACA	[英国]咨询建筑师协会

续表

机构团体外文名称	外文缩写	机构团体中文名称
Association of Consulting Engineers	ACE	[英国]咨询工程师协会
Association of Consulting Engineers of Canada		加拿大咨询工程师协会
Association of Consulting Management Engineers	ACME	[美国]管理咨询工程师协会
Association of Japanese Consulting Engineers	AJCE	日本咨询工程师协会
Association of Southeast Asian Nations	ASEAN	东南亚国家联盟
Australia Federation of Construction		澳大利亚施工承包商联合会
Bank for International Settlements	BIS	国际结算银行
Bank of China		中国银行
British Association of Standard	BAS	英国标准协会
British Engineering Standards Association	BESA	英国工程标准协会
British Standards Institution	BSI	英国标准学会
Bureau of Standards	BS	[美国]标准局
Canadian International Development Agency	CIDA	加拿大国际开发署
Canadian Standards Association	CSA	加拿大标准协会
Caribbean Common of Market	CCM	加勒比共同市场
Central American Federation	CAF	中美洲国家联盟
Central African Federation	CAF	中非洲国家联盟
Central American Common Market	CACM	中美洲共同市场
Chartered Institute of Building	CIOB	[英国]注册营造师协会
China Architecture Industry Society		中国建筑业协会
China Association of Engineering Consultants		中国建设监理协会
China Association of International Engineering Consultants	CAIEC	中国国际工程咨询协会
China Association of National Engineering Consultants	CANEC	中国工程咨询协会
China Exploration and Design Association		中国勘察设计协会

续表

机构团体外文名称	外文缩写	机构团体中文名称
China Import and Export Commodity Inspection Bureau	CCIB	中国进出口商品检验局
China Import and Export Commodity Inspection Corporation	CCIC	中国进出口商品检验公司
China International Contractors Association	CHINCA	中国对外承包工程商会
China International Economic and Trade Arbitration Commission	CIETAC	中国国际经济贸易仲裁委员会
China Investment Bank		中国投资银行
Coast Engineering Research Center	CERC	[美国]海岸工程研究中心
Commercial Court of Vienna		维也纳商会法庭
Commission of the European Communities	CEC	欧洲共同体委员会
Committee of European Construction Equipment	CECE	欧洲建筑设备委员会
Committee on International Ocean Affairs	CIOA	国际海事委员会
Concrete Reinforcing Steel Institute	CRSI	[美国]混凝土用钢筋学会
Confederation of International Contractors Associations	CICA	国际承包商联合会
Corps of Engineers of the United States Army	CE, US Army	美国陆军工程兵团
Council of Arab Economic Unity	CAEU	阿拉伯经济统一理事会
Court of Arbitration of the International Chamber of Commerce		国际商会仲裁庭
Economic Community of the West African States	ECWAS	西非国家经济共同体
Economic Development Institute	EDI	[世界银行]经济发展学院
Engineering Consulting Firms Association	ECFA	[日]工程咨询公司协会
Environmental Protection Agency	EPA	[美国]环境保护局
European clearing Union	ECU	欧洲清算联盟
European Development Fund	EDF	欧洲发展基金
European Economic Community	EEC	欧洲经济共同体

续表

机构团体外文名称	外文缩写	机构团体中文名称
European International Contractors' Association	EIC	欧洲国际承包商协会
European Investment Bank	EIB	欧洲投资银行
European Regional Development Fund		欧洲地区发展基金组织
Federal Trade Commission	FTC	[美国]联邦贸易委员会
Fédération Internationale des Ingénieurs-Conseils *	FIDIC	国际咨询工程师联合会
Federation of Civil Engineering Contractors	FCEC	[英国]土木工程师联合会
ILO Office, Beijing		[联合国]国际劳工组织北京局
ILO Regional Office for Asia and the Pacific		[联合国]国际劳工组织亚太地区局
Institute of Actuaries		[英国]保险精算师学会
Institute of London Underwriters		[英国]伦敦承保人学会
Institution of Civil Engineers	ICE	[英国]土木工程师学会
Institution of Structural Engineers	ISE	[英国]结构工程师学会
Inter-American Commercial Arbitration Commission	IACAC	泛美商业仲裁委员会
Inter-American Development Bank	IAIDB	泛美开发银行
Inter-Arab Investment Guarantee Corporation		阿拉伯地区投资保证公司
International Arbitration League	IAL	国际仲裁同盟
International Association for Earthquake Engineering	IAEE	国际地震工程协会
International Association of Engineering Geology	IAEG	国际工程地质学会
International Association of Geodesy	IAG	国际大地测量学会
International Association of Hydraulic Research	IAHR	[荷兰]国际水力学研究协会
International Association of Hydrology	IAH	国际水文学学会
International Association of Lawyers	IAL	国际律师协会

续表

机构团体外文名称	外文缩写	机构团体中文名称
International Bank for Reconstruction and Development	IBRD	[世界银行]国际复兴开发银行
International Center for the Settlement of Investment Disputes	ICSID	[世界银行]解决投资争端国际中心
International Chamber of Commerce	ICC	国际商会
International Development Association	IDA	[世界银行]国际开发协会
International Federation of Asian & Western Pacific Contractors' Associations	IFAWPCA	亚洲与西太平洋承包商协会国际联合会
International Federation of Prestressing	FIP	国际预应力协会
International Finance Corporation	IFC	[世界银行]国际金融公司
International Labour Organization	ILO	[联合国]国际劳工组织
International Law Commission	ILC	[联合国]国际(公)法委员会
International Legal Union	IAU	国际法律联盟
International Machinery Insurer's Association		国际机械保险人协会
International Monetary Fund	IMF	[联合国]国际货币基金组织
Internationale Standardisation Organization *	ISO	[联合国]国际标准化组织
International Society for Rock Mechanics	ISRM	国际岩石力学学会
International Society for Soil Mechanics and Foundation Engineering	ISSMEF	国际土力学与基础工程学会
International Standards Association	ISA	国际标准协会
International Trade Centre	ITC	国际贸易中心
International Union of Architects	IUA	国际建筑师联合会
International Union of Credit & Investment insurers		国际信用和投资保险联盟
International Union of Marine Insurance		国际海上保险联盟
International Water Resources Association	IWRA	国际水资源协会
Islamic Development Bank		伊斯兰发展银行

续表

机构团体外文名称	外文缩写	机构团体中文名称
Japan International Cooperation Agency		日本国际协力事业团
Joint Contracts Tribunal	JCT	[英国]合同审定联合会
Joint Engineering Management Conference	JEMC	[美国]工程管理联合会
Joint Negotiating Committee	JNC	[英国]联合谈判委员会
Lloyd's	LIDS	[英国]劳合社;劳埃德保险公司
London Court of Arbitration		伦敦仲裁法院
Management Research Society for Construction Industry	MRSCI	[日本]建筑业管理研究会
Mechanical Contractors' Association of America	MCAA	美国机械承包商协会
Multilateral Investment Guarantee Agency	MIGA	[世界银行]多边投资担保机构
Operation Evaluation Department	OED	[世界银行]执行评价局
Organization for Economic Cooperation and Development	OECD	[联合国]经济合作与发展组织(经合组织)
Organization of Petroleum Exporting Countries	OPEC	石油输出国组织
Overseas Construction Association of Japan, INC		日本海外建设协会
Overseas Economic Cooperation Fund	OECF	[日本]海外经济协力基金
Post Evaluation Centre	PEC	[联合国开发署]后评价中心
Post Evaluation Office	PEO	[亚洲开发银行]后评价办公室
Reinforced Concrete Association	RCA	[英国]钢筋混凝土协会
Royal Institute of British Architects	RIBA	英国皇家建筑师协会
Royal Institute of Chartered Surveyors	RICS	[英国]皇家注册测量师协会
South East Asia Treaty Organization	SEATO	东南亚条约组织
Specialist Engineering Contractor's Group	SECG	专业工程承包商联合体
Technical Assistance Board	TAB	[联合国]技术援助委员会

续表

机构团体外文名称	外文缩写	机构团体中文名称
The World Bank		世界银行
United Nation Economic & Social Commission for Asia and the Pacific		联合国亚太经社理事会
United Nations Commission on International Trade Law	UNCITRAL	联合国国际贸易法委员会
United Nations Development Programme	UNDP	联合国开发计划署
United Nations Environment Programme	UNEP	联合国环境规划署
United Nations Industrial Development Organization	UNIDO	联合国工(业开)发组织
World Association of Lawyers	WAL	世界律师协会
World Intellectual Property Organization	WIPO	[联合国]世界知识产权组织
World Organization of Dredging Association	WODA	世界疏浚协会
World Trade Organization	WTO	世界贸易组织

说明：凡在机构团体外文名称后标有"*"的为法文名称，其余均为英文名称。

附录二 世界各国及地区货币一览表

国家或地区 (中外文)		首都 (或首府)	货币 名 称		货币代码
			单位及简写	辅币及进位	
亚 洲					
中国	The People's Republic of China	北京 Beijing	人民币元(Renminbi Yuan,简写RMB ¥)	1元=10角(Jiao)=100分(Fen)	CNY
朝鲜	The Democratic People's Republic of Korea	平壤 Pyongyang	朝鲜圆(North Korean Won,简写NKW)	1朝鲜圆=100分(Jeon/Jun)	KPW
韩国	Republic of Korea	汉城 Seoul	韩国圆(South Korean Won,简写SKW)	1韩国圆=100分(Chon/Jun)	KRW
日本	Japan	东京 Tokyo	日元(Japanese Yen,简写¥)	1日元=100钱(Sen)	JPY
蒙古	The Mongolian People's Republic	乌兰巴托 UlaanBaator	图格里克(Tugrik,简写Tug)	1图格里克=100蒙戈(Mongos)	MNT
越南	The socialist Republic of Vietnam	河内 Hanoi	越南盾(Dong,简写D)	1盾=10角(Hau)=100分(Xu)	VND
老挝	The People's Democratic Republic of Laos	万象 Vientiane	新基普(Kip,简写K)	1基普=100阿特(At)	LAK
柬埔寨	Democratic Kampuchea	金边 Phnom·Penh	瑞尔(Riel)	1瑞尔=100仙(Sen)	KHR
缅甸	Union of Myanmar	仰光 Yangon	缅元(Kyat,简写Kt)	1缅元=100分(Pyas)	MMK

续表

国家或地区 （中外文）	首都 （或首府）	货币名称		货币代码
		单位及简写	辅币及进位	
泰国	The Kingdom of Thailand	曼谷 Bangkok	泰铢（Thai Baht，简写Bt）	1铢=100萨当(Satang)	THB
马来西亚	The Federation of Malaysia	吉隆坡 Kuala Lumpur	林吉特（Ringgit，简写M$）	1林吉特=100分(cents)	MYR
新加坡	The Republic of Singapore	新加坡 Singapore	新加坡元（Singapore Dollar，简写S$）	1元=100分(Cents)	SGD
印度尼西亚	The Republic of Indonesia	雅加达 Jakarta	印度尼西亚卢比（通称盾）(Indonesia Rupiah，简写Rp)	1盾=100仙(Sen)	IDR
文莱	The Sultanate of Brunei	斯里巴加湾 Seri Begawan	文莱元（Brunei Dollar，简写B$）	1元=100分(Cents)	BND
东帝汶	East Timor	帝力 Dili	帝汶埃斯库多（Timor Escudo）	1埃斯库多=100分(Centavos)	TPE
菲律宾	The Republic of Philippines	马尼拉 Manila	菲律宾比索（Philippine Peso，简写P）	1比索=100分(Centavos)	PHP
尼泊尔	The Kingdom of Nepal	加德满都 Kathmandu	尼泊尔卢比（Nepalese Rupee，简写NRe）	1卢比=100派沙(Paisa)	NPR
不丹	The Kingdom of Bhutan	廷布 Thimbu	努尔特鲁姆（Ngultrum，简写Nu）	1奴尔特鲁姆=100切特鲁姆(Chetrum)	BTN
巴基斯坦	The Islamic Republic of Pakistan	伊斯兰堡 Islamabad	巴基斯坦卢比（Pakistan Rupee，简写PRe）	1卢比=100派沙(Paisa)	PKR

续表

国家或地区 (中外文)		首都 (或首府)	货币名称		货币代码
			单位及简写	辅币及进位	
印度	The Republic of India	新德里 New Delhi	印度卢比(Indian Rupee，简写 Re)	1 卢比＝100 派沙(Paise)	INR
锡金	Sikkim	甘托克 Gangtok	印度卢比(Indian Rupee，简写 Re)	1 卢比＝100 派沙(Paisa)	
孟加拉国	The People's Republic of Bangladesh	达卡 Dhaka	塔卡(Taka，简写 Tk)	1 塔卡＝100 波依夏(Poisha)	BDT
斯里兰卡	The Republic of Sri Lanka	科伦坡 Colombo	斯里兰卡卢比(Sri Lanka Rupee 简写 SLRe)	1 卢比＝100 分(Cents)	LKP
马尔代夫	The Republic of Maldives	马累 Male	马尔代夫罗非亚(Maldive's Rufiyaa，简写 RF)	1 罗非亚＝100 拉列(Laari)	MVR
伊朗	Iran	德黑兰 Tehran	伊朗里亚尔(Iranian Rial，简写 Rl，复数 Rls)	1 里亚尔＝100 第纳尔(Dinars)	IRR
阿富汗	The Democratic Republic of Afghanistan	喀布尔 kabul	阿富汗尼(Afghani，简写 Af)	1 阿富汗尼＝100 普尔(Puls)	AFA
土耳其	The Republic of Turkey	安卡拉 Ankara	土耳其里拉(Turkish Lira，也称镑，简写 TL)	1 里拉＝100 库鲁(Kurus)	TRL
塞浦路斯	The Republic of Cyprus	尼科西亚 Nicosia	塞浦路斯镑(Cyprus Pound，简写 C£)	1 镑＝100 分(Cents)	CYP
叙利亚	The Syrian Arab Republic	大马士革 Dimashq	叙利亚镑(Syrian pound，简写 S£)	1 镑＝100 皮阿斯特(Piastres)	SYP

续表

国家或地区（中外文)		首都（或首府)	货币名称		货币代码
			单位及简写	辅币及进位	
黎巴嫩	The Republic of Lebanon	贝鲁特 Bayrut	黎巴嫩镑（Lebanese pound,简写 L£)	1 镑＝100 皮阿斯特(Piastres)	LBP
巴勒斯坦	Palestine	耶路撒冷 Jerusalem			PKR
以色列	The State of Israel	特拉维夫—雅法 Tel Aviv-Yafo	新谢克尔(New Sheqalim,简写 NIS)	1 新谢克尔＝100 阿高拉(Agora)	ILS
约旦	The Hashemite Kingdom Of Jordan	安曼 Amman	约旦第纳尔（Jordanian Dinar,简写 JD)	1 第纳尔＝1000 费尔(Fils)	JOD
伊拉克	The Republic of Iraq	巴格达 Baghdad	伊拉克第纳尔(Iraqi Dinar,简写 ID)	1 第纳尔＝1000 费尔(Fils)	IQD
科威特	The State of Kuwait	科威特 Kuwait	科威特第纳尔（Kuwait Dinar,简写 KD)	1 第纳尔＝1,000 费尔(Fils)	KWD
沙特阿拉伯	The Kingdom of Saudi Arabia	利雅得 Riyad	沙特里亚尔（Saudi Riyal,简写 SRL)	1 里亚尔＝20 库尔什（Qursh）＝100 哈拉拉(Halalah)	SAR
也门共和国	Republic of Yemen	萨那 Sana	也门里亚尔（Yemen Riyal,简写 YRI)	1 里亚尔＝100 费尔(Fils)	YER
阿曼	The Sultanate of Oman	马斯喀特 Masqat	阿曼里亚尔（Oman Riyal,简写 OR)	1 里亚尔＝1000 派沙(Baisa)	OMR
阿联酋	The United Arab Emirates	阿布扎比 Abu Dhabi	阿联酋迪拉姆(U.A.E. Dirham,简写 Dh)	1 迪拉姆＝100 费尔(Fils)	AED

续表

国家或地区 （中外文）	首都 （或首府）	货币名称		货币代码
		单位及简写	辅币及进位	
卡塔尔 The State of Qatar	多哈 Dawhah	卡塔尔里亚尔（Qatar Riyal，简写QR）	1里亚尔＝100迪拉姆（Dirhams）	QAR
巴林 The Shaikhdom of Bahrain	麦纳麦 Manamah	巴林第纳尔（Bahrain Dinar，简写BD）	1第纳尔＝1000费尔（Fils）	BHD
中国香港 Hongkong．China		香港元（Hongkong Dollar，简写Hk＄）	1元＝100分（Cents）	HKD
中国澳门 Macau，China		澳门元〔Pataca．简写Pat或P）	1元＝100分（Avos）	
中国台湾 Taiwan，China		新台币（New Taiwan Dollar，简写NT＄）	1元＝100分（Cents）	TWD
亚美尼亚 The Republic of Armenian	埃里温 Erevan	德拉姆(Dram)		
阿塞拜疆 The Republic of Azerbaijan	巴库 Baku	马纳特(Manat)		
格鲁吉亚 The Republic of Georgia	第比利斯 Tbilisi	库镑(Coupon)		
哈萨克斯坦 The Republic of Kazakhstan	阿拉木图 Alma-Ata	哈萨克斯坦腾戈(Kazakhstan Tenge)		
吉尔吉斯斯坦 The Republic of Kirghizstan	比什凯克 Biskek	索姆(Som)		

续表

国家或地区 (中外文)	首都 (或首府)	货币名称		货币代码
		单位及简写	辅币及进位	
塔吉克斯坦 The Republic of Tadzhikistan	杜尚别 Dusanbe	卢布(Rouble,简写 Rbl)	1 卢布＝100 戈比(Kopecks)	
土库曼斯坦 The Republic of Turkmenistan	阿什哈巴德 Ashabad	马纳特(Manat)		
乌兹别克斯坦 The Republic of Uzbekistan	塔什干 Taskent	苏姆(Sum)		UZS
非洲				
埃及 The Arab Republic of Egypt	开罗 Cairo	埃及镑(Egyptian pound,简写 E£)	1 镑＝100 皮阿斯特(Piastres)＝1000 米利姆(Milliemes)	EGP
苏丹 The Republic of The Sudan	喀土穆 Khartoum	苏丹镑(Sudanese Pound,简写 Sud£)	1 镑＝100 皮阿斯特(Piastres)＝1000 米利姆(Milliemes)	SDP
利比亚 The Socialist People's Libyan Arab Jamahiriya	的黎波里 Tarabulees	利比亚第纳尔(Libyan Dinar,简写 LD)	1 第纳尔＝1000 迪拉姆(Dirhams)	LYD
突尼斯 The Republic of Tunisia	突尼斯 Tunis	突尼斯第纳尔(Tunisian Dinar,简写 TD)	1 第纳尔＝1000 米利姆(Milliemes)	TND
阿尔及利亚 The Democratic People's Republic of Algeria	阿尔及尔 Alger	阿尔及利亚第纳尔(Algerian Dinar,简写 AD)	1 第纳尔＝100 分(Centimes)	DZD

续表

国家或地区（中外文）	首都（或首府）	货币名称		货币代码
		单位及简写	辅币及进位	
摩洛哥	The Kingdom of Morocco	拉巴特 Rabat	迪拉姆（Dirham，简写 DH）	1 迪拉姆 = 100 分（centimes）	MAD
毛里塔尼亚	The Islamic Republic of Mauritania	努尔克肖特 Nouakchott	乌吉亚（Ouguiya，简写 VM）	1 乌吉亚 = 5 库姆斯（Khoums）	
布基纳法索	Burkina Faso	瓦加杜古 Ouagadougou	非洲金融共同体法郎（Franc de la Communauté Financière Africaine，简写 CFAF）*	1 法郎 = 100 分（Centimes）	
塞内加尔	The Republic of Senegal	达喀尔 Dakar	非洲金融共同体法郎（Franc de la Communauté Financière Africaine，简写 CFAF）*	1 法郎 = 100 分（Centimes）	XOF
冈比亚	The Republic of The Gambia	班珠尔 Banjul	冈比亚达拉西（Gambia Dalasi，简写 GD）	1 达拉西 = 100 布图（Butut）	GMD
马里	The Republic of Mali	巴马科 Bamako	非洲金融共同体法郎（Franc de la Communauté Financière Africaine，简写 CFAF）*	1 法郎 = 100 分（Centimes）	GNP
几内亚	The Republic of Guinea	科纳克里 Conakry	几内亚法郎（Guinean Franc，简写 GF）	1 法郎 = 100 分（Centimes）	GNF
几内亚比绍	The Republic of Guinea Bissau	比绍 Bissau	几内亚比绍比索（Guinea Bissau Peso，简写 GBP）	1 比索 = 100 分（Centavos）	GWP

续表

国家或地区 （中外文）	首都 （或首府）	货币名称		货币代码
		单位及简写	辅币及进位	
塞拉利昂 The Republic of Sierra Leone	弗里敦 Freetown	利昂(Leone,简写 Le)	1 利昂＝100 分 (Cents)	SLL
利比里亚 The Republic of Liberia	蒙罗维亚 Monrovia	利比里亚元（Liberian Dollar,简写 L＄）	1 元＝100 分 (Cents)	LRD
加纳 The Republic of Ghana	阿克拉 Accra	塞地(Cedi, 简写 ₵)	1 塞地＝100 比塞瓦 (Pesewas)	GHC
多哥 The Republic of Togo	洛美 Lome	非洲金融共同体法郎 (Franc de la Communauté Financière Africaine,简写 CFAF)*	1 法郎＝100 分 (centimes)	XOF
贝宁 The Republic of Benin	波多诺伏 Porto-Novo	非洲金融共同体法郎 (Franc de la Communauté Financière Africaine,简写 CFAF)*	1 法郎＝100 分 (centimes)	XOF
尼日尔 The Republic of Niger	尼亚美 Niamey	非洲金融共同体法郎 (Franc de la Communauté Financière Africaine,简写 CFAF)*	1 法郎＝100 分 (centimes)	XOF
尼日利亚 The Federal Republic of Nigeria	拉各斯 Lagos	奈拉(Naira,简写 ₦)	1 奈拉＝100 考包(Kobo)	NGN
佛得角 The Republic of Cape Verde	普拉亚 Paria	佛得角埃斯库多(Cape Verde Escudo, 简写 CVEsc)	1 埃斯库多＝100 分 (Centiavos)	CVE

续表

国家或地区 (中外文)	首都 (或首府)	货币名称		货币代码
		单位及简写	辅币及进位	
乍得	The Republic of Chad	恩贾梅纳 Ndjamena	非洲金融共同体法郎 (Franc de la Communauté Financière Africaine, 简写 CFAF)*	1 法郎=100 分 (centimes)	XAF
科特迪瓦	Cote d' Lvoire	阿比让 Abidjan	非洲金融共同体法郎 (Franc de la Communauté Financière Africaine, 简写 CFAF)*	1 法郎=100 分 (centimes)	XAF
喀麦隆	The Republic of Cameroon	雅温得 Yaounde	非洲金融共同体法郎 (Franc de la Communauté Financière Africaine, 简写 CFAF)*	1 法郎=100 分 (centimes)	XAF
赤道几内亚	The Republic of Equatorial Guinea	马拉博 Malabo	非洲金融共同体法郎 (Franc de la Communauté Financière Africaine, 简写 CFAF)*	1 法郎=100 分 (centimes)	XAF
圣多美和普林西比	The Democratic Republic of Sao Tome and Principe	圣多美 Sao Tome	多布拉(Dobra)	1 多布拉=100 分(Centavos)	STD
中非共和国	The Central African Republic	班吉 Bangui	非洲金融共同体法郎 (Franc de la Communauté Financière Africaine, 简写 CFAF)*	1 法郎=100 分 (Centimes)	XAF

续表

国家或地区 （中外文）	首都 （或首府）	货币名称		货币代码
		单位及简写	辅币及进位	
加蓬	The Republic of Gabon	利伯维尔 Libreville	非洲金融共同体法郎（Franc de la Communauté Financière Africaine，简写 CFAF）*	1法郎＝100分（Centimes）	XAF
刚果	The People's Republic of The Congo	布拉柴维尔 Brazzaville	非洲金融共同体法郎（Franc de la Communauté Financière Africaine，简写 CFAF）*	1法郎＝100分（Centimes）	XAF
扎伊尔	The Republic of Zaire	金沙萨 Kinshasa	扎伊尔（Zaire，简写 Z）	1扎伊尔＝100马库塔（Makuta）＝10,000森吉（Sengi）	ZRZ
布隆迪	The Republic of Burundi	布琼布拉 Bujumbura	布隆迪法郎（Burundi Franc，简写 BuFr）	1法郎＝100分（Centimes）	BIF
卢旺达	The Republic of Rwanda	基加利 Kigali	卢旺达法郎（Rwanda Franc，简写 RF）	1法郎＝100分（Centimes）	RWF
乌干达	The Republic of Uganda	坎帕拉 Kampala	乌干达先令（Uganda Shilling，简写 USh）	1先令＝100分（Cents）	UGX
肯尼亚	The Republic of Kenya	内罗毕 Nairobi	肯尼亚先令（Kenya Shilling 简写 KSh）	1先令＝100分（Cents）	KES
埃塞俄比亚	People's Democratic Republic of Ethiopia	亚的斯亚贝巴 Addis Abeba	埃塞俄比亚比尔（Ethiopian Birr，简写 Br）	1比尔＝100分（Cents）	ETB

续表

国家或地区（中外文）		首都（或首府）	货币名称		货币代码
			单位及简写	辅币及进位	
索马里	The Somalia Democratic Republic	摩加迪沙 Muqdisho	索马里先令（Somalia Shilling，简写 So. Sh）	1 先令＝100 分(Cents)	SOS
吉布提	The Republic of Djibouti	吉布提 Djibouti	吉布提法郎（Djibouti Franc，简写 DF）	1 法郎＝100 分 (Centimes)	DJF
坦桑尼亚	The United Republic of Tanzania	达累斯萨拉姆 Dares Salaam	坦桑尼亚先令（Tanzania Shilling，简写 TSh）	1 先令＝100 分(Cents)	TZS
赞比亚	The Republic of Zambia	卢萨卡 Lusaka	赞比亚克瓦查(Zambian Kwacha，简写 ZK）	1 克瓦查＝100 恩韦 (Ngwee)	ZMK
安哥拉	The People's Republic of Angola	罗安达 Luanda	宽扎（Kwanza，简写 Kw）	1 宽扎＝100 勒韦(Lweis)	AOK
津巴布韦	The Republic of Zimbabwe	哈拉雷 Harare	津巴布韦元(Zimbabwe Dollar，简写 Z＄)	1 元＝100 分 (Cents)	ZWD
马拉维	The Republic of Malawi	松巴 Zomba	马拉维克瓦查(Malawi Kwacha，简写 MK）	1 克瓦查＝100 坦巴拉 (Tambala)	MWK
莫桑比克	The Republic of Mozambique	马普托 Maputo	莫桑比克梅蒂卡尔（Mozambique Metical，简写 MT）	1 梅蒂卡尔＝100 分 (Centavos)	MZM
博茨瓦纳	The Republic of Botswana	哈博罗内 Gaborone	普拉(Pula，简写 P)	1 普拉＝100 西比 (Thebe)	BWP
南非	South Africa	比勒陀利亚 Pretoria	南非兰特（South African Rand，简写 R）	1 兰特＝100 分(Cents)	ZAR

续表

国家或地区（中外文)	首都（或首府)	货币名称 单位及简写	货币名称 辅币及进位	货币代码
莱索托 The Kingdom of Lesotho	马塞卢 Maseru	鲁梯(Luti)	1 鲁梯=100 分(Lisentes)	ZAR
斯威士兰 The Kingdom of Swaziland	姆巴巴内 Mbabane	里兰吉尼(Lilangeni，简写E)	1 里兰吉尼=100 分 (Cents)	SZL
纳米比亚 Namibia	温得和克 Windhoek	南非兰特(South African Rand，简写R)	1 兰特=100 分(Cents)	ZAR
马达加斯加 The Democratic Republic of Madagascar	塔那那利佛 Tananarive	马尔加什法郎(Malagasy Franc，简写FMG)	1 法郎=100 分 (Centimes)	MGF
塞舌尔 The Republic of Seychelles	维多利亚 Victoria	塞舌尔卢比(Seychelles Rupee，简写Sey Re)	1 卢比=100 分(Cents)	SCR
科摩罗 The Federal Islamic Republic of Comoros	莫罗尼 Moroni	科摩罗法郎(Comoros Franc，简写CF)	1 科摩罗法郎=100 分 (Centimes)	KMF
毛里求斯 Mauritius	路易港 Port Louis	毛里求斯卢比(Mauritius Rupee，简写Mau Re)	1 卢比=100 分(Cents)	MUR

欧 洲

国家或地区（中外文)	首都（或首府)	货币名称 单位及简写	货币名称 辅币及进位	货币代码
欧洲联盟 European Union		欧元(EURO，简写€)	1 欧元=100 分(Cents)	EUR
罗马尼亚 Romania	布加勒斯特 Bucuresti	列伊(Leu，简称L)	1 列伊=100 巴尼(Bani)	ROL
保加利亚 The People's Republic of Bulgaria	索非亚 Sofija	列弗(Lev)	1 列弗=100 斯托丁基 (Stotinki)	BGL

续表

国家或地区（中外文）	首都（或首府）	货币名称 单位及简写	货币名称 辅币及进位	货币代码
南斯拉夫 The Federal Republic of Yugoslavia	贝尔格莱德 Belgrade	第纳尔（Dinar，简写 Din）	1 第纳尔＝100 帕拉（Paras）	YUN
克罗地亚 The Republic of Croatia	萨格勒布 Zagreb	第纳尔（Dinar，简写 Din）		HRK
斯洛文尼亚 The Republic of Slovenia	卢布尔雅那 Ljubljara	特拉（Tolar）		SIT
马其顿 Macedonia	斯科普里 Skopje			
波黑 The Republic of Bosnia and Herzegovia	萨拉热窝 Sarajevo			
阿尔巴尼亚 The People's Socialist Republic of Albania	地拉那 Tirana	列克（Lek）	1 列克＝100 昆塔（Qindarka）	ALL
希腊 The Greece Republic	雅典 AThens	希腊德拉克马（Greece Drachma，简写 Dr）	1 德拉科马＝100 雷普塔（Lepta）	GRD
意大利 The Republic of Italy	罗马 Roma	意大利里拉（Italian Lira，简写 Lit）	1 里拉＝100 分（Centimes）	ITL
圣马力诺 San Marino	圣马力诺 San Marino	意大利里拉（Italian Lira，简写 Lit）		ITL
梵蒂冈 Vatican City	梵蒂冈城 Vatican City	意大利里拉（Italian Lira，简写 Lit）		ITL

续表

国家或地区（中外文）	首都（或首府）	货币名称		货币代码
		单位及简写	辅币及进位	
马尔他 The Republic of Malta	瓦莱塔 Valletta	马尔他里拉(Malta Lira，简写 LM)	1 里拉＝100 分(Cents)＝1000 米尔(Mils)	MTL
西班牙 Spain	马德里 Madrid	比塞塔(Peseta，简写 Ptas)	1 比塞塔＝100 分(Centimos)	ESP
葡萄牙 The Republic of Portugal	里斯本 Lisboa	埃斯库多(Escudo，简写 Esc)	1 埃斯库多＝100 分(Centavos)	PTE
安道尔 The Principality of Andorra	安道尔 Andorra	法国法郎及西班牙比塞塔(Andorran Peseta)		ESP
英国 The United Kingdom of Great Britain and Northern Ireland	伦敦 London	英镑（Pound Sterling，简写£)	1 英镑＝100 新便士(New Pence)	GBP
爱尔兰 The Republic of Ireland	都柏林 Dublin	爱尔兰镑(Irish Pound，简写 Ir£)	1 爱尔兰镑＝100 新便士（New Pence)	IEP
荷兰 The Kingdom of NeTherlands	阿姆斯特丹 Amsterdam	荷兰盾（Florin 或 Guilder，简写 Fls 或 Fld)	1 荷兰盾＝100 分(Cents)	NLG
比利时 The Kingdom of Belgium	布鲁塞尔 Brussels	比利时法郎（Belgian Franc，简写 BF)	1 法郎＝100 分(centimes)	BEF
法国 The Republic of France	巴黎 Paris	法国法郎（French Franc，简写 FF)	1 法郎＝100 分(centimes)	FRF

续表

国家或地区	(中外文)	首都（或首府）	货币名称 单位及简写	辅币及进位	货币代码
摩纳哥	The Principality of Monaco	摩纳哥 Monaco Ville	法国法郎	1 法郎＝100 分 (centimes)	FRF
波兰	The Republic of Poland	华沙 Warsaw	兹罗提(Zloty，简写 Zl)	1 兹罗提＝100 格罗西 (Groszy)	PLZ
捷克	Czech	布拉格 Prague	克郎（Koruna，简写 KOS）	1 克郎＝100 赫勒 (Heller)	CSK
斯洛伐克	Slovak	布拉迪斯拉发 Bratislav	克郎（Koruna，简写 KOS）	1 克郎＝100 赫勒(Heller)	SKK
匈牙利	The Republic of Hungary	布达佩斯 Budapest	福林(Forint，简写 Ft)	1 福林＝100 菲勒(Filler)	HUF
德国	The Federal Republic of Germany	波恩 Bonn	马克（Deutsche Mark，简写 DM）	1 马克＝100 芬尼 (Pfennig)	DDM
奥地利	The Republic of Austria	维也纳 Vienna	奥地利先令（Austrian Schilling，简写 S）	1 先令＝100 格罗申 (Groschen)	ATS
瑞士	The Swiss Confederation	伯尔尼 Bern	瑞士法郎(Swiss Franc，简写 SF)	1 法郎＝100 分 (Centimes)	CHF
列支敦士登	The Principality of liechtenstein	瓦杜兹 Vaduz	瑞士法郎(Swiss Franc)	1 法郎＝100 分 (Centimes)	CHF
卢森堡	The Grand Duchy of Luxembourg	卢森堡 Luxembourg	卢森堡法郎（Luxembourg Franc，简写 LuxF）	1 法郎＝100 分 (Centimes)	LUF

续表

国家或地区 （中外文）	首都 （或首府）	货币名称 单位及简写	辅币及进位	货币代码
俄罗斯 Russian Federation	莫斯科 Moscow	卢布（Rouble，简写 Rbl）	1 卢布＝100 戈比（Kopecks）	SUR
白俄罗斯 The Republic of Belancs	明斯克 Minsk	卢布(Rouble,简写 Rul)	1 卢布＝100 戈比（Kopecks）	SUR
爱沙尼亚 The Republic of Estonia	塔林 Tallinn	克郎(Kroon)		
拉脱维亚 The Republic of Latvia	里加 Riga	拉特(Lats 或 Lati)		
立陶宛 The Republic of Lithuania	维尔纽斯 Vilnius	立特(Litas 或 Litai)		
摩尔多瓦 The Republic of Moldova	基希讷乌 Chisinau	列伊(Leu)		
乌克兰 Ukraine	基辅 Kiev	格里夫纳(Hryvnia)		SUR
芬兰 The Republic of Finland	赫尔辛基 Helsinki	芬兰马克（Finnish Markka,简写 F Mk）	1 马克＝100 盆尼（Pennia）	FIM
瑞典 The Kingdom of Sweden	斯德哥尔摩 Stockholm	瑞典克郎（Swedish Krona,简写 SKr）	1 克郎＝100 欧尔(Ore)	SEK
挪威 The Kingdom of Norway	奥斯陆 Oslo	挪威克郎（Norwayian Krone,简写 NKr）	1 克郎＝100 欧尔(Ore)	NOK

续表

国家或地区 （中外文）	首都 （或首府）	货币名称		
		单位及简写	辅币及进位	货币代码
丹麦	The Kingdom of Denmark	哥本哈根 Kobenhavn	丹麦克郎(Danish Krone，简写 D Kr)	1 克郎=100 欧尔(Ore)	DKK
冰岛	The Republic of Iceland	雷克雅未克 Reykjavik	冰岛克郎（Icelandic Krona，简写 Ikr)	1 克郎=100 奥拉(Aurar)	ISK

大 洋 洲

国家或地区		首都	单位及简写	辅币及进位	货币代码
澳大利亚	The Commonwealth of Australia	堪培拉 Canberra	澳大利亚元(Australian Dollar，简写 A$)	1 澳元=100 分(Cents)	AUD
新西兰	New Zealand	惠灵顿 Wellington	新西兰元(New Zealand Dollar，简写 NZ$)	1 新西兰元=100 分(Cents)	NZD
西萨摩亚	Western Samoa	阿皮亚 Apia	西萨摩亚塔拉(Western Samoa Tala 简写 WS$)	1 塔拉=100 分(Cents)	
汤加	The Kingdom of Tonga	努库阿洛法 Nuku'alofa	潘加（Pa'angn，简写 T$)	1 潘加=100 分(Centimes)	TOP
斐济	Fiji	苏瓦 Suva	斐济元（Fiji Dollar，写 F$)	1 斐济元=100 分(Cents)	FJD
巴布亚新几内亚	Papua New Guinea	莫尔兹比港 Port Moresby	基那(Kina，简写 K)	1 基那=100 托伊(Toea)	PGK
所罗门群岛	Solomon Islands	霍尼亚拉 Honiara	澳大利亚元(Australian Dollar，简写 A$)	1 澳元=100 分(Cents)	SBD
瓦努阿图	The Republic of Vanuatu	维拉港 Vila	瓦图(Vatu，简写 Vt)	1 瓦图=100 分(Centimes)	VUV

续表

国家或地区 (中外文)	首都 (或首府)	货币名称		货币代码
		单位及简写	辅币及进位	
瑙鲁 The Republic of Nauru	亚伦 Yaren	澳大利亚元(Australian Dollar,简写A$)	1 澳元=100 分(Cents)	AUD
基里巴斯 Kiribati	塔拉瓦 Tarawa	澳大利亚元(Australian Dollar,简写A$)	1 澳元=100 分(Cents)	AUD
帕劳 Palan	科罗尔			
密可罗尼西亚联邦 Micronesia	帕利基尔 Palikir			
图瓦卢 Tuvalu	富纳富提 Funafut	澳大利亚元(Australian Dollar,简写A$)	1 澳元=100 分(Cents)	AUD
美　　洲				
加拿大 Canada	渥太华 Ottawa	加拿大元(Canadian Dollar,简写Can$)	1 加元=100 分(Cents)	CAD
美国 The United States of America	华盛顿 Washington	美元(United States Dollar,简写US$)	1 美元=100 分(Cents)	USD
格陵兰(丹麦属地) Greenland(Den)	戈特霍布(努克) Godthab (Nuk)	丹麦克郎(Danish Krone)	1 克郎=100 欧尔(Ore)	DKK
墨西哥 The United States of Mexico	墨西哥城 Mexico City	墨西哥比索(Mexican Peso,简写Mex$)	1 比索=100 分(Centavos)	MXP

续表

国家或地区 （中外文）	首都 （或首府）	货币名称 单位及简写	货币名称 辅币及进位	货币代码
危地马拉 The Republic of Guatemala	危地马拉城 Guatemal City	格查尔（Quetzal，简写Q)	1格查尔=100分（Centavos）	GTQ
洪都拉斯 The Republic of Honduras	特古西加尔巴 Tegucigalpa	伦皮拉（Lempira，简写L)	1伦皮拉=100分（Centavos）	HNL
伯利兹 Belize	贝尔莫潘 Belmopan	伯利兹元（Belzean Dollar，简写B$)	1元=100分（Cents）	BZD
萨尔瓦多 The Republic of El Salvador	圣萨尔瓦多 San Salvador	萨尔瓦多科郎（Salvadoran Colon，简写C)	1科郎=100分（Centavos）	SVC
尼加拉瓜 The Republic of Nicaragua	马那瓜 Managua	金科多巴（Cordoba Oro，简写C$)	1科多巴=100分（Centavos）	NIO
哥斯达黎加 The Republic of Costa Rica	圣约瑟 San Jose	哥斯达黎加科郎（Costa Rican Colon，简写C)	1科郎=100分（Centavos）	CRC
巴拿马 Panama	巴拿马城 Panama	巴拿马巴波亚（Panamanian Balboa，简写B)	1巴波亚=100分（Centesimas）	PAB
古巴 The Republic of Cuba	哈瓦那 Havana	古巴比索（Cuban Peso，简写Cub$)	1比索=100分（Centavos）	CUP
海地 The Republic of Haiti	太子港 Port-au-Prince	古德（Gourde，简写G)	1古德=100分（Centimes）	HTG
多米尼克 The Dominican Republic	圣多明各 Santo Domingo	多米尼加比索（Dominican Peso，简写RD$)	1比索=100分（Centavos）	DOP

续表

国家或地区 (中外文)	首都 (或首府)	货币名称 单位及简写	货币名称 辅币及进位	货币代码
牙买加 Jamaica	金斯敦 Kingston	牙买加元(Jamaican Dollar,简写J$)	1元=100分(Cents)	JMD
特立尼达和多巴哥 The Republic of Trinidad and Tobago	西班牙港 Port of Spain	特立尼达和多巴哥元(Trinidad & Tobago Dollar,简写TT$)	1元=100分(Cents)	TTD
巴巴多斯 Barbados	布里奇顿 Bridgetown	巴巴多斯元(Barbados Dollar,简写BDS$)	1元=100分(Cents)	BBD
波多黎各(美) Commonwealth of Puerto Rico	圣胡安 San Juan	美元(United States Dollar,简写US$)	1美元=100分(Cents)	USD
格林纳达 Grenada	圣乔治 St. George's	东加勒比元(East Caribbean Dollar,简写EC$)	1元=100分(Cents)	XCD
巴哈马 Bahamas	拿骚 Nassau	巴哈马元(Bahamian Dollar,简写B$)	1元=100分(Cents)	BSD
多米尼加 Dominica Island	罗索 Roseau	东加勒比元(East Caribbean Dollar,简写EC$)	1元=100分(Cents)	XCD
圣卢西亚 ST. Lucia Island	卡斯特里 Castries	东加勒比元(East Caribbean Dollar,简写EC$)	1元=100分(Cents)	XCD
圭亚那 The Co-operative Republic of Guyana	乔治敦 Georgetown	圭亚那元(Guyana Dollar,简写G$)	1元=100分(Cents)	GYD
苏里南 Swrinam	帕拉马里博 Pramaribo	苏里南盾(Surinam Guilder,简写Surf)	1盾=100分(Cents)	SRG

续表

国家或地区（中外文）	首都（或首府）	货币名称 单位及简写	辅币及进位	货币代码
圣基茨和尼维斯 St. Kitts and Nenis	巴斯特尔 basseterre	东加勒比元（East Caribbean Dollar，简写 EC $）	1元=100分（Cents）	XCD
安提瓜和巴布达 Antigua and Barbuda	圣约翰 st: John's	东加勒比元（East Caribbean Dollar，简写 EC $）	1元=100分（Cents）	XCD
圣文森特和格林纳丁斯 St. Vincent and The Grenadines	金斯敦 Kingstown	东加勒比元（East Caribbean Dollar，简写 EC $）	1元=100分（Cents）	XCD
圭亚那（法） French Guiana	卡宴 Cayenne	法国法郎（French Franc）	1法郎=100分（Centimes）	GYD
委内瑞拉 The Republic of Venezuela	加拉加斯 Caracas	委内瑞拉博利瓦（Venezuelan Bolivar，简写 Bs）	1博利瓦=100分（Centimos）	YEB
哥伦比亚 The Republic of Colombia	圣菲波哥大 sta. Fe de Bogotá	哥伦比亚比索（Colombia Peso，简写 Col $）	1比索=100分（Centavos）	COP
巴西 The Federal Republic of Brazil	巴西利亚 Brasilia	巴西雷亚尔	1克鲁塞罗=100分（Centavos）	BRE
厄瓜多尔 The Republic of Ecuador	基多 Quito	苏克雷（Sucre，简写 Sl.）	1苏克雷=100分（Centavos）	ECS
秘鲁 The Republic of Peru	利马 Lima	秘鲁新索尔（Nuevo sol）		PEN
玻利维亚 The Republic of Bolivia	苏克雷 Sucre	玻利维亚诺（Boliviano）	1比索=100分（Centavos）	BOB

续表

国家或地区 (中外文)		首都 (或首府)	货币名称		货币代码
			单位及简写	辅币及进位	
智利	The Republic of Chile	圣地亚哥 Santiago	智利比索(Chilean Peso,简写Ch$)	1比索=100分 (Centavos)	CLP
阿根廷	The Republic of Argentina	布宜诺斯艾利斯 Buenos Aires	阿根廷比索(Peso Argentina)		ARS
巴拉圭	The Republic of Paraguay	亚松森 Asuncion	巴拉圭瓜拉尼(Paraguayan Guarani,简写G)	1瓜拉尼=100分 (Centimos)	PYG
乌拉圭	The Oriental Republic of Uruguay	蒙得维的亚 Montevideo	乌拉圭新比索(Uruguayan New Peso,简写NUr$)	1新比索=100分 (Centesimos)	UYP

说明：

1. 表中国家名称和首都(或首府)名称主要参照《最新实用世界地图册》(中外文对照),中国地图出版社编制出版,1996
2. 表中货币名称以1998年8月28日《金融时报》为准
3. 少数货币中标有"*"的为法文,其余为英文拼读

主要参考书目

1. The World Bank. Standard Bidding Documents: Procurement of Works, 1995
2. FIDIC. Conditions of Contract for Works of Civil Engineering Construction, 1992
3. FIDIC. Guide to the Client/Consultant Model Services Agreement, 1990
4. FIDIC. Guide to the Use of Conditions of Contract for Electrical and Mechanical Works, 1989
5. FIDIC. Guide to the Use of Conditions of Contract for Design-Build and Turnkey, 1996
6. FIDIC. Conditions of Subcontract for Works of Civil Engineering Construction, 1994
7. Owen Watson. Longman Modern English Dictionary, 1976
8. Henry Bosley Woolf. Webster's New Collegiate Dictionary, 1980
9. 陆谷孙. 英汉大词典. 上海:上海译文出版社, 1996
10. 新英汉词典编写组. 新英汉词典. 上海:上海外语教育出版社, 1992
11. 胡式如. 英汉经济管理词典. 上海:上海外语教育出版社, 1995
12. 张拴林. 英汉外贸保险词典. 北京:中国社会科学出版社, 1995
13. P.h.Collin. Dictionary of Law. 陈庆柏, 王景仙等译. 英汉双解法律词典. 北京:世界图书出版公司, 1998
14. P.h.Collin. Dictionary of Business. 周丽娟, 王献等译. 英汉双解商务词典. 北京:世界图书出版公司, 1998
15. 周国强. 英汉国际商贸词典. 合肥:安徽科学技术出版社, 1996
16. 孙德权. 英汉国际经贸词典. 北京:商务印书馆国际有限公司, 1994
17. 英汉法律词典编写组. 英汉法律词典. 北京:法律出版社, 1985
18. 赵祖康. 英汉道路工程词典. 北京:人民交通出版社, 1996
19. 张泽祯. 英汉水利水电技术词典. 北京:水利电力出版社, 1996
20. 虞家徕, 胡禧森. 英汉会计词典. 北京:石油工业出版社, 1982
21. 吕汝汉. 英汉金融财经词典. 北京:商务印书馆国际有限公司, 1996
22. 吴光华. 汉英大词典. 上海:上海交通大学出版社, 1993
23. 魏中明. 汉英水利水电技术词典. 北京:水利电力出版社, 1993
24. 张人琦. 汉英建筑工程词典. 北京:中国建筑工业出版社, 1995

跋

中国国际经济合作学会会长　王西陶

"国际工程管理教学丛书"是适用于大学的教科书,也适用于在职干部的继续教育。今年出版一部分,争取1999年出齐。它的出版和使用,能适应当今世界和平与发展的大趋势,能迎接21世纪我国对外工程咨询、承包和劳务合作事业大发展。

国际工程事业是比较能发挥我国优势的产业,也是改革开放后我国在国际经济活动中新崛起的重要产业,定会随着改革开放的不断扩大,在新世纪获得更大发展。同时,这套丛书不仅对国际工程咨询和承包有重要意义,对我国援外工程项目的实施,以及外国在华投资工程与贷款工程的实施,均有实际意义。期望已久的、我国各大学培养的外向性复合型人才将于本世纪末开始诞生,将会更加得力地参与国际经济合作与竞争。

我们所说的外向性复合型人才是:具有建设项目工程技术理论基础,掌握现代化管理手段,精通一门外语,掌握与国际工程有关的法律、合同与经营策略,能满足国际工程管理多方面需要的人才。当然首先必须是热爱祖国、热爱社会主义、勇于献身于国际经济建设的人才,才能真正发挥作用。

这套丛书是由有关部委的单位、中国国际经济合作学会、中国对外承包商会、有关高校和一些对外公司组成的国际工程管理教学丛书编写委员会组织编写的。初定出版20分册。编委会组织了国内有经验的专家和知名学者担任各分册的主编,曾召开过多次会议,讨论和审定各主编拟定的编写大纲,力求既能将各位专家学者多年来在创造性劳动中的研究成果纳入丛书,又能使这套丛书系统、完整、准确、实用。同时也邀请国外学者参与丛书的编著,这些均会给国际工程管理专业的建设打下良好的基础。以前,我们也曾编撰过一些教材与专著,在当时均起了很好的作用,有些作品在今后长时期内仍会发挥好的作用。所不同的是,这套丛书论述得更加详尽,内容更加充实,问题探讨得更加深入,又补充了过去从未论述过的一些内容,填补了空白,大大提高了可操作性,对实际工作定会大有好处。

最后,我代表编委会感谢国家教委、外经贸部、建设部等各级领导的支持与帮助。感谢中国水利电力对外公司、中国建筑工程总公司、中国国际工程咨询公司、中国土木工程公司、中国公路桥梁建设总公司、中国建筑业协会工程项目管理专业委员会、中国建筑工业出版社等单位,在这套丛书编辑出版过程中给我们大力协助并予以资助。还要感谢各分册主编以及参与编书的专家教授们的辛勤劳动,以及以何伯森教授为首的编委会秘书组作了大量的、有益的组织联络工作。

这套丛书,鉴于我们是初次组织编写,经验不足,会有许多缺点与不妥之处,希望批评指正,以便再版时修正。

1996 年 7 月 30 日